Education Policy and Social Class

In the **World Library of Educationalists**, international experts themselves compile career-long collections of what they judge to be their finest pieces – extracts from books, key articles, salient research findings, major theoretical and practical contributions – so the world can read them in a single manageable volume. Readers will be able to follow themes and strands of the topic and see how their work contributes to the development of the field.

Stephen J. Ball has spent the last 20 years researching, thinking and writing about some of the key and enduring issues in Education Policy and Sociology of Education. He has contributed 12 books and over 200 articles to the field.

In *Education Policy and Social Class*, Stephen J. Ball brings together 16 of his key writings in one place. Starting with a specially written Introduction, which gives an overview of his career and contextualises his selection within the development of the field, the chapters are divided into three sections:

- perspectives on policy research
- policy technologies and policy analysis
- social class and education policy.

This book not only shows how Stephen J. Ball's thinking has developed during his long and distinguished career, it also gives an insight into the development of the fields to which he contributed.

Stephen J. Ball is Karl Mannheim Professor of Sociology of Education at the Institute of Education, University of London. He is internationally renown for his research and writing in the field and has published widely in books and journals.

Contributors to the series include: Richard Aldrich, Stephen J. Ball, Jerome Bruner, John Elliott, Elliot W. Eisner, Howard Gardner, John K. Gilbert, Ivor F. Goodson, David Labaree, John White, E. C. Wragg.

World Library of Educationalists series

Other books in the series:

Lessons from History of Education
The selected works of Richard Aldrich
Richard Aldrich

Education Policy and Social Class
The selected works of Stephen J. Ball
Stephen J. Ball

Reimagining Schools
The selected works of Elliot W. Eisner
Elliot W. Eisner

Reflecting Where the Action Is
The selected works of John Elliott
John Elliott

Development and Education of the Mind
The selected works of Howard Gardner
Howard Gardner

Constructing Worlds through Science Education
The selected works of John K. Gilbert
John K. Gilbert

Learning, Curriculum and Life Politics
The selected works of Ivor F. Goodson
Ivor F. Goodson

The Curriculum and the Child
The selected works of John White
John White

The Art and Science of Teaching and Learning
The selected works of Ted Wragg
E. C. Wragg

Education Policy and Social Class

The selected works of Stephen J. Ball

Stephen J. Ball

Routledge
Taylor & Francis Group

LONDON AND NEW YORK

First published 2006
by Routledge
2 Park Square, Milton Park, Abingdon, Oxon OX14 4RN

Simultaneously published in the USA and Canada
by Routledge
270 Madison Ave, New York, NY 10016

Reprinted 2007

Routledge is an imprint of the Taylor & Francis Group an informa business

© 2006 Stephen J. Ball

Typeset in Sabon by
Newgen Imaging Systems (P) Ltd, Chennai, India
Printed and bound in Great Britain by
Cromwell Press, Trowbridge, Wiltshire

British Library Cataloguing in Publication Data
A catalogue record for this book is available
from the British Library

Library of Congress Cataloging in Publication Data
Ball, Stephen J.
    Education policy and social class: the selected works of
Stephen Ball / Stephen Ball.
        p. cm.
    Includes bibliographical references.
    1. Education and state – Great Britain. 2. Educational
sociology – Great Britain. 3. Educational equalization – Great
Britain. 4. Social classes – Great Britain. I. Title.

LC93.G7B33 2005
379.41–dc22   2005007302

ISBN10: 0-415-36397-7 (cased)
ISBN10: 0-415-36398-5 (limp)

ISBN13: 978-0-415-36397-6 (cased)
ISBN13: 978-0-415-36398-3 (limp)

CONTENTS

ACKNOWLEDGEMENTS

A life in social research is always and inevitably a social life, a life of relationships, collaborations, debts, favours, and obligations. Most importantly among these relationships are the literally thousands of people who have willingly submitted themselves to 'being researched' by me over a period of 35 years (so far!). I can only re-iterate the thank yous I offered at the time. But it has been pleasing to discover how many people have found 'being researched' a positive and indeed sometimes fulfilling experience – but this is not true of all. A life of research also contains many high and low points – 'Will any of this ever make sense?'; 'Do I really have anything of any worth to say here?'. Trinidad has always been there for me. I have also been lucky enough to be apprentice to a number of very special researchers – like Colin Lacey, Lawrence Stenhouse, Brian Davies, Tony Knight and Peter Woods, who taught me to think, write, see and work hard. And I have worked with a whole range of talented people from whom I have learned – Meg Maguire, Carol Vincent, Richard Bowe, Diane Reay, Alan Cribb, Sharon Gewirtz, Sheila Macrae, Sophie Kemp, Dave Gillborn, Rachel Herring, Hilary Radnor, Martin Thrupp, Alex Moore, John Fitz, Soile Pietikainen, Miriam David, Jackie Davies, Ivor Goodson, Naoko Ota, Stefan Larsson, Maria Tamboukou, Jennifer Wilson-Barnett, Sarah Bignold, Charles Batteson, Agnes van Zanten, Bethan Marshall, Geoff Whitty, Tony Green. Bob Burgess, Ann Gold, David Jones, John Smyth, Patricia Vanegas, Gustavo Fischmann, Silvina Gvirtz, Steven Crump, Clementina Marques Cardoso, Sam Neath, Christian Maroy, Dave Burrell, Tony Becher – traces of their influences are embedded throughout this text. I have also been lucky to have worked with and for people who have been enablers, who have made a point of making my lifer easier, of making things possible. In particular I would mention Tony Bailey, Margaret Brown, Caroline Gill, Paul Black, Dave Gillborn and Dylan Wiliam. Lastly there is Williams, Jasper and Smudge for being cute.

The following articles have been reproduced with the kind permission of the respective journals

'Big policies/small world: an introduction to international perspectives in education policy', *Comparative Education*, 1998, 34(2): 119–30.

'Circuits of schooling: a sociological exploration of parental choice of school in social class contexts', *The Sociological Review*, 1995, 43(1): 52–78.

' "Ethnic choosing": minority ethnic students, social class and higher education choice', *Race Ethnicity and Education*, 2003, 5(4): 333–57.

'Good school/bad school: paradox and fabrication', *British Journal of Sociology of Education,* 1998, 18(3): 317–36.

' "I heard it on the grapevine": "hot" knowledge and school choice', *British Journal of Sociology of Education,* 1998, 19(3): 377–400.

'Policy sociology and critical social research: a personal review of recent education policy and policy research', *British Education Research Journal,* 1997, 23(3): 257–74.

'Space, work and the "new urban economies" ', *Journal of Youth Studies,* 2000, 3(3): 279–300.

'The risks of social reproduction: the middle class and education markets', *London Review of Education,* 2003, 1(3): 163–75.

'The teacher's soul and the terrors of performativity', *Journal of Education Policy,* 2003, 18(2): 215–28.

'What is policy? Texts, trajectories and toolboxes', *Discourse,* 1993, 13(2): 10–17.

The following chapters have been reproduced with the kind permission of the respective publishers

'Educational studies, policy entrepreneurship and social theory', in R. Slee and G. Weiner with S. Tomlinson (eds), *School Effectiveness for Whom?* London: Falmer Press, 1998.

'Ethics, self-interest and the market form in education', in A. Cribb (ed.), *Markets, Managers and Public Service? Professional Ethics in the New Welfare State,* Centre for Public Policy Research, Occasional Paper No. 1, London: King's College, 1998.

'Discipline and chaos: the New Right and discourses of derision', *Politics and Policy Making in Education,* London: Routledge, 1990.

'Social justice in the head: are we all libertarians now?', in C. Vincent (ed.), *Social Justice, Identity and Education,* London: RoutledgeFalmer, 2003.

Chapters 8 and 9 are revised, re-edited and expanded from previously published papers and are partly drawn from 'Education for profit and standards in education: the ethical role of markets and the private sector in state systems', in J. Oelkers (ed.), *Futures of Education II: Essays from an Interdisciplinary Symposium,* Bern: Peter Lang, 2003; 'Market mixes, ethical re-tooling and consumer heroes: education markets in England', in J. Oelkers (ed.), *Economy, Public Education and Democracy,* Zurich: Peter Lang, 2003; 'School-based management: new culture and new subjectivity', in *da investigacao as practicas: estudos de natureza educacional,* 2002, 3(1): 59–76.

INTRODUCTION
The problem of policy

Life with its irrational reality and its store of possible meanings is inexhaustible.
(Weber, 1949, p. 48)

Having to re-read and re-consider what one has written over a period of three decades of research, commentary and analysis is both daunting and salutary. My first response to a long list of publications was that I had probably written too much, too quickly (and there are things I wish I had not written). The compulsion to write and the press to publish sometimes outstrip the availability of good ideas. But I was also made aware of how, through this writing, I had worked away at a set of consistent and coherent themes and concerns over a long period of time.

Writing is sometimes a chore, sometimes exciting, always a challenge, but it is an integral part of my scholarly practice and intellectual development. Neither in a practical nor epistemological sense do I see my texts as free-standing, finished pieces which once written and published close the book on some social issue or research question but rather as interpretational forays into the dynamic complexities of high modern society. Interpretations which always need further elaboration and more work, more thought, more research. It is only painstakingly over time that frameworks of interpretation – theoretically informed sets of linked concepts – can be developed. Such frameworks hopefully then have scope and applicability beyond the particularity of their empirical origins – middle range theory. Thus, reading back unearths sequences of work and recurring themes addressing specific concerns in journal articles, book chapters, conferences papers and some pieces which never saw the light of day at all, which are part of this process of development, re-evaluation and refinement. More recently I have taken to re-writing or rather re-working the same paper in different forms, as another way of achieving some coherent development of ideas (e.g. Ball, 2001, 2002, 2003). The presentation of ideas in seminars and conferences for different audiences can of course also be a vehicle for this kind of incremental thinking. If you are fortunate, both writing and presentations elicit sensible critical responses. And I am grateful to a multitude of colleagues who have, over the years, read and commented on drafts of papers. And I am especially grateful to that smaller group of people, they know who they are, who have argued with me, disagreed, criticised, made me think more and hopefully think better – many of whom I have researched and written with.

Over time, another crucial component for me in the dynamic and development of my work is theory. Theory can be both exciting and appropriately dangerous. It is constructive and invigorating, as well as violent and destructive. It plays a vital role in challenging cherished orthodoxies. Theory is for me not a perceptual straightjacket but a set of possibilities for thinking with. Theory should not bear down upon us and stultify our thinking, it should not be allowed to 'terrorise' us with its speculations, but can be used as a toolbox, as Foucault described his own work (see Chapter 3).

> What we need to recognise perhaps is that theory is a tool which can also have a 'transgressive' use, especially when, as Deleuze and Foucault (1977) put it, 'practice' seems to hit a wall.
>
> (Karakayali, 2004, p. 364)

I do not mean by this that any and all theories can or might be used, thrown together unsystematically and unreflexively, concepts can be 'used and troubled'. At the same time, as Patti Lather puts it, coherence and deliberation are important. Epistemologies and ontologies may clash and grate but the resultant friction can be purposeful and effective (see Ball, 1994) in providing different lenses through which to see and think about the social world. This means stepping back from simple certainties and thinking instead in paradoxes or holding onto ambivalence. I have I suppose taken on some of the post-modern suspicion of grand narratives, of elegant and all-embracing theories of everything which have their applications policed by guardians of interpretation who 'establish the conditions for who speaks and who gets heard' (Brantlinger, 1997) and which can provide off-the-shelf interpretational kits for every social phenomenon. In constrast the more I research, the more I come to see the social as complex, multi-facetted, elusive or as Bourdieu *et al.* (1991, p. 259) puts it 'complicated, confused, impure, uncertain', consequently parsimony seems dangerous and limiting, and two theories almost always better than one. Apple (1996, p. 141) writes about this as 'the issue of simultaneity, of thinking neo and post together, of actively enabling the tensions within and among them to help form our research'. Rather than attempting grand sweeps of ideas which encompass all or large parts of the social in their wake, my proclivity is to chip away at bits of the social, always looking for joins and patterns but equally aware of fractures and discontinuities. As Foucault explained his purpose was 'not to formulate the global systematic theory which holds everything in place, but to analyse the specificity of mechanisms of power . . . to build little by little a strategic knowledge' (Foucault, 1980, p. 145) and as Bourdieu often urged he wanted his readers to read his works as 'exercise books' rather than theories and was keen to 'remind us that "theory" should not be valued for its own sake' (Karakayali, 2004, p. 352). Part of the exercise of analysis is about 'appraising concepts as possibilities for future thinking' (Colebrook, 2000, p. 5) and in the process of particular analyses some concepts will not prove their worth, for me theory and research work together in this process. Analysis is an 'exercise in making things intelligible' (Parkin, 1979, p. 115) not what Dale (1992) calls 'theory by numbers', whereby the conceptual map of the social simply needs to be coloured-in rather than researched. It involves, as Bourdieu urges, the development of a set of concepts which are 'polymorphic, supple and adaptable, rather than defined, calibrated and used rigidly' (Bourdieu and Wacquant, 1992, p. 23).

Theory also works to provide the necessity and discipline of reflexivity and I think that Foucault has been important to me in allowing for the possibility of thinking about the social, and about the work of sociology, as a particular form of practice in relation to and within the social. As I argue in one of the papers (Chapter 4) in this collection 'epistemological development within the human sciences, like education, functions politically and is intimately imbricated in the practical management of social and political problems'. Bourdieu, with his continual emphasis on the need for reflexivity, has also been important to me. He was scathing in his rejection of what he called the 'intellectualist bias' which always arises when a researcher is insufficiently critical of the 'presuppositions inscribed in the act of thinking about the world' (Bourdieu and Wacquant, 1992, p. 39) and the failure to grasp 'the logic of practice' which stems from this. Part of Bourdieu's endeavour was to destabilise and re-invent the sociological habitus 'a system of dispositions necessary to the constitution of the craft of the sociologist in its universality' (Bourdieu, 1993, p. 271). His notion of sociology as a craft is appropriately modest but also thoroughly challenging. Unlike other theorists, Foucault and Bourdieu, at least in the way I read them, do not tell me how to think, but enable me to think about how I think.

Both Bourdieu and Foucault, in very different ways, offer the possibility of a form of social scientific practice which attempts to escape from the discursively constructed, and socially maintained traditions, categories and divisions of modernist thought. Both clearly saw social theory as socially produced, as a field or network of relations constantly subject to the play of power, both within and from without, and beset by struggles for positional advantage. However, taking seriously and engaging with their challenges and strictures does not mean simply giving up on what one was and becoming a different 'something' – a Bourdieurian/a Foucauldian – swapping new orthodoxies for old.[1] Rather indeed it means struggling against the complacencies and comforts of 'being something' – it means resisting orthodoxy for its own sake. Orthodoxies 'are patrons who need placating and stroking all the time' (Said, 1994, p. 89). But such struggles require, as Edward Said argued 'both commitment and risk, boldness and vulnerability' (p. 10) and it means accepting that work is always 'unfinished and necessarily imperfect' (p. 17) despite the increasingly emphatic high modernist demands for definitive statements and '... it doesn't make one particularly popular' (p. 17). As Wright-Mills (1970) put it: 'Fresh perception now involves the capacity to continually unmask and smash the stereotypes of vision and intellect which modern communications [i.e. modern systems of representation] swamp us'.

Doing social analysis means being difficult and constructive at the same time. Certainly part of what drives my work is the dissatisfactions that I have experienced with the tools and stereotypes available when I wanted to make sense of things. *The MicroPolitics of the School* (1987) was in a sense written for my students at the University of Sussex. For a number of years I struggled to teach a course on the theory of organisations and was constantly frustrated with the shortcomings of existing attempts to theorise schools as organisations. *Politics and Policymaking in Education* (1990), in a similar way, was written for my Urban Education students at King's, as an escape from the unreal, modernist, rational conceits of 'policy analysis' writing. *Class Strategies and the Education Market* (2003) was partly written in response to the impoverished (or absent) conceptualisation of class in much educational research. Stephen Crump has written about my work as a series of 'unsettlings' in that; it 'unsettles the location, function, power and growth of knowledge, especially for policy and research' (Section 1 and work on the national curriculum); it 'unsettles structured, systematic, deterministic, functional (yet disparate, contradictory and weak) theories of education and schooling processes' (micropolitics and policy work); it 'unsettles taken-for-granted articulations of different groups/classes within education' (work in Part 3 on race, class and gender in the 'education market'); and it 'unsettles explanations of the state' (work on the policy cycle, performativity and policy technologies in Part 2). My project then, in modest ways is, as Foucault might put it: 'to fragment what was thought unified, and show the heterogeneity of consistency' (Foucault, 1977, p. 144).

If I am to explain myself and my work I also have to say that I am an ethnographer, I construct, manage and analyse data using ethnographic methods and sensitivities (Ball, 1990, 1991). And clearly there are potential difficulties here in relation to theory, or at least some theory. Not Bourdieu, who started out as an ethnographer and returned to small-scale qualitative work at various moments in his long career but at face value there is no way of integrating a Foucauldian ontology with an ethnographic one which privileges the agency and meanings of actors. However, there are links to be made between the two, methodological and analytic possibilities and openings to be explored, and Maria Tamboukou and I have written about these (Tamboukou and Ball, 2004) and I will not rehearse them here. Being an ethnographer means that I work small. I am interested in events and specifics and locations, in contingencies, concatenations and contexts, in the odd as much as the typical. The critical case is a powerful analytical device. Foucault again has a relevance here, with his idea that things that are now self-evident 'are always formed in the confluence of encounters and chances, during the course of precarious and fragile history' (Foucault, 1988, p. 37); 'a cobbled patchwork of heterogeneous elements' (Ransom, 1997, p. 88) – 'a profusion of entangled events' (Foucault, 1977, p. 155). And his interest in small insignificant details, and the micro-analysis of power relations and importantly his belief that things 'can be unmade as long as we know how it was they were made' (Foucault in Ransom, 1997, p. 89). This, oddly perhaps, has resonances with Weber and his unwillingness to try to 'define social structure in any rigorous sense' (Lopez 2003, p. 67) and his commitment to the idea that society emerges as 'the effect of the particular complex historical "configurations" or "constellations" of individuals' meaningful actions'. Indeed Weber set himself '. . . to put an end to the use of collective concepts, a use which still haunts us' (cited in Frisby and Sayer, 1986, p. 86). All of this does not mean eschewing the search for principles of organisation and regularity, clearly not, for either Weber or Foucault – nor does it for me – but it does mean an avoidance of unthought-through pre-suppositions about structures and regularities, of taking rather than making an analysis.

Weber is clearly another sub-textual influence which runs through my work. In an effort to 'be something' I wrote in the Introduction to *Politics and Policymaking* in 1990, that 'I may be a Weberian neo-pluralist' (although I must admit to writing this at least a little tongue-in-cheek). But my book on the middle-classes (Ball, 2003) is firmly rooted in, via Parkin and Bourdieu, Weberian-class theory. But I have got side-tracked, I was writing about working small. Most of the data I have worked with over the past 15 years has consisted of interviews – people talking about themselves, their lives and their problems. I worry away at these materials, coding and re-coding them, arguing about them with colleagues, viewing them through various conceptual lenses, looking for links with other research, trying out interpretational possibilities for size, trying to develop the transposable frameworks referred to above, and always seeking to bring the promise of 'the sociological imagination' to bear, to make some sense of the 'interplay of man (*sic*) and society, of biography and history, of self and world'[2] (Wright-Mills, 1970, p. 10). The sociological imagination Wright-Mills explained: 'is the capacity to range from the most impersonal and remote transformations to the most intimate features of the human self' (p. 14) (see papers on performativity (Chapter 10) and on values and principles (Chapter 15)). This is in Apple's words 'the difficult problem of simultaneously thinking about both the specificity of different practices, and the forms of articulated unity they constitute' (p. 141). The conditions of our existence are concrete and practical and very real. We do make choices about our lives and ourselves but do not do so either within material conditions or with words over which we have control. Doing sociological work does not mean focusing exclusively on one or the other – choices or conditions, discourse or text – it involves developing ways of thinking about how the two work together within social practice.

The other statement I wish to make about working small and using ethnographic methods is that I do not see this exclusively as a matter of technique. Rigour is important, very important, but is only useful ultimately in combination with creativity, insight and the ability to 'think otherwise'. A great deal of 'social science' is marked by 'a certain emptiness, banality, impossibility, inappropriateness, unoriginality' (Woods, 1999, p. 11) – to all of which I have made my own contributions. Data does not speak for itself, analysis is not simply a matter of 'revealing' structures and patterns, ethnographic analysis is as much an art as it is a science. As that doyen of educational ethnography Peter Woods argues research requires a kind of 'controlled madness' (Woods, 1999, p. 11) and he believes firmly in research as a creative process and ethnography in particular as a very personal process. 'To a greater extent than other forms of research, it allows a working out of one's own destiny within the context of "public issues"' (Woods, 1999, p. 15). However, most researchers individually and collectively devote great deal of effort to obscuring the creative and personal aspects of research in the hope of acquiring some crumbs of symbolic capital which might come from aligning themselves with the objectivist vision. These efforts also support and are supported by an increasingly productive industry of research methods technologies and texts. The erasing of the social from social science does both political and ideological work and makes research seem both more and less than it is in reality. It rips it out of the context of its social production.

This then is a brief and inevitably inadequate attempt to provide a context for the papers which follow and to account for who I am and what I do, at least in terms of my writing, and for some of the influences and preoccupations that bear upon and run through my work. If I can again borrow Foucault's words, the point of all this for me, is to demonstrate that things are not as inevitable as all that, and that they can be different, although not necessarily in ways that we can easily imagine. Again somewhat like Foucault, I am wary of making recommendations for doing things differently within the discursive possibilities with which we are already thinking. I have a reputation for pessimism, of telling stories of despair. But despair need not be the end of things, indeed it may be a necessary stage towards something else, something beyond despair, something that is not just redemptive but properly radical. I suppose this is a version of Gramsci's 'pessimism of the intellect/optimism of the will'.

I have organised my selection of writings into three sections, although the sections do not constitute total separate bodies of work and the papers could have been divided and allocated in different ways. The papers in Part 1 outline the trajectory of my interest in and engagement with policy analysis and policy research and my attempts to develop a 'policy sociology' – a term coined by Jenny Ozga (1987). I will also explain my use of theory and the 'usefulness' of theory in policy research. The papers in Part 2 are some examples of the application of policy sociology to a range of contemporary issues arising from the reform of education – in particularly those of performativity and 'privatisation'. The papers in Part 3 address various aspects of my continuing interest in social class in and of itself and its relationships to policy. A full bibliography of my writing is in the appendix.

Notes

1   I have been described by one critic of my work as a post-modernist, which suggests that the writer does not know what post-modernism is, and as 'announcing the death of class' which suggests that they have not read any of my work – or even any of the titles of my books or papers. Being mis-read is an occupational hazard in sociology. Even if you do eschew 'being something', others are always eager to place you in some box or other, usually as a way of dismissing rather than engaging with what you are trying to do.
2   An ex-teacher recently told me after I had presented a paper at a conference that he knew he 'had to leave teaching, now I know why I left'.

References

Apple, M. (1996). 'Power, Meaning and Identity: Critical Sociology of Education in the United States'. *British Journal of Sociology of Education* 17(2): 125–44.
Ball, S. J. (1990). 'Self Doubt and Soft Data: Social and Technical Trajectories in Ethnographic Fieldwork'. *International Journal of Qualitative Studies in Education* 3(2): 157–72.
Ball, S. J. (1991). Power, Conflict, Micropolitics and all that! In *Doing Educational Research*, G. Walford (ed.). London, Routledge.

Ball, S. J. (1994). *Education Reform: A Critical and Post-Structural Approach*. Buckingham, Open University Press.
Ball, S. J. (2000). 'Performativities and Fabrications in the Education Economy: Towards the Performative Society'. *Australian Educational Researcher* 27(2): 1–24.
Ball, S. J. (2001). Performativities and Fabrications in the Eduation Economy: Towards the Performative Society. In *The Performing School: Managing Teaching and Learning in a Performance Culture*, D. Gleeson and C. Husbands (eds). London, RoutledgeFalmer.
Ball, S. J. (2003). 'The Teacher's Soul and the Terrors of Performativity'. *Journal of Education Policy* 18(2): 215–28.
Bauman, Z. (1998). *Work Consumerism and the New Poor*. Buckingham, Open University Press.
Bourdieu, P. (1993). *Sociology in Question*. London, Sage.
Bourdieu, P. and Wacquant, L. J. D. (1992). *An Invitation to Reflexive Sociology*. Chicago, University of Chicago Press.
Bourdieu, P., Chamboredon, J. C. and Passeron, J. C. (1991). *The Craft of Sociology: Epistemological Preliminaries*. Berlin and New York, de Guyer.
Colebrook, C. (2000). Introduction. In *Deleuze and Feminist Theory*. I. Buchanan and C. Colebrook (eds). Edinburgh, Edinburgh University Press.
Dale, R. (1992). Recovering from a Pyrrhic Victory? Quality, Relevance and Impact in the Sociology of Education. In *Voicing Concerns*, M. Arnot and L. Barton (eds). Wallingford, Triangle.
Devine, F. (1997). *Privilege, Power and the Reproduction of Advantage*. British Sociological Association Annual Conference, University of York, 7–10 April.
Foucault, M. (1977). *Language, Counter-Memory, Practice: Selected Essays and Interviews*. Ithaca, NY, Cornell University Press.
Foucault, M. (1980). *Power/Knowledge: Selected Interviews and Other Writings*. New York, Pantheon.
Foucault, M. (1988). *Politics, Philosophy. Culture: Interviews and Other Writings 1972–1977*. New York, Routledge.
Frisby, D. and D. Sayer (1986). *Society*. London, Tavistock.
Karakayali, N. (2004). 'Reading Bourdieu with Adorno: The Limits of Critical Theory and Reflexive Sociology'. *Sociology* 38(2): 351–68.
Lopez, J. (2003). *Society and its Metaphors: Language, Social Theory and Social Structure*. New York, Continuum.
Ozga, J. (1987). Studying Education Policy through the Lives of Policy Makers. In *Changing Policies, Changing Teachers*, S. Walker and L. Barton (eds). Milton Keynes, Open University Press.
Parkin, F. (1979). *Marxism and Class Theory: A Bourgeois Critique*. London, Tavistock.
Ransom, J. S. (1997). *Foucault's Discipline: The Politics of Subjectivity*. Durham, NC, Duke University Press.
Said, E. (1994). *Representations of the Intellectual*, Vintage Books.
Tamboukou, M. and S. J. Ball (eds) (2004). *Dangerous Encounters: Genealogy and Etnography*. Eruptions, New York, Peter Lang.
Weber, M. (1949). *The Methodology of Social Sciences*. Glencoe, The Free Press.
Woods, P. (1999). *Successful Writing for Qualitative Researchers*. London, Routledge.
Wright-Mills, C. (1970). *The Sociological Imagination*. Harmondsworth, Penguin.

PART 1

PERSPECTIVES ON POLICY RESEARCH

These papers address some general and basic theoretical and methodological issues involved in what I call, following Ozga, 'policy sociology'. The papers outline a form of analysis which involves the deployment of different kinds of theory to address different levels of analysis. This approach was first presented in my 1990 book, *Politics and Policy Making in Education* and one chapter from that book (Chapter 2 in this book) is included here, it serves to indicate the 'beginnings' of education reform and some of those diverse elements and force-relations that accumulated to give it its logic, and the beginnings of my method of analysis. Some of the analytical issues adumbrated here are further developed in the 1992 book *Reforming Education and Changing Schools: Case Studies in Policy Sociology*, written with Richard Bowe, and the paper *What is Policy? Texts, Trajectories and Toolboxes* (Chapter 3), which also introduces the 'policy cycle' as an heuristic device for analysing policies, and differentiates between discourse and text, stressing respectively the limits and possibilities of 'thinking' policy from the perspective of each. The *Policy Entrepreneurship* paper (Chapter 4) makes an explicit case for the role of theory as a form of intellectual violence and argues for a particular form of theoretically informed work in policy analysis. It also addresses the increasingly restrictive 'steering' of educational research by the state and the development of a hegemony of 'state relevance'. *Policy Sociology and Critical Social Research* (Chapter 1) lays out a framework for critical policy sociology, an aesthetics of critique, set over and against the dominant 'scientific' paradigm of public policy research. Finally, in this part, the *Big Policies/Small World* (Chapter 5) puts policy sociology into the context of globalisation and in relation to the global flow of policies, via the notion of 'policyscapes', a new global, policy commonsense, and a generic and 'magical' agenda of policy solutions is identified. Together the papers offer an overview of my approach to 'policy sociology' and of the main theoretical and conceptual tools which I employ in the practical analysis of policies and policy-making and the effects and consequences of policy.

CHAPTER 1

POLICY SOCIOLOGY AND CRITICAL SOCIAL RESEARCH

A personal review of recent education policy and policy research

British Education Research Journal, 1997, 23(3): 257–74

> If our task is understanding both how domination works and the possibilities of interrupting it, then one of the things we can do is learn from each other, to combine our critical efforts.
>
> (M. Apple (2003) *The State and the Politics of Knowledge*,
> New York, RoutledgeFalmer, p. 24)

Introduction

This paper expounds a personal and perhaps idiosyncratic view of education policy and education policy research in the UK during the past 15–20 years. The first part of the paper is concerned with the former and I discuss the transformation of public sector provision and civil society and the introduction of new forms of social regulation. The second part considers the latter and involves reflection on 'progress' in an emergent sub-field of educational studies – education policy research.[1] I am not using hard and fast boundaries or definitions of the field in my discussion which may introduce some imprecision and vagueness but that is probably inevitable. I will explore my concerns using a meta-analytical template and I will range across theoretical, epistemological and methodological issues.

The tone of the second part of the paper is generally critical, but is intended to be constructive and reflexive. I am rehearsing some of the weaknesses embedded in my own research practice and airing some ambivalences about the project of critical policy research. This is not an exercise in 'deep epistemology' – realism, essentialism, forms of explanation and all that – rather it is concerned with 'surface epistemology' – the relationships between conceptualisation, research conduct and design and interpretation. The discussion is framed to allow for at least some recognition of the social and personal aspects and agendas of research. Policy research is always in some degree both reactive and parasitic. Careers and reputations are made as our research flourishes upon the rotting remains of the Keynsian Welfare State (KWS). Both those inside the policy discourse and those whose professional identities are established through antagonism towards the discourse benefit from the uncertainties and tragedies of reform. Critical researchers, apparently safely ensconced in the moral high ground, nonetheless make a livelihood trading in the artefacts of misery and broken dreams of practitioners. None of us remain untainted by the incentives and disciplines of the new moral economy.

Transformations

I want to present the argument that during the last 15 years we have witnessed in the UK, and indeed in most other western and many developing societies, a major *transformation* (see below) in the organising principles of social provision right across the public sector. Forms of employment, organisational structures, cultures and values, systems of funding, management roles and styles, social relationships, pay and conditions, have all undergone change in similar directions. Heuristically these changes may be situated as a part of the transformation which Jessop represents as from the KWS to the Schumpeterian Workfare State (SWS) (Jessop, 1994). According to Jessop this transformation replaced the Fordist discourse of productivity and planning with a post-Fordist rhetoric of flexibility and entrepreneurialism. The SWS 'goes beyond the mere retrenchment of social welfare to restructure and subordinate it to market forces' (pp. 27–28). In the UK this restructuring process both as an economic strategy and a hegemonic project for the re-invigoration of civil society was articulated in the ideological politics of Thatcherite neo-liberalism.

> In narrow economic terms, the neo-liberal strategy demands changes in the *regulation* (governance) of both the public and private sectors. For the public sector, it involves privatisation, liberalisation, and an imposition of commercial criteria in any residual state sector.
>
> (Jessop, 1994, p. 30)

Pursuing a similar analysis of restructuring Hoggett suggests three points of emphasis in the UK case. They are:

1   the development of time and pay flexibilities (but not skill flexibilities);
2   the promotion of forms of external rather than internal decentralisation; and
3   the weakening and residualising of local government and the rudimentary democratic structures residing at district level within the NHS, by concentrating strategic control within central government or dissipating it into a myriad disaggregated local agencies and service units.

> (Hoggett, 1994, p. 44)

All of this is embedded within and contributes to changes in the technology of state control, what Hoggett calls 'remote control', or what is also called 'steering at a distance' (Kikert, 1991). I shall return to this later.

As above, most accounts of the transformation of the public sector concentrate on the processes of change, the new structures and new technologies of control. Less attention has been given to the transformation of the values and cultures of the public sector (Heelas and Morris, 1992) and the formation of new subjectivities (Rose, 1992). The key points of linkage between the restructuring and re-valuing (or ethical re-tooling) of the public sector are the discourses excellence, effectiveness and quality and the logics and culture of new managerialism in which they are embedded. Taking the latter first: Where neo-Taylorism focuses on intensifying systems of direct control, the new managerialism offers a 'people-centred' model of the organisation which views bureaucratic control systems as unwieldy, counterproductive for efficiency and repressive of the 'enterprising spirit' of all employees. Competitive success will be achieved by loosening formal systems of control (within what is tellingly termed a 'loose-tight structure') and instead motivating people to produce 'quality' and strive for 'excellence' themselves. Managers become leaders rather than controllers, providing the visions and inspirations which generate a collective corporate commitment to 'being the best'. This 'new' managerialism stresses a constant attention to 'quality', being close to the customer and the value of innovation (Newman and Clarke, 1994, p. 15). In the education sector the headteacher is the main 'carrier' and embodiment of new managerialism and is crucial to the transformation of the organisational regimes of schools (Grace, 1995). That is, the dismantling of bureau-professional organisational regimes and their replacement with market-entrepreneurial regimes (Clarke and Newman, 1992). In changing the conception, relationships and practices of headship the process of reform also effects a profound change in the subjectivity and values of leadership in schools. It is important however not to see these changes simply as located 'in' heads and 'in' schools. They should be seen as primarily located within the policy framework created by the 1988 and subsequent Education Acts which put into place the infra-structure and incentives of the market form.

A new moral economy

The critique of state planning and provision and advocacy of the market form, which are fundamental to the politics of public sector reform, draw directly upon the philosophy and economics of neo-liberalism and in particular the work of Hayek. From the neo-liberal perspective, both unionism, and bureau-professionalism are seen as contributory factors to the 'failures' of systems of planned public provision and as major obstacles in the way of the development of 'effective' social markets. In a variety of ways the deregulation, devolution and autonomy which are central to public sector reform have changed the possibilities for and meaning of union and professional activity. In education:

> The attempted fragmentation of the education service under LMS [Local Management of Schools] was accompanied by measures to introduce competition among schools and to fund them according to their success in attracting pupils...HRM [Human Resources Management] techniques are targeted at gaining the commitment of employees to the aims of the organisation. The new climate necessitates new mechanisms for controlling costs and teacher autonomy through a range of practices emphasising more casualised conditions of employment, flexibility, and controls on performance related not only to pay but to promotion and redundancy.
>
> (Sinclair *et al.*, 1995, pp. 266–7)

Education, like all other aspects of the public sector, is subject of and part of what Oakland calls 'the quality revolution', a rhetoric of quality improvement has been a key feature of government reforms in the UK (and many elsewhere) since the early 1980s and the concept of quality forms 'part of a wider Conservative government-led ideological narrative and organisational strategy of "the enterprise culture"' (Kirkpatrick and Martinez-Lucio, 1995). Much of the paraphernalia of quality is borrowed from the private sector – the public sector it was argued would benefit from exposure to market forces, commercial models of management and of quality improvement. The disciplines and effects of the market are rooted in a social psychology of 'self-interest, that great engine of material progress, [that] teaches us to respect results, not principles' (Newman, 1984, p. 158). Hence the new social markets are framed by a mix of incentives and rewards aimed at stimulating self-interested responses.

These incentives and rewards are intended to displace the 'out-dated' niceties of professional ethics. Ethical reflection is rendered obsolete in the process for goal attainment, performance improvement and budget maximisation. Value replaces values, except where it can be shown that values add value. More generally the disciplines and dynamics of the market form work to edge public sector organisations into a closer convergence with the private sector inasmuch that, paradoxically, performativity requires of public sector organisations as much attention to symbolic change and manipulation as it does to substantive change. It encourages organisations to become more and more concerned with their style, their image, their semiotics, with the way things are presented rather than with the way they actually work. The project of transparency through performativity indeed produces greater complexity and opacity as public sector organisations spend time, money and energy on impression management, marketing and promotion.

In all of this work on and in organisations performativity renders many professionals unrecognisable to themselves.[2] Corporatised, performative organisations, offer new 'possibilities' of quality and excellence, they provide 'the possibility for every member of an organisation to express "individual initiative" and to develop fully their "potential" in the service of the corporation' (Du Gay, 1996, p. 62). It also renders them dispensable, to be replaced by others trained according to different principles, unencumbered by the rigours of moral reflection – public sector technicians. Such technicians owe their allegiance to policy and to institutional survival rather than to any abstract value systems or ethical commitments. The notion of 'service', the investment of the self within practice, and professional judgement related to 'right' decisions, are devalorised. Ultimately, in these ways 'subjectivity and spirit' are 'plundered by capital itself as rage and desire' (De Lissovoy and McLaren, 2003, p. 141).

What is achieved in the introduction of the market form into public provision, is not simply a new mechanism of resource allocation and distribution but also the creation of a new moral environment for both consumers and producers (see Chapters 6 and 9).

Autonomy and discipline

In their various effects, I suggest, the 'practical autonomy' of LMS and GMS (Grant Maintained Status), and the 'borrowing' of techniques of HRM and TQM (Total Quality Management) by the 'new managers' of the public services, achieve the purposes of state policy without the presence of the state. The practice of teachers are overwhelmed by the inevitabilities and obviousness of these 'micro-disciplinary practices'. They play upon the insecurity of the disciplined subject. They are both feminised (Blackmore, 1995) and masculinist (Limerick and Lingard, 1995).[3]

These practices change that which they 'indicates', they changes meaning, they deliver re-design and ensure the 'alignment' of actors with the rigours of efficiency. They objectify and commodify public sector work, the knowledge-work of educational institutions is rendered into 'outputs', 'levels of performance', 'forms of quality'. The discourses of accountability, improvement, quality and effectiveness which surround and accompany these objectifications render existing practice fragile and indefensible. 'Teaching and learning, as a result are reduced to processes of production and provision that must meet market goals of transfer efficiency and quality control' (Boyles, 2000, p. 120).

This process of objectification contributes more generally to the possibility of thinking about social services like education as *forms of production*, as 'just like' services of other kinds and other kinds of production. The 'soft' services like teaching which require 'human interaction' are necessarily made just like the 'hard' services (book supply, transport, catering, instructional media) which can be standardised, calculated, qualified and compared. This involves the 'flattening' into 'crude representations' of complex human and social processes, it is as De Lissovoy and McLaren (2003, p. 133) represent it, a form of violence. The 'imperative of exchangeability depends upon the violence in the principle of identity' as when 'the student's knowledge is made identical to the test score that stands for it'. Within all of this the specificities of those human interactions involved in teaching and learning are erased. The practice of teaching is re-made and reduced to exogenously generated rule following and target achievement. This provides the logic for the substitution of specialist labour and specialist institutional cultures by generic management systems and cultures to 'manage' performance, improve quality and efficiency. Management is a promiscuous science. It has no necessary relation to substance or process. And in so far as management within the public sector does become separated off as a generic function then it enables what Wright (2001) calls 'bastard leadership' – leadership which is animated by the changing policy concerns of government, and the vicissitudes of the educational marketplace, rather than any commitment to substantive and situated values or principles.[4]

Some caveats to the above now need to be entered. First, the shift from neo-Taylorist management to new managerialism is by no means clear-cut. The use of performance indicators, specified contracting between purchasers and providers and the continued interventions of the state into organisational practices all tend to encourage the retention of organisational characteristics of 'machine bureaucracies' (Mintzberg, 1983). Second, not all organisations embrace change with equal alacrity or enthusiasm. There are pockets of resilience and counter-discursive activity (Mac an Ghaill, 1994). Laughlin (1991) usefully contrasts 'colonisation change', which involves 'major shifts in the cultural core of the organisation' with 'reorientation change' which absorbs the language of reform but not its substance. Third, in many public sector organisations it is possible to identify 'mixed messages' at work. In some circumstances, the market position of certain organisations allows them to escape from the full force of the disciplines of reform. Local and regional configurations of provision also differ and variations and differences have to be balanced out against general trends and patterns. Fourth, it is important not to mistake the heat and noise of reform and the rhetorics of marketisation for 'real' structural and values change. Altogether, policy analysis needs to be accompanied by careful regional, local and organisational research if we are to understand the degrees of 'play' and 'room for manoeuvre' involved in the translation of policies into practices or in the 'bite' of the disciplines of reform. Fifth, total transformation may neither be possible nor desirable within the logic of post-Fordism or the SWS.

> it has become increasingly apparent that within the restructuring of the state, bureau-professionalism cannot simply be dispensed with. Even reorganised departments and agencies require service deliverers with particular skills, service orientations and commitments... what is at stake is not the eradication of bureau-professionalism but the degree to which relevant clusters of skills and values can be subordinated to and accommodated within the new political and organisational logics embodied in managerialism.
>
> (Clarke *et al.*, 1994, p. 223)[5]

Despite these important provisos, I shall argue below that what has changed in the process of public sector restructuring over the past 20 years is, at least in terms of first order change, more important than what has stayed the same. The degree and extent of change becomes even clearer if we consider (very briefly) the concomitant re-imagining of civil society.

A new civility

> The imagination of civil society was the precondition and product of modernity. And so, just like the challenges associated with modernity, it too could not avoid a most bleak destiny after the initial burst of enthusiasm.
>
> (Tester, 1992, p. 176)

The point about Thatcherite neo-liberalism lies not so much in Margaret Thatcher's denial of the existence of society (interview for *Womans Own* 31 October 1987) as in her radical and bleak re-imagining of civil society. This rests upon a re-vivified competitive individualism and a new kind of consumer-citizen – the politics of temptation – to which her denial alludes.

This new citizenry are animated and articulated by Hayekian conceptions of liberty, 'freedom from' rather than 'freedom to', and the right to choice. 'Consumer democracy' is again both the means and the end in social and economic change. 'Active' choice will ensure a more responsive, efficient public sector and 'release' the 'natural' enterprising and competitive tendencies of citizens, destroying to so-called 'dependency culture' in the process. Replacing the latter with the virtues of self-help and self-responsibility (see Deem *et al.*, 1995, chap. 3). Again this is constitutive of the new moral economy discussed above. As Bagguley puts it; '...the state-civil society connection is now more complex than ever, if anything the simple Gramscian dichotomy is dissolving. The very *form* of the state, the *form* of civil society and the form of relationship between them involve radically new political technologies...market power...(Bagguley, 1994, p. 74). He goes on: '...market power is aimed at the *calculus* of the subject inside a proactive body' (p. 74) – the constitution of a new subjectivity.[6]

And so!

There are two main points I want to draw out of this lengthy account. First, how far is it appropriate to conceptualise the processes outlined as *change* or as *transformation*? Clearly, there are inherent problems in relation to the latter in so far as we lack baseline comparative data and are tempted to flirt with the dangers of golden ageism (see below) and see all aspects of reform negatively. But my point here is that we have a fairly clear view of the movements in structure, organisation, forms of relationship and language and values from 'the previous', and significantly little, in these respects, is now 'the same'. The sheer weight of change, or more precisely its scope and pervasiveness is also important. I am claiming therefore that the multi-faceted nature of restructuring, given the provisos about resilience and partiality enter earlier, amounts to a *transformation* in the form of public welfare. That is, a move from one state of affairs with a set of *dominant* characteristics, to a new state of affairs with a different, mutually exclusive set of dominant characteristics. (Hence some of my later concerns for researchers to be aware of policy ensembles, policy relations and levels of policy.) The second, closely related point concerns the nature of this transformation and I want to highlight two major categories of change. One is, drawing from Jessop and others, a change in the *mode of regulation*, 'The idea is of a unity encompassing a particular strategy of capital accumulation, a particular ensemble for social forms and class relations, and a particular hegemonic project' (Ball, 1990, p. 15). I take the market form and competition, contracting (by the state and by institutions) and various commodifications to be the key elements of this project.

Without a sense of the composite, inter-related, multi-faceted nature of change such a conception is difficult to capture or convey. The other aspect of restructuring is the formation of new 'professional' *subjectivities*. It is not simply that what we do is changed; who we are, the possibilities for who we might become, are also changed. There are 'new ways of saying plausible things about other human beings and ourselves' (Rose, 1989, p. 4). Thus, part of the transformation identified above is a 'transformation in the regime for the regulation of private conduct' (p. 226) central to which is 'the theme of enterprise' and the relations of 'exchange between discrete economic units pursuing their undertakings with boldness and energy, ever seeking the new endeavour and the path to advantage...' (p. 226).

I have concentrated thus far on general and generic features of the transformation of the public sector. I have done so for two reasons. One is substantive; that is to indicate the ways in which changes in education are part of a much broader and fundamental transformation across the public sector. There are sectorial variations and differences but these should not prevent us from seeing education against this backdrop of systemic change. The other is rhetorical; that is to highlight the general tendency in education policy research to neglect the commonalities and generalities of restructuring in the public sector.

Education policy research

It is simplistic to suggest any kind of uniform and direct relationship between social and political context and the preoccupations and dispositions of the academy. Equally however it would be naive to attempt to disconnect movements and trends in theory and research from the discourses of reform. Research is thoroughly enmeshed 'in' the social and 'in' the political and developments and innovations within the human sciences, like education, are intimately imbricated in the practical management of social and political problems. A quick skim through the papers presented at the British Educational Research Association conference indicates the extent to which education policy research is caught up in the agendas and purposes of the state and the governance of education. The vocabularies of research method may work to distance researchers from the subjects of their activity but, at the same time, it also constructs a gaze that renders the social landscape of education ever more visible. While there is a fetishistic preoccupation in some research with the mundane reflexivity of fieldwork interactions there is almost no reflexive attention paid to surveillant and disciplinary aspects of research – that is the work that research does as 'a subtle, calculated technology of subjection' (Foucault, 1977, p. 221). This takes on even more subtle dimensions as teachers are encouraged to undertake certain forms of research on their own practice – an auto-opticon. As Foucault argues 'power produces' and 'the individual and the knowledge that may be gained of him belong to this production' (p. 194).

Having said that education policy research displays a variety of stances, styles and preoccupation's which are positioned differently in relation to the processes and methods of reform and in relation to the traditions and practices of the human sciences. Perhaps perversely, I want to try to capture and explore some of that variety by use of a rather spartan and reified binary template. And I shall use the discussion of the template as a way of reviewing some specific examples of education policy research from the past 15 years, moving erratically and unevenly between the poles. In many respects these binaries may be seen as an elaboration of the policy science-policy scholarship dichotomy identified by (Fay, 1975) and used

Table 1.1 A template

a	
Policy oriented	Practice oriented
Multi-focus	Single focus
Multi-level	Single level
Temporal	Atemporal
Global/local	National/general
Linked focus	Detached
b	
Context rich	Context barren
Conceptually 'thick'	Conceptually 'thin'
c	
Social justice	Social efficiency
Critical	Incorporated
d	
Voiced	Silent

extensively by (Grace, 1995). Grace explains:

> Policy scholarship resists the tendency of policy science to abstract problems from their relational settings by insisting that the problem can only be understood in the complexity of those relations. In particular, it represents a view that a social-historical approach to research can illuminate the cultural and ideological struggles in which schooling is located...Whereas policy science excludes ideological and value conflicts as 'externalities beyond its remit...
>
> (Grace, 1995, p. 3)[7]

I will work through the template (Table 1.1) taking the binaries in related groups, identifying and adumbrating points and arguments, some of which will need to be developed more fully elsewhere. The first group deals with issues of definition and conception. As Elmore (1996) points out policy is additive, layered and filtered. He goes on to argue that:

> Education reform policy [and I would add education policy research SJB] typically embodies three distinctive conceits: (a) that the newest set of reform policies automatically takes precedence over all previous policies under which the system has operated; (b) that reform policies emanate from a single level of the education system and embody a single message about what schools should do differently; and (c) that reform policies should operate in more or less the same way in whatever settings they are implemented.

a

The first point I would make is in relation to the difference between 'policy-oriented' and 'practice-oriented' research. Clearly a great of research 'about' education or schooling is not 'about' policy at all. But in some of this research policy may be thought of as a significant present absence. Policy is ignored or theorised 'out of the picture'. This is particularly the case in research about classrooms, about teachers and about schools which treats them as free-standing and self-determining, as 'out of context'. That is, as out of their relational settings – as unaffected or unconstrained by the requirements of a National Curriculum, LMS, Local League Tables or competition. Such research takes patterns of teacher or headteacher activity to be exclusively constituted by educational principles and concerns and as not inflected and mediated by the new moral economy of the public sector. In a sense this kind of research slips neatly back into the unreflexive, 'blame-based' tactics of policy-makers wherein policies are always solutions and never part of the problem. 'The problem' is 'in' the school or 'in' the teacher but never 'in' policies.

There are overlaps here with the second binary. One of the generative effects of the flood of policy in the 1980s and 1990s is the flood of single-focus studies which concentrate exclusively on one policy bracketing out all others. The result is typically a reiteration of the 'policy-practice gap' with an implicit or explicit assumption that the gap represents an implementation failure on the part of teachers or schools. Critical or social justice researchers are as often as guilty of this kind of single-focus analysis as policy scientists – schools are presented as being not anti-racist enough or as not taking special needs seriously enough – without any attempt to consider the other things they are expected or required to take seriously and which compete for attention, effort and resources in the complexities of practice. I am not making the point as a way of 'excusing' 'bad practice'. Rather I am questioning the way in which policy studies are designed and focused and the relationship between design and focus and the interpretational claims that researchers make about research subjects. Policies pose problems to their subjects. (It may be possible for some to 'hide' from policy but that is rarely a common option.) When ensembles of uncoordinated or contradictory policies are in play then the resort to satisficing strategies and secondary accommodations may be the only reasonable and feasible response at certain points in time. As Elmore (above) indicates, when we focus analytically on one policy we conveniently forget that other policies are in circulation and that the enactment of one may inhibit or contradict or influence the possibility of the enactment of others.

My third binary presents a contrast between a conception of policy which treats policies as clear, abstract and fixed as opposed to one in which policies are awkward, incomplete, incoherent and unstable. (This relates to Elmore's points (b) and (c) above.) The first conception leads easily to the view that policies are or should be realised in the same way in every setting (part of the policymakers' dreamworld). The second begins with the assumption that local conditions, resources, histories and commitments will differ and that policy realisation will differ accordingly. Vincent's (1996) recent work on parent/teacher relations is a good example of the latter with her careful analysis of the role of school micropolitics as a key factor in the differential realisation of a home/school project in three primary schools. The third pairing also deals with a further aspect of the conceptualisation of policy and the design of policy research. Here the opposition is between those studies which are located at a single level of analysis – the school, classroom, LEA – and those which attempt to capture the dynamics of policy across and between levels; what I have called a 'policy trajectory' approach (Ball, 1994). The work of Edwards and Whitty, with Fitz and Gewirtz (Edwards *et al.*, 1989; Whitty *et al.*, 1993) remain the best examples of this genre of policy research in education. Both studies, of the Assisted Places Scheme and City Technology Colleges policies respectively, trace through the development, formation and realisation of those policies from the context of influence, through policy text production, to practices and outcomes (see Ball, 1994). The trajectory perspective attends to the ways in which policies evolve, change and decay through time and space and their incoherence. Here policymaking is a process which takes place within arenas of struggle over meaning (Taylor, 1997); it is the 'politics of discourse' (Yeatman, 1990).

There are of course further temporal aspects to the processes of policy and policy analysis but in practice most education policy research lacks any sense of time. The most obvious aspect of this neglect is a rampant ahistoricism. As Grace (1995) argues 'Many contemporary problems or crises in education are, in themselves, the surface manifestations of deeper historical, structural and ideological contradictions in education policy' (p. 3). There is clearly a dearth of policy research which takes Grace's imperative seriously. Indeed there is a distinct tendency of 'post-88ism'. That is, a good deal of policy research takes the changes introduced by the 1988 Education Reform Act as ground zero in the history of education, anything happening before 1988 becomes a kind of unexplored pre-history, creating a rubicon-like 'before-and-after' effect. A sense of significant continuities is lost sight of in the heat and noise of reform. But the 1988 watershed is important in other ways. For example, the tendency of 'golden ageism', the washing away of critical analysis of pre-88 policies, and thus the contrasting of the best of comprehensivism with the worst of market education. Power (1992) notes two aspects to this phenomenon. One is that policy post-88 is treated as potent and influential, as having a decisive impact on practice on the ground, whereas pre-88 policy was more usually viewed sceptically and as having minimal impact on practice.[8] Power's second point concerns the common deployment of a kind of analytic reversal: 'Take, for instance, explorations of the way in which educational psychologists or Education Welfare Officers were implicated, albeit "unintentionally," in the processes of differentiation, regulation and surveillance. Now that the influence of these kind of agencies is likely to be diminished, there is a tendency to perceive of them as some kind of benign buffer, trying to shore up the defences against even darker forces' (p. 496). Power's counsel alerts us not only to the problems of sloppy interpretative work but also again to the absence of decent baseline or longitudinal data which would allow for robust comparisons of pre- and post-1988 policy effects. Lastly, time is also a problematic in the interpretation of reform. We now have a series of studies which date from the earliest stages of reform up to the present time, most of which are snapshots.[9] There are two problems here. First, such time limited studies cannot deliver a sense of the processes of reform and change. Structural change is only one part and one moment in the reform process; change in consciousness, adaptation of practices, the arts of resistance and manoeuvre, 'values drift' (Gewirtz *et al.*, 1995) take place slowly, sometimes almost imperceptibly over time. Second, and related, there is a general problem concerning the status of 'findings' and 'conclusions' from such one-off studies. At what point is it valid to begin to draw conclusions about the effects of policy? After one year, or five, or ten? Again, in both cases here, practical and empirical issues are interwoven with the design of research, and the conceptualisation of policy.[10] All of this is crucial to and pointed up in my discussion above of the 'transformation' of the public sector.

Moving on, from time to space, I want to draw attention to both the insularity and abstractness of much education policy research. Policy research lacks a sense of 'place'; either in not locating policies in any framework that extends beyond the national level, or in not accounting for or conveying a sense of the locality in analyses of policy realisation. On the first point Brown and Lauder (1996) and Lingard (1996) illustrate the sort of framing of policy that a global perspective provides. And, as Brown and Lauder (1996) note: 'Knowledge, learning, information and technical competence are the new raw materials of international commerce' (p. 4). In effect the national/global relationship is another point of mediation in the policy process; an interface where pressures and constraints are mediated by 'local' concerns and preferences. As yet UK education policy researchers have paid relatively little attention to this interface except for some attempts to explore the issue of 'policy convergence' in education and the role in this of 'policy borrowing' (see Vanegas and Ball, 1996). For example, Whitty and Edwards (1992) investigation into 'whether cross-national networks of influence can be identified as an explanation of the apparent convergence in education policy' in the UK and USA. Halpin and Troyna (1995) conclude a review of such work by suggesting that all the evidence points to the importance of the symbolic role of 'borrowing' rather than practical transfer of the particularities of policy. Clearly, analysis of the flow and influence of policies between nations needs to be addressed with care; Popkewitz (1996) argues that: 'we can find a particular internationalisation of ideas as well as the particular "national" reflexivity about how such ideas are realised' (p. 47). This conception parallels my comments above about the institutional realisation of policies.

The second sense of place, the role of the local is, in a sense, a reversal of the above, and again I want to emphasise two aspects. First, there is the attempt, in some research, to identify particular characteristics of 'the local' which are significant in the realisation of policy. For example, recently researchers working of the development of markets in education have begun to examine and specify features of what Glatter (1996) call 'local competitive arenas' (see also Gewirtz *et al.*, 1995). However, a great deal of education research dis-locates schools and classrooms from their physical and cultural environment. They all begin to 'look' and 'sound' the same. The second aspect of locality relates to this latter point. That is, the failure of policy research to convey a sense of region or community or setting. But this is not simply a point about empirical description, although more of that would be very welcome, it is also about theorisation. As Cooke (1990) puts it:

> locality retains significance and social meaning in a contemporary period when the combined forces of modernity in the state, in multinational capital and in the mass media, have all but effaced the older social solidarities of community. The significance of this is that the modern nation state only gains its legitimacy from a practical division of functions between the centre where ... power increasingly lies and the locality, where its subject individuals live out their everyday working and consuming lives.
>
> (p. 132)

b

The next polarity refers back to the assertion made earlier that education policy research generally fails to acknowledge the generic quality of reform. That is, education is cut-off from the broader field of social policy change. I want to pick up on three facets of this isolationism. One is empirical/analytic, the simple failure to place education within the more general projects and ideologies of contemporary social policy. The other is interpretative, the lack of awareness of and use of concepts and theories applied and developed in these other fields. Recent exceptions to this are the take up of the concepts of 'quasi-markets' (Le Grand and Barlett, 1993), and 'post-fordism' (Hickox and Moore, 1992), and the more general impact and influence of feminist and postmodern theories. (There are also dangers in concept 'borrowing', especially when complex concepts are appropriated without any sense of their baggage of contestation or diverse interpretations.) I take the view that the interplay of theories, what McLennan (1996) calls 'combined' rather than 'additive' theorising, provides a rich source of concepts; for interpreting the policy process and policy effects; as ways of moving beyond the obvious; as ways of making links and envisioning relationships; for thickening up our descriptive registers. In order to go beyond the accidents and contingencies which enfold us, it is necessary to start from another position and begin from what is normally excluded. Theories offer another language, a language of distance, of irony, of imagination. And part of this, as Sheridan puts it is 'a love of hypothesis, of invention' which is also unashamedly 'a love of the beautiful' (Sheridan, 1980, p. 223) – as against the bland, technical and desolate languages of policy science and policy entrepreneurship. And indeed descriptive empiricism remains predominant in education policy research writing. My concern for theoretical interplay must clearly carry with it a particular concern to maintain coherence; but in the retreat from 'eliminative' reductionism (McLennan, 1996) theorists of all kinds now seem to acknowledge the need for and efficacy of multiple theories; 'of thinking neo and post together, of actively enabling the tensions within and among them to help form our research' (Apple, 1996, p. 141). In general terms these tensions (between structure, discourse and agency) revolve around what may be gained and what must be given away. It can mean having to deal in paradoxes and having to resist theoretical closure which does not or should not mean licensed incoherence.

> There is a world of difference (and no pun intended here) between emphasising the local, the contingent, and non-correspondence and ignoring any determinancy or any structural relationships among practices. Too often important questions surrounding the state and social formation are simply evacuated and the difficult problem of simultaneously thinking about both the specificity of different practices and the forms of articulated unity they constitute is assumed out of existence as if nothing existed in structured ways.
>
> (Apple, 1996, p. 141)[11]

I also want to underscore the point made earlier concerning the other aspect of isolationism; the substantive dis-connection of education policy research from the general arena of social policy. My concern here rests on a more general argument and relates to issues about the interpretation and theorisation of reform as outlined above. In failing to take account of the ways in which education is embedded in a set of more general economic and political changes education policy, researchers close down the possibilities for interpretation and rip the actors who feature in the dramas of education out of their social totality and their multiple struggles. We are thus, for example, unable to 'see' the impact and effects on different families of the development of multiple social markets and concomitant changes in the welfare state. Isolationism encourages the inherent tendency to 'over-estimate education's capacity to affect social inequalities by exaggerating its role in reproducing them' (Moore, 1996, p. 159).

c

Theory is important to research in another sense. Theory provides this possibility, the possibility of disidentification – the effect of working 'on and against' prevailing practices of ideological subjection. The point of theory and of intellectual endeavour in the social sciences should be, in Foucault's words, 'to sap power', to engage in struggle to reveal and undermine what is most invisible and insidious in prevailing practices (Troyna, 1994). This is very much a 'practical' concern addressed directly to the practices and interests of educational workers; but not at all in the sense meant by Bassey (1995) or Hargreaves (1996) in recent accounts of the role of research in education. Neither seem to envision the teacher as an intellectual. For Hargreaves teachers are 'experts' whose status must rest on demonstrable competence (p. 7); 'there is no virtue in expert teachers and newly qualified heads studying substantial bodies of educational theory and research that is mostly remote from practical application' (p. 7). For me, in contrast, theory provides the possibility of a different language, a language which is not caught up with the assumptions and inscriptions of policy-makers or the immediacy of practice (or embedded in tradition, prejudice, dogma and ideology – see below). It offers a potential location outside the prevailing discourses of policy and a way of struggling against 'incorporation'. To borrow Moore's formulation (Moore, 1996, p. 159), it maintains the boundary between critical research 'of' policy and research 'for' policy. 'The former positions the standpoint of the field, the latter is positioned by it' (p. 159).

Moore's binary addresses an increasingly critical and deep division within education policy research. A division between the new Benthamism and panopticism which is represented above by Hargreaves and the school effectiveness movement in general, with its emphasis upon performativity (Lyotard, 1984) and efficiency. And the various forms of critical/social justice research (socialist and deconstructive, Fraser, 1995) which place 'dignity' above 'price'.

Nonetheless, theory – work also has its own intrinsic problems of incorporation. Indeed, our use of theory is sometimes mantric, and simply gesturally featured. A process of concept matching, the search 'for a case of' – governmentality, patriarchy, state oppression, post-fordism. Theory as finger-pointing. Furthermore, much of what passes for theoretical informed research lacks any sense of critical distance or reflexivity about its own production and procedures and its claims to knowledge about the social. In the search for a point of vision, a place to see from, many policy researchers simply seek to reinhabit the old redemptive assumptions based upon an unproblematic organic role for themselves in a perpetual process of progressive, orderly growth or development achieved through scientific and technological 'mastery' or control over events or by the assertive re-cycling of old dogmas and tired utopias.

d

My final binary is epistemologically different in kind from the above and returns in some respects to the earlier concerns with the conceptualisation of policy itself and the way this is represented and reproduced in our analytical texts. The prevailing, but normally implicit view, is that policy is something that is 'done' to people. As first order recipients 'they' 'implement' policy, as second order recipients 'they' are advantaged or disadvantaged by it. I take a different view (see Ball, 1994). That is, as noted earlier: policies pose problems to their subjects, problems that must be solved in context. Solutions to the problems posed by policy texts will be localised and should be expected to display ad hocery and messiness. Responses indeed must be 'creative'. Policies do not normally tell you what to do, they create circumstances in which the range of options available in deciding what to do are narrowed or changed or particular goals or outcomes are set. A response must still be put together, constructed in context, off-set against or balanced by other expectations. All of this involves creative social action of some kind. This is what Bagguley calls 'the agency of the insubordinates' (p. 74). A first order response might result in colonisation (Laughlin, 1991). A second order response may produce despair, struggle or illicit circumvention (see e.g. Bagguley's account of non-poll-tax payers). I am also interested here in questions about the ontology of policy which are begged by such a conception. In particular, the way that we 'people' policy. Clearly, in some policy research there are no people as such. There is a deafening silence at the heart of these busy, abstract, tidy texts. Both the people that 'do' policy and those who confront it are displaced. And yet, alongside this, in many 'implementation' studies a 'peopling' is implicit. A set of recalcitrant, conservative and narrow-minded 'practitioners' is conjured up. They hide behind their closed-doors, resisting change, maintaining their naive commitments to progressivism, or anti-racism or class teaching (when they 'should' be doing investigations) or group-work (when they should be class teaching). Thus,

Hargreaves (1996), in reproducing a typically one sided imagery, quotes four grounds which Cox asserts that teacher use to justify their practices – tradition, prejudice, dogma and ideology. In other studies, of a different sort, equally shadowy characters emerge, romantic resisters, Althusserian 'heroes' (*sic*) striving against oppression or the 'bad' practices which policy-makers seek to foist upon them. As Power (1992) notes some of the former in pre-1988 research seem to have become the latter in post-1988 research even though their practices and perspectives have remained unchanged. These are cardboard cut-out people, one dimensional caricatures who fail to display the complexities, contradictions and paradoxes that you and I demonstrate in the face of change. I am not simply celebrating 'the quotation from data' here, that in itself does not guarantee that we are presented with authentic or complex social actors or capture a sense of events 'written…in letters of blood and fire' (Marx, 1977, p. 669; quoted in Bagguley, 1994). Rather it is the nature of the representation and conceptualisation of people within our texts as a whole and within our models of sociality that is the issue. My own research has been criticised in this respect, reviewing *Education Reform* (Ball, 1994) Nespor makes the point that:

> Policy and reform appear only in the interactions of politicians, administrators, teachers and researchers. Parents appear only as they are constructed in the language of the dominant conservative policy discourse – as 'consumers' or 'clients'. And while complaining that students are formulated as commodities and consumers by market discourse, Ball really does not talk about them in any other way in his own text. Is there no place for the standpoints of parents and students in critical policy analysis? How have academic and policy discourses accomplished the exclusion of such standpoints?
>
> (Nespor, 1996, pp. 380–1)

By thinking about what sort of people and 'voices' inhabit the texts of policy analysis we also need to think about how we engage with the social and collective identities of our research subjects – the 'teacher', 'parent', 'policymaker'; their gender, class, race, sexuality and physical ability. It is one thing to consider the 'effects' of policies upon abstract social collectivities. It is another to attempt to capture the complex interplay of identities and interests and coalitions and conflicts within the processes and enactments of policy (see Reay, 1991; Gillborn, 1995; Troyna *et al.*, 1993). It is important to recognise that social diversity and 'difference' are important bases for understanding the range of active social forces involved in and resistant to change – recognition is important. Equally however the effects of policy play upon and through the basic social facts of poverty, oppression and inequality. One challenge confronting education policy researchers therefore is engagement with the new intellectual and practical tasks identified by Nancy Fraser (1995, p. 69): 'that of developing a *critical* theory of recognition, one which identifies and defends only those versions of the cultural politics of difference that can be coherently combined with the social politics of equality'.

And then!

As noted already, there is a basic and apparently irredemable tension at the heart of education policy research. A tension between the concerns of efficiency and those of social justice. A tension which structures much of my previous discussion. Both sides of the tension are political – although the proselytisers of efficiency do not typically see it that way. And indeed, I find it difficult to imagine what non-political research might look like. Individual researchers must address, or try to resolve, the tension as they see fit; although it just may be that some of one side has to sacrificed to achieve more of the other. For me John Prunty provides a clear statement of good practice:

> The personal values and political commitment of the critical policy analyst would be anchored in the vision of a moral order in which justice, equality and individual freedom are uncompromised by the avarice of a few. The critical analyst would endorse political, social and economic arrangements where persons are never treated as a means to an end, but treated as ends in their own right.
>
> (Prunty, 1985, p. 139)

Acknowlegements

I am grateful to Alan Cribb, Louise Morely and Carol Vincent for their cogent criticisms of earlier drafts of this paper. The limits of available space have meant that I have not been able to take on board all of their comments.

Notes

1 In the past in an effort to be more precise I have used Jenny Ozga's term 'policy sociology', Ball, S. J. (1990). *Politics and Policymaking in Education*. London, Routledge.
2 As a result performativity drives resistance, drives professionalism, inside the practitioner – in doing so the alternatives to responsibility and excellence are either escape or madness.
3 Market power, unscrupulous competition and survivalist management are blended with passion, emotion and an emphasis upon communication and facilitation skills.
4 Although Gold *et al.* (2003) claim to have evidence of the continued existence in the UK of 'principled principals' (Wright, 2003).
5 Attempts with Licensed and Articled and Mums army, controls over PT, but also cost cutting exercises.
6 Furthermore, the new discourse of consumer-citizenship both obscures and, at the same time, positions the 'underclass' 'beyond' civil society, as 'non-citizens', the dependent 'others'.
7 I have also suggested a third category to extend and compliment Fay's categories, that of the policy entrepreneur (see Chapter 4).
8 Of course it might be argued that post-88 policy is different in kind, more pervasive and broader in scope, more directive and interventionary, more firmly tied to statutory requirements; that practice pre-88 was under-determined by policy whereas practice post-88 is over-determined.
9 My colleagues and I have tried to address this in a series of related studies in a set of schools over a seven year period; see Bowe, R. *et al.* (1992). *Reforming Education and Changing Schools: Case Studies in Policy Sociology*. London, Routledge. Gewirtz, S. *et al.* (1995). *Markets, Choice and Equity in Education*. Buckingham, Open University Press.
10 Clearly the strictures of research funding encourage a quick-turn-around, snapshot style of research.
11 This dual perspective captures the paradoxical analysis embedded in this paper; that is an argument for structural transformation set against an argument for diverse local policy realisation.

References

Apple, M. (1996). 'Power, Meaning and Identity: Critical Sociology of Education in the United States'. *British Journal of Sociology of Education* 17(2): 125–44.
Bagguley, P. (1994). Prisoners of the Beveridge Dream? The Political Mobilisation of the Poor Against Contemporary Welfare Regimes. In *Towards a Post-Fordist Welfare State?* R. Burrows and B. Loader (eds). London, Routledge.
Ball, S. J. (1990). *Politics and Policymaking in Education*. London, Routledge.
Ball, S. J. (1994). *Education Reform: A Critical and Post-Structural Approach*. Buckingham, Open University Press.
Ball, S. J. (1995). 'Intellectuals or Technicians? The Urgent role of Theory in Educational Studies'. *British Journal of Educational Studies* 43(3): 255–71.

Bassey, M. (1995). *Creating Education Through Research*. Newark/Edunburgh, Kirklington Moor Press/British Educational Research Association.

Blackmore, J. (1995). Breaking Out from a Masculinist Politics of Education. In *Gender and Changing Educational Management*. B. Limerick and B. Linguard (eds). Sydney, Hodder.

Bowe, R., Ball, S. J. and Gewirtz, S. (1992). *Reforming Education and Changing Schools: Case Studies in Policy Sociology*. London, Routledge.

Boyles, D. (2000). *Amercian Education and Corporations: The Free Market Goes to School*. New York, Falmer Press.

Brown, P. and H. Lauder (1996). 'Education, Globalisation and Economic Development'. *Journal of Education Policy* 11(1): 1–25.

Clarke, J. and J. Newman (1992). *The Right to Manage: A Second Managerial Revolution*. Milton Keynes, Open University.

Clarke, J., Cochrane, A. and McLaughlin, E. (1994). Mission Accomplished or Unfinished Business? The Impact of Managerialization. In *Managing Social Policy*. J. Clarke, A. Cochrane and L. McLaughlin (eds). London, Sage.

Cooke, P. (1990). *Back to the Future: Modernity, Postmodernity and Locality*. London, Unwin Hyman.

Deem, R., Brehony, K. and Heath, S. (1995). *Active Citizenship and the Governing of Schools*. Buckingham, Open University Press.

De Lissovoy, N. and P. McLaren (2003). 'Educational "accountability" and the violence of capital: a Marxian reading of post-structuralist positions'. *Journal of Education Policy* 18(2): 131–144.

Du Gay, P. (1996). *Consumption and Identity at Work*. London, Sage.

Edwards, T., Fitz, J. and Whitty, G. (1989). *The State and Private Education: An Evaluation of the Assisted Places Scheme*. Lewes, Falmer.

Elmore, R. F. (1996). 'School Reform, Teaching and Learning'. *Journal of Education Policy* 11(4): xxx.

Fay, B. (1975). *Social Theory and Political Practice*. London, Allen and Unwin.

Foucault, M. (1977). *Discipline and Punish*. New York, Pantheon Press.

Fraser, N. (1995). 'From Redistribution to Recognition? Dilemmas of Justice in a "Post-Socialist" Age'. *New Left Review* 212: 68–93.

Gewirtz, S., Ball, S. J. and Bowe, R. (1995). *Markets, Choice and Equity in Education*. Buckingham, Open University Press.

Gillborn, D. (1995). *Racism and Antiracism in Real Schools*. Buckingham, Open University Press.

Glatter, R., Bagley, C. and Woods, P. (1996). Modelling Local Markets in Schooling. In *Markets in Education: Policy, Process and Practice*. N. Foskett (ed.). Conference Proceedings. University of Southampton.

Gold, A., Evans, J., Earely, P., Halpin, D. and Collarbone, P. (2003). 'Principled Principals? Values Driven Leadership: Evidence from Ten Case Studies of "Outstanding" School Leaders'. *Educational Management and Administration* 31(2): 127–38.

Grace, G. (1995). *School Leadership: Beyond Education Management: An Essay in Policy Scholarship*. London, Falmer.

Halpin, D. and Troyna, B. (1995). 'The Politics of Education Policy Borrowing'. *Comparative Education* 31(3): 303–10.

Hargreaves, D. (1996). Teaching as a Research-based Profession: Possibilities and Prospects. *Teacher Training Agency Annual Lecture*. London, TTA.

Heelas, P. and Morris, P. (eds) (1992). *The Values of the Enterprise Culture: The Moral Debate*. London, Routledge.

Hickox, M. and Moore, R. (1992). Education and post-Fordism: A New Correspondence? In *Education for Economic Survival: from Fordism to Post-Fordism?* P. Brown and H. Lauder (eds). London, Routledge.

Hoggett, P. (1994). The Modernisation of the UK Welfare State. In *Towards a post-Fordist Welfare State?* R. Burrows and B. Loader (eds). London, Routledge.

Jessop, B. (1994). The Transition to post-Fordism and the Schumpeterian Workfare State. In *Towards a post-Fordist Welfare State?* R. Burrows and B. Loader (eds). London, Routledge.

Kikert, W. (1991). *Steering at a Distance; A New Paradigm of Public Governance in Dutch Higher Education*. Eurepean Consortium for Political Research, University of Essex.

Kirkpatrick, I. and M. Martinez-Lucio (1995). Introduction. In *The Politics of Quality in the Public Sector*. I. Kinkpatrick and M. Martinez-Lucio (eds). London, Routledge.

Laughlin, R. (1991). 'Can the Information Systems for the NHS Internal Market Work?' *Public Money and Management* Autumn: 37–41.

Le Grand, J. and W. Barlett (eds) (1993). *Quasi-Markets and Social Policy*. Basingstoke, Macmillan.

Limerick, B. and B. Linguard (eds) (1995). *Breaking Out from a Masculinist Politics of Education*. Yearbook of the Australian Council for Educational Administration. Sydney, Hodder.

Lingard, B. (1996). 'Educational Policy Making in a Postmodern State'. *The Australian Educational Researcher* 23: 65–91.

Lyotard, J.-F. (1984). *The Postmodern Condition: A Report on Knowledge*. Manchester, Manchester University Press.

Mac an Ghaill, M. (1994). Public Service in the Market: The Birmingham Catholic Partnership. In *Cooperating in the Education Marketplace*. M. Lawn and M. Mac an Ghaill (eds). Birmingham, Educational Review Publications.

McLennan, G. (1996). 'Post-Marxism and the "Four Sins" of Moderist Theorising'. *New Left Review* 218: 53–74.

Mintzberg, H. (1983). *Structure in Fives: Designing Effective Organisations*. Englewood Cliffs, NJ, Prentice Hall.

Moore, R. (1996). 'Back to the Future: The Problems of Change and Possibilities of Advance in the Sociology of Education'. *British Journal of Sociology of Education* 17(2): 145–62.

Nespor, J. (1996). 'A Review of: Stephen J Ball, Education Reform'. *International Journal of Qualitative Studies in Education* 9(3): 380–1.

Newman, J. and J. Clarke (1994). Going about Our Business? The Mangerialization of Public Services. *Managing Social Policy*. J. Clarke, A. Cochrane and E. McLaughlin (eds). London, Sage.

Newman, S. (1984). *Liberalism at Wits End*. Ithaca, NY, Cornell University Press.

Popkewitz, T. (1996). 'Rethinking Decentralisation and State/Civil Society Distinctions: The State as a Problematic of Governing'. *Journal of Education Policy* 11(1): 27–52.

Power, S. (1992). 'Researching the Impact of Education Policy: Difficulties and Discontinuities'. *Journal of Education Policy* 7(5): 493–500.

Prunty, J. (1985). 'Signposts for a Critical Educational Policy Analysis'. *Australian Journal of Education* 29(2): 133–40.

Reay, D. (1991). 'Intersections of Gender, Race and Class in the Primary School'. *British Journal of Sociology of Education* 12(2): 163–82.

Rose, N. (1989). *Governing the Soul: The Shaping of the Private Self*. London, Routledge.

Rose, N. (1992). Governing the Enterprising Self. *The Values of the Enterprise Culture*. P. Heelas and P. Morris (eds). London, Routledge.

Sheridan, A. (1980). *Michel Foucault: The Will to Truth*. London, Tavistock.

Sinclair, J., Seifert, R. and Ironside, M. (1995). Market-driven Reforms in Education: Performance, Quality and Industrial Relations in Schools. In *The Politics of Quality in the Public Sector*. I. Kirkpatrick and M. M. Lucio (eds). London, Routledge.

Taylor, S. (1997). 'Critical Policy Analysis: Exploring Contexts, Texts and Consequences'. *Discourse* 18(1): 23–35.

Tester, K. (1992). *Civil Society*. London, Routledge.

Troyna, B. (1994). 'Critical Social Research and Education Policy'. *British Journal of Educational Studies* 42(1): 70–84.

Troyna, B., Hatcher, R. and Gewirtz, D. (1993). *Local Management of Schools and Racial Equality*. London, Commission for Racial Equality.

Vanegas, P. and S. J. Ball (1996). *The Teacher as a Variable in Education Policy*. BERA annual meeting, Lancaster, UK.

Vincent, C. (1996). *Parents and Teachers: Power and Participation*. London, Falmer.

Whitty, G. and T. Edwards (1992). *School Choice Policies in Britain and the USA: Their Origins and Significance*. AERA annual meeting, San Francisco.

Whitty, G., Power, S. and Halpin, D. (1993). *Specialisation and Choice in Urban Education: The City Technology College Experiment*. London, Routledge.

Wright, N. (2001). 'Leadership, "Bastard Leadership" and Mangerialism: Confronting Twin Paradoxes of the Balir Education Project'. *Educational Management and Administration* 29(3): 275–90.

Yeatman, A. (1990). *Bureaucrats, Technocrats, Femocrats: Essays on the Contemporary Australian State*. London, Falmer Press.

CHAPTER 2

DISCIPLINE AND CHAOS
The New Right and discourses of derision

Politics and Policy Making in Education, London: Routledge, 1990

> [I]n any society the production of discourse is at once controlled, selected, organized and redistributed according to a number of procedures whose role is to avert its powers and its dangers, to master the unpredictable event.
>
> (Foucault, 1981, p. 53)

In this chapter and the following one, I intend to examine the impact of the so-called New Right on education policy in two different but related ways. First, I will introduce and discuss the substantive views of the New Right and, via the concept of *discourse*, I shall then argue that these views have come to constrain the possibilities of policy and policy debate.

Discourse provides a particular and pertinent way of understanding policy formation, for policies are, pre-eminently, statements about practice – the way things could or should be – which rest upon, derive from, statements about the world – about the way things are. They are intended to bring about idealised solutions to diagnosed problems. Policies embody claims to speak with authority, they legitimate and initiate practices in the world, and they privilege certain visions and interests. They are power/knowledge configurations *par excellence*. Indeed, Foucault suggests that there are two arenas within which 'procedures of exclusion', the control over discourses, is most strict in our society; they are sexuality and politics. 'We know very well that we are not free to say anything, that we cannot speak of anything when and where we like, and that just anyone, in short, cannot speak of just anything' (Foucault, 1981, p. 62).

What is presented here, then, is a discursive account of education policy through the 1970s and 1980s. It is not an account of events as such and it is by no means exhaustive, although I will suggest that certain events are of special discursive significance. Rather I am concerned with a number of emergent theories and key issues in policy debate and the manner and effects of their articulation (see Laclau and Mouffe, 1985). In particular, I shall draw attention to the way in which these emergent discourses were constructed to define the field, articulate the positions and thus subtly set limits to the possibilities of education policy.

The New Right and education: the beginnings

Foucault distinguishes between beginnings and origins. The latter provide a basis from which causality and narrative can be deployed. Origins, once found, are often taken to constitute an explanation of things; they are also commonly the starting point for the evolution or development of things. In contrast, an interest in the former (beginnings) involves not a reconstitution of the past but rather an attempt to make the past intelligible.

I take as my beginnings, then, not one point in time but, in fact, two. The first, the year 1969, is the date of publication of the first of the *Black Papers* (Cox and Dyson, 1969), a series of right-wing, populist pamphlets which mounted a trenchant critique of all aspects of progressive and comprehensive education. The second, the year 1976, is the date of Labour Prime Minister James Callaghan's much-publicised speech at Ruskin College, Oxford, in which he appeared to take up basic aspects of the *Black Paper* criticisms, and in which he initiated The Great Debate on education. Something of the differences between origins and beginnings is highlighted in the following comment made in interview by Stuart Sexton.

> The turning point, not just in education, was in turning away from Heath-minded conservatism, to the re-emphasis of individual freedom and the market, that things worked better if you let people run their own show, rather than bureaucrats, etc. That was really brought in and encouraged by Mrs Thatcher when she assumed leadership of the party.
>
> It irritates me when people claim that the 1976 Callaghan Ruskin speech was the turning point when it jolly well wasn't. It was an attempt by the then Labour government to recapture some of the initiative we had captured. Norman St John Stevas' Parent Charter speech in Stockport was more important a year previously. It got less publicity because it wasn't James Callaghan. Callaghan said nothing new but it was the Labour government saying it, climbing on the band wagon. They then carried on the bad old ways under Shirley Williams anyway and if you look at that 1976 Education Act...

Nonetheless, Sexton, like a large number of the rest of my respondents, identified the Ruskin speech as being of major discursive significance. The speaker, the setting and the nature of the text all came together to provide legitimation for a conception of the problems and possibilities of education and to empower certain groups and constituencies to speak authoritatively about education and to marginalise other groups.

1969

The first of the *Black Papers* (Cox and Dyson, 1969) on education was primarily concerned with Higher Education and the political involvement of students in the events of 1968. For many of the writers in the collection the causes of such student unrest were seen to lie in the lack of respect for and challenge to traditional authority (both the authority of texts and of institutions); and indeed much of this critique arises from inside the academic establishment. Typically, C. L. Mowat argues: 'We forget at our peril the mediaeval origin of universities as guilds analogous to the craftmen's guilds, in which the masters, journeymen and apprentices were all bretheren but not all equal' (Cox and Dyson, 1969, p. 13). The basis of the critique is within the tradition of what Williams (1962) calls 'old humanism'. It contains both a defence of the elitist, liberal curriculum and an attack on the destabilising effects of progressivism. The discourse being generated here links education with traditional social and political values and with social order. In the rest of the series the criticisms tend to focus more particularly on schools and especially upon comprehensive schools, the products of Department for

Education and Science (DES) Circular 10/65, and progressive primary schools, the progeny of the Plowden Report. But the underlying concerns are essentially the same no matter what the specific object of critique. A new ideology of education was being synthesised under the 'mobilizing myth' (Levitas, 1986, p. 8) of education in 'crisis'. State education was portrayed as having disintegrated into chaos; and, having established an imagery of crisis and chaos, the *Black Papers* writers were not slow to offer their solution. The call was both for a return to pre-comprehensive, pre-progressive forms and methods (the reinvention of tradition or cultural restoration) and for new ways of exerting discipline in and over education.

> In the name of 'equality of opportunity' the egalitarian seeks to destroy or transmogrify those schools which make special efforts to bring out the best in talented children...in his impatience the egalitarian takes the alternative course of levelling down the higher standards towards a uniform mediocrity...This leads him to decry the importance of academic standards and discipline – and indeed learning itself.
>
> (Maude, 1969, p. 6)

Through the *Black Paper* opus, as a whole, three major substantive themes are reiterated, each of which involves direct criticism of comprehensive and progressive education. The first is that academic standards are in decline, particularly standards of literacy and numeracy. For many commentators the nation had to look no further to explain Britain's economic decline. The oil price rises (of 1973 and 1974) and the world trade crisis aside, Britain's recession could be blamed on comprehensive schools, progressive primary education and bad teachers...and all this despite the absence of clear evidence of decline in standards and the existence of counter evidence of no decline (Bullock, 1975), and more pupils than ever before leaving school with examination passes (Wright, 1977). Crucially, as part of a complex, interrelated discourse of critique, this refrain remained largely impervious to disconfirmation. It entered into the generally accepted 'what we all know about school', precisely because of its composite interdependence with other thematic choices in the discourse. In this way, the discourse is self-generating, self-reinforcing, it constitutes an 'imposition of the real' (Baudrillard, 1988) – where the opposition between things as presented and what's really going on begins to dissolve. Signs take on a life of their own, their own circulation. Schools in public debate are 'imaged', judgement and rational critique become impossible. The second and third themes have the same dubious empirical status but, taken together, they do powerful political and ideological work, effectively deconstructing the fragile possibilities of comprehensive schooling.

The second theme is that of dangerous, politically motivated teachers preaching revolution, socialism, egalitarianism, feminism and sexual deviation. Here the link is between comprehensive schools and social disorder. Teachers of English, guardians of national literacy, were in particular indicted on this count. Attempts by a painfully small number of teachers to bring aspects of working-class culture into the school curriculum and to develop forms of critical literacy were regarded as massively subversive. Thornbury (1978, pp. 136–7) captures the mood of ideological subversion in his description of English teachers in London.

> Young English teachers in the 1960s revived the romantic nineteenth-century notion of 'enthusiasm', encouraging the working class child to remain a literary primitive...Many of the new English teachers indoctrinated themselves and

their classes in attitudes critical to the police, local government bureaucracy, industry and employers. They did not hesitate to encourage this ideology in the children's writing, or classroom discussion...The new wave of English teachers was committed to the comprehensive school, to unstreaming, subject integration and team teaching.

Brian Cox took up this theme again in the 1980s in a more generalised attack, claiming that education policy since the 1960s had been dominated by left-wing educationalists, 'whose aim is revolution, not by armed over-throw of the government, but by transformation of institutions from within' (1981, p. 5).

Significantly education did not stand alone in the 1970s as an object of political suspicion; this kind of analysis can clearly be situated within the context of the general Conservative Party attack on socialism, trade unionism and egalitarianism which was being formulated in the early 1970s. The shadow cabinet conclave at Selsdon Park in 1970 produced an election strategy which centred on the issue of law and order and which was aimed to fuel a national disquiet based on the idea of 'a nation under threat'.

The reaction, into which the *Black Papers* fitted, was to a loss of legitimacy in traditional authority, including the authority of the state, which was increasingly evident in the late 1960s. (What Habermas [1976] calls the 'legitimation crisis'.) Established values of all kinds were subjected to challenge. This leads on directly to the third educational theme of the *Black Papers*, that of indiscipline. Again the comprehensive schools and progressive primaries were identified with a decline in standards, this time standards of behaviour. The comprehensive and open-plan primary classrooms were portrayed as unruly and ill-disciplined, with the teachers unable or unwilling to assert their control. The schools were subject, it was argued, to vandalism and disfiguring graffiti. Lack of classroom control spilled over into the rest of the school and thence onto the streets. The rising level of juvenile crime, particularly street crimes, were in part laid at the door of the comprehensive school (the other 'popular' explanation treated such crimes, newly dubbed as 'mugging', as essentially crimes of black youth, see Hall *et al.*, 1978). Teachers and black youth provided relatively unpopular and susceptible groups (in very different ways) which could be constructed as specific scapegoats for general social problems. The streets and the classrooms were no longer safe places to be. A 'moral panic' was being constructed, and taken up with enthusiasm in the media, with teachers 'named' and cast in the role of 'folk devils' (Cohen, 1980).

This formed the basis for a powerful and effective 'symbolic crusade', a 'moral enterprise' where 'someone takes the initiative on the basis of interest and uses publicity techniques to gain the support of the organizations that count' (Cohen, 1980, p. 112). In this respect the *Black Paper* writers possessed the sort of legitimating values, enterprise and power which Cohen (1980) suggests are the necessary basis for successful moral entrepreneurship. The crusade was to save the future, by turning to the past, to save the school system. It was made clear that teachers could no longer be trusted with the education of the nation's children. All aspects of the progressivism of the comprehensive school – curriculum, teaching methods and social relationships – were being thoroughly debunked in the critical discourse of the *Black Papers*. However, the degree of impact achieved would have been inconceivable without the ideological support of the greater part of the media for the educational project of these cultural restorationists. The *Daily Mail* and, more recently, the *Sun* and the *Daily Star* have played a particularly important role in a sustained campaign of 'teacher-bashing' (CCCS, 1981). Furthermore, a number of key events provided particular focus for the elaboration of the discourse of critique.

In particular, the events at William Tyndale primary school brought the possibility of linking all three of the *Black Paper* themes. Here were politically motivated teachers, making no attempt to teach traditional basic skills, who were deliberately abdicating from their responsibility to discipline and control their pupils. It revealed teachers to be unaccountable to their community and their employers. It

> showed that teachers could run the schools in ways that clearly contradicted many of the shared assumptions on which the education system rested. Teachers could be in effective day to day control of the schools, and they could use that control in ways not welcome to the school managers or its funding authority.
>
> (Dale, 1979, p. 96)

Within the framework of the emerging rightist education discourse the lessons of Tyndale were obvious – teachers needed to be made more accountable, they needed to be more closely monitored and controlled. A similar message could be constructed out of Neville Bennett's much-publicised report, *Teaching Styles and Pupils' Progress* (1976). The analysis of data from a variety of primary classrooms purported to show that children did notably better on a whole range of measures in formal rather than informal classroom regimes. Significantly the BBC *Horizon* programme based on the book was entitled *Lesson for the Teacher*. Teachers were being told again that they had got it wrong.

There are many other examples to choose from, headlines, articles and television programmes mobilised and reiterated a set of simple myths, slogans, silences, stereotypes and emphases. They all pointed to crisis, to schooling out of control. There is little or no space in this discursive terrain for alternative interpretations. The blame was clear. And many parents, fearful for the future of their children, were ready to accept an analysis which would apparently lead towards a shift of control over education away from teachers to them. The discourse is not one of despair, for the construction of blame also constructs solutions (a point to which I shall return below). As with the other expressions of cultural regressive, the cultural restorationists with their emphasis on the heritage, the known and the valued, could tap the evident popular distrust of the new and the difficult. In this way elitist conceptions of art, literature, music and education could actually be passed off as popular. Traditional patterns of the distribution of cultural capital were thus reinforced.

In more general terms, the *Black Papers* anticipated and contributed to two key aspects of contemporary Conservative politics or what has come to be called Thatcherism. First, in the sphere of cultural politics they provided an intellectual basis for and legitimation of anti-progressivism (not only in education but also in art, music, and the theatre). Progressivism is identified unequivocally (but mistakenly) with egalitarianism. (The more recent incorporation of progressive methods into vocational education schemes has illustrated the absence of an inevitable relationship between progressivism and liberation [Bernstein 1975]. And this is one more indication of the possibility for words and concepts to be wrenched out of one discursive ensemble and reassembled in an entirely different metonymical relation in another discourse.) Progressivism is also linked to the decline of traditional values and the purportedly concomitant potential for social unrest. It also relates to the Thatcherite critique of permissiveness generally.

The second key aspect pointed to a relationship between the decline in traditional values and moral decay, which is also linked to the devaluation of the family, and the family writ large – the nation. Here a set of sacred objects, statements and concepts are thematically welded into a powerful regularity. Racial politics (and immigration laws) are bound with a rediscovery of Nation (massively underpinned by the jingoistic effects of and exploitation of the Falklands war). These in turn are articulated with attacks on trade unionism ('the enemy within') and student radicalism. The whole package is tied in turn to the virtues of the traditional family which are set over and against the 'rise' in sexual permissiveness, pornography, abortion and homosexuality. These affinities within the discourse capture and evoke a whole range of commonsense fears and concerns. A great deal of the popularism of Thatcherism has its basis in this corpus. The discourse is realised in the style and practice of Thatcherism which Hall and Jacques (1983) describe as a form of 'authoritarian populism'. Keith Joseph provides an apt illustration of the populism and the discursive packaging.

> We were taught that crime, violence, wife-beating, child-beating were the result of poverty; abolish poverty, and they would disappear…By now, we are in a position to test all these fine theories in the light of experience…Real incomes per head have risen beyond what anyone dreamed of a generation back; so have education budgets and welfare budgets; so also have delinquency, truancy, vandalism, hooliganism, illiteracy, decline in educational standards. Some secondary schools in our cities are dominated by gangs operating extortion rackets against small children. Teenage pregnancies are rising; so are drunkenness, sexual offences and crimes of sadism…the decline is spreading. We know that some universities have been constrained to lower their standards for entrants from comprehensives, discriminating against the more talented because they come from grammar or independent schools…If equality in education is sought at the expense of quality, how can the poisons created help but filter down?
>
> (*The Times*, 21 October 1974)

Returning to education specifically, Macdonell suggests 'any discourse concerns itself with certain objects and puts forward certain concepts at the expense of others' (1986, p. 3). Thus, in this area of concern it is sensible to consider that which is excluded or displaced in the new emergent dominant discourse. In other words what previous possibilities, for example, for comprehensive schooling are rendered impossible by the intervention and take up of the *Black Papers*? What is the world that we have lost?

It is all too easy in a field of ideological struggle, like education, to respond to retrenchment and restructuring by romanticising the past. However, it is difficult to point with any confidence to a period in the recent educational history of England that could be described as the golden age of the comprehensive school. The Centre for Contemporary Cultural Studies (CCCS) (1981) review of educational policy in the 1960s makes it clear that the 'noise' of educational reform in the emergence of comprehensive schooling was often not matched by real changes in educational practices. The reviewers also argue that while 'There was a distinctive social democratic "moment" in the formulation of policy' in the 1960s, 'it was always caught within sharp limits' (p. 111). And they highlight the incoherent nature of the policies and reforms being advanced in this period, which were 'uneasily adjacent, often incompatible and held loosely together by ambiguous key terms' (p. 106). Their conclusion on the 1960s is that while the implementation of circular 10/65 (via which the Labour government of 1964–70 made its only *request* to Local Authorities for comprehensive reorganisation, there being no legal framework for such reorganisation until 1976) 'encouraged a national movement towards comprehensives...the meaning of the movement was never in any way radical' (p. 129). Throughout the short period of so-called progressive consensus (say 1965–69) the meaning and practice of comprehensive schooling remained a focus of conflict and indecision. The discourse of reform was fractured, incoherent and often contradictory. Several ideological models, in effect a set of contesting discourses, were invested in aspects of practice in schools (see Ball, 1981) and in the arenas of policy formation.

Neither the teacher unions, nor the DES, nor the LEAs (Local Education Authorities), nor the Labour Party were clear in their support for or vision of comprehensive schooling. There was no politically significant institutional site from which the discourse of comprehensive education could be mounted without equivocation. The failure of the discourse was therefore a failure of both theory and practice.

In some sense the lack of coherent definition and positive guidance allowed for a convenient policy hiatus. While this hiatus gave some grassroots innovators room for manoeuvre, it also gave the much larger number of conservatives or doubtfuls the room to carry on more or less as they had before. The tendency to regard 1965 and the introduction of comprehensives as a point of break in English educational history also tends to obscure the extent of continuity from previous practice. More than anything else the policy hiatus allowed a version of the grammar school curriculum to become firmly and unproblematically established in most comprehensives (Ball, 1981; Riseborough, 1981; Reynolds and Sullivan, 1987). To a great extent when critics of current government policy look back to the previous period with regret and a sense of loss, that which is considered lost is the small minority of attempts at innovation in a small minority of schools, and, perhaps more importantly, the possibilities for change, unrealised for the most part, which the situation in the late 1960s seemed to offer.

In general terms the inchoate, fragmented and contested discourse of comprehensive education failed to win the hearts and minds of parents and employers. There was certainly no attempt by the Labour Party to fashion a broad-based national political discourse into which comprehensive education would naturally fit. Indeed many of the major Labour politicians of the Wilsonian period were only too willing to parade their personal belief in the efficacy of grammar schooling as the best route of social mobility for bright working-class pupils. This further undermined any possibility of consolidated class support for comprehensives. The hegemony of the grammar school and the O-level curriculum was never successfully challenged (except within a handful of varietist schools such as Countesthorpe College, Sutton Centre, Vauxhall Manor, Stantonbury), and such support as was forthcoming from the Labour Party was articulated in traditional Fabian terms, as a project of improving class access. There was little or no attempt to examine and reconstruct the ideological form and content of the education on offer – what is to count as being educated. Thus the discourse of comprehensive education was a discourse of vagary, of uncertainty and of polarity, embracing as it did extremes from the most radical to the most pragmatic (many Conservative LEAs sanctioned the building or reorganisation of comprehensives straightforwardly on the basis of cost-effectiveness). In effect, the comprehensive movement failed to bring off a meaningful discursive formation. The dispersion of statements (Foucault, 1972, p. 38) addressed to comprehensive education remained arbitrary and chaotic, and lacked the rules of formation (the conditions of existence) for a discursive formation. The voices of the public educators, always muted and somewhat discordant, were thus rendered silent within policy debate.

Against this discursive background, as political and economic conditions began to change in the early 1970s, it is hardly surprising that comprehensive education provided a soft target for Conservative critics. But the irony embedded in this argument is that the motifs of crisis, or chaos, and of rampant unremitting change appear ever more circumstantial and illusory. They are built upon a small number of exceptions. The thrust of comprehensivism was poorly rooted and represented in practice and easily dismantled by critique.

The offensive of the Right against comprehensive education contains throughout a number of distinct but discursively related aspects and bases. In contrast to the comprehensive movement, the Conservatives have sucessfully managed to integrate and maintain and manage a high degree of contradiction and incoherence within their critical educational discourse. Indeed, the disparate aspects of the discourse have served all the more effectively to outflank putative resistance.

1976

There are a number of symbolic, practical and pragmatic reasons why the bulk of my analysis of education policy begins from the year 1976. The main symbolic reason is the presentation in that year of James Callaghan's Ruskin speech and the ensuing Great Debate. As noted already a number of my respondents had comments to make about the significance – political and educational – of the speech and its aftermath. Whatever Callaghan's intention, the speech gave powerful encouragement and added legitimacy to the 'discourse of derision' mounted by the *Black Papers*. In discursive terms it marked the end to any possibility of serious public opposition to the critique of comprehensivism and progressivism. It cleared the ground for a shift of emphasis on the Right from critical deconstruction to radical reconstruction. The shaky edifice of comprehensive theory and practice in areas of the curriculum, assessment and ped-agogy could now be dismantled with impunity. Hold-outs against change, defenders of comprehensivism, could now be picked off as both subversive, damaging to the interests of children and the nation, and reactionary, irrationally persisting with old, disreputable ways. In terms of policy the sayable and unsayable were thenceforward carefully demarcated. A classic division between madness and reason is erected: the madness of egalitarianism, social engineering and democracy in education over and against the reason of tradition, discipline and authority. To engage in the discourse of madness would be to court exclusion from the arenas of policy. From 1976, only cer-tain policies were possible, only certain policies were sane or rational. Thus, in those places where policy was being made only certain concepts, conceptions, proposals and pleas were utterable or at least hearable. And indeed only certain interests had the right to speak, to plea, to be heard. Some old interests and lobbies were now being firmly excluded, the folk-demon teachers and their unions were one such group, teacher educators and academics another, the LEAs would soon be another. In contrast, new voices were being listened to in the corridors of power, in particular, the voices of industry, given special credence by Callaghan's Great Debate, and the various voices of the now increasingly well-organised and articulate New Right. Digby Anderson, Director of the New Right, Social Affairs Unit, explained:

> We are interested in taking things which have not been looked at very critically and doing something on them...in the late 70s it was fairly clear there was an

orthodoxy about education, it wasn't difficult to know where to go to find the sorts of things that might be interesting and provoke better debate. And I don't think anyone would deny that the breadth of the education debate has improved ... we have pushed back the boundaries of what is sayable, and now there are a number of things which are sayable which weren't sayable ten years ago.

The deconstructive/reconstructive thrust of the *Black Papers*/New Right discourse works at a variety of levels producing a series of 'binary oppositions with positive and negative poles' (Kenway, 1987, p. 42). Two of these oppositions are funda-mental to the whole edifice of critique and response in the assault on education policy making. One is the setting of expertise and against commonsense. The role of expert knowledge and research is regarded as less dependable than political intuition and commonsense accounts of what people want. The other rests on what Kenway calls the 'people-powerbloc distinction': 'Powerless individuals were juxtaposed against a self-serving, unresponsive bureaucracy' (p. 42). (I shall examine more of these juxtapositions and polarities in more detail later.)

Interestingly and crucially these fundamentals represent opposing conceptions of power/knowledge relations in education policy. As Kenway also points out, the effectiveness of such polarities is related both to the divisions they generate – parents against teachers, scholarly research against the popular media – and the *unities* they conjure up – parents as a group, of a kind, teachers as a group, of a kind. The interests of all parents are cast together as the same; the culpability of all teachers is cast together as the same. 'Disparate and contradictory interests [are] activated and welded into a common position' (Kenway, 1987, p. 43). In effect the discourse of the *Black Papers* constructed a new social-subject in the field of education policy, a subject which would be crucial in the development of the New Right's policy initiatives in the 1980s – the concerned parent; the parent as consumer of education. And through and around this new subject another key polarity was established, a polarity of control – professional control versus accountability. Out of the ashes of William Tyndale, of *Teaching Styles and Pupil Progress* and The Bullock Report rose the phoenix of *parental choice*.

In all this, then, the power/knowledge ensemble of the education policy establishment, the triangle of tension (teacher unions, DES and LEAs) was profoundly dismembered. Again the concerned parent is cast as a figure of reason and sanity naturally opposed to and set against the wild experimentation and unorthodoxies of the uncaring teachers (like those of William Tyndale) and 'loony left' authorities like Inner London Education Authority (ILEA), Brent and Haringey. As Hall explains '... the work of ideological struggle is therefore equiv-alent to the work of articulating/disarticulating discourses from their previously secured position in an ideological field' (1980, p. 174). But clearly the discourse of the concerned parent does not stand alone in the New Right's ideological work. It is at the centre of a series of interpenetrating discourses and both affects and is affected by them. For example, the discursive themes of standards and excellence articulate straightforwardly with the role and concerns of the archetypal con-cerned parent in terms of basic elements of the general political discourse of Thatcherism, that is possessive individualism and personal initiative. Thus, the concerned parent aims to do the best for his or her child, given the harsh realities of the competitive world. The child needs a decent education and good qualifica-tions which will enable him or her to get on. The emphasis is upon individual betterment and competition. The parent's duty is to ensure that they choose the best education for their child, even if that means that the children of others will have less than the best education. In this condensation excellence is a competitive acquisition, it is a form of differentiation, of comparison. Education is thus displaced from its political and collective context, and notions of mass or common schooling no longer have a valid or logical role to play in this scenario. The concerned parent is thus recruited as a discursive subject of Thatcherism. If the parent makes a poor choice, it is said, then that is his or her problem.

In classic Foucauldian terms the 'dividing practices' provided for by this discursive complex both *totalise* and *individualise* the social-subject, the concerned parent. All parents are taken to have shared interests in opposing liberalising reforms in education but they compete individually, via their children, for the scarce rewards of educational success.

We should note a further significant element of these educational and political discourses. Many of the key elements in these discursive ensembles – individualism, choice, competition, etc. – are ramified from recently re-emergent Conservative philosophies, particularly that of Neo-liberalism. Neo-liberalism, which we will shortly examine more closely, rests firmly upon notions of freedom of choice, market forces and quality by competition (strongly counterposed to the worth or possibility of equality). Excellence and standards, and the advocacy of practices like streaming, corporal punishment and the use of formal exams, all pursued dedicatedly in the *Black Papers*, also resonate with some of the root concepts of neo-conservativism – tradition and authority, order and place.

Political philosophy and social policy

The last of the *Black Papers* was published in 1977. From that point on the discursive cudgels of the conservative educational offensive were taken up by a variety of related and overlapping New Right agencies and groups, ranging from the Centre for Policy Studies, The National Council for Educational Standards and the Social Affairs Unit to the Institute of Economic Affairs and The Adam Smith Institute. What makes them markedly different from the rather informally produced *Black Papers* is the degree and sophistication of their organisation and strategies for dissemination (see Labour Research, 1987, Vol. 76, No. 10; Bosanquet, 1983), and the extent to which their critiques and proposals are theoretically informed by philosophies of neo-liberalism and neo-conservatism. CCCS make the point that:

> Little could be said by way of characterizing the Conservative Party's educational 'thought' from the inter-war years into the early 1960s. The whole idea would be paradoxical. There was no right wing figure comparable to Tawney (Eliot's writing was remote from prescription, Bantock's never found much resonance), while little importance was attached to the whole area of social policy except as reluctantly found necessary.
>
> (CCCS, 1981, p. 191)

By the 1980s, the intervention of the crusading, radical, New Right had changed all that. Neo-liberal texts, particularly the work of Hayek, and monetarist theories like those of Friedman, are paraded as a basis for social and economic policy making. And neo-liberal and neo-conservative philosophers like Adam Smith and Edmund Burke are being re-examined and reworked by contemporary Conservative intellectuals like Roger Scruton and Peter Quinton (see Salisbury Review).

Before looking specifically at the engagement of these theoretical discourses with education policy, I want to sketch very briefly and schematically the main theoretical tenets of neo-liberalism and neo-conservatism.

Neither of these assemblages of economics, philosophy and social theory are of a piece. They each encompass a range of positions and perspectives. Neo-liberalism, for example, is used as a generic term to cover Friedman's economic liberalism, Nozick's libertarianism (the advocacy of the minimal state), and Hayek's Austrian economics. For our purposes Hayek is most pertinent and most influential, Nozick (1974), even in these circles is regarded as somewhat of an extremist. He argues for no state intervention beyond the protection of life and property and thus the absolute freedom of the market.

Hayek's work rests on a critique of socialism, statism and Keynsianism. He is opposed to trade unionism, to government interventions into the economy and to state welfare. They each, he argues, distort and inhibit the free and efficient work-ings of *the market*. Trade unions artificially push wages above the level which would be set by the free market. They also advantage some workers, those in strong unions, and thus disadvantage others, ununionised or in weak unions. Democracy itself is a major problem in all this; according to Hayek 'political feeling aroused in a democracy would have certain practical results in terms of rising public expendi-ture and growing centralisation' (Bosanquet, 1983, p. 14). State welfare is wasteful, depresses competition (i.e. without state benefits unemployed workers would be motivated to accept jobs at lower wages and thus drive down wages generally) and reduces incentives. Indeed Hayek suggests that collectivism has an effect of moral distortion, the national character can be damaged (1986, p. 159). Also welfare involves the substitution of state judgements about output for those of the market. State judgements are inevitably biased, the market is not. Furthermore, according to Hayek, welfare payments are based upon coerced transfers of income between individuals. Government intervention in the economy is also unfair and inefficient and once started is difficult to stop. It leads to socialism and what Hayek graphi-cally calls 'the road to serfdom'. Mrs Thatcher is a very orthodox Hayekian in this regard. 'I have' she said 'always regarded part of my job as – and please do not think of it in any arrogant way – killing Socialism in Britain' (*Financial Times*, 14 November 1985). According to Hayek, government failure is more common and more likely than economic failure. The market embodies a superior rationality. Governments once embarked upon social or economic expenditure programmes are confronted by and susceptible to interest and client group pressures for more or new expenditures. And elections are imperfect public-choice mechanisms, they encourage governments to attempt to buy support.

Much of Hayek's analysis of the ills of collectivism are focused on a rebuttal of Keynsian economics (Table 2.1). Keynsianism is identified with a politicised econ-omy, an economy where decisions are made by public agencies, and with economic strategies which rely heavily on government expenditure and thus on high taxes and high levels of public sector borrowing. The result, it is argued, is inflation and government overload, or what is called 'ungovernability' (King, 1975). Overload is used in two senses; the first is the vast and increasing responsibilities of modern democratic governments, and the concomitant increases in intervention in and control over people's lives; the second is the extent to which the increases in state expenditures outrun the growth in the national product to the point where the state has insufficient resources to meet its accumulated responsibilities. This also relates to Friedman's 'theory of bureaucratic displacement'; the theory suggests that 'increases in expenditure will act rather like "black holes" in the economic universe, simultaneously sucking in resources and shrinking in terms of "emitted" production' (Friedman and Friedman, 1980, p. 155). (The National Council for Educational Standards has devoted considerable time and energy to attempting to

Table 2.1 Proscriptions: criticism of Keynsian economics

1	State and public intervention in the economy, especially attempts to control levels of unemployment by government spending produces a *politicized economy*, which restricts competition and generates inflation.
2	Socialism is atavistic, based on the politics of envy. All government decisions are less likely to work than the trial and error of the market.
3	State intervention and public spending encourages pressure group policies, interest groups press for increased and expanded shares of government expenditure.
4	Politics based on public spending solutions to economic problems encourage *promisory democracy*, the use of expenditure promises to influence voters.
5	Notions of *social justice* or *redistribution* are politically biased, relying as they do on partisan definitions of *need* and worth.
6	Welfare and citizenship rights rely on the *coerced* transfer of income between individuals and are *unfair*, i.e. high taxes.
7	High taxes and transfer of income reduces initiative, incentive and creativity *and* personal responsibility, create dependence and distort the national character.
8	State provision of services eradicates *choice* and *competition*, reduces *efficiency*, stifles innovation and removes personal *liberty*.
9	State professionals are an inefficient, self-serving clique determined to maintain restricted access, restrictive practices and resist innovations.
10	Trade Unions distort the market and competition by artificially raising wages above the real market level and are unfair because they damage the interests of some workers and advantage others.
11	To implement the politicised economy and policies of social redistributive justice requires massive state concentrations of power and gives rise to practical and financial *ungovernability*.

prove this maxim.) All this can lead to a decline in public confidence and a loss of legitimacy by the state. Thus: 'By attacking Keynsianism as a discredited and failed theory New Right economists were trying to knock out the lynchpin on which so much of post-war intervention in the economy rested' (Gamble, 1986, p. 40).

As an alternative to all this Hayek argues for two things: for free markets and for individual freedom. Markets, according to Hayek, are better than central planning authorities at coping with rapid social and technological change and with uncertainty, by continuous adaptation to unpredictable change (see Table 2.2). Decentralised markets also maximise creative entrepreneurship, that is the search for new ways to make profits. 'Through the pursuit of selfish aims the individual will usually lead himself to save the general interest, the collective actions of organised groups are almost invariably contrary to the general interest' (Hayek, 1976, p. 138). Furthermore, the market is unprincipled, it allows no moral priorities in its patterns of distribution. It may not produce equality, indeed equality would be unhelpful in market terms, but it is not unfair. 'Since inequality arises from the generation of innumerable individual preferences it cannot be evil unless these preferences are themselves evil' (Joseph and Sumption, 1979, p. 78). It produces a natural economic order and the poorest, the losers in the market, will benefit from the progress of the society as a whole. There are no intentional effects in the market, no possibility of things like institutional racism – that would be arbitrary and inefficient. The market is spontaneous. There is no one to blame for failure but the failures themselves. Fault must lie in the culture, the family, or the individual. For Hayek, as for Mrs Thatcher, society is a meaningless aggregation. There can be no commonly agreed social definitions of either need or worth, so attempts at

Table 2.2 Prescriptions for the market

1   Decentralised markets maximise creative entrepreneurship and are better at coping with uncertainty and rapid social and technological change – ensuring progress and civilisation.
2   Markets render no moral priorities or claims to justice, it is neutral – a natural order.
3   Inequalities are *fair* because the market is unprincipled, its effects are unintentional, there is no deliberate bias – hence no racism or sexism.
4   Inequalities are inevitable and acceptable – indeed necessary. Inequality produces incentives.
5   This provides for maximum *LIBERTY*. Liberty is the absence of coercion, maximum control over one's own behaviour, an absence of interpersonal constraint (freedom *from*). This leaves us with the *real* choice, even if between exploitation wages and starvation.
6   The key is *market competition* based on *economic individualism*. The privatised provision of *all* services produces *efficiency* and *choice* for the individual *consumer* (which produce greater expenditure).
7   The state should have minimal responsibility for maintaining property rights, and the legal framework of the market, and national defence.
8   Liberty ensures the creation and dispersal of knowledge. Choice in the market encourages the pursuit of new ideas and methods.
9   Extensions of market relations and privatisation are extensions of freedom. Hence attacks on the welfare state and union rights as a moral crusade.

social justice are always biased and unfair because only some are selected to bene-fit. These are political judgements, they require a concentration of power and thus smack of totalitarianism. These are the enemies of freedom.

Hayek's definition of freedom is very precise and very narrow. It is a freedom 'from', rather than a freedom 'to', that is an absence of coercion. Thus, it differs fundamentally from post-war conceptions of freedom that rest upon notions of citizenship rights. It is solely a freedom to have control of one's own behaviour, the removal of interpersonal constraints. It is a freedom to choose. Even if the choice is between starvation and exploitative labour, for Hayek this is a real choice. It is real freedom. You can starve if you want to. There are always alternatives in the market.

> The fact that the opportunities open to the poor in a competitive society are much more restricted than those open to the rich does not make it less true that in such a society the poor are much more free than a person commanding much greater material comfort in a different type of society.
>
> (Hayek, 1986, pp. 76–7)

Thus, freedom is market freedom, very much the basis of 'on yer bike' Tebbitism. State activity can only serve to reduce freedom, thus the role of the state in Hayek's view must be limited to the maintenance of those property rights and legal procedures which provide the conditions necessary for the market to operate. All else – health care, pensions, education, etc. – can be left to the market. Clearly both the rhetorical commitment in the early phases of Thatcherism to the 'rolling back of the state', and the privatisation programme of the latter period rest on these twin premises of individual liberty and market freedom. Property rights rather than person rights are celebrated. However, while it is arguable that the impact of the New Right on economic policy has been more rhetorical than ideological, it certainly has provided an impetus for a whole variety of social policy initiatives in social security, health and education, aimed at destroying the basis of the post-war political consensus. My general point here is that the role of the New Right, as well as its direct impact on policy in some areas, has been discursive, that is it has facilitated a discursive reworking of the parameters of political possibility and acceptability. Some aspects of the once unproblematic consensus are now beyond the pale, and policies which might have seemed like economic barbarism twenty years ago now seem right and proper.

> Those who stress the political orthodoxy of Thatcherism are in one sense right but only to the extent that they fail to take note of the deeper shifts in which yesterday's outrage becomes tomorrow's norm, in which what was only a short while ago unthinkable becomes today's green paper and the policy of the future.
>
> (Schwarz, 1987, p. 125)

But clearly, that which is the New Right, and indeed that which is Thatcherism, does not begin and end with economic orthodoxies and a minimal state. In fact, aspects of the New Right present a very different view of the role of the state and give emphasis to social rather than economic orthodoxies; that is neo-conservatism.

In the renewed theoretical project of neo-conservatism freedom is again a central concept, but again it is a concept which is narrowly defined in a careful metonymical relation to a set of other concepts, like nation, authority and human nature. Specifically, freedom is taken to lie in a willing subordination to the nation. Thus, according to Roger Scruton, 'the value of individual liberty is not absolute, but stands subject to another and higher value, the authority of established government' (1980, p. 19) or Peregrine Worsthorne, 'social discipline is a much more fruitful theme for contemporary conservatism than individual freedom' (1978, p. 150). While the neo-liberals see the community as founded upon economic relations, the neo-conservatives see it as founded upon social bonds arising out of a common culture and sense of national identity, held together, and, if necessary, enforced by strong government. Thus, the essence of social order here is neither individualism nor the mutuality or collectivity of society, but nation. Here there is no such thing as society, there are individuals and there is the nation. The citizen is interpellated not by choice but by duty. The social-subject of neo-conservatism is the loyal, law-abiding family man (or housewife/mother), holder of and believer in traditional values and sober virtues. Over and against this ideal citizen/parent is set an alternative subject: the carrier of alien values or alien culture, the agitator/trade unionist, sexual deviant, or working, single-parent mother, permissive/liberal, and progressive teacher – in other words 'the enemy within', the traitor.

In all this family and nation, morality and law are bound together in a discursive unity. The 'naturalness' of the traditional family, of fixed gender roles and 'normal' sexuality, of family loyalty and allegiance, fit neatly to the 'naturalness' of national loyalty, of order and place, of historic continuity. And out of this comes a 'natural' fear and suspicion of 'outsiders' and the rejection of alien values which undermine social cohesion.

> There is a natural instinct in the unthinking man...to accept and endorse through his actions the institutions and practices into which he is born. The instinct is rooted in human nature.
>
> (Scruton, 1980, p. 119)

Thus, cultural variation becomes a social 'problem', a threat to the preservation of national identity. Racism is simply a defence, a natural reaction; but it is a racism based on assumptions not of innate superiority but rather of cultural difference, and implicit cultural superiority. As a result, not surprisingly, the neo-conservatives are vehemently opposed to internationalism (like the idea of a European State) and multi-culturalism.

> The enemy, the 'multiculturalist', is presented in purely negative terms as activists and agitators. They 'damage', prompt a 'backlash', 'purge', 'sanitise' and commit 'multiracialist assault'. They also argue (passionately), 'impede', 'assert', 'insist' and 'issue guidelines'. They are emotional rather than reasonable, and deviant by association and by assumed political attitudes.
>
> (Seidel, 1986, p. 118)

This ensemble of strength and allegiance, nation and culture, nature and normality is often portrayed by commentators as the basis in Thatcherism of 'authoritarian populism' (Hall, 1983). These aspects of Thatcherism are taken to articulate with certain popular prejudices and baser forms of jingoism which are fostered in the tabloid press, and with the resonant traditional themes of order, standards and duty. As noted already, Thatcherism operates via these themes in terms of commonsense, oppositions which set normal against abnormal, order against chaos, the hard-working against the scrounger, discipline against decay, nature against ideology.

> ...the successes of Thatcherism in shifting the ideological conjuncture – in imposing and normalising the springs of authoritarianism – go very deep, especially on the issues of race, law and order (such that principled, rather sensible liberals can be branded treacherous) and family and sexual life. And indeed one mark of the power of this cultural transformation is precisely the fact that it has been so speedily normalised...
>
> (Schwarz, 1987, p. 145)

Clearly, as we may see, when taken together, the neo-liberal and neo-conservative elements of the New Right display a number of vital contradictions. The existence of these contradictions must sound for any analyst of contemporary politics a series of important warning bells. First, there is the obvious danger of holding too firmly to the loose aggregation which is commonly referred to as the New Right. Second, there is the danger of attempting to translate directly between philosophical discourses and political action. Thatcherism represents an amalgam of and a selection from these philosophical discourses and clearly the emphases within Conservative policies have shifted several times since 1979. Thus, Jessop *et al.* (1984) suggest that 'Thatcherism must be seen...more as an alliance of disparate forces around a self-contradictory programme' (p. 38). Furthermore, pragmatism, expedience and so-called intuition all play their part in forging a distinctive set of policy discourses inside government. Opposition from dissenting ministers and civil servants, contradictory advice from advisers, and, on occassion 'popular' dissent (for example, over NHS cuts) all mediate and disrupt the relationships between philosophies and policies. And Thatcherism is not necessarily homo-logous with Conservatism. Dimitri Coryton, Chairman of the Conservative Education Association:

> she [Mrs Thatcher] is very much the outsider, she hasn't gone through that 30 year period of building up colleagues in the House of Commons...so when

she did come to power, she actually drew to her some fairly bizarre and peculiar individuals. People who were not part of the mainstream, and who were, in the case of education, often not really all that well informed. The basis was ideology not practical experience and they have the messianic fervour of the ideologue. The expert is dismissed as a vested interest so the inexpert ideologue has the field.

Alan Hazelhurst MP, Mark Carlisle's PPS (Parliamentary Private Secretary):

There was a fairly important sea change, with the election of Mrs Thatcher and a feeling of dissatisfaction with the 'failure' of the Heath years, and those of us who came into parliament in 1970 originally, as the supporters of the party and the then party leader, were put into eclipse. People were looking for new brooms and questions were asked: 'Are you really part of the new system...?' When you're in government, especially now perhaps, things get led from the top and I think you get one or two things appearing in the manifesto and are genuinely surprised by what you find.

The work of the New Right intellectuals in and around the party is not just one of advocacy, it is also one of opposition – that is opposition to policies which are regarded as ideologically unsound, in their terms (like, as we shall see, the National Curriculum). Policies within the Conservative Party are a matter of continuing dispute, although disputation is neither always welcome nor easy, 'it's especially difficult at the present time to be dissenting voices within the Conservative Party. You are set upon more savagely if you are dissenting, it doesn't matter who you are.' (Alan Hazelhurst); ideological purity, expedience and career advancement, among others, are factors which come into play in particular policy struggles.

There are also ways in which the different philosophical emphases work effectively together either by impacting on different fields of government policy or by mutual reinforcement, for example in relation to civil liberties or the role of the strong state acting to preserve the freedom of the market (see Levitas, 1986, p. 103).

References

Ball, S. J. (1981) *Beachside Comprehensive*, Cambridge, Cambridge University Press.
Baudrillard, J. (1988) *Selected Writings* (ed. M. Poster), Oxford, Polity Press.
Bennett, N. (1976) *Teaching Styles and Pupil Progess*, London, Open Books.
Bernstein, B. (1975) 'Visible and Invisible Pedagogies', in *Class, Codes and Control*, Vol 3, London, Routledge and Kegan Paul.
Bosanquet, N. (1983) *After the New Right*, London, Heinemann.
Bullock Report, The (1975) *A Language For Life*, London, HMSO.
CCCS (1981) *Unpopular Education*, London, Hutchinson.
Cohen, P. (1980) *Folk Devils and Moral Panics*, Oxford, Martin Robertson.
Cox, C. B. (1981) *Education: The Next Decade*, London, Conservative Political Centre.
Cox, C. B. and Dyson, A. E. (eds) (1969) *Fight For Education: A Black Paper*, London, The Critical Quarterly Society.
Dale, R. (1979) 'The Politicisation of School Deviance: Reactions to William Tyndale', in L. Barton and R. Meighan (eds) *Schools, Pupils and Deviance*, Driffield, Nafferton.
Foucault, M. (1972) *The Archeology of Knowledge*, London, Tavistock.
Foucault, M. (1981) 'The Order of Discourse', in R. Young (ed.) *Untying the Text*, London, Routledge and Kegan Paul.
Friedman, M. and Friedman, R. (1980) *Free to Choose*, London, Secker and Warburg.

Gamble, A. (1986) 'The Political Economy of Freedom', in R. Levitas (ed.) *The Ideology of the New Right*, Oxford, Polity Press.

Habermas, J. (1976) *Legitimation Crisis*, London, Heinemann.

Hall, S. (1980) 'Popular-Democratic vs Authoritarian Populism: Two Ways of "Taking Democracy Seriously" ', in A. Hunt (ed.) *Marxism and Democracy*, London, Lawrence and Wishart.

Hall, S. (1983) 'The Great Moving Right Show', in S. Hall and M. Jacques (eds) *The Politics of Thatcherism*, London, Lawrence and Wishart.

Hall, S., Critcher, C., Jefferson, T., Clarke, C. and Roberts, B. (eds) (1978) *Policing the Crisis*, London, Macmillan.

Hayek, F. (1976) *Law, Legislation and Liberty, Vol. 2: The Mirage of Social Justice*, London, Routledge and Kegan Paul.

Hayek, F. (1986) *The Road to Serfdom*, London, Routledge and Kegan Paul.

Jessop, B., Bonnett, K., Bromley, S. and Ling, T. (1984) 'Authoritarian Popularism, Two Nations and Thatcherism', *New Left Review*, No. 147.

Joseph, K. and Sumption, J. (1979) *Equality*, London, John Murray.

Kenway, J. (1987) 'Left Right out: Australian Education and the Politics of Signification', *Journal of Education Policy*, 2(3): 189–204.

King, A. (1975) 'Overload: problems of governing in the 1970s', *Political Studies*, 23: 284–96.

Labour Research (1987) Web of Reaction: right-wing groups and activists, 76, 10, pp. 7–12, London, Labour Research Department.

Laclau, E. and Mouffe, C. (1985) *Hegemony and Socialist Strategy*, London, Verso.

Levitas, R. (1986) 'Competition and Compliance: The Utopias of the New Right', in R. Levitas (ed.) *The Ideology of the New Right*, Oxford, Polity Press.

Macdonell, D. (1986) *Theories of Discourse*, Oxford, Blackwell.

Maude, A. (1969) 'The Egalitarian Threat', in C. B. Cox and A. E. Dyson (eds) *Fight for Education*, London, The Critical Quarterly Society.

Nozick, R. (1974) *Anarchy, State and Utopia*, Oxford, Blackwell.

Reynolds, D. and Sullivan, M. (1987) *The Comprehensive Experience*, Lewes, Falmer Press.

Riseborough, G. (1981) 'Teachers' careers and comprehensive schooling: an empirical study', *Sociology*, 15(3): 352–81.

Schwarz, B. (1987) 'The Thatcher Years', in R. Miliband, L. Pantich and J. Saville (eds) *Socialist Register 1987*, London, Merlin Press.

Scruton, R. (1980) *The Meaning of Conservatism*, Harmondsworth, Penguin.

Seidel, G. (1986) 'Culture, Nation and "Race" in the British and French New Right', in R. Levitas (ed.) *The Ideology of the New Right*, Oxford, Polity Press.

Thornbury, R. (1978) *The Changing Urban School*, London, Methuen.

Williams, R. (1962) *The Long Revolution*, Harmondsworth, Penguin.

Worsthorne, P. (1978) 'Too much Freedom', in M. Cowling (ed.) *Conservative Essays*, London, Cassell.

Wright, N. (1977) *Progress in Education*, London, Croom Helm.

CHAPTER 3

WHAT IS POLICY?
Texts, trajectories and toolboxes

Discourse, 1993, 13(2): 10–17

> All my books...are little tool boxes...of people want to open them, to use this sentence or that idea as a screwdriver or spanner to short-circuit, discredit or smash systems of power, including eventually those from which my books have emerged...then so much the better.
>
> (Cited in Patton, 1979, p. 115)

This paper is an exercise in theoretical heurism. It is intentionally tentative and open-ended. I realise that on occasion I resort to aphorism rather than argument. It rests in part on an oddly unfashionable position in educational and sociological research. That is, that in the analysis of complex social issues – like policy – two theories are probably better than one, or to put it another way, the *complexity* and *scope* of policy analysis – from an interest in the workings of the state to a concern with contexts of practice and the distributional outcomes of policy – precludes the possibility of successful single theory explanations. What we need in policy analysis is a toolbox of diverse concepts and theories – an applied sociology rather than a pure one. Thus, I want to balance the modernist theoretical project of abstract parsimony against a somewhat more post-modernist one of localised complexity. This polarisation, between parsimony and complexity, and the dilemmas it highlights are very much to the fore in recent debates in the UK about the conception and purposes of 'policy-sociology' (Ozga, 1987, 1990; Ball, 1990). Thus, Ozga (1990) suggests that it is important to 'bring together structural, macro-level analysis of education systems and education policies and micro level investigation, especially that which takes account of people's perception and experiences' (p. 359). Now that is what I mean by scope and I agree strongly with Ozga's plea. But she goes on to criticise approaches which generate 'a view of policy making which stresses ad hocery, serendipity, muddle and negotiation' (p. 360). Now that is part of what I mean by complexity (or at least one aspect of it) and I disagree with the exclusory thrust of Ozga's plea. We cannot rule out certain forms and conceptions of social action simply because they seem awkward or theoretically challenging or difficult. The challenge is to relate together analytically the ad hocery of the macro with the ad hocery of the micro without losing sight of the systematic bases and effects of ad hoc social actions. To look for the iterations embedded within chaos. As I see it, this also involves some rethinking of the simplicities of the structure/agency dichotomy. This task is one which Harker and May (1997, p. 177) identify as central to Bourdieu's sociology, that is 'to account for agency in a constrained world, and show how agency and structure are implicit in each other, rather than being the two poles of a continuum'. We live and think structures rather than simply being oppressed or limited by them.

One of the conceptual problems currently lurking within much policy research and policy sociology is that more often than not analysts fail to define conceptually what they mean by policy. The meaning of policy is taken for granted and theoretical and epistemological dry rot is built into the analytical structures they build. It is not difficult to find the term policy being used to describe very different 'things' at different points in the same study. For me, much rests on the meaning or possible meanings that we give to policy; it affects 'how' we research and how we interpret what we find. Now let me add quickly that I do not exempt myself from these criticisms; although in work done with Richard Bowe we have tried to be careful and explicit about our understanding and use of the term policy (Bowe and Ball with Gold, 1992).

Now typically in a piece of writing which begins like this one I would now offer my own definitive version of the meaning of policy and with a few rhetorical flourishes and a bit of fancy theoretical footwork, I would solve all the problems that I have pointed up. But I cannot do that or at least I cannot do that very simply. The reason is that I hold my own theoretical uncertainties about the meaning of policy and in recent writing on policy issues, I actually inhabit two very different conceptualisations of policy. For the time being I will call these; *policy as text and policy as discourse*. In simple terms the differences between these two conceptualisations are rather dramatic and in sociological terms rather hoary and traditional and they reiterate the Bourdieurian dichotomy signalled earlier. But the point I am moving on to is that policy is not one or the other, but both, they are 'implicit in each other'. Policy discourses (and I am using that term here in the Foucauldian sense, as a regulated practice that accounts for statements, rather than the linguistic sense of language in use) produce frameworks of sense and obviousness with which policy is thought, talked and written about. Policy texts are set within these frameworks which constrain but never determine all of the possibilities for action. As an aside, but an important aside, the question 'what is policy?', should not mislead us into unexamined assumptions about policies as 'things'; policies are also processes and outcomes (more of which later).

Policy as text

Here, somewhat under the influence of literary theory, we can see policies as representations which are encoded in complex ways (via struggles, compromises, authoritative public interpretations and reinterpretations) and decoded in complex ways (via actor's interpretations and meanings in relation to their history, experiences, skills, resources and context). A policy is both contested and changing, always in a state of 'becoming', of 'was' and 'never was' and 'not quite'; 'for any text a plurality of readers must necessarily produce a plurality of readings' (Codd, 1988, p. 239). Now this conception is not simply one which privileges the significance of readings of policy by its subjects. While that is important – authors cannot control the meanings of their texts – policy authors do make concerted efforts to assert such control by the means at their disposal, to achieve a 'correct' reading and some texts are framed by or have embedded in them the weight, and measure, or requirement. We need to understand those efforts and their effects on readers and to recognise the attention that readers pay to the writers' context of production and communicative intent (Giddens, 1987, pp. 105–7). But, in addition, it is crucial to recognise that the policies themselves, the texts, are not necessarily clear or closed or complete. The texts are the product of compromises at various stages (at points of initial influence, in the micropolitics of legislative formulation, in the parliamentary process and in the politics and micropolitics of interest group articulation). They are typically the cannibalised products of multiple (but circumscribed) influences and agendas. There is ad hocery, negotiation and serendipity within the state, within the policy formulation process. Now if this sounds like a restatement of the epistemology of pluralism, it is not meant to be. There is a difference between agenda control and ideological politics and the processes of policy influence and text production within the state. Only certain influences and agendas are recognised as legitimate, only certain voices are heard at any point in time within the commonsense of policy. The point is that quibbling and dissensus still occur within the babble of 'legitimate' voices and sometimes the effects of quibbling and dissensus result in a blurring of meanings within texts, and in public confusion and a dissemination of doubt. We only have to look at Edwards *et al.* (1989, 1992) studies of the Assisted Places Scheme and City Technology Colleges to see that sometimes it is actually difficult to even identify analytically what a policy is and what it is intended to achieve. These studies also point up a second issue. Policies shift and change their meaning in the arenas of politics; representations change, key interpreters (secretaries of state, ministers, Chairs of Councils) change (sometimes the change in key actors is a deliberate tactic for changing the meaning of policy). Policies have their own momentum inside the state; purposes and intentions are re-worked and re-oriented over time. The problems faced by the state change over time. Policies are represented differently by different actors and interests – Kenneth Baker's Grant Maintained Schools scheme as against Margaret Thatcher's; Margaret Thatcher's National Curriculum as against John Major's, Kenneth Baker's, Kenneth Clarke's and Ron Dearing's. At all stages in the policy process we are confronted both with different interpretations of policy, and with what Rizvi and Kemmis (1987) call 'interpretations of interpretations'. And these attempts to represent or re-represent policy sediment and build up over time, they spread confusion and allow for play in and the playing-off of meanings. Gaps and spaces for action and response are opened-up or re-opened as a result. Thus, the physical text that pops through the school letterbox, or where ever, does not arrive 'out of the blue', it has an interpretational and representational history, neither does it enter a social or institutional vacuum. The text and its readers and the context of response all have histories. Policies enter existing patterns of inequality, e.g. the structure of local markets, local class relations, local distributions of facilities and resources. They 'impact' or are taken up differently as a result (see Ball *et al.*, 1995 on the middle-class use of local education markets). Policy is not exterior to inequalities, although it may change them, it is also affected, inflected and deflected by them.

It is also important not to reify policy – not to identify policy solely with a set of texts. Some texts are never even read first hand. A study of the Maths National Curriculum found that 7 per cent of its sample of Maths teachers never read any National Curriculum documents (Brown, 1992); a study of assessment at Key Stage 1 found that a significant number of teachers in the 32 case study schools fundamentally misunderstood the premises and methods of School Attainment Tasks and teacher assessment and employed these misunderstandings to organise their classroom practice (Gipps and Brown, 1992). Sometimes policies are 'enacted' on the basis of confusion. But there may often be key mediators of policy in any setting who are relied upon by others to relate policy to context or to gate keep; e.g. Headteachers (Wallace, 1988) or heads of department (Bowe *et al.*, 1992). But also certain policy texts may be collectively undermined (e.g. the 1993 teacher unions' stand against National Testing for 14-year-olds and the publication of school test results for 7- and 14-year-olds) or may generate mass confusion and de-moralisation. Pollard (1992, p. 112) provides a very good example of both the mediation and de-legitimation of a text; the Schools Examination and Assessment Council *Guide to Teacher Assessment* (1990).

> This document, which was intended to provide INSET support to schools, seriously failed to connect with primary teacher's views about learning or with the practicalities of the circumstances in which they work. For instance, it was suggested that 'lessons' are planned with direct reference to Attainment Targets and suggested, unproblematic ally, that the National Curriculum has set out the order in which children would learn. To teachers and advisers who retained child-centred beliefs and an awareness of the diverse patterns by which children learn, this was like a red rag to a bull.
>
> There was also enormous hilarity and anger over the impracticality of many of the suggestions which were made. In particular, the authors of the materials seemed to have no awareness of the demands of teaching with large class sizes and made a number of simplistic and naive suggestions. The credibility of the document was thus heavily undercut. SEAC was then humiliated by an article on the materials by Ted Wragg in *The Times Educational Supplement* entitled 'Who put the "Ass" in Assessment?' and a large number of schools and LEAs actively discouraged the circulation or use of the *Guide*.

Nonetheless, policies *are* textual interventions into practice; and although many teachers (and others) are proactive, 'writerly' readers of texts, their readings and reactions are not constructed in circumstances of their own making. Policies pose problems to their subjects. Problems that must be solved in context. It may be possible for some to 'hide' from policy but that is rarely a common option. I must be very clear, policy 'matters: it is important, not the least because it consists of texts which are (sometimes) *acted on*' (Beilharz, 1987, p. 394). The point is that we cannot predict or assume, much to the chagrin of politicians, how they will be acted on in every case in every setting, or what their immediate effect will be, or what room for manoeuvre actors will find for themselves. Action may be constrained differently (even tightly) but it is not determined by policy in the sense of an absolute uniformity across settings. Solutions to the problems posed by policy texts will be localised and should be expected to display ad hocery and messiness. Responses indeed must be 'creative'; but I use the term carefully here and in a specific sense. Given constraints, circumstances and practicalities, the translation of the crude, abstract simplicities of policy texts into interactive and sustainable practices of some sort involve productive thought, invention and adaptation. Policies do not normally tell you what to do, they create circumstances in which the range of options available in deciding what to do are narrowed or changed or particular goals or outcomes are set. A response must still be put together, constructed in context, off-set against other expectations. All of this involves creative social action not robotic reactivity. Thus, the enactment of texts relies on things like commitment, understanding, capability, resources, practical limitations, co-operation and (importantly) inter-textual compatibility. Furthermore, sometimes when we focus analytically on one policy or one text we forget that other policies and texts are in circulation and the enactment of one may inhibit or contradict or influence the possibility of the enactment of others. (I could illustrate most of these points with data from our Education Reform Act study; Bowe *et al.*, 1992.) And the more ideologically abstract any policy is, the more distant in conception from practice (as in the example above), the less likely it is to be accommodated in unmediated form into the context of practice; it confronts 'other realities', other circumstances, like poverty, disrupted classrooms, lack of materials, multi-lingual classes. Some policies change some of the circumstances in which we work, they cannot change all the circumstances. Riseborough (1992) in a detailed analysis of the policy responses of one primary Headteacher, draws our attention to the importance of 'secondary adjustments' in teachers' engagement with policy. '...teachers can create, through a repertoire of individual and collective, "contained" (i.e. "fitting in without introducing pressure for radical change") and "disruptive" (i.e. attempts to radically alter the structure or leave) strategies, an empirically rich under-life to policy intention' (p. 37). Generally, we have failed to research, analyse and conceptualise this under-life, the 'secondary adjustments' which relate teachers to policy and to the state in different ways. We tend to begin by assuming the adjustment of teachers and context to policy but not of policy to context. There is a privileging of the policymaker's reality. The crude and over-used term resistance is a poor substitute here which allows for both rampant over-claims and dismissive under-claims to bring about the way policy problems are solved in context. I also want to avoid the notion that policy is always negatively responded to, or that all policies are coercive or regressive. Some emancipatory policies are subject to creative non-implementation (education history is littered with examples). And some policies may be deployed in the context of practice to displace or marginalise others (see Troyna, 1992).

In all this discussion of interpretation and creativity I am not trying to exclude power. Textual interventions can change things significantly, but I am suggesting that we should not ignore the way that things stay the same nor the ways in which changes are different in different settings and different from the intentions of policy authors (where these are clear). Power, as Foucault points out, is productive; 'relations of power are not in superstructural positions, with merely a role of prohibition or accompaniment; they have a directly productive role, where ever they come into play' (1981, p. 94). Policies typically posit a restructuring, redistribution and disruption of power relations, so that different people can and cannot make claims to be able to do different things; again 'relations of power are not in a position of exteriority with respect to other types of relationships (economic processes, knowledge relationships, sexual relations), but are immanent in the latter...' (p. 94). Power is multiplicitous, overlain, interactive and complex, policy texts *enter* rather than simply change power relations. Hence again the complexity of the relationship between policy intentions, texts, interpretations and reactions. From a rather different theoretical starting point Offe (1984, p. 106) offers a similar view:

> the real social effects ('impact') of a law or institutional service are not determined by the wording of laws and statutes ('policy output'), but instead are generated primarily as a consequence of social disputes and conflicts, for which state policy merely establishes the location and timing of the contest, its subject matter and 'the rules of the game'. In these cases of extra-political or 'external' implementation of social policy measures state social policy in no way establishes concrete 'conditions' (for example, the level of services, specific insurance against difficult living conditions). Instead, it defines the substance of conflict and, by differentially empowering or dis-empowering the relevant social groups, biases the extent of the specific 'utility' of the institutions of social policy for these groups.

What Offe is saying, I think, is that practice and the 'effects' of policy cannot be simply read-off from texts and are the outcome of conflict and struggle between 'interests' in context. (The use of the market form within policy and the relative advantage that this allows middle class families to achieve is a case in point; see Chapter 16.)

Thus, I take it as axiomatic that there is agency and there is constraint in relation to policy – this is not a sum-zero game. Policy analysis requires not an understanding that is based on constraint *or* agency but on the changing relationships between constraint *and* agency and their inter-penetration. Furthermore, such an analysis must achieve insight into both overall and localised outcomes of policy.

But I also want to use this quotation as a transition point in order to move on to the *other* things that I want to say about policy. First, I want to take up the point made that state policy 'establishes the location and timing of the contest, its subject matter and 'the rules of the game'. This I think highlights the importance of policy *as* and *in* discourse. Second, I want to return to the problem of the 'effects' of policy.

Policy as discourse

In the above there is plenty of social agency and social intentionality around. Actors are making meaning, being influential, contesting, constructing responses, dealing with contradictions, attempting representations of policy. Much of this stuff of policy can be engaged with by a realist analysis in the different contexts of policy. But maybe this *is* a new pluralism. Maybe this *is* caught within an ideology of agency; by dealing with what is or can be done it misses what Ozga calls 'the bigger picture'. In other words, perhaps it concentrates too much on what those who inhabit policy think about and the relations between thought and action and misses and fails to attend to what they do not think about. Thus, we need to appreciate the way in which policy ensembles, collections of related policies, exercise power through a *production* of 'truth' and 'knowledge', as discourses. Discourses are 'practices that systematically form the objects of which they speak ... Discourses are not about objects; they do not identify objects, they constitute them and in the practice of doing so conceal their own invention' (Foucault, 1977a,b, p. 49). Discourses are about what can be said, and thought, but also about who can speak, when, where and with what authority. Discourses embody the meaning and use of propositions and words. Thus, certain possibilities for thought are constructed. Words are ordered and combined in particular ways and other combinations are displaced or excluded. 'Discourse may seem of little account' Foucault says 'but the prohibitions to which it is subject reveal soon enough its links with desire and power' (1971, pp. 11–12). Discourse is 'irreducible to language and to speech' (1974, p. 49) it is 'more' than that. We do not speak a discourse, it speaks us. *We are* the subjectivities, the voices, the knowledge, the power relations that a discourse constructs and allows. We do not 'know' what we say, we 'are' what we say and do. In these terms we are spoken by policies, we take up the positions constructed for us within policies. This is a system of practices (marketing one's courses, promoting one's institution) and a set of values and ethics (forcing unproductive colleagues to take early retirement so that they do not have to be counted in the departmental performativity returns). 'Discourses get things done, accomplish real tasks, gather authority' (Said, 1986, p. 152). And we have to note the de-centring of the state in this, discourses are non-reductionist. The actions of the state are here also the product of discourse, points in the diagram of power, although discourses are typically formed and legitimated in particular institutional sites like the state. It is a necessary but not sufficient concept in the development of an 'analytics of power' – 'The state can only operate on the basis of other, already existing power relations' (Rabinow, 1986, p. 64) – like racism and like patriarchy. I am not arguing that the state is irrelevant, or that is should not play a key role in policy analysis (see Ball, 1990). But serious attention needs to be given to the play of state power within 'disaggregated, diverse and specific (or local) sites' (Allan, 1990) and the ways in which particular fields of knowledge are sustained and challenged in these settings, around particular 'events'. Discourses of different sorts, with different histories, clash and grate against one another. Dominant discourses pre-suppose their opposite. The existence of 'other' discourse, 'outlaw' discourses, always presents the possibility of some kind of 'disidentification' (Pecheux, 1982).

In Foucault's terms we would see policy ensembles that include, for example, the market, management, appraisal and performativity as 'regimes of truth' through which people govern themselves and others. This is based upon the production and transformation and effects of true/false distinctions (Smart, 1986, p. 164) and the application of science and hierarchisation to 'problems' in education – like standards, discipline, the quality of teaching, efficient use of resources. These new 'sciences' of education are inhabited and disseminated and legitimated by a set of 'specific' intellectuals – the Spinks and Caldwells, Sextons, Hargreaves and Hopkins', and Fidlers and Bowles' (see Chapters 1 and 4). The point of all this is that an exclusive focus upon 'secondary adjustments', particularly if this takes the form of 'naive optimism', may obscure the discursive limitations acting on and through those adjustments. We may only be able to conceive of the possibilities of response in and through the language, concepts and vocabulary which the discourse makes available to us. Thus, Offe may be right in stressing that struggle, dispute, conflict and adjustment take place over a pre-established terrain. The essence of this is that there are real struggles over the interpretation and enactment of policies. But these are typically set within a moving discursive frame which articulates and constrains the possibilities and probabilities of interpretation and enactment. We read and respond to policies in discursive circumstances that we cannot, or perhaps do not, normally think about. Also embedded in this is the intellectual work done on and in the 'politics of truth' by the advocates and technicians of policy change, and the 'will to power' and desire of those who find themselves the beneficiaries of new power relations, where power is 'exercised in the effect of one action on another action' (Hoy, 1986, p. 135). 'Power may be understood in the first instance as the multiplicity of force relations in the sphere in which they operate and which constitute their own organization' (Foucault, 1981, p. 92) (see Chapter 10). Thus, in these terms the effect of policy is primarily discursive, it changes the possibilities we have for thinking 'otherwise', thus it limits our responses to change, and leads us to misunderstand what policy is by misunderstanding what it does. Further, policy as discourse may have the effect of redistributing 'voice'. So that it does not matter what some people say or think, only certain voices can be heard as meaningful or authoritative.

Now the danger here of course is that of 'naive pessimism'. As Jameson (1984, p. 57) puts it:

> the more powerless the reader comes to feel. In so far as the theorist wins, therefore, by constructing an increasingly closed and terrifying machine, to that very degree he [*sic*] loses, since the critical capacity of his work is thereby paralyzed, and the impulses of negation and revolt, not to speak of those of social transformation, are increasingly perceived as vain and trivial in the face of the model itself.

But in practice in complex modern societies, as noted already, we are enmeshed in a variety of discordant, incoherent and contradictory discourses, and 'subjugated knowledges' cannot be totally excluded from arenas of policy implementation (see Riseborough, 1992). 'We must make allowance for the complex and unstable process whereby discourse can be both an instrument and an effect of power, but also a hindrance, a stumbling block, a point of resistance and a starting point for an opposing strategy' (Foucault, 1981, p. 101). But we do need to recognise and analyse the existence of 'dominant' discourses, regimes of truth, erudite knowledges – like neo-liberalism and management theory – within social policy. At present I can offer no satisfactory closure on the issue of policy as discourse except, weakly perhaps, to reiterate my earlier point about needing more than one good theory to construct one half-decent explanation or account. I tried this composite theory approach in my 1990 study of the politics of educational reform in the UK.

Policy effects

I want now to take up some problems remaining in the first section of this paper in a different way. That is by exploring how we might begin to conceptualise policy effects in a way that is neither theoretically high-handed nor trivialising. This also takes me back to my disagreement with Ozga, noted above, about the nature of localised responses to policy as being ad hoc, serendipitous etc. In this respect both those writers who celebrate agency and their critics misunderstand, or are at least imprecise about, what might be meant by the effects or impact of policy. I want to distinguish initially between the generalities and specifics of policy effect.

Again I want to make myself clear; the earlier discussion of policy texts is not intended to convey a conception of policy effects as typically minimal or marginal. It is not that policies have no effects, they do; it is not that those effects are not significant, they are; it is not that those effects are not patterned, they are, although it is possible to think of policies that just fail to work. But to reiterate, responses (as one vehicle for effects) vary between contexts. Policies from 'above' are not the only constraints and influences upon institutional practice. One difficulty in discussing effects is that the specific and the general are often conflated. The general effects of policies become evident when specific aspects of change and specific sets of responses (within practice) are related together. A neglect of the general is most common in single-focus studies which take one change or one policy text and attempt to determine its impact on practice. Taken in this way the specific effects of a specific policy may be limited but the general effects of ensembles of policies of different kinds may be of considerable significance in terms of their effects for social justice. I would suggest that in the UK at least (probably also the US, Canada, Australia and New Zealand) the cumulative and general effects of several years of multiple thrusts of educational reform on teachers' work have been profound. Here teachers' work is a general category which encompasses a variety of separate reforms related to curriculum, assessment, performativity, organisation, pay and conditions (see Chapters 7 and 10). Again though such a generalisation has to be handled carefully in at least two senses. (1) There is a danger of idealising the past and portraying a situation in which teachers once had autonomy and now do not (again this is not a zero-sum issue). A formulation like that of Dale (1989) of a shift from licensed to regulated autonomy is a useful tool in thinking about this. What he attempts to capture is a qualitative shift from one kind of autonomy to another; thus he has to specify the different characteristics of the two kinds. (2) The generalisation will not encompass the experience of all types of teachers in all types of situation. Two examples: Teachers in the UK who find themselves in oversubscribed schools of high reputation which can thus select students may find their conditions of work and freedom for manoeuvre very different from teachers in undersubscribed schools of poor reputation which must take what students they can get and will be funded at a lower level accordingly. Furthermore, the recent changes in the UK have had very different implications for classroom teachers and Headteachers. The latter, in some respects, and also depending on which schools they are responsible for, find their freedom for manoeuvre and powers in relation to erstwhile colleagues enhanced rather than diminished. They are beneficiaries, at least to an extent, in the redrawing of the diagram of power. This kind of attention to policy 'effects' also highlights some other difficulties inherent in the 'policy as text' perspective. A concentration upon the interpretational responses of individual actors can lead to a neglect of the compound and structural changes effected by state policies. In particular, such a focus may lead to a neglect of the pervasive effect of institutional reconfiguration.

But there is a further important distinction to be made in regard to effects. A distinction between what might be called first order and second order effects. First order effects are changes in practice or structure (which are evident in particular sites and across the system as a whole). And second order effects are the impact of these changes on patterns of social access and opportunity and social justice. Walker (1981, p. 225) articulates the distinction thus:

> the essential aspect of *social* policies is their distributional implications or outcomes. Social policies may be made implicitly or explicitly, by a wide range of social institutions and groups, including the state. The task of social policy analysis is to evaluate the distributional impact of existing policies and proposals and the rationales underlying them. In such analyses attention will be focused...on the behaviour of organisations, professionals and classes in order to balance descriptions of the institutional framework through which the welfare state is administered with analysis of the social production and maintenance of inequality.

One important analytical strategy which provides a mechanism for linking and tracing the discursive origins and possibilities of policy, as well as the intentions embedded in, responses to and effects of policy, is that employed by Edwards *et al.* (1989, 1992) in their APS (Assisted Places Scheme) and CTC (City Technology Colleges) studies. They are what I would call policy trajectory studies. They employ a cross-sectional rather than a single level analysis by tracing policy formulation, struggle and response from within the state itself through to the various recipients of policy. Richard Bowe and I attempted to give some conceptual structure to the trajectory method by adumbrating three contexts of policy-making (Bowe *et al.*, 1992) – *the context of influence, the context of policy text production and the context(s) of practice*. Each context consists of a number of arenas of action – some private and some public. Each context involves struggle and compromise and ad hocery. They are loosely-coupled and there is no simple one direction of flow of information between them. But in theoretical and practical terms, this model requires two further 'contexts' to make it complete. First, we must add the relationship between first order (practice) effects and second order effects – that is *the context of outcomes*. Here analytical concern is with the issues of justice, equality and individual freedom. Policies are analysed in terms of their impact upon and interactions with existing inequalities and forms of injustice. The question of the fifth context is then begged, *the context of political strategy*; the identification of a set of political and social activities 'which might more effectively tackle inequalities' (Troyna, 1993, p. 12). This is an essential component of what Harvey (1990) calls *critical social research* or the work of those Foucault calls 'specific intellectuals', which is produced for strategic use in particular social situations and struggles. As Sheridan (1980, p. 221) puts it: 'the Foucauldian genealogy is an unmasking of power for the use of those who suffer it'. This is what Foucault calls 'the real political task' in our society, 'to criticize the working of institutions which appear to be both neutral and independent, and to criticize them in such a manner that the political violence which has always exercised itself obscurely through them will be unmasked so that we can fight them' (Rabinow, 1984, p. 6). But Foucault's method also carries stark messages for the over-ambitious researcher/reformer; for the genealogical method, Sheridan goes on to say, 'is also directed against those who would seize power in their name' (p. 221).

References

Allan, J. (1990). 'Does Feminism Need a Theory of "The State"?', in Watson, S. (ed.), *Playing the State: Australian Feminist Interventions*. NSW, Allen and Unwin.

Ball, S. J. (1990). *Politics and Policy Making in Education*. London, Routledge.

Ball, S. J. (1994). 'Culture, Crisis and Morality: The Struggle Over the National Curriculum', in Atkinson, P., Davies, B. and Delamont, S. (eds), *Discourse and Reproduction: Essays for Basil Bernstein*. New York, Hampton Press.

Ball, S. J., Bowe, R. and Gewirtz, S. (1995). 'Circuits of Schooling: A Sociological Exploration of Parental Choice in Social Class Contexts', *Sociological Review*, 43(1): 52–78.

Beilharz, P. (1987). 'Reading Politics: Social Theory and Social Policy', *Australia and New Zealand Journal of Sociology*, 23(3): 388–406.

Bowe, R., Ball, S. J. with Gold, A. (1992). *Reforming Education and Changing Schools*. London, Routledge.

Brown, M. (1992). *National Curriculum Mathematics – National Evaluation*. Personal Communication.

Codd, J. (1988). 'The Construction and Deconstruction of Educational Policy Documents', *Journal of Education Policy*, 3(5): 235–48.

Dale, R. (1979). 'The Politicisation of School Deviance: Reactions to William Tyndale', in Barton, L. and Mieghan, R. (eds), *Schools, Pupils and Deviance*. Driffield, Nafferton.

Edwards, T., Fitz, J. and Whitty, G. (1989). *The State and Private Education: An Evaluation of the Assisted Places Scheme*. London, Falmer.

Edwards, T., Gewirtz, S. and Whitty, G. (1992). 'Whose Choice of Schools? Making Sense of City Technology Colleges', in Arnot, M. and Barton, L. (eds), *Voicing Concerns*. Wallingford, Triangle.

Foucault, M. (1971). *L'ordre du discours*. Paris, Gallimard.

Foucault, M. (1974). *The Order of Things*. London, Tavistock.

Foucault, M. (1977a). *The Archeology of Knowledge*. London, Tavistock.

Foucault, M. (1977b). 'The Eye of Power', in Gordon, C. (ed.) (1980), *Power/Knowledge*. New York, Pantheon.

Foucault, M. (1980). *Power/Knowledge: Selected Interviews and other Writings, 1972–77*, in Gordon, C. (ed.), Brighton, Harvester Press.

Foucault, M. (1981). *The History of Sexuality*, Vol. 1. Harmondsworth, Penguin.

Gewirtz, S., Ball, S. J. and Bowe, R. (1993). 'Parents, Privilege and the Education Market Place', *Research Papers in Education*, 9(1): 3–29.

Giddens, A. (1987). *Social Theory and Modern Sociology*. Cambridge, Polity Press.

Gipps, C. and Brown, M. (1992). *National Assessment in Primary Schools Project*. Seminar Paper, Institute of Education, University of London.

Harker, R. and S. May (1997). 'Code and habitus: comparing the accounts of Bernstein and Bourdieu', *British Journal of Sociology of Education*, 14(2): 169–79.

Harvey, L. (1990). *Critical Social Research*. London, Allen and Unwin.

Hoy, D. (1986). 'Power, Repression, Progress: Foucault, Lukes and the Frankfurt School', in Hoy, D. (ed.), *Foucault: A Critical Reader*. Oxford, Blackwell.

Jameson, F. (1984). 'Postmodernism or The Cultural Logic of Late Capitalism', *New Left Review*, 147: 61–84.

Offe, C. (1984). *Contradictions of the Welfare State*. London, Hutchinson.

Ozga, J. (1987). 'Studying Education Policy through the Lives of Policy Makers', in Walker, S. and Barton, L. (eds), *Changing Policies, Changing Teachers*. Milton Keynes, Open University Press.

Ozga, J. (1990). 'Policy Research and Policy Theory: A Comment on Fitz and Halpin', *Journal of Education Policy*, 5(4): 359–62.

Patton, P. (1979). 'Of Power and Prisons', in Morris, M. and Patton, P. (eds), *Michel Foucault: Power/Truth/Strategy*. Sydney, Feral Publications.

Pecheux, M. (1982). *Language, Semantics and Ideology*. Macmillan, Basingstoke.

Pollard, A. (1992). 'Teachers Responses to the Reshaping of Primary Education', in Arnot, M. and Barton, L. (eds), *Voicing Concerns*. Wallingford, Triangle.

Rabinow, P. (1986). *The Foucault Reader*. Harmondsworth, Penguin.

Riseborough, G. (1992). 'Primary Headship, State Policy and the Challenge of the 1990s', *Journal of Education Policy*, 8(2): 123–42.

Rizvi, F. and Kemmis, S. (1987). *Dilemmas of Reform*. Geelong, Deakin Institute for Studies in Education.

Said, E. (1986). 'Foucault and the Imagination of Power', in Hoy, D. (ed.), *Foucault: A Critical Reader*. Oxford, Blackwell.

Sheridan, A. (1980). *The Will to Truth*. London, Tavistock.

Smart, B. (1986). 'The Politics of Truth and the Problem of Hegemony', in Hoy, D. (ed.), *Foucault: A Critical Reader*. Oxford, Blackwell.

Troyna, B. (1992). ' "The Hub" and "the Rim": How LMS Buckles Antiracist Education', paper presented at the *8th ERA Research Network Seminar* (12 February 1992).

Troyna, B. (1993). 'Critical Social Research and Education Policy', paper presented to the *Conference New Directions in Education Policy Sociology* (30–31 March), also forthcoming in the *British Journal of Educational Studies*.

Walker, A. (1981). 'Social Policy, Social Administration and the Social Construction of Welfare', *Sociology*, 15(2): 255–69.

Wallace, M. (1988). 'Innovation For All: Management Development in Small Primary Schools', *Education Management and Administration*, 16(1): 15–24.

CHAPTER 4

EDUCATIONAL STUDIES, POLICY ENTREPRENEURSHIP AND SOCIAL THEORY*

R. Slee and G. Weiner with S. Tomlinson (eds), *School Effectiveness for Whom?* London: Falmer Press, 1998

> The sociology that each sociologist can perform of the social conditions of his sociological practice and his relation to sociology...it the precondition for his making his unconscious presuppositions explicit and for a more complete internalization of a more adequate epistemology.
>
> (Bourdieu *et al.*, 1991, p. 72)

In this paper I reflect upon my practice as an educational researcher and theorist and, in more general terms, consider the current state of the field of educational studies within which my practice is located. In doing so, I shall allow myself to be playful and perhaps at times outrageous but always with serious intent. I am not attempting to be definitive. What I offer here is coming close to an approximation of something I might hope to say more clearly in the future. The spirit of what I am attempting, and some of the substance I wish to argue, are conveyed rather effectively in the following quotation from Michel Foucault:

> I wouldn't want what I may have said or written to be seen as laying any claims to totality. I don't try to universalize what I say; conversely what I don't say isn't meant to be thereby disqualified as being of no importance. My work takes place between unfinished abutments and anticipatory strings of dots. I like to open out a space of research, try it out, then if it doesn't work try again somewhere else. On many points...I am still working and don't yet know whether I am going to get anywhere. What I say ought to be taken as 'propositions', 'game openings' where those who may be interested are invited to join in; they are not meant as dogmatic assertions that have to be taken or left en bloc...
>
> (Foucault, 1991, pp. 90–1)

My proposition, then, my 'game opening' here, is that educational studies is in a sorry state and in danger of becoming worse. That is to say, using Bernstein's terms, the weak grammars of educational studies, those concepts, relations and procedures upon which it rests, are becoming weaker (Bernstein, 1999). The serial segmented structures, those differentiating rituals which distinguish us from each other and from other fields of knowledge, are becoming more detached and insulated from one another. As Basil Bernstein might put it, the invisible light that shines wanly within the knowledge structures of educational studies is in danger of being snuffed out entirely.

It is hardly novel to suggest that the discourses and knowledge structures of educational studies are shifting in response to the political and ideological repositioning of the academy and of scholarship in the UK. It is important to make it clear that the state of affairs I am addressing here is, at least in part, symptomatic of a more wholesale reworking of the relationship between higher education and research and the state (Ball, 2004a,b). However, the resultant changes in the practices of scholarship seem particularly marked and particularly paradoxical in the field of educational studies. More specifically, what I have called the sorry state of educational studies seems to me to stem in part from both the wholesale appropriation of other 'unreflexive' and utilitarian languages *and* the internal lack of dynamism, exacerbated by intellectual isolationism as educational studies pointedly ignores significant theoretical developments in cognate fields. The problem with educational studies, I am arguing, is that we are both too open to other discourses and not open enough.

This state of affairs is my topic. I want to spend some time exploring the problems with educational studies as I see them; I shall then consider the role of theory in reconstituting a new present for educational studies and conclude with some brief thoughts about the nature of theorising and the problem with theory. While bearing in mind the initial disclaimer quoted above, I will have, necessarily, to indulge in some generalisations. I must also acknowledge from the start that I will leave my argument only partially developed and I will leave it with embedded contradictions. At times I will be likely to appear self-destructive and perhaps intellectually schizophrenic. I shall leave the reader to judge. I must also acknowledge that what I say may have somewhat less relevance to some disciplines within educational studies than it does to others.

To begin I want to take as my particular case in point my own field of practice – the sociology of education – but, as I say, I intend my thesis to be more generalised. I shall rehearse a kind of vulgar history of the discipline in order to establish what I call the *reincorporation* of educational studies.

British sociology of education had its beginnings in, that is it was initiated and primarily disseminated from, the London School of Economics. The methods and politics of the subject were, from the late 1930s to the late 1960s, driven by the methods and politics of the LSE. This placed education as part of the post-war social reconstruction of Britain and as part of the establishment of a modern welfare state. The concerns of researchers were focused *initially* upon the problems of mass participation in the education system and the debilitating effects, for some children, of economic and material deprivation. The sometimes unarticulated assumption of the handful of education researchers at work at this time appeared to be that if these extrinsic sources of inequality could be removed or ameliorated, then the repeatedly evident and apparently tight bond between educational attainment and social class could be broken; leaving residual differences which could be explained in others ways – like in terms of intelligence or selection bias. Crucially, the particular focus upon social class differences served to establish social class as the major, almost the only, dependent variable in sociological research for the next forty years. During this period, through the work of particular 'universal intellectuals', the sociology of education aspired to, and occasionally achieved, a positive and influential relationship with policy-making. Particular policy solutions, based upon the outcomes of empirical research, were pursued, particularly in relation to Labour Party policy-making. Both the discipline and its politics and its relationships to policy were set within the grooves of an unproblematic progressive, utopian modernism. This was the enlightenment project writ small. Research linked to ameliorative state policies focused upon the achievement of equality *and* prosperity – the better educated we are the better off we are, individually and collectively. The discourse of this policy optimism was founded upon notions like the 'wasted pool of talent' and 'compensatory education'.

As we know this dual optimism (that attached to the welfare state and that embedded in the practices and discourses of the discipline itself) did not last. In the 1970s, the academic discourse of programmatic optimism was to be dramatically and decisively replaced by one of radical pessimism. The interpretations of the causes and solutions of inequality scattered to the winds. Policy became an irrelevance as the reproduction of unequal social relations were discovered to be lurking stubbornly in every classroom nook and cranny and every staffroom conversation; while at the same time they were rooted in the abstract needs of the state and the inevitable and inescapable requirements and workings of the economy. The teacher as cultural dope was now the subject of derision from all sides for failing to deliver either fairness or prosperity. A relationship between research and policy (at least at national level) was now not just pointless but also politically incorrect. Educational researchers found themselves grounded between negativity and complicity. With the collapse of the relationship between educational research and policy and the beginnings of a growing suspicion of liberal expertise within educational politics, the vacuum in the arena of educational policy-making was skillfully filled by the organic intellectuals of the new right.

In the 1980s, things became more complicated as class analysis was displaced as the primary variable and race, gender and, later, disability and sexual orientation came to the fore both in analytical perspectives and in a new but tentative liaison between theory and practice. But race and gender studies were only two parts of a more thorough-going fragmentation of the sociology of education as some researchers began to turn their attention to and then attach themselves to the industry of educational reform. While some one-time and would-be sociologists and other educational researchers now reinvented themselves as feminists or anti-racists, and indeed brought to educational studies a much needed infusion of invigorating new theory, others began to take on new identities as 'school effectiveness researchers' and 'management theorists'. Around this latter kind of work, a new relationship *to* policy or rather *inside* policy was forged. Issues related to system design, analysis of provision and social justice were replaced by implementation studies focused on issues like 'quality', 'evaluation', 'leadership' and 'accountability'.

In the 1990s, whole areas of the sociology of education, specifically, and educational studies generally have been thoroughly reincorporated into the political project and discourse of policy and of educational reform. In some respects the discipline has come full circle. This reincorporation can be interrogated by rehearsing Brian Fay's distinction, also used by Gerald Grace, between policy science and policy scholarship (Fay, 1975). Fay defines policy science as 'that set of procedures which enables one to determine the technically best course of action to adopt in order to implement a decision or achieve a goal. Here the policy scientist doesn't merely clarify the possible outcomes of certain courses of action, he actually chooses the most efficient course of action in terms of the available scientific information' (p. 14). This Fay suggests is a type of 'policy engineering': the 'policy engineer ... is one who seeks the most technically correct answer to political problems in terms of available social scientific knowledge' (p. 14). Here policy is both de-politicized and thoroughly technicised; the perview of the policy scientist is limited to and by the agenda of social and political problems defined elsewhere and by solutions already embedded in scientific practice, this is what Fay calls 'the sublimation of politics' (p. 27). It also produces, I suggest, another effect, that is; by a combination of financial restructuring and Faustian deal-making, it plays its part in 'the taming of the academy'. As a result, research perspectives and research funding are increasingly tightly tied to the policy agendas of government. The already weak autonomy of higher education having been re-defined as part of the cause of the nation's economic problems is closed down further HE policy by HE policy. Further, this problem-solving technicism rests upon an uncritical acceptance of moral and political consensus and operates within the hegemony of instrumental rationalism or as Fay puts it 'man (*sic*) must plan, and the function of the social sciences is to provide the theoretical foundation that makes this planning possible' (p. 27). In this scientific and technical project for research the debates and conflicts which link policies to values and morals is displaced by bland rationalist empiricism, and the best we can aspire to is to be 'integrated critics' (Eco, 1994). But again, other effects are produced here. Firstly, this instrumental, rational empiricism is implicated and interested in the social construction of those subjects about whom it speaks and in relation to whom it construes problems and constructs solutions. It has produced what Donzelot calls the 'landscape of the social' within which it then acts (I return to this later). Furthermore, in this 'will to knowledge' and the complex interplay between knowledge and the objects of its concern, the very nature of 'the social' is captured and constrained by social science's classifications and nosologies and by the drive to achieve parsimonious and totalising conceptions of social structures and processes. The epistemic assumptions of order, structure, function, cause and effect are variously mobilised to represent 'the social' and in doing so work to exclude many of the mobile, complex, ad hoc, messy and fleeting qualities of lived experience. We become locked into the simple but powerful and very productive assumption that 'the social' is susceptible to parsimonious and orderly totalising conceptions. Or to use a slightly different lexicon, drawing again from Foucault, we can say that:

> In appearance, or rather, according to the mask it bears, historical consciousness is neutral, devoid of passions and committed solely to truth. But if it examines itself and if more generally, it interrogates the various forms of scientific consciousness in its history it finds that all these forms and transformations are aspects of the will to knowledge: instinct, passion, the inquisitor's devotion, cruel subtlety and malice...

> (1977, p. 162)

Perhaps it would be helpful at this point if I were to develop an example of policy science at work in a way which begins to illustrate some of the variety of points I have adumbrated above. 'Management theory' offers one example on which I have written previously (Ball, 1990, 1994) so let me move away from that slightly by considering the relationships between management theory and school effectiveness research. Again my style of analysis draws on Foucault, in particular I shall employ his 'master trope' – reversal. I will thus be seeking the negative activity of discourse.

Management theories as modes of objectification place human beings as subjects – to be managed. This is a 'discourse of right' which legitimates the exercise of authority. Its primary instrument is a hierarchy of continuous and functional surveillance. Effectiveness research can be seen to have played a crucial role in laying the groundwork for the reconceptualisation of the school within which management discourse operates and has played its part in providing a technology of organisational measurement and surveillance. By technology here I refer to 'coherent or contradictory forms of managing and activating a population' which, like Bentham's panopticon, lend themselves to polyvalent tactical applications. First, effectiveness studies and school-difference studies re-centred the school as the focus of causation in explanations of student performance and variations in levels of achievement; displacing or rendering silent other explanations related to the embeddedness of education in social and economic contexts. And in so far as the gaze of 'effectiveness' provided a scientific basis for the possibility of 'blaming' the school, it fitted perfectly (in terms of theoretical unity) into the discourses of derision which targeted schools as 'causes' of general social and economic problems within society at large. In addition, the focus on measurable outcomes also articulated directly with the political process of the commodification of education involved in the creation of an education market. Second, this research provided a scientific concomitant to the political re-emphasis on excellence, diversity and selection and the attempt to develop methods of appraisal which can be used to identify (and punish) 'weak' and 'inadequate' teachers and this feeds into systems of incentive and performance related pay. Third, the effectiveness studies developed a technology of control which enables the monitoring and 'steering' of schools by applying 'neutral' indicators; and in its ambition effectiveness research continually attempts to 'tap' and measure more of that which is schooling, including 'the "deep structure" of pupil attitudes and perceptions' (Reynolds, 1990, p. 21). Thus, significant discursive and disciplinary work is done by effectiveness research, which is even further reaching in its implications when linked to notions of accountability, school review and school development planning. Here we may see the play and effects of power and domination at work in the direct relationships and immediate structures of school organisation. These are 'the panopticisms of every day' which are constructed and enacted 'below the level of emergence of the great apparatuses and the great political struggles' (Foucault, 1979a, p. 223).

In effect, through such schemes, teachers are entrapped into taking responsibility for their own 'disciplining'. Indeed teachers are urged to believe that their commitment to such processes will make them more 'professional'. Moreover, effectiveness is a technology of normalisation. Such research both constructs a normative model of the effective school and abnormalises the ineffective or 'sick' school. In relation to the concepts of 'review', 'development' and 'self-evaluation' it then draws upon the 'confessional technique' (an admission of transgressions and a ritual of atonement) as a means of submission and transformation. The secular confession is founded on the notion of normal as against abnormal transposed from the religious opposition of sin and piety. Such a transposition is most clearly evident in the methods of 'appraisal'.

The normalising effects of 'effectiveness' are noted by Laurie Angus. In a review of school effectiveness literature, he comments that 'predictability and efficiency are valued to the extent that schools would surely become dramatically more boring places than they are already' (Angus, 1993, p. 343). He goes on to suggest that:

> not only is there a lack of engagement with sociological (or other theory), but also effectiveness work is largely trapped in a logic of common sense which allows it, by and large, to be appropriated into the Right's hegemonic project…it advocates an isolationist, apolitical approach to education in which it is assumed that educational problems can be fixed by technical means and inequality can be managed within the walls of schools and classrooms provided that teachers and pupils follow 'correct' effective school procedures.
>
> (p. 343)

By such means 'normalising judgments' are turned upon the whole school and each school is set in a field of comparison – which again articulates with other current aspects of educational policy. An 'artificial' order is laid down, 'an order defined by natural and observable processes' (Foucault, 1979a, p. 179). The definitions of behaviour and performance embedded in the order and the norm are arrived at 'on the basis of two opposed values of good and evil' (p. 180). The good school and the bad school, effective and ineffective practice. Through 'value-giving' measures the constraint of a conformity that must be achieved is introduced.

If self-examination fails, the expert, the consultant, the moral disciplinarian are at hand to intervene with their models of 'effective practice'. In this role the scientific and the moral are tightly intertwined. In effect, given the logic of management, ineffectiveness is seen as a disorder of reason and as such susceptible to cure by the use of appropriate techniques of organisation.

I could go on but my point here is to begin to explore an aspect of educational study and educational research by employing a different theoretical language and theoretical perspective, to focus upon unintended and overlooked consequences, so as to render our practice critically problematic. I am also seeking to demonstrate some of the ways in which our research and 'scientific' conceptualisations can be tied back into broader political projects and social processes and to the functions of managing and neutralising social problems. A facade of objectivity obscures this process and further empowers the research enterprise with the capacity to categorise, professionalise and contain a specified social problem.

By employing this kind of critical reflexivity we can re-envision educational studies as a whole as a disciplinary technology, part of the exercise of disciplinary power. Management, effectiveness and appraisal, for example, as I have suggested, work together to locate individuals in space, in a hierarchical and efficiently visible organisation. In and through our research, the school and the teacher are captured within a perfect diagram of power; and the classroom is increasingly one of those 'small theatres', in which 'each actor is alone, perfectly individualized and constantly visible' (Foucault, 1979a, p. 200). It is thus that *governmentality* is achieved through the minute mechanisms of everyday life and the application of 'progressive' and efficient technical solutions to designated problems. Governmentality being that 'ensemble formed by the institutions, procedures, analyses and reflections, the calculations and tactics, that allow the exercise of this very specific albeit complex form of power, which has as its target population' (Foucault, 1979b, p. 20).

It is in this way that epistemological development within the human sciences, like education, functions politically and is intimately imbricated in the practical management of social and political problems. The scientific vocabulary may distance the researcher (and the manager) from the subjects of their action but, at the same time, it also constructs a gaze that renders the 'landscape of the social' ever more visible. Through methodical observation the 'objects of concern' identified in this landscape are inserted into a network of ameliorative or therapeutic practices. The point is that the idea that human sciences like educational studies stand outside or above the political agenda of the management of the population or some how have a neutral status embodied in a free-floating progressive rationalism are dangerous and debilitating conceits.

But now I have run ahead of myself and I want to return to Fay's work to consider the alternatives to policy science more closely.

Fay (1975) offers two alternatives to policy science; one is interpretive social science, and the other is critical social science. Both are familiar enough I think not to require extensive discussion here, except to say this: Fay argues that 'an interpretative social science promises to reveal to the social actors what they and others are doing, thereby restoring communication by correcting the ideas that they have about each other and themselves' (p. 90).[1] Now that may be an over-simplification, but I shall let that go at present and note Fay's comment that interpretative social science is deeply conservative in that 'it leads to reconciling people to their social order' (p. 91). That may be equally contestable but again I shall leave that argument for another time. Fay's second alternative, critical social science, rests on the proposition that 'social theory does not simply offer a picture of the way that a social order works; instead, a social theory is itself a catalytic agent of change within the complex of social life which it analyses' (p. 110). Now this is an attractive and popular intellectual position for policy scholars. It is a position I find, at least some of the time, personally comfortable and conducive. But is it a real *alternative* to the failings that Fay finds in policy science? Only partially I think. We need to think carefully here about the use and meaning of terms, especially those in Fay's final phrase 'a catalytic agent of change within the complex of social life which it analyses'. I have three nagging and related problems with this formulation. First, social science, here, is set over and against the social, social life, which it acts upon and analyses but is not part of. The critical social scientist is not seen as part of the struggle for 'truth' but is placed above and outside it with clean hands and clean conscience, representing the 'conscience of society as a whole'. Social scientists are not seen to have interests, careers or identities at stake here, they are free moral agents, unencumbered by everyday ideological limitations and personal ambitions. The second worry is that 'the critical' in critical social science is too limited and does not extend to a reflexive consideration of the ways in which social science constitutes 'the social' and its own ethical subjects; in this case the 'falsely conscious' and those of 'raised consciousness'. This spartan and familiar duality, upon which the critical social scientist then works, does significant injustice to the 'complex of social life' to which Fay himself refers and trades on a rather simplistic notion of unified and stable social subjects. Third, in the educative, revelationary role which Fay attributes to the critical social scientist, an uncritical rationalism and progressive humanism are smuggled back into the social scientist's practice, in the form of 'consciousness raising'; which is achieved by offering to social actors 'an alternative conception...of what they are' – a simple essentialism. I am not arguing that Fay's model of critical social science is irredeemably flawed but its epistemological emphases are in danger of collapsing it back into that which it seeks to distinguish itself from. Cohen makes the point more dramatically:

> I propose to withdraw the automatic 'cognitive advantage' of university critical writing, on the grounds that no such advantage is warranted: our writings are outfitted for the grooves of 'reason', 'society', 'need' – each of which is a cosmos of mythology unto itself. In making this withdrawal, I am more of less expressing 'no confidence' in the essential activities of the modern university.
>
> (1993, p. x)

So can I discern still another position in all this? Is there another, a fourth way? In the way things like this are supposed to work it is probably incumbent upon me to attempt to do so. But I will make my attempt in a rather elliptical fashion I am afraid. Before doing so I shall return once more to Fay's distinctions.

I want to extend Fay's nosology – alongside policy scholarship, policy engineering and policy science we also now need to recognise the role in educational studies of *policy entrepreneurship.* I intend the term to carry a variety of meanings but it rests primarily on the proselytising, and in some cases the sale, of 'technically correct answers'. The policy entrepreneur is committed to the application of certain technical solutions to organisations and contexts which are taken *a priori* to be in need of structural and/or cultural change. The entrepreneur's interests, in terms of identity and career, are bound up directly and immediately, rather than once removed, as in the case of policy science and critical social science, with the success of their dissemination. We might pick out 'the self-managing school' as an example of one such focus of dissemination, 'enterprise in higher education' is another, 'teacher appraisal' another, 'mentoring' and 'partnership' in initial teacher education are others. However, currently, particularly under New Labour, school effectiveness provides the clearest example of the power and effect of policy entrepreneurship.

As almost a mirror image of the school, family, social class nexus of the educational studies of the 1950s and 1960s school effectiveness provides a new *zeitgeist* for educational reform in the 1990s. Social contexts and social demographies are stripped away to 'expose' and position schools in isolation; to be inspected, evaluated and compared by 'the difference' they make. The social patterns and economic trends which link together large numbers of failing schools, especially in the secondary sector, are systematically neglected in the attention given to leadership, vision, management, and ethos. The gaze of research has shifted once more, away from the pathologies of the home, the workings of capital, and political biases and distortions, to land upon the skills and competences of teachers and headteachers. Indeed teachers and headteachers generally are rendered as ensembles of skills and competences – depersonalised and stripped of commitments, passions and desires (Ball, 2004). School effectiveness is the most asociological of the new educational studies and perhaps for that reason the most attractive to politicians, of virtually all persuasions. By removing context and complexity school effectiveness renders education eminently manageable and malleable. It translates directly into judgment and 'improvement'. It feeds into what Thrupp (1998) calls the 'politics of blame'. 'Savage Inequalities' (Kozol, 1991) are magically tamed, decoupling education from homelessness, unemployment, poverty and racism. Institutional turbulence, social segregation and social mix, and resource allocation are set aside in favour of an arid, technical reductionism. Concomitantly education is depoliticised in at least two senses. Firstly, 'Knowledge and curriculum are generally regarded as unproblematic and it is assumed that students must simply learn them' (Angus, 1993, p. 343). Secondly, home–school relationships are homogenised and reduced to the anodyne rhetoric of partnership. 'Neglect of pupil cultures and family cultures, which are also class cultures means a neglect of agency' (Hatcher, 1996, p. 40).

One again there is an intellectual trade between government and educational studies, a new economy of ideas and a new generation of single-idea policy advisers. It might be said that in all this, the referent that we call 'school' has disappeared and become a floating 'target' of signification by policy solutions. The promotion of humanity is subordinated to the promotion of efficiency. School effectiveness is in some sense the zenith of modernist intellectualism, a final accommodation between popular meaning and social research. An accommodation which, perhaps not surprisingly gives rise to *Sun-style* headlines – 'Failing Schools Named'; 'Incompetent Teachers to be Sacked' – strident in their simplifying terror. Of course all of this fits neatly with various other punitive populist measures on the New Labour agenda – curfews for young people, zero tolerance (on the streets and in schools), the harassing of beggars, workfare. The use-value of such research is clear. It cuts through the cultural overcoding which typifies much academic writing to achieve statist forms and language. A form of writing that 'exceeds what is expected of it', that offers 'semantic fixes' of a variety of sorts.

Furthermore, school effectiveness is now among the UK's invisible exports – its entrepreneurs tour the world with their powerpoint presentations to deliver effectiveness 'gigs' to various audiences keen for a policy 'high' to 'fix' their school or school system. In Africa school effectiveness software is now available for sale. In the UK, school effectiveness seminars do good business in out-of-town hotels.

It is possible again to situate such developments in a broader social and political context. In the era of late modernity the urge to represent is verging on the obsessional and forms of certainty have become valuable commodities as we seek to know the world a little better than those with whom we compete and assert greater and more detailed control over our environment. Unmediated knowledgability has its attractions and its price in many fields of the human sciences (cf. Beck, 1992).

This then is my backcloth. In epigrammatic form I want to suggest now that we have too much knowledge and not enough understanding. I want to put some epistemological distance between myself and the developments I have been reviewing. I want to celebrate theory. I wish to argue that the absence of theory leaves the researcher prey to unexamined, unreflexive preconceptions and dangerously naive ontological and epistemological *a prioris*. I shall wail and curse at the absence of theory and argue for theory as a way of saving educational studies from itself.

As a further aside, it is important to note that the collapse of, or abandonment of theory within educational studies has its parallels elsewhere in the field of education for example in the removal of theory work from teacher education courses and the concomitant reduction of teacher development to a matter of skills and competencies and on the job learning. Teaching like educational studies is thus reconstituted and depoliticised. It is changed from being an intellectual endeavour to being a technical process. Indeed this coincidence of change is in no way surprising, these technologies are all part of the same contemporary *dispositif* – the unity of a discourse through a period of time, 'a limited space of communication'.

But how can theory help? What is the point of theory? The point is that theory can separate us from 'the contingency that has made us what we are, the possibilities of no longer seeing, doing or thinking what we are, do or think' (Mahon, 1992, p. 122). Theory is a vehicle for 'thinking otherwise'; it is a platform for 'outrageous hypotheses' and for 'unleashing criticism'. Theory is destructive, disruptive and violent. It offers a language for challenge, and modes of thought, other than those articulated for us by dominant others. It provides a language of rigour and irony rather than contingency. The purpose of such theory is to de-familiarise present practices and categories, to make them seem less self-evident and necessary, and to open up spaces for the invention of new forms of experience. Now such a register, I realise, grates upon the Anglo-Saxon, positivist, utilitarian ear. We prefer our intellectualism expressed in the more sober tones and nuances of semantic deliberation and rational planning. Within the British tradition intellectualism, science or scholarship often only seem to be regarded as valid and useful when weighed and measured by concrete outcomes. Shilling (1993) made just this point in a review of a collection of papers drawn from work in the sociology of education. He took it as a sign of the times that the editors 'should have to justify the sociology of education, and by implication their own collection, by a highly reflexive positioning of it within an essentially utilitarian tradition of research based upon measuring the social outcomes of educational policies' (p. 103). He goes on to describe the sociology of education as 'a discipline which has been in decline in Britain for far too long' (p. 103). In effect the sociology of education and educational studies are in a state of 'intellectual stagnation', most particularly we are experiencing what Randall Collins refers to as the 'loss of cultural capital', that is the neglect of significant ideas, concepts and theories. Or as Shilling puts it in his review: 'Quite simply, the contributors to this volume have paid insufficient attention not only to previous traditions in the sociology of education, but to the most important current developments in sociology. Contemporary sociological theories in such areas as modernity, postmodernity, structuration, self-identity, the civilising process, consumption, and the body have much to offer the study of education' (1993, p. 111). All of this relates back to my initial point about the dangers of isolation, but it also illustrates again the basic transition, both cultural and structural, which is under way in educational studies, a transition from intellectual intelligence to technical rationalism.

But the point about theory is not that it is simply critical. In order to go beyond the accidents and contingencies which enfold us, it is necessary to start from another position and begin from what is normally excluded. Theory provides this possibility, the possibility of disidentification – the effect of working 'on and against' prevailing practices of ideological subjection. The point of theory and of intellectual endeavour in the social sciences should be, in Foucault's words, 'to sap power', to engage in struggle to reveal and undermine what is most invisible and insidious in prevailing practices (see Siraj-Blatchford, 1994). Theories offer another language, a language of distance, of irony, of imagination. And part of this, as Sheridan puts it is 'a love of hypothesis, of invention' which is also unashamedly 'a love of the beautiful' (Sheridan, 1980, p. 223) – as against the bland, technical and desolate languages of policy science and policy entrepreneurship. However, in taking such a stance, intellectuals cannot simply seek to re-inhabit the old redemptive assumptions based upon an unproblematic role for themselves in a perpetual process of progressive, orderly growth or development achieved through scientific and technological 'mastery' or control over events or by the assertive re-cycling of old dogmas and tired utopias. 'The regime of "truth" gave the intellectual, whose business truth was, a certain "universal" status' (Sheridan, 1980, p. 222). This is no longer available or desirable. The process of disidentification also involves a transformation of intellectuals and their relationship to the 'business of truth'. The post-epistemological theorist will eschew the scientific claim to originality, discovery and the improvement of the human condition. What I am groping towards here is a model of the educational theorist as a cultural critic offering perspective rather than truth; engaged in what Eco calls 'semiotic guerrilla warfare' (Eco, 1994). Or to put it another way:

> Criticism is a matter of flushing out that thought (which animates everyday behaviour) and trying to change it: to show that things are not as self-evident as one believed, to see that what is accepted as self-evident will no longer be accepted as such . . . As soon as one can no longer think things as one formerly thought them, transformation becomes both very urgent, very difficult and quite possible.
>
> (Foucault, 1988a, p. 154)

For Foucault, freedom lies in our ability to transform our relationship to the past, to tradition and much less in being able to control the form and direction that the future will take. In the mad scramble of late modernist life we seem to need to latch on to elusive images of who we are and what our existence means. But in the place of such rigid and anterior norms and discourses, we must, as Richard Rorty suggests, locate a playing field on which ideas are toyed with and radical ironies explored. In Rorty's post-epistemological view, edifying conversations, rather than truth-generating epistemological efforts must be the staple of a post-structural social science (Rorty, 1979). To quote Foucault again 'I think that there are more secrets, more possible freedoms, and more inventions in our future than we can imagine in humanism as it is dogmatically represented on every side of the political rainbow' (Foucault, 1988b, p. 15).

But will any theory do? I think not! We must consider *how* as well as *why* we employ theory. Theory can, and often does, function to provide comforting and apparently stable identities for beleaguered academics in an increasingly slippery world. Theory can serve to conjure up its own anterior norms and lay its dead hand upon the creativity of the mind. Too often in educational studies, theory becomes no more than a mantric reaffirmation of belief rather than a tool for exploration and for thinking otherwise. Such mantric uses of theory typically involve little more than a naming of spaces. This is what Dale (1992) calls 'theory by numbers', whereby the map simply needs to be coloured in rather than researched. We all too easily become stuck in what Althusser (1975) calls a 'descriptive theory', a transitional phase in theory development, based upon a 'special kind of obviousness' (p. 133). 'Every descriptive theory' he argues 'thus runs the risk of "blocking" the development of the theory...'. The paradox of critical social science is that our rational, humane utopias are always formed within the discourses, dispositifs and epistemes from which we seek to escape. It is the past that is the problem here not the future.

There is another sense in which we need to think about how we theorise and that relates to the ambition of our enterprise and the style and scope of our endeavours. On the one hand, there is a kind of theorising that is parsimonious, certain and closed. This is also typically a hard-edged, in some ways peculiarly male form of knowledge. More often than not critical social science takes this form and is as a result both too sure of itself and too bold in its ambitions. On the other, there is a kind of theorising that rests upon complexity, uncertainty and doubt and upon a reflexivity about its own production and its claims to knowledge about the social. What I am trying to convey here is beautifully expressed by Teresa de Lauretis who describes feminist theory as requiring

> leaving or giving up a place that is safe, that is 'home' – physically, emotionally, linguistically, epistemologically – for another place that is unknown and risky, that is not only emotionally but conceptually other; a place of discourse from which speaking and thinking are at best tentative, uncertain, un-guaranteed.
> (Lauretis, 1990, p. 138)

Disindentification as a practice for educational studies will almost certainly involve a loss of identity, of universal status, it will threaten our certainty and our sense of usefulness. But maybe those things have been swept away anyway. The question is do we reiterate our tired, anterior, mantric theories, do we do what ever we have to, to make ourselves useful as technicians of social management, or do we re-invent ourselves as public intellectuals and cultural critics?[2]

I realise in all this that I am teetering between fatalism and skepticism (Sawicki, 1991, and others note the same problem), an uncomfortable but nonetheless sometimes productive position to find oneself in. Perhaps I am occupying what De Lauretis calls the 'eccentric' perspective. Nonetheless, I take some heart from a comment by Andre Gorz, who wrote 'The beginning of wisdom is the discovery that there exist contradictions of permanent tension with which it is necessary to live and that it is above all not necessary to seek to resolve'.[3]

Notes

*   This is a twice reworked paper; a first version was given as the Annual Address to the Standing Conference for Studies of Education, at the Royal Society of Arts, London, 4 November 1994, a second appeared as an article in the *British Journal of Educational Studies* 1995 43(3) under the title 'Intellectuals or Technicians: The Urgent Role of Theory in Educational Studies'. I am grateful to the editors for their permission to re-use the paper.
1   Rorty (1989, p. xvi), for example, places ethnography rather differently.
2   One of the most common responses to the original version of this text was to ask whether I am leaving myself and educational studies open to the criticism that the point of philosophy is not simply to describe the world, but to help to change it. My text may be read as deficient in those terms but I intend to convey very much the opposite message. I would see a specific and situated politics, a politics of the immediate, of the every day, of the personal as the logical concomitant of my arguments. Furthermore, I am counseling both boldness and modesty. Boldness in relation to the specifics of power; both in our own backyards and in our research sites. Modesty in our normative claims and in our general political ambitions. But this is a dangerous politics very different from the safe, fictive revolutionism that remains a la mode in some parts of the academy.
3   I am grateful to Jo Boaler, Alan Cribb, David Halpin, Iram Siraj-Blatchford, Maria Tamboukou and Jack Whitehead for their comments on earlier versions of the text. Some of which I have acted upon, others of which remain as food for thought, for further writing and further conversations.

References

Althusser, L. (1975) *Lenin and Philosophy and Others Essays* (London, Verso).

Angus, L. (1993) The Sociology of School Effectiveness. *British Journal of Sociology of Education* 14(3): 333–45.

Ball, S. J. (1990) Management as Moral Technology: A Luddite Analysis. *Foucault and Education: Disciplines and Knowledge* (London, Routledge).

Ball, S. J. (1994) *Education Reform: A Critical and Post-Structural Approach* (Buckingham, Open University Press).

Ball, S. J. (2004a) *Education for Sale: The Commodification of Everything! Annual Education Lecture* (London, King's College London).

Ball, S. J. (2004b) *Educational Reform as Social Barberism: Economism and the End of Authenticity*. Scottish Educational Research Association Annual Lecture (Perth, SERA).

Beck, U. (1992) *Risk Society: Towards a New Modernity* (Newbury Park, CA, Sage).

Bernstein, B. (1999) Vertical and Horizontal Discourse: An Essay. *British Journal of Sociology of Education* 20(2): 157–73.

Bourdieu, P. , J. Chamboredon and J. Passeron (1991) *The Craft of Sociology: Epistemological Preliminaries* (Berlin, Walter de Gruyter).

Cohen, S. (1993) *Academia and the Luster of Capita* (Minnesota, MN, Minnesota University Press).

Dale, R. (1992) Recovering from a Pyrrhic Victory? Quality, Relevance and Impact in the Sociology of Education. *Voicing Concerns* (Wallingford, Triangle).

de Lauretis, T. (1990) Eccentric Subjects: Feminist Theory and Historical Consciousness, *Feminist Studies* 16(1): 133–46.

Eco, U. (1994) *Apocolypse Postponed*. Lumley, R. (ed.) (London, BFI Publishing).

Fay, B. (1975) *Social Theory and Political Practice* (London, Allen and Unwin).

Foucault, M. (1977) *Language, Counter-Memory, Practice: Selected Essays and Interviews* (Ithaca, NY, Cornell University Press).

Foucault, M. (1979a) *Discipline and Punish* (Harmondsworth, Peregrine).

Foucault, M. (1979b) On Governmentality, *Ideology and Consciousness* 6(1): 5–22.

Foucault, M. (1988a) *Michel Foucault: Politics, Philosophy and Culture – Interviews and Other Writings 1977–1984* (New York, Routledge).

Foucault, M. (1988b) Truth, Power, Self: An Interview with Michel Foucault. *Technologies of the Self* (Amherst, MA, The University of Massachusetts Press).

Foucault, M. (1991) Questions of Method. *The Foucault Effect: Studies in Governmentality* (Brighton, Harvester/Wheatsheaf).

Hatcher, R. (1996) 'The limitations of the new social democratic agendas: class, equality and agency', in Hatcher, R. and Jones, K. (eds), *Education under the Conservatives: The Response to the New Agenda of Reform* (Stoke-on-Trent, Trentham).

Kozol, J. (1991) *Savage Inequalities* (New York, Crown Publishing).

Mahon, M. (1992) *Foucault's Nietzscean Genealogy: Truth, Power and the Subject* (Albany, NY, SUNY).

Reynolds, D. (1990) Research on School/Organizational Effectiveness: The End of the Beginning. *Management and Policy: Retrospect and Prospect* (London, Falmer).

Rorty, R. (1979) *Philosophy and the Mirror of Nature* (Princeton, NJ, Princeton University Press).

Sawicki, J. (1991) *Disciplining Foucault: Feminism, Power and the Body* (New York, Routledge).

Sheridan, A. (1980) *Michel Foucault: The Will to Truth* (London, Tavistock).

Shilling, C. (1993) The Demise of the Sociology of Education in Britain. *British Journal of Sociology of Education* 14(1): 105–21.

Siraj-Blatchford, I. (1994) *Praxis makes Perfect: Critical Educational Research for Social Justice* (Ticknall, Education Now Books).

Thrupp, M. (1998) The Politics of Blame: How can teacher education best respond? *Delta* 50(2): 163–68.

CHAPTER 5

BIG POLICIES/SMALL WORLD

An introduction to international
perspectives in education policy

Comparative Education, 1998, 34(2): 119–30

> One by one, modernity stripped man of all 'particularlistic' trappings and
> pared him to the (assumed) 'all-human' core – that of the independent,
> autonomous, and thus essentially non-social moral being.
>
> (Bauman, 1993, p. 82)

One of the tensions which runs through all varieties of policy analysis is that
between the need to attend to the local particularities of policy-making and policy-
enactment and the need to be aware of general patterns and apparent commonalities
or convergences across localities (see Whitty and Edwards, 1998). That tension is
central to this paper and my primary emphasis is upon the general and common
elements in contemporary, international education policy but I will also address
the processes of translation and recontextualisation involved in *the realisation or
enactment of policy* in specific national and local settings. However, one immediate limitation upon the generality of my discussion is its focus upon western and
northern, developed economies; although a great deal of what I have to say has
considerable relevance to countries like Colombia, Chile, Portugal, Japan and
some of the ex-Warsaw Pact nations of eastern Europe. The paper has three main
sections. The first sketches in a set of generic 'problems' which constitute the
contemporary social, political and economic conditions for education and social
policy-making. The second discusses the idea of ideological and 'magical' solutions
to these problems and the dissemination of these solutions. The third and last
returns to the issue of recontextualisation.

Post-modernity and the global economy

As Brown and Lauder (1996) explain: 'The significance of globalisation to questions of national educational and economic development can be summarised in
terms of a change in the rules of eligibility, engagement and wealth creation' (p. 2).
As regards *eligibility*, individual governments, even the apparently most powerful,
have experienced a reduction in their ability to control or supervise the activities
of Multinational Corporations (MNCs) and to maintain the integrity of their
economic borders. This results in the loss of 'Keynesian capacity'; that is the ability to pursue independent reflationary policies. However, it is important not to
overstate the case here and succumb to what Weiss (1997) calls the 'myth of the
powerless state'. She argues that within the processes of globalisation 'domestic

state capacities differ' (p. 26) and that 'the proliferation of regional agreements suggest that we can expect to see more and more of a different kind of state taking shape in the world arena, one that is reconstituting its power at the centre of alliances formed either within or outside the state' (p. 27) (see also Taylor *et al.*, 1997, chap. 4). In other words, we need to be wary of what Harvey (1996) calls 'globaloney'. The 'globalisation thesis' can be used to explain almost anything and everything and is ubiquitous in current policy documents *and* policy analysis. We also need to acknowledge here the national changes in *the form and scope* of state activities in many western economies. Contracting, deregulation and privatisation have reduced, in both practical and ideological terms, the capacity for direct state intervention. That is not to say that these devices do not provide new forms of state steering and regulation (see below). The *rules of engagement* describe the relationship between governments, employers and workers. The key change here, at least in the West is from a fordist, welfare corporatism to a 'market-model' wherein 'the prosperity of workers will depend on an ability to trade their skills, knowledge and entrepreneurial acumen in an unfettered global market place' (Brown and Lauder, 1996, p. 3). And *the new rules of wealth creation* are replacing the logic of fordist mass-production with new 'knowledge-based' systems of flexible production. However, there are three crucial caveats to the last point. First, fordist production systems in the West have not so much been replaced as 'exported', cheap labour and unregulated conditions of labour in some developing economies make the relocation of mass production an attractive proposition to MNCs. Furthermore, while MNCs are increasingly dominant, a great deal of capital activity remains 'nationalistic'. Second, even within the developed western and Asian Tiger economies, the new logic of flexible specialisation and 'just-in-time' production (Swynegedouw, 1986) is not an inclusive one – low skill, insecure jobs, especially in the service sectors, are the main areas of expansion of work in all of these economies. And these 'new' jobs are also bringing about the feminisation of the labour market. Harvey (1989) makes a key point that: 'Under conditions of flexible accumulation, it seems as if alternative labour systems can exist side by side within the same space in such a way as to enable capitalist entrepreneurs to choose at will between them' (p. 187). Thus, third, the polarisations of fordist/post fordist – modernist/post-modernist economies are not so much alternative forms of capital and regulation as 'a complex of oppositions, expressive of the cultural contradictions of capitalism' (Harvey, 1989, p. 39). The two general points then that I want to make here are; that things have changed but not absolutely; and that while these changes have produced new 'first order' problems, in terms of the demand for new skills for example, they have also produced new 'second order' problems, like threats to the maintenance of political legitimacy and authority. Not everyone has an equal 'stake' in the success of the new economic order. The core/periphery structure of the global economy and global and national labour markets appears to be closely paralleled in the emerging 'star'/'sink' school polarisations within 'market reformed' education systems.

Now there is no way that I can follow through properly all aspects of this account of the role of globalisation on education in the space available here (see Harvey, 1989; Brown and Lauder, 1996; Taylor *et al.*, 1997; Jones, 1998). And indeed, I am not concerned to convey the full complexity of these global changes but to isolate some of those aspects of change which might allow us to understand struggles taking place over education policy. However, I do want to pick out two further specific and related aspects of global change which I will suggest have particular significance in making sense of the current 'turn' in education and social policy-making. They are, in short, *uncertainty* and *congestion*.

Harvey suggests that the rhythm and content of daily life has become both more ephemeral and volatile, commodity production increasingly emphasises 'the values and virtues of instantaneity and disposability' (1989, p. 286) and is increasingly focused upon 'sign systems rather than with commodities themselves' (p. 287). The latter, among many other factors has contributed to a 'crisis of representation' (p. 298). All of this provides a context for the 'crack-up of consensus' (p. 286). It constitutes in part of what Pfeil (1988) calls the 'postmodern structure of feeling' and forbears 'the terror of contingency from which all possibility of eventful significance has been drained' (p. 386).

> The central value system, to which capitalism has always appealed to validate and gauge its actions, is dematerialized and shifting, time horizons are collapsing, and it is hard to tell exactly what space we are in when it comes to assessing causes and effects, meanings or values.
>
> (p. 298)

In other words 'disorganised capitalism' (Lash and Urry, 1987) may be beginning to dissolve the conditions of consensus and social cohesion upon which it depends in order to continue. One particular, and very material, aspect of the new politics of uncertainty is the very dramatic change in the trajectory of economic growth and patterns of employment which provided the basis for the massive post-war expansion in the middle-classes and the creation of the so-called 'new middle class'. Their 'imagined futures' and those of their off-spring, are now under threat from the 'unmanaged congestion' in the old and new professions and in management positions (Jordon *et al.*, 1994). One effect of this has been a loss of support among the new middle classes for efforts to democratise education and social policy. Education is being 'transformed back into an "oligarchic" good' (Jordon *et al.*, 1994, p. 212) and progressive experimentation in educational methods is being replaced by a set of re-invented traditional pedagogies and/or a set of 'improvement' or 'modernising' pedagogies.

Magical solutions?

If these various 'policyscapes' (Appadurai, 1990) of global change adumbrate a set of 'problems' and challenges for education and social policy, what then are the 'solutions' in play among which makers of policy might 'choose' as modes of response? As I shall go on to suggest 'choose' is an inappropriate word here. Brown and Lauder suggest two ideal types of response: neo-fordism, which 'can be characterised in terms of creating greater market flexibility through a reduction in social overheads and the power of trade unions, the privatisation of public utilities and the welfare state, as well as the celebration of competitive individualism' (p. 5); and post-fordism, which can 'be defined in terms of the development of the state as a "strategic trader" shaping the direction of the national economy through investment in key economic sectors and in the development of human capital' (p. 5). This latter is close to Hutton's (1995) Rhineland model of capitalism. In practice, as ever is the case, the differences between states or political parties in these terms often seems to be more a matter of emphasis than any 'clear blue water'. While superficially at least, the neo-fordist 'solution' seems to be in the ascendant in education policy-making, aspects of the post-fordist scenario are clearly in evidence even in the practices of the most neo-liberal of governments. Having said that, the differences between the positions are not insignificant.

This policy dualism is well represented in contemporary education policies which tie together individual, consumer choice in education markets with rhetorics and policies aimed at furthering national economic interests. Carter and O'Neill (1995) summarise evidence on the state of education policy-making in their two volume collection on international perspectives on educational reform by identifying what they call 'the new orthodoxy' – 'a shift is taking place' they say 'in the relationship between politics, government and education in complex Westernised post-industrialised countries at least' (p. 9). They cite five main elements to this new orthodoxy:

- improving national economics by tightening a connection between schooling, employment, productivity and trade;
- enhancing student outcomes in employment related skills and competencies;
- attaining more direct control over curriculum content and assessment;
- reducing the costs to government of education; and
- increasing community input to education by more direct involvement in school decision-making and pressure of market choice.

I shall return to the substance of this reform package below. Avis *et al.* (1996) make a similar claim about post-compulsory education and training and what they call the 'new consensus'. Indeed the European Union White paper on education and training, *Towards the Learning Society* (European Union, 1995) announces; 'The end of the debate on educational principles' (p. 22). Concepts like the 'learning society', the 'knowledge based economy' etc. are potent policy-condensates within this consensus. They serve and symbolise the increasing colonisation of education policy by economic policy imperatives; although Levin (1998) suggests that it is sometimes the politics of the sign rather than the substance of policies that moves across national borders.

It would be ridiculous to claim that there is one or even one set of key ideas or influences which underpin this package. However, it would be equally ridiculous to ignore the links and correspondences which run through it. Five elements or sets of influences are identifiable. I will adumbrate these very crudely. Some of these have an analytic status, others are more substantive. One is *neo-liberalism* or what might be called the ideologies of the market. These set the spontaneous and unplanned but innovative responses of the market form over and against the partisan, inefficient bureaucracy of planned change. This has been of particular importance in the UK in the formation of those policies often referred to as 'Thatcherism' (see Ball, 1990), and the UK education reforms certainly provided a test-bed to which other governments at least attended when contemplating their own reforms (see Whitty and Edwards 1998). A second, is *new institutional economics*, 'which sought to explain the workings of social life and its various institutions, and the construction of relationships and co-ordination of individual and collective behaviour, in terms of the choices and actions of the rational actor' (Seddon, 1997, p. 176). This involves the use of a combination of devolution, targets and incentives to bring about institutional redesign. It draws both on recent economic theory and various industrial practices, sometimes referred to as Mitsubishiism – the replacement of task specification by target-setting (see below). In education, the impact of such ideas is evident in the myriad of 'site-based management' initiatives in countries and states around the world and the social psychology of institutional reinvention is proselytised in texts on 'The Self-Managing School' and 'School Improvement'. Chubb and Moe (1990) also articulate what they describe as 'a theoretical perspective linking the organisation and performance of schools to their institutional environments' (p. 185). A third influence, which inter-weaves with both of the above is what Lyotard (1984) calls *performativity* – 'be operational (that is, commensurable) or disappear' (Lyotard 1984, p. xxiv). 'Performativity is a principle of governance which establishes strictly functional relations between a state and its inside and outside environments' (Yeatman, 1994, p. 111). In other words, performativity is a steering mechanism. A form of indirect steering, or steering at a distance which replaces intervention and prescription with target setting, accountability and comparison (*cross ref*). Furthermore, as part of the transformation of education and schooling and the expansion of the power of capital, performativity provides sign systems which 'represent' education in a self-referential and reified form for consumption. And indeed many of the specific technologies of performativity in education (Total Quality Management, Human Resources Management etc.) are borrowed from commercial settings. Number four, is *public choice theory*, this is a particularly important component of US attempts at education reform (see again Chubb and Moe, 1990) but choice is a key aspect of Hayekian, neo-liberalism as well (see OECD, 1994, for a review of choice policies in six countries). Fifth, and finally, there is *new managerialism*, that is the insertion of the theories and techniques of business management and the 'cult of excellence' into public sector institutions. Managerialism is, in this sense, both a delivery system and a vehicle for change. This 'new' managerialism stresses a constant attention to 'quality', being close to the customer and the value of innovation (Newman and Clarke, 1994, p. 15). In the education sector the headteacher is the main 'carrier' and embodiment of new managerialism and is crucial to the transformation of the organisational regimes of schools (Grace, 1995). That is, the dismantling of bureau-professional organisational regimes and their replacement with market-entrepreneurial regimes (Clarke and Newman, 1992). New management also involves 'new' forms of employee involvement. In particular through the cultivation of 'corporate culture' via which managers 'seek to delineate, normalize and instrumentalize the conduct of persons in order to achieve the ends they postulate as desirable' (Du Gay, 1996, p. 61). Such developments are deeply paradoxical. On the one hand, they represent a move away from Taylorist, 'low-trust' methods of employee control. Managerial responsibilities are delegated, initiative and problem-solving are highly valued. On the other hand, new forms of surveillance and self-monitoring are put in place; e.g. appraisal systems, target-setting, output comparisons (see Muller, 1998, for a discussion of different forms of self-regulation – competence-based and performance-based). This is what Peters and Waterman (1982) referred to 'simultaneously loose and tight' or what Du Gay (1996) calls 'controlled de-control'.

The dissemination of these influences internationally can be understood in at least two ways. First, and most straightforward, there is a flow of ideas through social and political networks; the 'inter-national circulation of ideas' (Popkewitz, 1996). Such flows are facilitated by processes of policy borrowing (Halpin and Troyna, 1995) – both the UK and New Zealand have served as 'political laboratories' for reform – and by the dissemination and lobbying activities of groups like the Heritage Foundation, the Mont Pelerin Society and Institute of Economic Affairs; although the effects here should not be over-estimated. The movement of graduates, especially from US universities, is also important (see Vanegas and Ball, 1996). In some contexts this movement 'carries' ideas and creates a kind of cultural and political dependency which works to devalue or deny the feasibility of 'local' solutions. As Max-Neef puts it:

> If as a Latin American economist I wish to become an expert in Latin American development problems, it is necessary to study in the United States or in Europe to be respectable in the eyes of both my Southern and Northern colleagues. It goes without saying that it is not only dangerous but absurd.
>
> (Max-Neef *et al.*, 1991, p. 98)

There is also the activity of various 'policy entrepreneurs', groups and individuals who 'sell' their solutions in the academic and political marketplace – the 'self-managing school' and 'school effectiveness' and 'choice' are all current examples of such entrepreneurship which takes places through academic channels – journals, books etc. – and via the performances of charismatic, travelling academics. Last, there is the sponsorship, and enforcement in some respects, of particular policy 'solutions' by multi-lateral agencies (Jones, 1996, 1998). The World Bank is particularly important here, as Jones puts it; 'The Bank's preconditions for education can only be understood as an ideological stance, in promoting an integrated world system along market lines'. But it is equally important to understand a second aspect of the dissemination or institutionalisation of these influences upon reform; their establishment as the new orthodoxy. That is as a discursive framework within which, and limited by which, solutions are 'thought'. There is a concomitance, if not a correspondence, here between the logic of globalisation – as a world free-trading system – and the new terrain of thinking about social policy. 'Notions of the public good shift in order to accommodate reduced expectations about accountability, regulation and taxation, which in turn lead to not only reduced but transformed expectations about what public services and infrastructure consist of' (Jones, 1998). This concomitance is most obvious in what Brown and Lauder call neo-fordism; 'the route to national salvation in the context of the global knowledge wars is through the survival of the fittest, based on a extension of parental choice in a market of competing schools, colleges and universities' (pp. 6–7). That is: 'education systems have been made objects of micro-economic reform with educational activities being turned into saleable or corporatised market products as part of a national efficiency drive' (Taylor *et al.*, 1997, p. 77). Such reforms rest upon two starkly opposed chronotopics – the grey, slow bureaucracy and political correct, committee, corridor-grimness of the city-hall, welfare state as against the fast, adventurous, carefree, gung-ho, open-plan, computerised, individualism of choice, autonomous 'enterprises' and market responsiveness.

This last point serves to remind us that policies are both systems of values and symbolic systems; ways of representing, accounting for and legitimating political decisions. Policies are articulated both to achieve material effects and to manufacture support for those effects. In particular here I want to suggest that advocacy of the market or commercial form for educational reform, as the 'solution' to educational problems is a form of 'policy magic' or what Stronach (1993) calls 'witchcraft': 'a form of reassurance as well as a rational response to economic problems' (p. 6). One of the attractions here is the simplicity of the formula on which the magic is based.

> social markets/institutional devolution = raising standards (of educational performance) = increased international competitiveness

Such simplicities have a particular attraction when set within the 'conditions of uncertainty' or what Dror (1986) calls 'adversity'. In Stronach's terms, the repetitive circularities of 'the market solution' display 'the logics of witchcraft and the structures of ritual' (p. 26). It links individual (choice) and institutional (autonomy/responsiveness) transformation to universal salvation. A transformation from mundane citizen to archetype, from dependent subject to active consumer/citizen, from dull bureaucracy to innovative, entrepreneurial management.[1] 'Ritual typically associates a personal with a cosmic pole, around which prosperity, morality and civilization are clustered' (p. 23). Minor personal and physical changes are linked to large-scale transformation. Again then all of this is founded upon the play of opposites, order against chaos, and the redress of crisis. Employing a similar language Hughes and Tight (1995) argue that concepts such as 'the stakeholder' and the 'learning society' represent powerful myths for projecting futuristic visions which determine the on-going principles on which education policy and practice are based. And as Newman (1984, p. 159) puts it 'The libertarian revolt against the modern state is first and foremost a campaign for the hearts and minds of the American people'.

For politicians the 'magic' of the market works in several senses. On the one hand, it is a 'hands off' reform, a non-interventionary intervention – a basic trope of the conjurer; 'now you see it now you dont!'. It distances the reformer from the outcomes of reform. Blame and responsibility are also devolved or contracted out (see below). And yet by use of target-setting and performative techniques 'steering at a distance' can be achieved, what Kikert (1991) calls 'a new paradigm of public governance'. On the other hand, these policies also carry with them political risks, insofar, as noted already, they may disable direct forms of control and can leave the politician 'in office' but not 'in power'.

As indicated above, one key facet of the policy process and the formulation of new orthodoxies is critique. New policies feed off and gain legitimacy from the deriding and demolition of previous policies (see Ball, 1990) which are thus rendered 'unthinkable'. The 'new' are marked out by and gain credence from their qualities of difference and contrast. In education in particular part of the attraction of a new policy often rests on specific allocation of 'blame' from which its logic derives. Blame may either be located in the malfunctions or heresies embedded in the policies it replaces and/or is redistributed by the new policy within the education system itself and if often personified – currently in the UK in the 'incompetent teacher' and 'failing school' (see Thrupp, 1998, on the politics of blame).

Stated in more general terms two complexly related policy agendas are discernible in all the heat and noise of reform. The first aims to tie education more closely to national economic interests. While the second involves a de-coupling of education from direct state control. The first rests on a clear articulation and assertion by the state of its requirements of education. While the second gives at least the appearance of greater autonomy to educational institutions in the delivery of those requirements. The first involves a reaffirmation of the state functions of education as a 'public good'. While the second subjects education to the disciplines of the market and the methods and values of business and redefines it as a competitive private good. In many respects educational institutions are now being expected to take on the qualities and characteristics of 'fast capitalism' (Gee and Lankshear, 1995). And this involves not only changes in organisational practices and methods but also the adoption of new social relationships, values and ethical principles.

We can see these two political agendas being played out in terms of an ensemble of generic policies – parental choice and institutional competition, site-based autonomy, managerialism, performative steering, curricula fundamentalism – which nonetheless have local variations, twists and nuances – *hybridity* – and different degrees of application – *intensity*. The purest and most intense versions of this ensemble are evident in places like England, New Zealand and Alberta (Canada). Mixed and low intensity versions are evident in places like France, Colombia and many US and Australian states. Places like Portugal and Sweden display hybrid but low intensity versions. (See discussion of recontextualisation below.)

While previous regimes of unthinkability derived rhetorical energy from the critique of elitism, one of the mechanisms involved in the establishment of the new orthodoxy in education has been a critique of the press for equity and social justice as part of the diagnosis of the existing 'inadequacies' of education – what I have called elsewhere 'the discourse of derision' (Ball, 1990; see also below). The World Bank sees equity as one of the residual concerns of governments in marketised education systems. But as a part of the logic of the new orthodoxy the social and welfare purposes of education are systematically played down and directly or in effect education is increasingly subject to exchange value criteria. That is, education is not simply modelled on the methods and values of capital, it is itself drawn into the commodity form. Within all this equity issues do not so much disappear entirely as become 'framed and reframed'; 'competing discourses are "stitched together" in the new policies' (Taylor, 1995, p. 9). The meanings of equity are refracted, reworked and realised in new ways 'glossing over the different perspectives of key players' (p. 10).

In effect, in education and social policy generally the new orthodoxy, the market solution, is a new master narrative, a deeply fissured but primary discourse encompassing 'the very nature of economics and therefore the potential range and scope of policies themselves' (Cerny, 1990, p. 205). The discourse constructs the topic and as with any discourse, it appears across a range of texts, forms of conduct and at a number of different sites at any one time. Discursive events 'refer to the one and the same object…there is a regular style and… constancy of concepts…and "strategy" and a common institutional, administrative or political drift and pattern' (Cousins and Hussain, 1984, pp. 84–5). Thus, we see this discourse at work as much in the 1980s Hollywood 'male-rampage' movies (Pfeil, 1995), part of what Ross describes as 'the desperate attempts, under Reagan, to reconstruct the institution of national heroism, more often than not in the form of white, male rogue outlaws for whom the liberal solution of "soft" state-regulated law enforcement was presented as having failed' (Ross, 1990, p. 33); as in the UK in the commodification of academic research; in the celebration of the parent-chooser – hero of so many market policy texts in education; in the re-furbished, customer-friendly, competitive school; the 'quality-guru' educational consultants and quick-fix policy entrepreneurs; Channel One television in US schools, 'designer-label' uniforms in Japanese high schools; 'early-learning' educational games shops; and niche-marketing, 'hothouse', nursery schools. 'Educational democracy is redefined as consumer democracy in the educational marketplace. *Buying* an education becomes a substitute for *getting* an education' (Kenway, 1993, p. 116). It is not simply that publicly provided school systems are being inducted into quasi-market practices but that education in its various forms, at many points, in a variety of ways is inducted into the market episteme – a non-unified, multiple and complex field of play which realises a dispersion of relationships, subjectivities, values, objects, operations and concepts.

Localism and recontextualisation

While it may well be possible to discern a set of principles or a theoretical model underlying policy – neo-liberalism, new institutional economics, public choice theory or whatever – these rarely, if ever translate into policy texts or practice in direct or pristine form. National policy-making is inevitably a process of bricolage; a matter of borrowing and copying bits and pieces of ideas from elsewhere, drawing upon and amending locally tried-and-tested approaches, cannibalising theories, research, trends and fashions, and not infrequently a flailing around for anything at all that looks as though it might work. Most policies are ramshackle, compromise, hit-and-miss affairs, that are reworked, tinkered with, nuanced and inflected through complex processes of influence, text production, dissemination and ultimately recreation in contexts of practice (Ball, 1994).

Policy ideas are also received and interpreted differently within different political architectures (Cerny, 1990) national infrastructures (Hall, 1986) national ideologies – a national ideology is 'a set of values and beliefs that frames the practical thinking and action of agents of the main institutions of a nation-state at a given point in time' (van Zanten, 1997, p. 352), and business cultures (Hampden-Turner and Trompenaars, 1994). The latter conducted research on 15,000 business managers in seven different countries and identified distinct contrasts in the mind-sets and ideologies of their respondents. Unfortunately, comparative educational research on the formation, reception and interpretative of policy in these terms is thin on the ground (see Dale and Ozga, 1993, on the new right in the UK and New Zealand, and van Zanten, 1997, on the education of immigrants in France).

In our attempts to understand education policies comparatively and globally, the complex relationships between ideas, the dissemination of ideas, and the recontextualisation (see Bernstein, 1996) of ideas remains a central task. As Bernstein puts it: 'Every time a discourse moves, there is space for ideology to play' (p. 24). Recontextualisation takes place within and between both 'official' and 'pedagogic' fields. The former 'created and dominated by the state' and the latter consisting of 'pedagogues in schools and colleges, and departments of education, specialised journals, private research foundations' (p. 48). These fields are constituted differently in different societies. The new orthodoxies of education policy are grafted onto and realised within very different national and cultural contexts and are affected, inflected and deflected by them. See for example Taylor *et al.* (1997) case studies of Papua New Guinea, Malaysia and Australia. They conclude that: 'there is no essential determinacy to the ways in which globalisation pressures work, since for various globalisation pressures there are also sites of resistance and counter movements' (p. 72) (see Colclough and Lewin, 1993, p. 256, for a similar argument). The fields of recontextualisation are, as Muller (1998) puts it 'fields of contest' involving 'various social fractions with different degrees of social power sponsoring' different 'pedagogic regimes'. The five generic policies adumbrated above are polyvalent, they are translated into particular interactive and sustainable practices in complex ways. They interact with, interrupt or conflict with other policies in play and long-standing indigenous policy traditions. They enter rather than simply change existing power relations and cultural practices. We can generalise here from Offe's (1984, p. 186) comment that

> ...the real social effects ('impact') of a law or institutional service are not determined by the wording of the laws and statutes ('policy out'), but instead are generated primarily as a consequence of social disputes and conflicts, for which state policy merely establishes the location and timing of the contest, its subject matters and 'the rules of the game'.

Such disputes and conflicts take place at a number of levels – national, local and institutional. Policy analysis requires an understanding that is based not on the generic or local, macro or micro, constraint or agency but *on the changing relationships between them and their inter-penetration*.

Conclusion

What I have tried to do in this paper is not only to take several things seriously, but also take them together. To recognise the 'problems' of globalisation which frame and 'produce' the contemporary 'problems' of education. To identify a set of generic 'solutions' to these problems and acknowledge their effects in educational reform and restructuring. But also to suggest that these 'solutions' have a magical form and ritual function. That they become an inescapable form of reassurance, they discursively constrain the possibilities of response and are borrowed, enforced and adopted through various patterns of social contact, political and cultural deference and supra-national agency requirements. Finally, to register nonetheless the importance of local politics and culture and tradition, and the processes of interpretation and struggle involved in translating these generic solutions into practical policies and institutional practices.

I want to end by returning to that side of my argument which is concerned with the generic aspects of education policy rather than its specifics, and to Offe's 'real social effects'. My point is that careful investigation of local variations, exceptions and hybridity should not divert attention from the general patterns of practical and ideological, first and second order, effects achieved by the ensemble of influences and policy mechanisms outlined above. That is to say, even in their different realisations, this ensemble changes the way that education is organised and delivered but also changes the meaning of education and what it means to be educated, what it means to learn. One key aspect of the reworking of meanings here is the increasing commodification of knowledge (which again parallels changes in the role of knowledge in the economy). Educational provision is itself increasingly made susceptible to profit and educational processes play their part in the creation of the enterprise culture and the cultivation of enterprising subjects (see Kenway, 1993). The framework of possibilities, the vocabularies of motives and bases of legitimation (including values and ethics) within which educational decisions are made are all discursively re-formed. But crucially also, these mechanisms and influences are not just about new organisational forms or 'worker incentives' or rearticulated professional ethics – they are about access to and the distribution of educational opportunity in terms of race, class, gender and physical ability. The diversification and re-hierarchisation of schooling in various educational marketplaces display an uncanny concomitance with widespread middle-class concerns about maintaining social advantage in the face of national and international labour market congestion. Thus, both in relation to patterns of convergence in education policy and the re-contextualisation of policy we need to be asking the question; 'whose interests are served?'.

Acknowledgement

I am grateful to Alan Cribb, Ben Levin and Carol Vincent for their comments on previous drafts of this paper.

Note

1   Of course the policies of welfarism can be subjected to a similar sort of analysis.

References

Appadurai, A. (1990) Disjuncture and difference in the global cultural economy. In: M. Featherstone (ed.), special issue of *Theory, Culture and Society; Global Culture: Nationalism, Globalisation and Modernity* (London, Sage).

Avis, J., Bloomer, M., Esland, G., Gleeson, D. and Hodkinson, P. (1996) *Knowledge and Nationhood: Education, Politics and Work* (London, Cassell).

Ball, S. J. (1990) *Politics and Policymaking in Education* (London, Routledge).

Ball, S. J. (1994) *Education Reform: A Critical and Post-Structural Approach* (Buckingham, Open University Press).

Bernstein, B. (1996) *Pedagogy Symbolic Control and Identity* (London, Taylor and Francis).

Brown, P. and Lauder, H. (1996) Education, globalisation and economic development, *Journal of Education Policy*, 11(1): 1–25.

Carter, D. S. G. and O'Neill, M. H. (1995) *International Perspectives on Educational Reform and Policy Implementation* (Brighton, Falmer).

Cerny, P. (1990) *The Changing Architecture of Politics: Structure, Agency and the Future of the State* (London, Sage).

Chubb, J. and Moe, T. (1990) *Politics, Markets and America's Schools* (Washington, DC, The Brookings Institution).

Clarke, J. and Newman, J. (1992) Managing to survive: dilemmas of changing organisational forms in the public sector, *Social Policy Association Conference*, University of Nottingham.

Colclough, C. and Lewin, K. (1993) *Educating all the Children* (New York, Oxford University Press).

Cousins, M. and Hussain, A. (1984) *Michel Foucault* (London, Macmillan).

Dale, R. and Ozga, J. (1993) Two hemispheres – both new right? In: R. Lingard, J. Knight and P. Porter (eds), *Schooling Reform in Hard Times* (London, Falmer).

Dror, Y. (1986) *Policy Making Under Adversity* (New Brunswick, NJ, Transaction Books).

Du Gay, P. (1996) *Consumption and Identity at Work* (London, Sage).

European Union (1995) White paper on education and training, teaching and learning: towards the learning society (Brussel, EU).

Gee, J. and Lankshear, C. (1995) The new work order: critical language awareness and 'fast capitalism' texts, *Discourse*, 16(1): 5–20.

Grace, G. (1995) *School Leadership: Beyond Education Management: An Essay in Policy Scholarship* (London, Falmer).

Hall, P. (1986) *Governing the Economy* (Cambridge, Polity Press).

Halpin, D. and Troyna, B. (1995) The politics of education policy borrowing, *Comparative Education*, 31(3): 303–10.

Hampden-Turner, C. and Trompenaars, F. (1994) *The Seven Cultures of Capitalism; Value Systems for Creating Wealth in the United States, Britain, Japan, Germany, France, Sweden and the Netherlands* (London, Piatkus).

Harvey, D. (1989) *The Condition of Postmodernity* (Oxford, Basil Blackwell).

Harvey, D. (1996) *Justive, Nature and the Geography of Difference* (Oxford, Basil Blackwell).

Hughes, C. and Tight, M. (1995) The myth of the learning society, *British Journal of Educational Studies*, 45(2): 290–304.

Hutton, W. (1995) *The State We're In* (London, Jonathan Cape).

Jones, P. W. (1998) Globalisation and internationalism: democractic prospects for world education, *Comparative Education*, 34(2): 143–55.

Jordon, B., Redley, M. and James, S. (1994) *Putting the Family First: Identities, Decisions and Citizenship* (London, UCL Press).

Kenway, J., Bigum, C. and Fitzclarence, L. (1993) Marketing Education in the Post-Modern Age, *Journal of Education Policy*, 8(1): 105–22.

Kikert, W. (1991) Steering at a distance; a new paradigm of public governance in Dutch Higher Education, *European Consortium for Political Research*, University of Essex.

Lash, S. and Urry, J. (1987) *The End of Organised Capitalism* (Cambridge, Polity Press).

Levin, B. (1998) An epidemic of education policy: what can we learn for each other? *Comparative Education*, 34(2): 131–42.

Lyotard, J.-F. (1984) *The Postmodern Condition: A Report on Knowledge* (Manchester, Manchester University Press).

Max-Neef, M. A., Elizalde, A. and Hopenhayn, M. (1991) *Human Scale Development: Conception, Application and Further Reflections* (New York, The Apex Press).

Muller, J. (1998) The well-tempered learner: self-regulation, pedagogical models and teacher education policy, *Comparative Education*, 34(2): 177–93.

Newman, J. and Clarke, J. (1994) Going about our business? The mangerialization of public services. In: J. Clarke, A. Cochrane and E. McLaughlin (eds), *Managing Social Policy* (London, Sage).

Newman, S. (1984) *Liberalism at Wits End* (Ithaca, NY, Cornell University Press).

OECD (1994) *School, a Matter of Choice* (Paris, OECD).

Offe, C. (1984) *Contradictions of the Welfare State* (London, Hutchinson).

Peters, T. and Waterman, R. (1982) *In Search of Excellence* (London, Harper Row).

Pfeil, F. (1988) Postmodernism as a 'structure of feeling'. In: L. Grossberg and C. Nelson (eds), *Marxism and the Interpretation of Culture* (London, Macmillan).

Pfeil, F. (1995) *White Guys: Studies in Postmodern Domination and Difference* (London, Verso).

Popkewitz, T. (1996) Rethinking decentralisation and state/civil society distinctions: the state as a problematic of governing, *Journal of Education Policy*, 11(1): 27–52.

Ross, A. (1990) Ballots, bullets or batman: can cultural studies do the right thing, *Screen*, 31(1): xx.

Seddon, T. (1997) Markets and the English: rethinking educational restructuring as institutional design, *British Journal of Sociology of Education*, 18(2): 165–86.

Stronach, I. (1993) Education, vocationalism and economic recovery: the case against witchcraft, *British Journal of Education and Work*, 3(1): 5–31.

Swynegedouw, E. (1986) The socio-spatial implications of innovations in industrial organisation. *Working Paper no. 20* (Lille, Johns Hopkins European Centre for Regional Planning and Research).

Taylor, S. (1995) Critical policy analysis: exploring contexts, texts and consequences (Red Hill, School of Cultural and Policy Studies, Queensland University of Technology).

Taylor, S., Rizvi, F., Lingard, B. and Henry, M. (1997) *Educational Policy and the Politics of Change* (London, Routledge).

Thrupp, M. (1998) The Politics of Blame: How can teacher education best respond? *Delta*, 50(2): 163–68.

van Zanten, A. (1997) Schooling immigrants in France in the 1990s: success or failure of the republican model of integration? *Anthropology and Education Quarterly*, 28(3): 351–74.

Vanegas, P. and Ball, S. J. (1996) The teacher as a variable in education policy, *BERA annual meeting*, Lancaster, UK.

Weiss, L. (1997) Globalization and the myth of the powerless state, *New Left Review*, 225: 3–27.

Whitty, G. and Edwards, T. (1998) School choices policies in England and the United States: an exploration of their origins and significance, *Comparative Education*, 34(2): 211–27.

Whitty, G., Power, S. and Halpin, D. (1998). *Devolution and Choice in Education* (Buckingham, Open University Press).

Yeatman, A. (1994) *Postmodern Revisionings of the Political* (New York, Routledge).

PART 2

POLICY TECHNOLOGIES AND POLICY ANALYSIS

Introduction

These papers 'apply' the perspectives and tools of 'policy sociology' to a set of specific policies initiatives and policy contexts. There are four main themes running through this body of work: (1) The development of performativity, management and markets as policy technologies for the management of reformed education systems (*The Teachers' Soul and the Terrors of Performativity* (Chapter 10) *and Good School/Bad School* (Chapter 7)). (2) The consequences of these technologies for social relations and practical ethics in educational organisations (*Ethics, Self-Interest and the Market Form in Education* (Chapter 6), *Standards in Education* (Chapter 9), *and Ethical Re-tooling* (Chapter 8)). (3) The effects of these technologies on the well-being, identities and practices of educational professionals (*The Teachers' Soul*). The papers explore ways in which policy changes and the work of policy technologies insinuate themselves into the lives and 'souls' of teachers, researchers and scholars. (4) The changes involved in all of this in the role and nature of the state and the emergence of, for want of a better term, a post-welfare state political settlement. That is, the emergence of a new set of social relations of governance and 'novel functional and scalar distributions of responsibility' (Dale 2002). This novelty arises from the changing roles and relationships of the state, capital and public sector institutions, and citizens, or what Cerny (1990) calls the 'changing architecture of politics'. A shift from the welfare state to what he called the competition state – 'a shift in the focal point of party and governmental politics from the general maximization of welfare within a national society . . . to the promotion of enterprise, innovation and profitability in both private and public sectors – a shift with significant ramifications for liberal democracy' (Cerny, 1990, p. 204). One major facet of these changes is the direct participation of for-profit companies in education services delivery (see Chapter 9) . The increasing participation of the private sector in the management, delivery and funding of public sector services is evident at a national level – with England, Greece, Germany, Spain and Portugal taking the lead in Europe – and at regional level within the European Community. The European Community sees 'partnerships' with business as 'an effective framework for mobilizing all available resources for the transition to the knowledge based economy' (Lisbon, 2000, para 41). As Robertson (2002, p. 2) explains 'For key economic actors, like the large transnational firms IBM, Cisco and Nokia, amongst others, participating in the creation of a European educational space means generating the conditions for their investment in the lucrative education market without the impediments of existing institutional arrangements'. Thus, within the EC, policy-making arenas are porous with these firms and others involved in setting and specifying the policy agenda for education in their own interests. In the United States, the Whittle

Corporation's Edison Project, Educational Alternatives Inc., Alternative Public Schools, Sylan Learning Centres, Eduventures and Huntington Learning Centres are all interested in making money from running state schools or alternatives to state schools. All of this raises new questions which policy research needs to address, and requires the development of new conceptual tools. These papers are intended to contribute to the beginings of these tasks.

References

Cerny, P. (1990). *The Changing Architecture of Politics: Structure, Agency and the Future of the State*. London, Sage.

Dale, R. (1992). Recovering from a Pyrrhic Victory? Quality, Relevance and Impact in the Sociology of Education. In M. Arnot and L. Barton (eds), *Voicing Concerns*. Wallingford, Triangle.

Robertson, S. (2002). *Changing Governance/Changing Equality? Understanding the Politics of Public–Private Partnerships in Education in Europe*. European Science Foundation – Exploratory Workshop, 3–5 October, Barcelona.

CHAPTER 6

ETHICS, SELF-INTEREST AND THE MARKET FORM IN EDUCATION

A. Cribb (ed.), *Markets, Managers and Public Service? Professional Ethics in the New Welfare State,* Centre for Public Policy Research, Occasional Paper No.1, London: King's College, 1998

We create our values through our choices.

(Jean-Paul Sartre)

If, then, education is concerned with values and their subjectivity, it follows that the management of schools cannot avoid these issues, and that it needs to be aware of, and be ready to examine, the values, principles, and attitudes proposed for its practice.

(Bottery, 1992, p. 2)

In England now we have all of the components of a market form in place underpinning the provision of compulsory and Further education (although the specifics of the form are different). There are six key elements to the market form; choice/open enrolment; diversity; competition/per capita funding; autonomy/LMS (Local Management of Schools); information; and managerialism. The outcomes of the interactions of these elements are intended to raise educational standards and improve the efficiency of schools by modelling the state system on a 'romanticised' and sanitised version of the dynamics of the free market.

The development of this market form has been driven by an assortment of theoretical and ideological commitments and projects; none of which translate into policy straightforwardly and directly. Policy is rarely like that. However, I would suggest that it has its beginnings in simple Hayekian economics. Hence Keith Joseph, UK Secretary of State for Education 1981–86, and neo-liberal guru to Margaret Thatcher, explained his commitment to choice and school autonomy, in an interview I conducted with him in 1990, thus:

> I think that national agencies tend to be producer lobbies, like nationalised industries. One of the main virtues of privatisation is to introduce the idea of bankruptcy, the potential of bankruptcy. That's why I like opting out...of course I wanted vouchers. Simply because you transfer in one go from the producers to the consumers...I don't want to claim that all consumers are wise, of course not, but some will be able to exercise choice which they can't exercise now.
>
> (Interview with Keith Joseph, quoted in Ball, 1990, p. 63)

Hayek's world view, which is fundamental to both his critique of state provision and his advocacy of the market form, is rooted in a psychology of self-interest and interest maximisation and a form of 'moral naturalism'; it mixes the idea of risk behaviour with a strong dose of traditionalism. The new social markets are framed by a mix of incentives and rewards aimed at stimulating self-interested responses on the part of producers and consumers; although at the same time, in relation to bureau-professional, state provision (Clarke and Newman, 1992) advocates of the market, Hayek and others, argued that 'self-interest' combined with producer-capture encouraged complacency and unresponsiveness. That is, within public organisations 'a kind of reciprocity with employees and key interest groups is created that, along with the executive's self-interest, tends to foster the maximisation of budgets rather than profits (i.e. consumer or client satisfaction)' (Boyd, 1982, p. 115). Self-interest then is the problem and the solution. There is no recognition in these critiques of the possibility of altruism, service or commitment as aspects of the work or motivation of public professionals. And indeed altruism is suspect as a source of partisanship. The logic of the critique is also the logic of the alternative; that decision-making will be organised and change brought about in response to the rewards and sanctions of the market framework. Thus, decisions will be driven by financial calculation rather than principled educational thinking and will be more likely to result in educational 'improvements' as a result. Bottery (1992) notes that free market economics rest upon two basic assumptions 'The first is that the market, and hence competition between people, is natural to the human condition . . . The second assumption is that humanity is composed of individuals, who are basically selfish . . . The market, then, merely gives expression to a basic urge . . .' (p. 86). However, like Bottery, I would take the view that 'market-place institutions, instead of providing a structure for natural inclinations, in fact produce the conditions under which the mentality occurs' (p. 87).

What is achieved in the establishment of the market form in education, as in other sectors of public provision, is a new moral environment for both consumers and producers, a new framework for judging social behaviour. Thus, schools are being inducted into what Plant (1992, p. 87) calls a 'culture of self interest'. The market celebrates the ethics of what Nagel (1991) calls the 'personal standpoint' – the personal interests and desires of individuals – and obscures and deprecates the egalitarian concerns of the 'impersonal standpoint'. What Nagel calls 'the duality of standpoints' and sees as the basis for practical ethics and moral stability – that is the nexus of equality and partiality – is thus collapsed.[1] Within markets, in theory at least, personal motives are given absolute preference over impersonal values. Within the market form both consumers and producers are encouraged, by the rewards and punishments of 'market forces', and legitimated, by the values of the personal standpoint, in their quest for positional advantage over others, what Kenway (1990, p. 155) calls the 'cult of selfishness'. More generally this is part of what Bottery (1992, p. 93) terms the 'pauperisation of moral concepts in the public sphere'. The idea of the deliberate and planned pursuit of the 'common good' is rendered meaningless within the disciplines of competition and survival. I suggest that we can already see these market values, and the 'deformed ethics' to which they give rise, at work in the UK school system.[2]

What I want to do now is to give some substance to my analysis through an exploration of some specific dilemmas produced by, or heightened within, the pressures and incentives of the education market. In doing so, I will contrast the 'market response', the response constructed by the logic of market incentives, with what I shall call a 'professional response'; that is a response based upon Nagel's 'impersonal standpoint' and informed by a 'service ethic'. In other terms

Grace (1995, p. 144) writes of this as the 'dilemma of *professional community versus continuous advantage* which was one of the outcomes of a market for schooling'. To be clear, I am trying not to trade here upon some kind of romantic, golden age of comprehensivism, when all decisions in schools were driven purely by educational principles. Nonetheless, I am assuming the possibility of a set of 'resolutions' which are set within a moral framework of service and social justice which are qualitatively different in kind from those naturalised within the morality of the market. Teaching has always involved making decisions within a complex and rich field of contradictions, dilemmas and priorities (see Berlak and Berlak, 1981) – a 'range of tensions "in" teachers, "in" the situation and "in" society, over the nature of control teachers exert over children in school' (p. 135). Indeed, as Berlak and Berlak argue, teaching acts can be viewed 'as a simultaneous resolution to multiple dilemmas' (p. 165). I suggest that school administration and management can be seen in a similar way. Thus, Glatter (1996) also argues for attention to be given to the study of organisational dilemmas and presents a set of examples of strategic dilemmas facing schools in the competitive climate 'now existing in many areas of England and Wales' (p. 6). The market simplifies or 'flattens' or brings a powerful set of biases into this complex of dilemmas and encourages and legitimates a new 'dominant pattern of resolution' (Berlak and Berlak, 1981, p. 203).

My examples are not thought-experiments but rather they are actual cases drawn from a series of three research studies on aspects of the market in education.[3] In some instances they refer to general trends or patterns, in others specific events or decisions or policies from particular schools and colleges are used. In my discussion of these data do not intend to position myself as an 'ethical virtuoso' (Hunter, 1994, p. 177) nor to I speak from any moral high-ground. I do not under-estimate the pressures nor the situated legitimacy – the obviousness – which attend at least some of the decisions involved. Many of the dilemmas and resolutions discussed here have very direct parallels in the world of higher education in which I practice.

Each of the dilemmas identified here require detailed discussion to do full justice to the range of issues involved and that is not possible given the limits of available space (see Chapters 7, 8 and 9). Nonetheless, even in schematic form, they serve to give some sense of the sorts of tensions thrown up by the disciplines of the market form and the patterns of resolution and of 'appropriate' behaviour that are produced. What I intend to do is to deal with some of the dilemmas fairly superficially and explore others in more depth.

1. The first dilemma concerns the provision of information to year 11 students about their choices and opportunities for post-16 education. Very simply a professional response would be to ensure that the student has maximum information upon which to base a choice. Given the regime of per-capita funding the market (income maximisation) response for an 11–18 school is to restrict information about alternative routes and encourage students to 'stay-on'. Thus, Colleges of Further Education find themselves 'banned' from visiting 11–18 schools to talk about their courses and brochures from competing institutions are not made available to students in 11–18 schools. Extracts A and B offer illustrations of the market response at work on each side of the conjunction/transition at 16 (see Ball *et al.*, 1997, for further discussion).

A recent NFER survey of 256 maintained sixth forms also found that such schools were motivated by 'protectionism' in failing to circulate information about

Issue	Professional response	Market response
Information for post-16 choice	Student interest	School recruitment
Institutional response to difficult or disruptive student	Various strategies for discipline and support involving family and support services	Immediate exclusion – cheaper, good for school reputation and exam performance
Entry to A-level course for under-achieving student	Match students to appropriate course even if student goes elsewhere	Accept students in order to fill-up courses
Response to persistent Year 11 truant	Mobilise support to keep student at school or find alternative provision	Remove student from roll and improve exam statistics
LEA response to local schools' use of exclusion	Oppose schools' applications at appeal	Maintain low profile and ensure good relations to prevent 'opting out'
Student participation in school productions	Music and drama are for all students	Use only 'best' students who will convey 'best' impression of school to audiences
Design of school brochures and prospectuses	Information to parents	Marketing school, careful impression management
Provision of SEN support within school	Targeting of monies on SEN and use of other resources	Re-distribution of monies to 'valued' students
Preparing students for GSCE (1)	Maintain a full and varied curriculum and diverse pedagogies	Narrow curriculum to exam-related work and teach exam skills
Preparing students for GSCE (2)	Maximise performance of all students	Target C/Ds with money, resources and encouragement
'Turnaround' of students on FE training courses	Length and structure of course based on educational needs and principles	Length and structure of course based on income maximisation and contract renewal
Recruitment, choice and ethnic mix	Encourage diversity	View intake in relation to choosers' preferences

Extract A: The Opportunities for Choice document is vetoed by the Head, is has full page spreads on Colleges of FE. We do not take students to 6th form Colleges but we do take them to Careers 2000. There are limits to the flow of information... The bums on seats argument is used all the time to close down issues. And sometimes we shoot ourselves in the foot. Like I have 23 in my A-level English class and it changes the mode of delivery. We probably contravene the Trades Description Act in what we sell as A-levels. A small number of those students may be should not be there, should not be encouraged to stay on to do those kinds of courses.

(Head of Careers, 11–18 GM school)

Extract B:...we are not trying to pull you away from the school but why didn't you come to somewhere where they can offer all the subjects that you wanted instead of setting yourself an impossible task where you are either going to fail or not do as well as you could do by trying to take one in the evening and you know I just think that schools are influencing people through some monetary pressures in ways that are not necessarily giving information and pushing their own things. Some schools just don't pass on information but others actually give misinformation out of ignorance I like to think rather than malice because they don't really know what goes on in Colleges.

(Admissions Tutor Bracebridge Further Education College)

other providers (Shagen *et al.*, 1996). Smith (1996) an FE College Lecturer, outlines a similar situation based upon her own experience and concludes that:

> Unless the competitive atmosphere between educational institutions is eroded, and eroded quickly, the new vision for 16-to-19-year olds proposed by the Dearing review, and apparently welcomed so warmly by the Government, will be destroyed by the market-led culture that that same government has deliberately created.

(p. 13)

2. The second dilemma refers to the massive national increase in numbers of expulsions from schools since the 1988 Education Reform Act and particularly since the introduction of Local League Tables: 12,500 students were permanently excluded from schools in England in 1994/95, 84 percent of them from secondary schools (*Guardian*, 14.9.96, p. 4). African-Caribbean boys are significantly over-represented among those excluded. Some schools appear to be using expulsions as a way of disposing of problematic and costly students, protecting or enhancing examination performance, and bolstering their disciplinary profile. In relation to the latter, a strong line on expulsion is used to indicate a firm disciplinary regime to potential parent applicants (see e.g. in extract G). Here the interests of the school within the marketplace take precedence over the problems of individual students. In a MORI survey conducted in 1993 nearly half of Local Education Authority Directors identified competition between schools as a major factor behind the increase in exclusions (reported in *Time Out*, 10.7.96, p. 13). From the point of view of individual schools the removal of a difficult student means that student becomes someone else's problem. This may indicate a general shift from an education system orientation, and a sense of general professional social responsibility, to a narrower, institutional survival orientation.

3. Dilemma 3 is related to the first. In this case it is the 'temptation' faced by Colleges and schools to allow insistent but 'unsuitable' students on to post-16 courses in which they are very unlikely to succeed. It is clear from our research on the post-16 sector (Ball *et al.*, 1997a) that some institutions will bend or lower their entry requirements and give unrealistic advice and encouragement in order to retain the choices of students who might otherwise have gone elsewhere. (See extract A for example.) This is a kind of 'bidding-down' process where again income maximisation takes primacy over professional judgment. Significantly, 25 per cent of students on General National Vocational Qualification (GNVQ)

Intermediate and Advanced courses fail or drop out (Ainley and Green, 1996, p. 23). The National Foundation for Educational Research (NFER) study reported above also found that schools were worried that Colleges are accepting students on courses that are beyond their ability, with disastrous consequences for the young peoples' self esteem (Shagen *et al.*, 1996).

4. Dilemma 4 is similar to 2 and focuses upon a schools' response to truanting students, especially those in years 10 and 11. The incentives of both cost and performance maximisation leads to an approach of minimum support and effort for the retention of truants and instead their early removal from the school roll. Students 'off' roll do not count in the calculation of local league table percentages and if retained incur additional costs in terms of pastoral support and administrative effort, and may be 'damaging' the reputation of the school. One LEA Admissions and Exclusions Officer in our research drew attention to a 'significant dip' in the official year 11 roll of schools across her LEA, which she attributed to a determined effort by schools to remove students who would threaten their League Table position.

5. Dilemma 5 is again related to 4. This time the focus is upon the ethics of the LEA and the balance between the interests of students and parents appealing against 'exclusion', as against the interests of the LEA itself in maintaining good relations with schools that expel and thus minimising the number of schools considering 'opting out'. This question is the degree of rigour with which the LEA monitors, and reports to Appeals Panels, the procedures followed by schools when 'expelling' students.

6. Dilemmas 6 and 7 are also related. Number 6 takes the level of tension between market and professional concerns down to the classroom. In the education marketplace one of the ways in which schools are able to 'present' themselves to their 'customers' is through public events. Perhaps not surprisingly, drama and music productions attract much larger numbers of parents or potential parents into school than do Governors' meetings for parents or Parent Teacher Association socials. The former are also much more likely to be reported in the local press. The issue here is the blurring of the distinction, in relation to productions, between educational as opposed to promotional or marketing purposes. Again the issue is whether is it the recruitment or reputational concerns of the school that are to the fore or the educational experiences of students. Extract C illustrates the issues and concerns here, and perhaps also gives some indication of the way in which calculability and exchange relationships have come to the fore in the micropolitics of schools (see Ball, 1997).[4]

Extract C: The Head takes a genuine interest in the Arts and we have a very good position in the curriculum, compared with a lot of other schools, but the quid pro quo if you like is a thriving kind of public face and most of the teachers are actually committed to that, funnily enough...I mean they enjoy doing it, they get a lot out of it...but it's a lot of work, particularly to maintain the programme that they want...a problem with performance, the public performance in education, although it's educationally beneficial, very, for those students involved, it is inevitably selective, and what you're doing is concentrating on the able students...at the expense, well you haven't got the time to spend so much on others, although of course we try and get...other people involved as much as we can...the performance...we've got so much keenness to be involved, and if you're doing what we're doing at the moment... like we're going into a thing...with the National Theatre, organising a youth theatre project, we might be able to get...actually to the National...the

pressure's on and we're not gonna pick kids that can't do it, and anyway one of
the things that the principal would say is, we don't want anyone who can't act
involved really...she doesn't like people in the orchestra who can't play instruments, who've only just started, although you can get away with that to an
extent, but she's against that, so there is that...I think it's unfortunate but performance is really aimed at...the kids who benefit are the ones who are able...

(Head of Arts, GMS school)

7. Dilemma 7 represents a more general tension in the education market
between information-giving and impression management. Schools have become
much more aware of and attentive to the 'need' to carefully organise the ways in
which they 'present' themselves to their current and potential parents. Two of the
16 secondary schools which were case studies in Gewirtz *et al.* (1995) employed
Public Relations Consultants to help them in this respect. Most schools have
marketing committees and devote considerable time, energy and expense to the
design of brochures, prospectuses and school events and it was noted in the case of
school prospectuses:

* the use of more sophisticated production techniques and the resulting
  'glossification' of school imagery;
* the commercialisation of texts and an associated focus on 'visual images' and
  explicit indicators of 'quality'; and
* a growing emphasis on middle-class symbolism.

(Gewirtz *et al.*, 1995, p. 127)

The last point refers to the use of drama and music as social-class surrogates; both as
forms of appeal and indirectly forms of selection aimed at maximising middle-class
recruitment. It is interesting to note that 35 of the 41 GMS schools which responded
to the change of regulations earlier this year concerning selection of students indicated that they would select on the basis of aptitude or talent in Music or Drama
(Parliamentary answer 11 June 1996). The professionalisation of marketing is much
more developed in FE Colleges, everything including the photographs in and colour
of the prospectus is carefully planned and tested for market effects (Ball *et al.*, 1997)
(see extracts D and E). 'It's not what we do, what we teach, what we provide, it's
what we look like, some may observe cynically' (Callinan, 1994, p. 5).

Extract D: It could be you see because I don't think you attract women into
the College by showing a lot of pictures of men do you, but on the other hand
if you get the impression that it is a College that looks as if it has lots of
females and treats them well you will get lots of women and that will always
attract the males anyway...

(Marketing Manager Burbley FE College)

Extract E: Particularly sixteen year olds like red it is a colour they seem to
like, because when we get the prospectus we quite often go into groups in
College and say well right here is the new prospectus what do you think and
they tell you, don't they.

(Marketing Manager Mersely FE College)

Returning to the school sector, in more general terms, the emphasis on 'selling' schools (see extract F) effects and inflects a whole range of interactions between schools and their social environment (see Glatter, 1996).

Extract F:...she [the Head] likes to get people competing against each other in different areas of the school, and it works, I don't know how effectively it works all the time so...certainly within the school I'd say that applied very strongly...and in the first few years it was idiotic really...some of the things people felt they had to get up to...but I think in...I think Mrs Carnegie would prefer a much harder sell on the school than actually happens...at the moment I think what's really happening is that she...she tends to say that sort of thing a lot...a fair amount within the school and hopes that it will become reality, whether it actually is reality at present, I'm not at all sure.

(Deputy Year Tutor, GMS school)

There are two aspects to this as regards ethics. One is the means employed, as with brochures and productions. The other is the relationship between the sell and the actuality. (This is the question raised in extract F.) Local League Tables, publicity and marketing, even Ofsted Inspections, in different ways all give emphasis to the importance of ways of 'representing' the school for purposes of choice or evaluation, which may be complexly un-related to the actualities of day-to-day practice. Thus, Carol Fitzgibbon has drawn attention to the increasing use of consultants by schools preparing themselves for Ofsted inspections (*Guardian*, 21 June 1996). Extract G gives one example of the care which now goes into the preparation of such things as the Headteacher's address to parents at Open evenings.

Extract G: We sat down beforehand in the Senior Management Team and said; 'What do we want the Head to say?'. And, basically, it was, appear traditional, conservative with a small 'c' and emphasise traditional things like hard work, discipline. Emphasise the fact that the authority don't particularly like it that we exclude quite significant numbers of pupils, more than they would like us to exclude. Particularly for fighting and particularly for bullying. Emphasise the fact that our examination results, in terms of number of GCSEs, have improved by 25% over the last three years, which is not too bad. And keep it short, sharp and keep it to those areas...And we are a caring institution. We have a sophisticated pastoral system, it's the backbone of the school and that was emphasised. And people, round and about, have got the impression that the pastoral system is very good. It's got a very good special needs department. Now that in itself might cause problems, because if you're known to be the school to deal effectively with SEN kids you will get a higher proportion of those kids which has resource implications and implications for the image of the institution and what the institution turns out and you may well be less comprehensive than you would want to be. So she didn't over emphasise it. And talked about pastoral in a way that means more than looking after the welfare of children and that an integral part of it is what they achieve in terms of examination results.

(Deputy Head LEA Comprehensive School)

As a further aspect of this extract H indicates how the concern for favourable 'representation' confronts subject teachers in the way in which they are expected to organise and present examination results. The new values of the market are disseminated in this way through the practices of the whole school.

Extract H: I'm rushing around like a loony today trying to put together this exam results display she wants...I didn't have any data to do it with and I've had to collect that and then I've had to find a way of presenting the results in a way that looks good...GCSEs and A level results against the national average...that's presented us with some problems, because obviously with four subjects the results are uneven...I've found a way of doing the A-level that looks alright, I'm struggling a bit with the GCSE.

(Head of Department, GM school)

---

8. Dilemma 8 concerns a set of issues discussed in detail in previous work (Gewirtz *et al.*, 1995). That is, the changing 'value' attributed to SEN (Special Educational Needs) work and SEN students in schools concerned with the relationship between recruitment and performance in Public Examinations and local reputation. As extract G indicates, and as we found more generally, schools with histories of excellence in SEN downplaying this expertise for fear of 'putting off' parents of 'high achieving' students. Again this is in part a matter of managing the messages given by schools to their 'consumers' (Glatter, 1996). But here there are also 'real' effects in terms of the time, effort and resources devoted to SEN work. Certainly a much higher profile is now given to schemes and programmes for 'high achievers' and concerns have been raised about the way in which special and social needs monies are actually used now that schools control their own budgets and can vire between budget headings (Spalding, 1993).

9 and 10. Dilemmas 9 and 10 are complex and closely related. They focus on the impact of Public Examination performance on classroom pedagogies and priorities especially in years 10 and 11. Current research indicates a whole variety of ways in which the curriculum offered in years 10 and 11 has been narrowed and culled in order to focus students' work more exclusively upon examination performance. The nature of classroom work has been re-oriented and 'made less exciting' as a result.

Extract I: It's not as exciting for the children, it's not as exciting for me. I mean, I'm not fully didactic yet, and hopefully I never will be, but personally I feel I don't have the time to spend enough time doing practicals – it's a very practical subject – but...I feel that if I'm going to help – certainly the brighter pupils – to get the As to Cs then I just have to somehow give them the information...

(Main Grade Teacher, 11–18 LEA School)

While it could well be argued that as a response to a general process of certification inflation this narrowing works in the best interests of students, the second dilemma does not respond so readily to such an interpretation. This refers to the 'targeting' of resources and teachers' efforts on students identified as working on the C/D border in GCSE examination terms (see Gillborn and Youdell, 2000). We have identified a variety of tactics here, including in one school the use of a specialist to work with such students on examination technique. There are questions here about equity in the distribution of resources, attention, and esteem in all this (see extract J) ; also about the educational value of such work; and indeed again, about the 'meaningfulness' in educational terms of the 'improvements' thereby achieved. A new kind of labelling of students is brought into play.[5] This is part of an internal economy of student worth which is also pointed up in extract L.

Extract J: I don't know, I mean on paper you might be able to claim that it is. Maybe it is, I mean if I am getting these pupils who are D border, getting them to C's, yes, the standard is being raised, or as far as that exam measures it, yes, the standard's being raised. Yes, that is raising standards in a sense, I would accept that but, I'm sort of talking it through myself really . . . but I'm not sure it's the best way to go about raising standards, not that I know what the best way is, but . . . there's something about it that . . . if the only way we're getting standards done is by going . . . everyone going really out of their way to focus on particular individuals . . . and not thinking about raising the standards of everyone, focusing on a few, bringing them from one grade to another grade.

11. Dilemma 11 refers to the Further Education sector and the impact of the pressures of funding on the 'turnaround' of students on National Vocational Qualification (NVQ) Training courses. Again individual practitioners find themselves caught between institutional income maximisation, and the chances of obtaining future contracts from their local Training and Enterprise Council (TEC), which press towards quick 'turnaround' and their professional judgment about the provision of a worthwhile and effective learning experience for students. The activities of some private providers point up these pressures at work and the shifts under way in this area of provision.

Extract K: For the other training there is competition. Because certain NVQs you can get through quite quickly and obviously that is financially better for you and I have got my educational values more than my financial ones. It falls within a tight balance. Well, can you afford to do this which takes two-and-a-half years, because at the end of the day the trainee achieves not just a qualification but achieves in terms of self-worth and employment, when you could do another NVQ that you could roll over in six months and some providers roll over in a month.

(Network Training Manager, Riverway Tertiary College)

12. Finally, dilemma 12 cuts across sectors and returns to the issue of recruitment. In this guise the concern is again with the pressures created by the market framework to maximise the recruitment of 'high achieving' students. But here this is cross-cut with matters of equal opportunity and racism. To what extent do schools and colleges respond to the racism of highly 'valued', middle-class white parents. Again this is partly played out in relation to image and 'representation', that is the extent to which any institution presents itself as multi-ethnic to its potential

consumers, but it also has implications for values, practices and social relationships within the institution. The FE College Marketing manager quoted in extract L conveys a very immediate sense of the dilemmas here at work within his institution.

Extract L: The problem is that teachers tend to you know you see a lot of black youngsters they do over react that is true. Well the view has been put that we to give you an example of that, we do insist on a no smoking policy in the College so it means at certain times of the day the steps just behind you there are absolutely packed with students obviously puffing away you see and most of them tend to be black and to be girls as well, you know both white and black and black males and it has been said to me once or twice that we should try and get rid of that really and people have quoted parents saying that they find it quite off putting if they come to the College for the first time to push their way through that kind of mob you know. A lot of the white middle class parents don't care for all these black students and you know you have to be careful not to alienate them because they are our bread and butter you know but you can't be seen to agree with them either. I don't think the black youngsters are in themselves violent but it is just that people perceive them to be violent you know. I heard on the radio coming into work this morning how many old people are fearful of being beaten up on the street, of course they are about the safest group that there are, it is just this feeling and I think it is the same with what we have here, I say West Indians tend to be quite out going I think is the word and if you are not used to that, it can be off putting. Yes it is a slight problem. People here compare us with Darcy College, I don't know if that is one of the Colleges you are looking at, it is a sixth form college and of course they do 'A' levels in a nice white middle class group and hence a lot of teachers obviously teaching 'A' levels would like us to get that sort of set up here you know, but I think in the main we accept the whole equal opportunities thing and as I say if you look at the prospectus I hope you find the right balance you know.

(Burbley FE College Marketing Manager)

Here an older ethics represented by equal opportunities policies are in direct confrontation with the new ethics of the market which give emphasis to a more calculative approach to recruitment. For the competitor, Darcy College, mono-culturalism is, in effect, part of its image and its 'sell' to white, middle-class parents (see Ball *et al.*, 1997a,b).

Commentary

Now clearly, as already indicated, the dilemmas outlined above would be susceptible to a good deal more elaboration and interrogation than has been possible here. However, it is the very existence (and recognition by practitioners) of these dilemmas, or the particular form that they now take, that are of primary concern in the analysis I am offering here. I have tried to suggest that the moral framework of the education market both produces new kinds of ethical dilemmas for those now working in educational institutions and establishes a, largely implicit, values environment in which the market response to these dilemmas, and particular patterns of resolution, is acceptable and palatable. In other words, the logic of the market displaces explicit values-talk with a language of pragmatism which has the effect of marginalising or subordinating educational and social justice values issues. To a great extent the discourse of competition excludes the lexicon of values and this is replaced by a lexicon of expediency, pragmatics and financial necessity. Writing about these issues in relation to school leadership Grace (1996, p. 152) reports from his research that: 'what has changed...are the moral codes and moral certainties which headteachers could invoke in constructing a response to the value dilemmas of school leadership'.

Furthermore, the moral framework of the market interpolates a new kind of professionalism or indeed perhaps two new kinds. One is what might be called, after Hoyle (1974), 'narrow professionality'. That is a professionalism based upon a direct and limited identification of career and responsibility with the 'success' and 'failure' of one's school, or department or classroom. A professionalism based upon exactly the sort of self-interest which was so roundly criticised by the market advocates as a feature of bureaucratic schooling. Another aspect of the complex effects of this 'narrowing' is the reorientation of some schools from the needs of their communities to the interests of their clients.

> ...as a GM head it forces you to look inwards into your institution, in a way it's rather like a public school head, I'm looking into my institution very much.

The other kind we might call 'market or entrepreneurial professionality'; a professionalism based upon expertise in the arts of the market – competition, income generation, marketing. As noted earlier, management plays a key role in the market framework, in particular in delivering change and transforming the consciousness and subjectivity of educational workers (Clarke and Newman, 1992; Gewirtz *et al.*, 1995) and the establishing of a new ethical framework is a key part of this transformation. Yeatman (1993) makes the point that management provides 'teleological promiscuity'; a system of means that can be turned to different ends without a primary concern for the ends themselves; see also (Spybey, 1984).

There clearly are enthusiasts and converts to the market in education and arguably there is a 'new breed' of entrepreneurial headteachers coming into post. But I am not suggesting any kind of simple and total colonisation of institutional decision-making by the disciplines of the market. For many practitioners their responses are pragmatic rather than enthusiastic. There are on-going micro-political struggles over values which take place within some schools and the classroom work of many teachers is not tainted directly by the market logic. Furthermore, individuals inhabit and struggle with the sorts of ethical dilemmas which are created by the market through different aspects of their professional identity (or their old and new identities). Again, as Grace (1996, p. 145) puts it:

> There was evidence from this study that despite the 'distaste' which marketing the school created for some headteachers and despite the moral and professional dilemmas which they perceived and experienced, there appeared to be an iron law of inevitability about market intensification in certain localities. In these circumstances, institutional survival was at stake, and the headteachers understood this.

However, in the play between old and new identities at least some of the dilemmas outlined above can be given different sorts of 'spins' which in some instances enables a sense of propriety and integrity to be maintained. For example, selection can be re-worked as a means of ensuring a 'comprehensive' entry. In other ways the primacy of immediate concerns for institutional survival mean that what are identified here as dilemmas are not always recognised or interpreted or articulated *in that way* by those who inhabit them. I am not suggesting a deliberate duplicity here, rather a resolution of values tensions through a process of translation between different 'vocabularies of motives'. But it is important not to lose sight of the key point here that it is the policies which created the new moral framework that is producing these dilemmas and the climate within which values drift takes place.

It is not that we have got to the stage whereby all responses of all schools can be simply 'read-off' from the incentives of the market. First, we have to recognise that the market does not have the same impact on every institution in every setting. Schools are positioned differently in the market. But our research does indicate a process, we call 'values drift', at work across schools. That is a discursive shift from professional to market values (Gewirtz *et al.*, 1993, 1995); although individual schools have different starting points, and they are moving at different rates. Some headteachers have embraced the shift with urgent enthusiasm. Others are pushed reluctantly and slowly. It is very difficult to escape entirely from the discursive and financial incentives which drive the movement; although different local contexts, local histories and market configurations do effect the pace of movement. Second, there are pockets of concerted resilience and counter-discursive activity. In some locations the Catholic church is an important buttress against drift and shift. (In others it is decidedly not.) Grace (1996) sees the market as posing a particular challenge to Catholic headteachers. In his research; 'the moral dilemma for educational leaders...[was] constituted by a recognition that "playing the market" made it more difficult to serve the poor and the powerless' (p. 177). Some groups of schools are attempting to re-invent collaboration and co-operation and minimise competition; for example, the Birmingham Catholic Partnership (Mac an Ghaill, 1994); Education 2000 in Letchworth (Monck, 1996); and the North Lowestoft Schools Network (Harbour, 1996).

To sum up, the market is not simply a value-free, mechanistic alternative to partisan planning, as some advocates and choice-politicians suggest. Together with the cognate technologies of enterprise and entrepreneurship it is a transformational force which carries and disseminates its own values. Choice and market systems re-interpolate key actors – families, children and teachers; re-position schools; and re-works and re-values the meaning of education (Gewirtz *et al.*, 1993; Ball, 1994). Families are re-interpolated as consumers of education (Hughes, 1994, pp. 66–70). The education market re-socialises and de-socialises; encouraging competitive individualism and instrumentality. Writing in more general terms Ranson (1995, p. 442) argues that 'the economic, social and political transformations of our time are altering fundamentally the structure of experience: the capacities each person needs to flourish, what it is to live in society, the nature of work and the form taken by the polity'. Within all this, children themselves are positioned differently and evaluated differently in the education market, they are commodified. In systems where recruitment is more or less directly related to funding, then the educational and reputational 'costs' of the child become part of the 'producers' response to choosers. This also occurs, as we have seen, where exclusivity is a key aspect of a school's market position. Further, in a whole variety of ways education itself is reworked as a commodity.

The research on which this paper draws indicates a shift taking place in schools and colleges from what I have called 'professional' values or the values of 'professional community' (Grace, 1996) to the values of the market (see also Gewirtz *et al.*, 1993). Where there is competition to recruit, non-market values and professional ethics are being de-valued and displaced by the 'need' to 'sell' schools and colleges and make and manage 'image' in the marketplace. The incentives of the education market encourage commercial responses and marginalise professional ethics. Furthermore, the discourses of policy which animate and infuse the market provide a climate of legitimation and vocabulary of motives which make new ways of action thinkable, possible and acceptable and 'old' ways seem less appropriate. Thus, within the educational context the pedagogy of the market 'teaches' and disseminates a new morality. Bottery (1992) argues that 'if morality is defined as...that area concerned with the ways in which people, individually or in groups, conceptualise, treat and affect themselves and other living beings...then ultimately the management of the school is concerned with the moral education of those within it' (p. 3).[6] I have also suggested that the changes in the ethico-political terrain of education which I have begun to map are part of a broader set of shifts in 'the categories and explanatory schemes according to which we think ourselves, the criteria and norms we use to judge ourselves, the practices through which we act upon ourselves and one another' (Rose, 1992, p. 161). Social welfare is on the way towards thorough-going incorporation into the ontology of the market.

Notes

1   My colleague Alan Cribb has made the point to me that it is important not to see Nagel's 'personal standpoint' as simply an expression of self interest. It also conveys aspects of identity, self worth, sense of purpose etc. And paradoxically perhaps the 'personal standpoint' is also impoverished and narrowed by the processes I am describing here. The reduction in the scope of professional judgement in teaching is also a reworking and subversion of teachers' identity and self worth.

2   Another aspect of the influences which play upon education policy, derived from what Dale calls 'new institutional economics', is 'mainstreaming'. The argument that the public sector should no longer be treated as special, as different from the private sector.

3   Economic and Social Research Council (ESRC) funded projects nos. 235544, 23251006 and 232858.

4   The hestitancies evident within the delivery of the account perhaps give some indication of the discomfort and personal ambivalence felt by this teacher. Old and new incentives and commitments are difficult to reconcile.

5   A colleague recently told me of a school in which she is researching which holds separate assemblies for a/b, c/d and e/f labelled students.

6   I am very grateful to Alan Cribb, Trinidad Ball, Diane Reay, Agnes van Zanten and Stephen Crump for their insightful comments on an earlier version of this paper, to Sharon Gewirtz, Richard Bowe, Diane Reay, Sheila Macrae and Meg Maguire who collaborated in the various projects upon which the paper draws, and to colleagues at King's and Rene Descartes for their questions.

References

Ainley, P. and Green, A. (1996). 'Missing the Targets: The New State of Post-16 Education and Training'. *Forum*, 38(1): 22–3.

Ball, S. J. (1990). *Politics and Policymaking in Education*. London, Routledge.

Ball, S. J. (1997). Performativity and Fragmentation in 'Postmodern Schooling'. In *Postmodernity and the Fragmentation of Welfare: A Contemporary Social Policy*. J. Carter (ed.). London, Routledge.

Ball, S. J., Bowe, R. and Gewirtz, S. (1994). 'Competitive Schooling: Values, Ethics and Cultural Engineering'. *Journal of Curriculum and Supervision*, 9(4): 350–67.

Ball, S. J., Macrae, S. and Maguire, M. M. (1997a). *The Post-16 Education Market: Ethics, Interests and Survival*. London, School of Education, King's College London.

Ball, S. J., Macrae, S. and Maguire, M. M. (1997b). *Race and Racism in a Post-16 Education Market*. London, School of Education, King's College London.
Berlak, A. and Berlak, H. (1981). *Dilemmas of Schooling: Teaching and Social Change*. London, Methuen.
Bottery, M. (1992). *The Ethics of Educational Management*. London, Cassell.
Boyd, W. (1982). 'The Political Economy of Future Schools'. *Educational Administration Quarterly*, 18(3): 111–30.
Callinan, D. (1994). 'FE Public Image – substance or Illusion?' *College Management Today*, 2(4): 5.
Clarke, J. and Newman, J. (1992). *The Right to Manage: A Second Managerial Revolution*. Milton Keynes, Open University.
Gewirtz, S., Ball, S. J. and Bowe, R. (1993). 'Values and Ethics in the Marketplace: The Case of Northwark Park'. *International Journal of Studies in Education*, 3(2): 233–53.
Gewirtz, S., Ball, S. J. and Bowe, R. (1995). *Markets, Choice and Equity in Education*. Buckingham, Open University Press.
Gillborn, D. and Youdell, D. (2000). *Rationing Education: Policy, Practice, Reform and Equity*. Buckingham, Open University Press.
Glatter, R. (1996) Managing Dilemmas in Education: The tightrope walk of strategic choice in more autonomous institutions. In *School Administration: Persistent Dilemmas in Preparation and Practice*. E. Hickox and R. Stevenson (eds). Westport, CT, Greenwood Publishing.
Grace, G. (1995). *School Leadership: Beyond Education Management: An Essay in Policy Scholarship*. London, Falmer.
Harbour, M. (1996). The North Lowestoft Schools Network. In *Consorting and Collaborating in the Education Marketplace*. D. Bridges and C. Husbands (eds). Hove, Falmer.
Hoyle, E. (1974). 'Professionality, professionalism and control in teaching'. *London Educational Review*, 3(2): 15–17.
Hughes, M., Wikeley, F. and Nash, T. (1994). *Parents and their Children's Schools*. Oxford, Basil Blackwell.
Hunter, I. (1994). *Rethinking the School: Subjectivity, Bureaucracy, Criticism*. St Leonards, Allen and Unwin.
Kenway, J. (1990). Class, Gender and Private Schooling. In *Power and Politics in Education*. D. Dawkins (ed.). Lewes, Falmer Press.
Lane, R. E. (1983). 'Political Education in a Market Society'. *Micropolitics*, 3(1): 39–65.
Mac an Ghaill, M. (1994). Public Service in the Market: The Birmingham Catholic Partnership. In *Co-operating in the Education Marketplace*. M. Mac an Ghaill and M. Lawn (eds). Birmingham, Educational Review Publications.
Monck, L. and Husbands, C. (1996). Education 2000 Letchworth. In *Consorting and Collaborating in the Education Marketplace*. D. Bridges and C. Husbands (eds). London, Falmer.
Morrell, F. (1989). *Children of the Future*. London, Hogarth Press.
Nagel, T. (1991). *Equality and Partiality*. Oxford, Oxford University Press.
Plant, R. (1992). Enterprise in its place: the moral limits of markets. In *The Values of the Enterprise Culture*. P. Heelas and P. Morris (eds). London, Routledge.
Ranson, S. (1995). 'Theorising Educational Policy'. *Journal of Education Policy*, 10(4): 427–48.
Rose, N. (1992). Governing the Enterprising Self. In *The Values of the Enterprise Culture*. P. Heelas and P. Morris (eds). London, Routledge.
Shagen, S., Johnson, F. and Simkin, C. (1996). *Sixth Form Opportunities: Post Compulsory Education in Maintained Schools*. Windsor, NFER/Nelson.
Smith, M. (1996). 'My View'. *The Independent*, 13.
Spalding, B. (1993). 'Money Talks Louder than Special Needs Code'. *Times Education Supplement*, 19 November.
Spybey, T. (1984). 'Traditional and Professional Frames of Meaning for Managers'. *Sociology*, 18(4): 550–62.
Yeatman, A. (1993). 'Corporate Managerialism and the Shift from the Welfare to the Competition State'. *Discourse*, 13(2): 10–17.

CHAPTER 7

GOOD SCHOOL/BAD SCHOOL
Paradox and fabrication

British Journal of Sociology of Education, 1998, 18(3): 317–36

Introduction

While this paper can be read, I hope, as a free-standing and ended, if not finished, piece of analysis, it is one of a series of related and incomplete 'attempts' at conceptualising 'reformed'[1] schools. The relatedness and incompleteness is part of the point of the exercise. What I am trying to do here is move beyond the neat and totalising, essentialist, one-off forms of analysis that are normally applied to schools as organisations, both in characterisations in research and in public evaluations; i.e. failing/successful, effective/ineffective etc.

The basis of and motivation for this concern for an analysis 'otherwise' are very practical. They stem from the problems involved in trying to establish some analytic 'truths' about a set of schools which are subjects of an ESRC-funded research study (Grant no. 235544) – see below. The schools, through the data which stand for them, refuse to submit to comprehensive, closed or totalising forms of analysis. As recalcitrant realities the schools demand more. Put simply, schools, school managements, school cultures are not 'of a piece'. Schools are complex, contradictory, sometimes incoherent organisations, like many others. They are assembled over-time to form a bricolage of memories, commitments, routines, bright ideas and policy effects. They are changed, influenced and regularly and increasingly interfered with. They drift, decay and re-generate. Furthermore, as 'values' organisations they interweave affective, ideological and instrumental engagement – although a good deal of this is conveniently ignored or set aside in much of the contemporary work on school organisations. Furthermore, despite important commonalities, organisations and managements are not sector indifferent. There are particular inherent tensions in the work practices, values and 'attitudes' of teachers between technocratic and substantive/humanistic orientations (see below; Yeatman, 1993).

Finally, schools, like other organisations, are produced and articulated by disparate discourses (knowledges and practices) that sometimes grate and collide, or at least sit uneasily together. These disparate discourses provide resources of order and effect, and vocabularies of motives for organisational practices and fables and are particularly visible in critical events and moments as well as in various odd and 'unpromising places'. What we access and understand as 'the school' is thus an effect of the interweaving of certain historic and more immediate (and sometimes future, possible) discourses. These discourses are typically entangled and confused and they are obscured by micropolitical struggles, tactical plunderings, disguises and ploys.

This paper is drawn from a research study of 'the changing values and cultures of secondary schools' conducted collaboratively with Sharon Gewirtz and Diane Reay. The research involves detailed ethnographic case studies of four very different secondary schools, of which Martineau was one. The case studies were conducted mainly between January 1995 and December 1996 – although some work is on-going. Data were collected by interviewing a cross-section of staff (and some governors) in each school (approximately 110 to date) and from observations of school committees and events (approximately 120 to date) and shadowing staff with a view to analysing management practices, decision-making roles and social relationships. Particular attention was paid to the organisational language employed in the schools and we also focused upon 'critical decision-making events' – defined as decision-making activities around issues which involved value conflicts and dilemmas. The analysis of data employs Straussian coding techniques (Strauss, 1987), which focus on the identification of key categories and concepts through a process of close open coding of transcripts and observational data. These categories were subject to continuous interrogation and refinement as new pieces of data (indicators) were collected, by constant comparison – 'by making comparisons of indicator to indicator the analyst is forced into confronting similarities, differences, and degrees of consistency of meaning among indicators' (Strauss, 1987, p. 25). The analysis was on-going and was used to guide further data collection and questioning, and 'theoretical sampling' was used to address major, emergent issues.

This paper was read and commented on, in detail, by one of Martineau's middle managers, Ms Rice. Her general response was: 'I think you have captured the flavour of the school remarkably well; I recognise the Martineau you describe and the attitudes of those who work in it'. Some of her other comments are included in the text below.

As will become apparent I will be attempting to problematise the concept of a 'good school', that is to step outside of the rather rigid parameters of the 'official' and commonsense discourses which currently reduce the idea of a 'good school' to a set of simple performativities and representations.[2] This will involve an exercise of reversal. That is the linking of various quality assurance procedures, advocated by Ofsted and others, to achieve 'good' schools, to such 'bad' effects as the intensification of teachers' work (often on administrative tasks unrelated to the teaching/learning process), a reduction in teacher collegiality, and the production of fabricated indicators and manufactured representations of 'the school'. An alternative version of the 'good' school is implicit in this reversal. But I am not intending here to assert one conception of a 'good' school over and against the other, rather to demonstrate the antagonism between the two. Given the limits of space and the primary purposes of this paper, the alternative will remain implicit.

Alongside my argument that TQM, School Development Planning and Inspections work as sophisticated disciplinary technologies I am also suggesting that procedures and techniques which are intended to make schools more visible and accountable, paradoxically encourage opacity and the manipulation of representations – or at least produces a significant slippage between certain key signifiers and the signified. That is to say, documents produced in these technologies of surveillance become increasingly reified, self-referential and dislocated from the practices they are 'meant' to stand for or account for.

Martineau

Martineau is a 'good school', just about everybody thinks so. It is the only state girls' school in Northwark. It is oversubscribed and it's intake has grown markedly since it became Grant Maintained (that is 'opted-out' of Local Authority control) in 1991/92 (to 283 in 1994 and increasing again in 1995 – the school over recruits, to allow for 'bleeding'). When the school introduced a partially selective entry policy in 1995,

344 students sat examinations for the 90 places available. Martineau won a capital grant award of £500,000 as part of the government's technology initiative, followed by another of £800,000 for science facilities and major plant maintenance. It was also successful in its bid to be part of Toyota's Science and Technology Fund. The total budget in 1994 was a little over £5m. Its performance in public examinations has improved steadily, especially since 1990 and it regularly captures second position in the Local League table. It achieved 49 per cent A–C passes at GCSE (General Certificate of Secondary Education) in 1993/94, 47 per cent in 1994/95 (making it top of the local state league table). On occasion the Headteacher, Mrs Carnegie, describes it to parents as a 'feminist school'. Its is also an ethnically mixed school.

1990/91	Black	White	S. Asian	Chinese	Other
Year 7	31.4	45.7	20.9	0.5	1.4
Year 11	32.8	35.6	27.9	3.1	—

The school is committed to self-improvement and has employed an educational consultant to introduce the principles and methods of TQM throughout the school.

The Headteacher is clear in her support for the principle of Comprehensive education but describes herself as a pragmatist when it comes to school policy and decision-making. The move to GM status was initiated to escape from the anti-comprehensive policies of the LEA: 'this difficult decision was taken for reasons of philosophy, but also as an answer to resolve the problem of capital monies'. The Headteacher went on to say that 'The first year of GM was an exhilarating one. It revealed the LEA as an emperor without clothes...'. The Headteacher provides strong and visionary leadership but also pursues a policy of maximum delegation to her *senior* staff. She is also absolutely clear about her managerial prerogatives and gives particular emphasis to the establishment and use of clear systems throughout the school: 'we must be one of the most systems-based schools in the country' (TQM development session). In SMT (Senior Management Team – that is Head, Finance Officer, 2 deputy Heads and four senior teachers) meetings she is vigorous and some-times combative but always willing to foster and listen to debate. Interestingly the SMT discussions, even of the grimmest issues, are punctuated with laughter and snippets of the Headteacher's dry humour. She frequently shares her educational 'beliefs' with staff [this I believe is a sophisticated 'steering' technique] *and* con-stantly praises them. She provides 'a mission as well as a sense of feeling great' (Peters and Waterman, 1982, p. 323). But she can also be quite critical of individuals and groups of staff in public 'she shoots from the hip' as one teacher put it, and is generally regarded as having 'favourites'. Nonetheless, in interviews with staff favourable comments far outweighed the negative. She is very involved in local and national educational circles and offers her staff a clear view of the directions of education policy. The senior deputy was very clear about the Headteacher's strengths and particularly her ability to inspire loyalty and make her staff feel valued.

> I think she has the capacity for a start to inspire the most tremendous loyalty. You have seen the way she and I will snap at each other in senior team meet-ings, well I say snap, that sounds as though it's destructive, it's not. I view the tension between her and me on certain issues as a creative one. Even if it goes beyond the creative and does become difficult at times, we both know that we come from the same...you know we come through the same door, even if we cross the room in slightly different ways, and what we actually care most about

is children's education and there's nothing that will move us from that...she cares very much about the staff, and cares not in a sort of cuddly, lovey dovey sort of way, but through making sure that staff are well treated, that their conditions of service are as good as they can possibly be, that they get their INSET entitlement, it's all those sorts of things, that people can go to her and talk, people have very open access to Kristen really, so there's that. There's no doubt that her kind of involvement in sort of outside areas...I think makes people feel that the school has a status, and they enjoy that status, they enjoy that feeling of being in a school...that's perceived as being in the forefront...they quite enjoy all these sort of national commissions, research projects, such as yours that we get in here, it's a feel good factor...which is incredibly important. There is no doubt with Kirsten what her principles are...

The second deputy offered a similar account.

She's incredibly well informed, and far seeing. She shares...she's always had this notion of shared headship, that certainly the deputies, and I think increasingly actually the senior teachers as well, in a sense share the headship and although there are certain things that are very firmly on her plate and no one else's, as it were, there is a lot of free discussion and she listens to what we say...and takes on board the kinds of things that are being said, even though as I say, she may well have to put them aside. She is generally a very consultative sort of person, she likes to work by consultation and by consensus, wherever she can. But on the other hand, she's not afraid...when occasion demands it, of saying no, I want it done this way, and of being top down. But that is comparatively rare, and more often than not, even when she's operating in that kind of mode, she has already talked things through with at least the deputies, if not the whole senior team, and so it's a kind of top down in that respect. She cares hugely about the pupils and about their experience of education, she cares about the school and that it should be and should be seen to be a successful and worthwhile institution, and that rubs off all over the place, on the staff and on the pupils.

And the Head of Year Tutors also talked about a potent combination of missionary leadership and collective endeavour:

I think she is an inspired leader. To be perfectly honest I would not have come to the school without Kirsten...I think she has enormous stature. I think she is responsive to her staff, but in no way intimidated by them. I do know some heads who are intimidated by their staff. I think on the whole she manages extremely well, I mean she occasionally shoots from the hip and then thinks about it, but she's always big enough to say look, that was a mistake, let's do it another way...I enjoy her management style. I think there's quite a lot of fun about it...in that we're...I mean the things which are being discussed are very serious, and they are taken seriously, they are thought about...I think she's educationally very literate, but she doesn't make it dour.

Running through all of the accounts of the Head's style and interactions is a dualism; a strong but open, valuing but critical leadership style. The Librarian:

there's a very strong Headteacher, personality wise, a very...I wouldn't say...not dominant, but leading...she's a good...she's a very strong leader, her own ideas...and then there's quite a quiet team who support her I think, the senior team...and then there are a lot of very talented teachers who are...fairly career oriented I think, you now, will stay here for so long and then move on...kind of thing, quite a young staff as well. I think it's quite dynamic...and they're prepared to make it work, and certainly prepared to go for the output, to get good results, and to show that they're getting good results.

In many respects leadership at Martineau embodies the 'pop management' prescriptions of Peters and Waterman.

> The top performers create a broad, uplifting, shared culture, a coherent framework within which charged-up people search for appropriate adapta-tions. Their ability to extract extraordinary contributions from very large numbers of people turns on the ability to create a highly valued sense of purpose. Such purpose invariably emanates from love of product providing top-quality services, and honouring innovation and contribution from all.
>
> (1982, p. 51)

All of this is meant to give a flavour of things, I will return to the Headteacher's leadership style and methods later.

Clearly no institution is all good, whatever the standpoint of evaluation, institutions like schools are diverse and complex. No school is of a piece either in terms of efficacy or ideology. Education is value laden and prone to dispute and conflict, although little of that is apparent on the surface of things at Martineau. Furthermore, schools, like other institutions, may be inherently contradictory. They may be productive and oppressive, liberating and inefficient, purposeful and unfair. I intend to explore here some aspects of such contradictions.

Let us return to Martineau's emphasis on systems. I want to highlight three related tools and methods of system and speculate about their 'deeper' organisa-tional impact and effects. They are TQM, SDPing (School Development Planning) and preparing for Ofsted Inspection. The three are heavily inter-related. They all play their part in fostering and developing Martineau's corporate culture. TQM receives the most detailed discussion.

TQM

Here, echoing Willmott (1993) I want to explore the 'dark side' of the project of corporate culture 'by drawing attention to the subjugating and totalitarian impli-cations of its excellence/quality prescriptions' (p. 515). Also, I want to suggest ways in which the 'practical autonomy' of LMS, GMS and TQM may be seen as achieving the purposes of state policy through a combination of 'micro-disciplinary practices' and 'steering at a distance'. The first concern is with the moral signifi-cance of management tools like TQM and Corporate Culture and their attempt at the 'governance of the employee's soul' (p. 517) and their colonisation of the 'softer features of organisation' (p. 518). The task and duty of management is 'no longer restricted to authorising and enforcing rules and procedures' it becomes rather that 'of determining how employees should *think* and *feel* about what they produce' (p. 522) and 'every conceivable opportunity is taken for imprinting the core values of the organisation upon its (carefully selected) employees' (p. 523). When put together a regime of quality and market discipline provide a 'cross-disciplinary ideology for organising professional work' (Kitchener and Whipp, 1995, p. 207).

The TQM development and training programme has been going on for two years. All staff, teaching and non, have been involved and considerable staff development time has been devoted to it. As far as Martineau is concerned three key aspects of the approach have made an impact.

(1) The emphasis on everybody working to together, the fostering of common aims, shared mission etc. What in more sinister tones might be called something like incorporation.

> I've always thought that the way that you work with people was absolutely crucial because unless you have people working with you then what you try to do is probably impossible, in running a school...people are central to the whole thing, whether it's the staff or the children or the parents or whatever, because unless you can get to a position where you can all work together and have a kind of common sense of purpose, then you're not gonna get very far, education is so complex.
>
> (2nd Deputy)

> One of the things that took us into TQM originally was that the senior team were concerned about what appeared to be a huge gap between senior and middle managers, and...not that we were at each others throats in any sense like that, it wasn't that sort of gap, but it was the sort of gap that...middle managers had really very little understanding of what it was that senior managers had to deal with and the kind of decisions we had to make and how difficult some of these decisions actually were. And we also felt rather I think, that all sorts of things were coming to senior team which had no real need to. So that was part of the reason why we started to look at our systems and then started to look at TQM...and I think...certainly all the senior team feel, and I've heard it also from a number of middle managers...that that gap has narrowed markedly, so that there is now a much better understanding on their part of the way that we have to operate...
>
> (2nd Deputy)

> I think there are elements of it which have become ingrained, I think there are...parts of the process which have been very valuable, like...particularly one that I found very interesting, working on my expectations of senior team...and theirs of mine...and mine of my team and theirs of me, and I thought that threw up a lot of very interesting stuff, which I think we've been able to address. So I think the process has been valuable. I think some of the things are reflected in the way in which the school runs. I think on a day-to-day level for main grade teachers...I think they'd say, what, TQM? They would say right first time, but it would be slightly ironic, I have to say.
>
> (Year Tutor)

The final comment in the last extract is important and I shall return to it.

A further aspect of the presentation of TQM by the consultant was a critique of traditional, hierarchical management structures and processes and in their stead an argument for a team structure. Whether as a result of TQM or other influences and concerns an emphasis on a differentiated team structure based on Groups – groups of departments under a Head of Group (Hog) has become a major defining characteristic of the culture structure and relationships of staff at Martineau.

> This is TQM, but it doesn't work, well it does, but it doesn't work...it works very well in the Groups, but then it's done as though we're almost competing companies, rather than all contributing to the corporate image really, this is where this corporate image thing doesn't...in some ways...I mean...I think

the corporate thing would work better if it there were more kind of . . . you see, there's nothing that's whole school. It's very nice the senior team but they don't actually have much to do with anything.

(Hog 1)

This differentiated team structure is seen by virtually all interviewees as being used to develop a sense of competition between the Groups in order to encourage and stimulate harder work and higher 'standards' of work by staff. This competition was viewed with different degrees of cynicism and amusement by all the non-SMT staff interviewed in a language which spoke either of empires, factions, divide and rule, fragmentation and suspicion or hard work and effort or increasing hard work and work loads.

I think the line manager system they've got seems to work fairly well . . . but I also think it's a little bit . . . divisive in that . . . the recent impression of Group against Group . . . I get the impression it's a sort of divide and rule sort of scenario almost. I mean it's not . . . that rigid but that's the impression you get, everybody's bidding against each other . . . for certain outcomes . . . and I think the nature of the school itself . . . I don't think that's maybe the most effective way of doing things.

(Main Grade Teacher 1)

I've noticed it this year more than last year . . . after this year you come back and you go through the results, and there is a very big thing about . . . how has this department done or this Group against that Group, you know, it's how are the maths results compared to the science results, and the science results compared to the history results. I mean it may be like that in all schools, but here it seems like, if you've got bad results compared to somebody else . . . you are going to be frowned upon by other members of staff at the school, you can expect them to be in the staff room saying . . . oh look geography have done really badly . . . and it's not . . . you don't get the impression that . . . oh look at it, the school has done really well . . . we are above the national average, the school has been very successful. It is that science are doing really well, maths aren't . . . they're not coming up to scratch, you know . . . or whatever. I don't think it's enough sort of togetherness, if you like, not everyone pulling for the school, for success . . . for Martineau as a whole . . . it is people pulling for science success or for humanities success.

(Main Grade Teacher 1)

I think one of the things here though, is that you can get very bogged down and easily . . . marginalised from the system as a whole because of this Group allegiance thing. That is so strong here, you know, this thing that people don't go to the staff room, you socialise on an individual level, you sort of suss out who you can talk to as it were. I've got the vibes so far that there's a lot of vying here and there and points scoring . . . to get things or be seen in a certain way.. almost a little bit of divide and rule.

(Main Grade Teacher 2)

the Group team is kind of all empowering and all kind of encompassing and it doesn't really recognise what's going on in other parts of the school much, or other teachers in other areas are treated with a bit of suspicion. They're not really one of us, and the teams are deliberately held up against each other sometimes, like this is good practice, and in the Arts they do this, why aren't you doing it, or in English they've done X, Y, Z, isn't this marvellous.

(Hog 1)

She likes to get people competing against each other in different areas of the school, and it works, I dont know how effectively it works all the time though, certainly within the school I'd say that applied very strongly, and in the first few years it was idiotic really, the sort of things people had to get up to...

(Deputy year tutor)

although the senior team is a team, middle managers are not allowed to be a team, and we can't call ourselves a team, we've got the senior team, got middle managers...CP teams. Group teams...I think that's quite interesting. It seems to me that the language is actually bearing out the reality, and we are more likely to kind of be set against one another than functioning as a small team.

(Hog 2)

it comes from the top, the tone is set at the beginning of the year when those with good results are praised and those who aren't are either ignored or mentioned in an unfavourable light, and at any meeting where Mrs Carnegie is in the chair, there will usually be an allusion to something very good that one Group has done, that the rest of us ought to be doing, but aren't...

(Hog 2)

Competition and fragmentation were driven by a combination of praise and blame and more tangible rewards (resourcing, capitation, facilities etc.) to Groups and individuals. TQM is packaging and systematising basic control techniques such as the ones teachers use in the classroom. Some of the interviewees also made the point that the emphasis on competition worked through to an individual level.

The thing I've found is that there's a need to kind of prove yourself, in order to be respected. You have to do something...where you're obviously making a unique contribution...I had a minor triumph a few weeks ago...

(Responsible Teacher)

All of this resonates strongly with Du Gay's notion of the 'post-entrepreneurial revolution' which 'provides the possibility for every member of an organisation to express "individual initiative" and to develop fully their "potential" in the service of the corporation' (1996, p. 62). One side-effect of competition and hard work, which was noted by several interviewees and evident to the researcher, was the 'de-socialisation' of staff relationships. The staff room was hardly used, especially at lunch times and most staff social activities had ceased. Staff relations were changed and narrowed with an emphasis on business-like and procedural exchanges. Paradoxically then the emphasis on common endeavour and teamwork is realised in part by and obscures a strong sense of competition and social dislocation.

(2) The orientation to the customer.

there's a strong sense of...maybe again TQM has had a bearing on this, as a sort of get it right first time, as far as you can...but also...we are very aware of the proper presentation of things...people aren't satisfied with poorly presented things. You know, we feel...it's part of the way we value people if you like. You know, if you present on scrappy bits of paper or an ill thought INSET or what-ever, it doesn't do anyone any good, so yes there's a tremendous sense of style...

(1st Deputy)

I think TQM has a value in that, in making us think in terms of customers... which is how I regard my parents, and...to a certain degree the students now.

I don't think it changes the fundamental relationship but I think one is very definitely aware that numbers need to be kept up, that we need to have high targets not only for the students but to make sure that the school goes on functioning as well as it does, and I think the introduction of selection has made this very clear.

(Year tutor)

Mrs C always makes it clear that pupils and parents are our customers, and she's always ahead of the game, anticipating was happening.

(Year Tutor at TQM meeting 15.2.95)*

[* but perhaps only some customers, some parents and pupils, other are not wanted or their consumer interests are not a high priority].

As Willmot (1993, p. 522) suggests 'employees are simultaneously required to recognise and *take responsibility for* the relationship between the security of their employment and their contribution to the competitiveness of the goods and services they produce'. Approaches like TQM immerse employees in the logic of the market (Gewirtz *et al.*, 1995, for fuller discussion).

(3) The emphasis on quality and linked to that continuous evaluation and improvement.

I was kind of lukewarm about TQM, I thought it was great, it was fine, but I wasn't madly keen... or madly anti... and I think... the interesting thing... I like to be a little sceptical about some of these things, because... you know, these things come and go... the pattern of equality doesn't come and go actually, so in that sense I would espouse it fully, but I think some of the techniques are really helpful and... that whole sort of... notion of continuous improvement, the continuous search for excellence, the continuous stress on quality, looking at the relationships between people and how they enhance the quality of institution, looking at some of the problem solving approaches as well... the sort of barriers and solutions... stopping us, how we're gonna solve it, and working through those problems. I think it has been very very useful for this school, and I think by and large it may well be seen as a management tool, I don't know whether we've captured the hearts and minds of absolutely everybody.

(1st Deputy)

Again note the final comment.

I know right first time is a wonderful sort of off the tongue phrase, isn't it, for TQM, but that also has been part of my philosophy... to try and get things as near right as you can, but at the same time constant evaluation, this is something that I suppose has developed in me over the years, that you've got to keep checking things out.

(2nd Deputy)

As the consultant explained, TQM involves a 'shift from reliance on outside agencies for judgement of quality to internal monitoring of self-regulation' and 'Ofsted will look at procedures of monitoring in place'. He then asked 'How good are you at monitoring your performance and monitoring the performance of your team?' Viewed critically, TQM instils and rests upon self-surveillance and mutual surveillance. Professionality is replaced by accountability, collegiality by competition (a strong theme across most transcripts), costing and surveillance. These are forms of power which are realised and reproduced through social interaction, within the everyday life of institutions. They do not so much bear down upon but take shape within the practices of the institution itself and construct individuals and their social relations through direct interaction. This is, at least in some respects, a constructive rather than coercive power. It does not simply constrain and oppress it articulates a mode of personal existence which is inscribed within the 'minute arts of self-scrutiny, self-evaluation, and self-regulation' (Rose, 1989, p. 222 and see Ball, 1990, on teacher appraisal). The systems were a source of ambivalence for most staff providing them with both security *and* constraint, a sense of support *and* over burdensome paperwork. The form of power I am referring to here realised and invested and embodied within the professional selves and sense of efficacy and personal, everyday, mundane interactions of the teachers.

> When I think of the mechanics of power, I have in mind rather its capillary form of existence, at the point where power returns into the very grain of individuals, touches their bodies, and comes to insert itself into their gestures and attitudes, their discourses, apprenticeships and daily lives.
> (Foucault, 1980 quoted in Gordon (ed.) *Power/Knowledge*)

Technologies like TQM work, in part, on the body, they use-up and exhaust bodies, submitting them to harsh regimes of stress, pressure, performativity and surveillance. I have come to realise that virtually all the meetings I attended at Martineau, especially those of the Groups and Year Tutors can be seen as enactments of self-monitoring; the development or checking of procedures for personal or group accountability – recording and making activities visible. Enormous amounts of time are spent ensuring that students are correctly labelled, reports are completed, records up to date etc. As noted already, debate or controversy are rare. They are displaced or subsumed by adherence to systems and the demands of performativity. An Arts and PE Group discussion of 'setting' is one exception I witnessed.[3]

All of this keeps the gaze in place. Here the professional teacher is here defined by grasp of and careful use of systems and procedures, and by the narrow and superficial rewards and identities that this delivers through a regressive self-regulation. Submission to the compelling logics of TQM and the attractions of corporate culture involves a giving up of or restriction of self or the substitution of an organisational subjectivity, what might be called, in a different language, alienation. One young English teacher managed to convey a sense of this in interview although significantly she commented 'I'm actually working this through as I'm talking to you'.

> So in terms of the systems that have been set up, in terms of the general management...I suppose I am thinking more logistical and financial, yes, it puts things in place that make it easier. In terms of the personal and how it's making you, the teacher, feel in what you are doing...that's perhaps where I have the problem. But you see, perhaps ultimately you kind of...because you're also focused on the children, cos that's what...well that's what I've come into it for...you have to put that to one side and it comes out at other times, and with the other pluses that come from the system, that are beneficial for the children, you then work with, you put your own personality if you like, into working with those. So again it's a double edged sword...yes, it makes things set up in a very practical...you know, it gives good messages to the children, that everything is here and they can work and we expect and all of that, but then how you are personally feeling, I don't know. I'm gabbling, aren't I? I'm really gabbling.

> how much personal do you have to sacrifice for having the rest there...is probably what would be my...You see, I think one of the strategies behind it, and I think Peter Waters [the TQM consultant] said it, you don't have to like each other, as long as you can work within the systems...well...I'm sorry, I'm not a product, and I don't...you know, and that really gets me.
>
> (Main Grade Teacher 2)[4]

This may exemplify Giddens' (1991) point that where there is an institutionalised 'existential separation' from 'the moral resources necessary to live a full and satisfying existence' (p. 91), a situation he sees as endemic in late modernity, the individual may experience personal meaninglessness (cf. Broadfoot's, 1996, discussion of the technology of educational measurement).

TQM is a method and arguably a culture; it is a '*systematic and totalising approach to the design and strengthening of the normative framework of work*' (Willmott, p. 524). It is an 'intellectual technology' and thus has attractions to some teachers, but it is also a 'relay device' effectively linking government 'mentalities' and policies, with 'everyday organisational realities'. It has made its impact on Martineau, in part through the development process, and some ideas have stuck and have become part of the 'thinking as usual' of the staff. Particularly the senior and middle managers. But the role of TQM and its impact, in the terms I have outlined above, should neither be over or under-estimated. On the one hand (as we discuss in a further paper), this and other techniques of 'reforming education and changing schools' do play a role in the reconstitution of the teacher and teachers' work. On the other hand, as has been noted in commercial contexts, culture-strengthening programmes quite commonly elicit suspicious and sceptical responses from workers. These may generate a kind of calculative compliance and/or a distancing of self from corporate values – 'cool alternation' (Berger and Luckmann, 1966).

> It's very easy to be totally cynical about it...but I think the feeling within our Group is...we don't quite know why Martineau is spending so much money on it, because we don't feel that the hierarchy of this school actually...not only doesn't it run really on TQM principles, it doesn't want to. So we're kind of buying into something we don't believe in, that goes more against the grain of what we do than with it. So there's a sort of puzzlement...if you look at any of the sort of A4 hand outs you get after the TQM sessions, there's...examples of good practice or a good model for team management or a good model for team work, and we loved that one with all the different teams that goes down to being a pseudo team, we think middle managers are a pseudo team and Curriculum Group teams are pseudo teams, but...I don't think most of us find it really has any bearing on our practice.
>
> (Hog 2)

> where you have a lot of people who've been working in a particular way for a very long time, they're not gonna change their viewpoint...there are a lot of...not cynical people, but people who are...well there are a few cynical ones, but...there's no way that you can change your working practice if everyone else isn't doing that, and what happens is that TQM becomes a joke. For instance, whenever something goes wrong, you know...at the meeting, it's the fault of TQM...so in a sense it's almost backfired.
>
> (Main Grade Teacher 1)

I think the image and developing a school ethos stuff...because it's a comparatively new school, I think all that was very important, and again a lot of it I thought was pretty silly, like the flagpole...but it doesn't actually do any harm, and...I'm not sure that's where the school ethos comes from actually.

(Deputy Year Tutor)

All these responses are quite complex and the last is particularly interesting. The nostrums of TQM do not in any straightforward sense translate into and determine day-to-day practice, but they do have various indirect effects. However, I would suggest at least in some respects the introduction of TQM is a symbolic policy. It is intended to *stand for* an approach to management in the school which is business-like and innovative. It is part of the representation of the school as dynamic and adventurous. It plays a part in maintaining the school's national profile. I am not suggesting that it has not 'real' effects within the school but there may be a significant gap between the degree of adoption of TQM (among senior managers or teaching staff) and the costs and effort devoted to it. This may be one part of a more general strategy of 'talking up' the school in the marketplace, within which there is a mismatch between the 'sell' and 'the reality'.

she [the Head] likes to get people competing against each other in different areas of the school, and it works, I don't know how effectively it works all the time so...certainly within the school I'd say that applied very strongly...and in the first few years it was idiotic really...some of the things people felt they had to get up to...but I think in...I think Mrs Carnegie would prefer a much harder sell on the school than actually happens...at the moment I think what's really happening is that she...she tends to say that sort of thing a lot...a fair amount within the school and hopes that it will become reality, whether it actually is reality at present, I'm not at all sure.

(Deputy Year Tutor)

TQM is symptomatic of the responses of schools to the competitive pressures produced by the current policy framework of education in England. It does 'work', as I hope to have demonstrated, in a number of ways to shift the organisational culture of Martineau, and in combination with other disciplinary technologies provides an apparatus of surveillance and the legitimation of certain kinds of relationships. Undoubtedly both the cultural changes and the apparatus of surveillance contribute to Martineau's 'success' in an intensely competitive local market both in terms of performance and in giving the school a distinctive profile, locally and nationally.

SDPing

Set alongside TQM, in the academic year 1994–95, was the process of reviewing and re-writing the School Development Plan. SDPs were pioneered in a number of schools and LEAs in the 1980s and were subsequently adopted and promulgated by the Department for Education. The School Management Task Force report (HMSO, 1990) identified SDPs which incorporated a management and staff development policy as a major characteristic of successful schools. Logan *et al.* (1994) take a more sanguine view of SDPing, and see it as having a potential for 'organisational learning' and/or sophisticated power assertion. When the latter is to the fore they suggest it 'denies the moral aspects of management' and go on to argue that: 'The central dilemmas raised in SDP revolve around the issue, whose interest is the school now serving – the state, system, teachers, community or pupils? How are interests being served and why? That is, the critical issues of SDP are educational and professional, not bureaucratic and procedural' (p. 49). As I have tried to indicate at Martineau it is the bureaucratic and procedural issues that are very much to the fore. It is important to see TQM and SDPing as part of a complex web of tactics and procedures which tie the details of organisational life to the steering requirements of the state.

> also linking TQM to Ofsted because I think that's quite important, and that we use this management tool, we've now taken on board, and clearly ... there is a very clear link there to ... the kind of stuff Ofsted wants.
>
> (2nd Deputy)

All of this is represented in the creation or development of school 'systems' (see below). Meadmore *et al*. (1995) convey a similar duality, which it is important to retain analytically: 'devolution as a management strategy and a power/knowledge technology is currently a means to bring about desired change. However, just as it is dangerous to position all practices of government as being repressive forms of state control, so is it equally cavalier to position them as transformational' (p. 22). They also note that; 'what is in the best interests of the state must be carefully balanced with measures to increase the happiness and life chances of individuals. It is this balance which is crucial to an interpretation of devolution' (p. 10). This touches directly upon the central paradox with which this paper is concerned.

In the language of Mortimore and MacGilchrist (1994) the Headteacher of Martineau sees the SDP as a co-operative plan, which Mortimer and MacGilchrist define as involving 'the teaching staff in the process. The plan is multi-purpose serving both the efficiency and effectiveness of the school through school wide improvements and the professional development of teachers' (p. 2); although the professional development aspects are fairly minimal at Martineau. The Headteacher wrote to staff about the SDP in January 1995 as follows:

> The Senior Team found that some Development Plans are top down and mechanistic whereas we feel that Martineau's development Plan is organic and comes from grass roots thinking. Our development plan rests on findings flowing from INset Days, Diagnostic Windows and feedback from Team and other meetings.
>
> (Head's Policy Paper No. 40)

This is, I would suggest, a rather 'romantic' view, the SDPing appears to be strongly driven and framed by the SMT and within the team by the Headteacher, although the plan is inflected by other inputs from the team and from other 'influential' or persistent staff or staff groups. However, the outcomes of the SDP process cannot simply be seen as an assertion of the management agenda. [Ms Rice commented 'agree with your use of "romantic." Its inconceivable that our school could ever emerge with a SDP that didn't absolutely reflect the head's priorities and requirements'.] This planning process also displays some of the discursive differences at work within the SMT and the tensions, 'in' the teachers and 'in' the school, between humanistic/substantive and technical/managerial orientations. These tensions are not played out in terms of a simple binary, as Yeatman presents them below, but are represented in different parts of SMT discussions or different stances by the same people in relation to different issues.

> This tension between technical and substantive aspects of professional identity is one that is imported into the public service as a result of its new classing. It is a cultural conflict between humanistic intellectuals (who have primarily a substantive orientation) and the technical intelligentsia. It is a tension which

exists between different sections of public servants (for instance social workers *vis-a-vis* finance officers) and it exists also *within* the consciousness of many middle and upper level public servants.

(Yeatman, 1993, p. 348; see also Spybey, 1984)[5]

Again viewed critically, the School Development Plan is a key method for the imprinting of core values, for the transmission and interpretation of external priorities, and concomitantly for excluding or containing rival 'ends' or values. It is a means of cultural engineering. The Plan as text comes to 'stand for' and symbolise the school. The SDP, as at Martineau, begins and ends with a closed 'openness', an appearance and rhetoric of open goal setting framed by a tight agenda of actual and possible goals – hence an SMT 'think tank' discussion at a Professional Development Day began from the Headteacher's question 'where are we going' and was quickly linked in the discussion to the need to be 'checking that policies are working' (2nd Deputy). Nonetheless, at least on paper, the SDP turns out to have some contradictory features. It illustrates the way in which residual substantive discourses can reassert themselves at particular moments or within particular events.

Thus, one theme that recurs in the SMT discussions around the SDP is a nascent tension between a set of instrumental, performance or behavioural priorities which relate to the reputation, image and market position of the school and a set of priorities concerned with equal opportunity. These latter, for example, emerged in the SMT professional development day 'think tank' discussion (3.12.94) in relation to the school's move away from mixed-ability grouping to setting; 'we have become de facto a streamed school' (2nd Deputy). 'Shall I be frank...I was initially strongly in favour of the move to setting, now I am not so sure, we have the same groups of students in bottom sets across the subjects and they are mostly afro-Carribean students from Streetly, and they dont identify with us as a school and they have become behavioural problems' (Acting Senior Teacher). As a result of this meeting three priorities were identified in the draft SDP: Curriculum, setting, and special needs.

The SDP was then discussed (to varying degrees), and responded to, in all the keys arenas of the staff, mainly Groups and Years, and individually through Diagnostic Windows; although the Head was clear in introducing the Diagnostic Windows discussion at SMT (2.2.95) that the exercise was 'consultative not negotiation' (Headteacher). But commenting on the windows the Head concluded that there was 'amazing support for priorities'; this meeting was over-shadowed by a discussion of potential of budget cuts[6] – see below. But it was also reported by the Head that through their 'diagnostic windows' Humanities [who else] noted that 'equal opportunities' 'had been neglected for some years' as a school priority and was 'absent from the SDP' and was not represented in a project partnership; this was supported by the senior deputy [the most frequent SMT articulator of humanistic/substantive concerns] 'I think that very strongly' (1st Deputy). Nonetheless, on both occasions, once raised, the equal opportunity concerns were swiftly reincorporated into the *evaluation* procedures of SDPing. They were translated into matters of technical discrepancy and the values dimensions of the issues involved remained buried. ['I see it as an example of the head's skill in managing a potentially contentious area' (Ms Rice)]. Thus, it was decided that setting be 'monitored'. Technical discourse and practices can nullify or deflect potentially 'discrepant' values and concerns in this way – but at the Staff meeting (13.2.95) both Equal Opportunities and Setting were announced as SDP priorities. A third example of the substantive-technicist tension, related to financial priorities, and arose in discussion of the school's response to the 1995 local government Spending Assessments and the possibility of a cut in the school's budget; top of the Headteacher/Finance Officer's 16 suggestions for budget saving was 'winding up ESOL', in order to save the school's 25 per cent contribution to its funding.

The further implementation (and reworking) of the SDP is also of interest. The curriculum priority became a 'curriculum review' focused around a costing exercise led by the Administrative Officer (significant in itself). This relates to an interest and concern expressed by the Head in the think tank – an analysis of the cost of delivering different subjects (staffing, resources, rooms, support etc.) – and appears to be quite different from the actual discussion, which concentrated on the need to take account of the Dearing Curriculum review. The setting priority was to come under the consideration of a Project Partnership [working party] to be lead by the Head herself. As regards the Equal Opportunity policy 'we have asked the Student Council, staff and the Governors to review our current Equal Opportunities policy' (Memo from the Head). This may be read in two ways; either as an opening up of the issue for widespread debate, or as a diffusion tactic. Without a Project Partnership formally there is no clear focus for the review (as compared to setting and curriculum) and the locus of the review is policy (text) not practice. Without a Project Partnership format there is no mechanism or pressure to systematically collect information or take evidence.

Again it could be argued that symbolism is as important as substance here. In at least two senses. The SDP symbolises and 'stands for' the corporate consensus of the school. It is a version of the school constructed for viewing, for inspection (internally and externally) (Ball, 1997). As the focus of activities around an 'agreed' set of priorities, the SDP is a touchstone of shared endeavour which displaces or subsumes differences, disagreements and value divergencies. As a process it also symbolises an openness, a participative system of management which allows for the widespread expression of views and concerns. In both cases commonality and openness are reduced to an event. They are synthesised and represented in a particular opportunity to participate. The implication may be that once passed the opportunity is lost.

Ofsteding

The third, and again inter-related technology at work in Martineau is that required by the arrival, at some point, of the Ofsted Inspectors. The school will come under scrutiny from the outside and has a lot to live up to. While Ofsteding is not imminent at Martineau, mention of Ofsted expectations were common. Senior staff attended meetings outside at which these expectations were spelt out and the book of inspection criteria was key reading among the SMT. The Ofsted expectations became a focus for common interest within the school and a rationale for regular monitoring and checking of 'systems' and procedures. This provided an interesting set of possibilities for displacement. The locus of power or blame for additional work, overbearing paperwork, meticulous surveillance was often located with Ofsted and not directly with the SMT who frequently positioned themselves as ciphers for outside pressures. But, as we have seen, the school management is also implicated in the generation of surveillance paperwork. And there is a further paradox here, embedded in what Lyotard (1979) calls 'the law of contradiction'. That is to say, increasing precision in the specification, collection and collation of indicators of performance requires greater and greater time which must be diverted away from the activities the indicators are supposed to represent (see Elliott, 1996, for a discussion of this).

What are important here are appearances; having policies for..., being seen to..., making sure the figures look good. Public performances like Ofsted inspections, local league table position, and artistic events in the school, dance, drama and music, all 'needed' to be carefully stage-managed to give the right impression. All this is oddly reminiscent of John Gray's comments on the Soviet system of planned production.

> the soviet manager has an incentive to comply with the quantitative production targets that he or she has been set, regardless of the quality of the products, and to fabricate statistics regarding output.
>
> (Gray, 1993, p. 68)

I observed several instances when the management of figures for public consumption was discussed. At a year heads' meeting with the senior deputy she talked about attendance figures and the need for 'the Judicious use of authorised absences' (1st Deputy). At a SMT meeting on Staffing analyses the Head asked the senior teacher responsible; 'How do we show the contact ratio in the best light' (for Ofsted). And in interview the Head of one subject talked about the very direct pressure coming from the Head to get the exam results presented in a particular way.

> I'm rushing around like a loony today trying to put together this exam results display she wants...I didn't have any data to do it with and I've had to collect that and then I've had to find a way of presenting the results in a way that looks good...GCSEs and A level results against the national average...that's presented us with some problems, because obviously with four subjects the results are uneven...I've found a way of doing the A-level that looks alright, I'm struggling a bit with the GCSE.
>
> (Hog 2)

On the one hand, the issue again is that of appearances – the simulacrumic organisation? An organisation for 'the gaze', and for avoidance of 'the gaze'.

> the propaganda of the system here, I don't know...I take results. yes, that sounds good, and I see what happens in my own classroom and...do I sometimes even get taken in by the whole machinery of...this is how wonderful we are...am I actually starting off on the completely wrong premise, are we not, have we got gaping holes, that me as part of the system has not been showing or has not noticed yet, or might notice if they weren't covered up, and are they being. I do feel a bit like that sometimes.
>
> (Main Grade Teacher 2)

> I've noticed now she's [the Head] getting much stronger on the development plan than she was recently...she's suddenly...well it's probably to do with OFSTED...but she's trying to...when I first came here it wasn't that important, she said I don't want it to be something...I just want it to be a document that people will look at...and they did look at priorities...but other things came along, like setting I mean things like that suddenly happened, and even though they're not on the plan.
>
> (Hog 1)

But the organisational responses to or anticipations of Ofsted do also have first order effects on teachers' practices and second order effects on students' school experience.[7]

In a different way from previously, substantive and technicist tensions, and compromises, are evident once again. As before, in some circumstances, in subtle and not so subtle ways, 'the sell' and image become more important than and/or are set over and against substantive issues. To reiterate, income maximisation, reputation enhancement and indicators of 'quality' do also have immediate effects upon professional practice. They reorient attention and effort and have the 'tendency to reduce the organisational entities involved to calculable and ultimately financial inputs and outputs' (Yeatman, 1993, p. 351). Yeatman suggests that professional, technocratic managers are 'teleological promiscuous' (p. 349); a system of means that can be turned to different ends without a primary concern for the ends in themselves.

> the Headteacher takes a genuine interest in the Arts and we have a very good position in the curriculum, compared with a lot of other schools, but the quid pro quo if you like is a thriving kind of public face and most of the teachers are actually committed to that, funnily enough...I mean they enjoy doing it, they get a lot out of it...but it's a lot of work, particularly to maintain the programme that they want...a problem with performance, the public performance in education, although it's educationally beneficial, very, for those students involved, it is inevitably selective, and what you're doing is concentrating on the able students...at the expense, well you haven't got the time to spend so much on others, although of course we try and get...other people involved as much as we can...the performance...we've got so much keenness to be involved, and if you're doing what we're doing at the moment...like we're going into a thing...with the National Theatre, organising a youth theatre project, we might be able to get...actually to the National...the pressure's on and we're not gonna pick kids that can't do it, and anyway one of the things that the Headteacher would say is, we don't want anyone who can't act involved really...she doesn't like people in the orchestra who can't play instruments, who've only just started, although you can get away with that to an extent, but she's against that, so there is that...I think it's unfortunate but performance is really aimed at...the kids who benefit are the ones who are able...
>
> (Hog 1)[8]

Conclusion[9]

In its investments in TQM and through the various other technologies of quality at work in the school Martineau is definitively positioned within the 'quality revolution' (Oakland, 1991); although I have tried to indicate that the new managerial discourse of quality is not the only one in play at Martineau. Nonetheless, quality does a great deal of micro-disciplinary work in the school but this work is part of a bigger picture, a larger transformation. The concept of quality forms 'part of a wider Conservative government-led project of change in the public sector' (Kirkpatrick and Martinez-Lucio, 1995, p. 8) and is also 'part of a larger ideological narrative and organisational strategy of the "enterprise culture"' (pp. 10–11).

However, it would be a mistake to represent Martineau as a paradigm case of a 'quality' organisation. Organisational control at Martineau is made up of bits of 'new' management (TQM, SDP) and entrepreneurism, and bits of 'old' management (hierarchy, separation of policy and execution), and educational commitments especially to the education of girls. These produce a heady mix of feminism, surveillance, initiative, competition and corporate culture. The staff are 'encouraged' to commit themselves to the corporate culture in exchange for a sense of virtuousness and resourcefulness but they are also subject to a considerable amount of micro-management – checking that reports were done etc. A mass of trivia which 'used up' time that might have been devoted to substantive discussion. The combination of innovations and changes stemming directly from government policies and from Martineau's responses to those policies – as a set of loquacious tactics of power – produces a set of contradictory experiences and responses from teachers. They are invigorated and empowered by new demands and skills, exhausted by additional work, and, in some cases, alienated from their selves and their colleagues. They make sense of their work lives typically very positively within these dissonances – although over-work and stress are commonly referred to in interviews. As one Senior Teacher explained:

> Mrs C never keeps still, just when you think you are comfortable we're off again – you cant be complacent. Its nice to be in an institution where you are constantly reviewing your practice and the practice of others.

This is no simple or simplistic story of oppressive power at work. Rather we see here the 'polymorphous techniques of power' (Foucault, 1981) and its effects of 'refusal, blockage and invalidation, but also incitement and intensification' (p. 11). Almost all staff speak proudly and positively about their school and compare it favourably with other schools they know of. The undoubted achievements of the school provide staff with a very strong sense of effectivity. Martineau is an inherently 'flexible' organisation where an 'organic' complementarity is established between 'the greatest possible realisation of the intrinsic abilities of individuals at work' and the 'optimum productivity and profitability of the corporation' (Du Gay, 1996, p. 71). What I am struggling to envision here is a sense of the social and personal costs and moral significance of all this. To draw attention to the rates of exchange in play within the 'quality revolution'. But importantly, flexibility and the apparatus which makes is possible, are part of a piece-meal improvisation, not a simple expressive or repressive relation between the individual and the state. Management at Martineau is a hybrid of old and new (fordist and post-fordist) management paradigms; reflecting perhaps the particular lcoal contingencies of a hybrid market/bureaucratic school system.

Put epigrammatically, the point here is that it is what makes Martineau good that makes it bad. What counts as good and bad, of course, rests on what qualities of institutions are valued. That valuing is to a great extent determined by the indicators and technologies of quality which are predominant at any point in time.

Acknowledgements

I would like to thank various colleagues who commented on this paper, particularly Judyth Sachs, I took at least some of their advice. The comments of two anonymous referees were also useful. I am also grateful to all the staff at Martineau for their tolerance over several years.

Notes

1   I use the term deliberately loosely here to signal both the school as object of the processes of reform, and the school as a reforming subject , in much the same way that we talk of a 'reformed' alcoholic.
2   The school effectiveness movement is an important source of performative technologies (and I have written about these elsewhere). See also Elliott, 1996.
3   Even here the debate turned more on the knock-on effects of other clusters' setting procedures on the constitution of Arts teaching groups at GCSE.
4   The mode of speech, the 'gabbling' are significant here. Both in indicating the creation of a response, based on previously unarticulated concerns, and the difficult, personal and emotional nature of the response.
5   We may need to think of a third kind of entrepreneurial intelligentsia, a form of professionality founded on the ethics, arts and skills of income maximisation, image manipulation and marketing.

6   The use of these individual written forms tended to fragment and personalise responses and discussions at meetings were stultified by the working through of fixed and pre-determined agenda items. The convenience and formalism of the management technique produced particular kinds of response.
7   These are explored elsewhere in our research writing.
8   Again I would suggest that the form of utterance is significant here. The broken pattern of speech suggests something of the speaker's discomfort and sense of dilemma.
9   This paper covers a lot of ground and works, for the most part, in terms of generalities. It lays out a set of arguments and concerns which need further development and more grounding in data. It is intended to provide an agenda of possibilities for thinking about school reform and reformed schools.

References

Ball, S. J. (1990) Management: A luddite Perspective. In: S. J. Ball (ed.), *Foucault and Education* (London, Routledge).

Ball, S. J. (1997) Performativity and Fragmentation in 'Postmodern Schooling'. In: J. Carter (ed.), *Postmodernity and the Fragmentation of Welfare – A Social Policy for New Times* (London, Routledge).

Berger, P. and Luckmann, T. (1966) *The Social Construction of Reality: A Treatise on the Sociology of Knowledge* (Harmondsworth, Penguin).

Broadfoot, P. (1996) Educational Assessment: The Myth of Measurement. In: P. Woods (ed.), *Contemporary Issues in Teaching and Learning* (London, Routledge).

Du Gay, P. (1996) *Consumption and Identity at Work* (London, Sage).

Elliott, J. (1996) *Quality Assurance, The Educational Standards Debate, and the Commodification of Educational Research*, paper presented at the Annual Meeting of the British Educational Research Association, University of Lancaster.

Foucault, M. (1981) *The History of Sexuality: An Introduction* (Harmondsworth, Penguin).

Gewirtz, S., Ball, S. J. and Bowe, R. (1995) *Markets, Choice and Equity in Education* (Buckingham, Open University Press).

Giddens, A. (1991) *Modernity and Self-Identity* (Cambridge, Polity).

Gordon, C. (ed.)(1980) *Power/Knowledge: Michel Foucault Selected Interviews and Other Writings 1972–1977* (Brighton, Harvester Press).

Gray, J. (1993) *Beyond the New Right: Markets, Government and the Common Environment* (London, Routledge).

Kanter, R. M. (1990) *When the Giants Learn to Dance* (London, Unwin Hyman).

Kirkpatrick, I. and Martinez-Lucio, M. (1995) Introduction. In: I. Kirkpatrick and M. Martinez Lucio (eds), *The Politics of Quality in the Public Sector* (London, Routledge).

Kitchener, M. and Whipp, R. (1995) Quality in the Marketing Change Process: the Case of the National Health Service. In: I. Kirkpatrick and M. Martinez Lucio (eds), *The Politics of Quality in the Public Sector* (London, Routledge).

Logan, L., Sachs, J. and Dempster, N. (1994) *Who said Planning was Good for Us?: School Development Planning in Australian Primary Schools* (Queensland, Griffith University).

Lyotard, J.-F. (1979) *The Postmodern Condition: A Report on Knowledge* (Manchester, NH, Manchester University Press).

Meadmore, D., Limerick, B., Thomas, P. and Lucas, H. (1995) *Devolving Practices: Managing the Managers*, unpublished paper, Queensland University of Technology, Red Hill.

Mortimore, P. and MacGilchrist, B. (1994) *School Development Planning*, Final Project Report to the ESRC (London, Institute of Education).

Oakland, J. (1991) *Total Quality Management* (London, Heinemann).

Peters, T. and Waterman, R. (1982) *In Search of Excellence* (London, Harper Row).

Rose, N. (1989) *Governing the Soul* (London, Routledge).

Spybey, T. (1984). Traditional and Professional Frames of Meaning for Managers, *Sociology*, 18(4): 550–62.

Strauss, A. (1987) *Qualitative Analysis for Social Scientists* (New York, Cambridge University Press).

Willmott, H. (1993) Strength is Ignorance; Slavery is Freedom: Managing Culture in Modern Organisations, *Journal of Management Studies*, 30(4): 215–52.

Yeatman, A. (1993) Corporate Managerialism and the Shift from the Welfare to the Competition State, *Discourse*, 13(2): 10–17.

CHAPTER 8

EDUCATIONAL REFORM, MARKET CONCEPTS AND ETHICAL RE-TOOLING

This chapter is a re-edited version of three papers: J. Oelkers (ed.), 'Education for profit and standards in education: the ethical role of markets and the private sector in state systems', *Futures of Education II: Essays from an Interdisciplinary Symposium*, Bern: Peter Lang, 2003; J. Oelkers (ed.), 'Market mixes, ethical re-tooling and consumer heroes: education markets in England', *Economy, Public Education and Democracy*, Zurich: Peter Lang, 2003; 'School-based management: new culture and new subjectivity', in *da investigacao as practicas: estudos de natureza educacional*, 2002, 3(1): 59–76

In this paper I address what may seem like two quite distinct tasks. First, I want to problematise and begin to clarify the use of the terms market, private and competition as applied to recent developments in the governance and delivery of education services in England. That is, I point to the need for a more precise and careful use of these terms; although I do this as a sociologist rather than an economist. Second, I shall explore some aspects and effects of the dual function of 'education markets' in England. That dual function being the re-making of consumer and producer behaviours and social relationships. So, in the second part of the paper I intend to concentrate on changes in the moral economy of society – an ethical re-tooling – legitimated, encouraged and made possible by the values of the market regime. The application of the market form to public sector institutions and exchanges encompasses, requires and legitimates a variety of changes that are structural and procedural but also brings in to play new values and new kinds of social relationships.

One source of research findings deployed here is a series of Economic and Social Research Council (ESRC) funded studies of local, lived markets at work conducted by colleagues and I (Gewirtz *et al.*, 1995; Ball, 1997; Ball *et al.*, 1998, 1999, 2000; Reay *et al.*, 2001; Vincent and Ball, 2001). Other research related to social polarisation in English school markets is also quoted in passing. Given the scope of the paper, the material used are merely illustrative snapshots or vignettes which offer a brief glimpse of complex and evolving social and economic processes.

The literature on social and educational markets in England is extensive but is also narrowly focused and primarily discursive. Political argument and policy-making have out-run research. Key components of the dynamics of the market are still relatively poorly understood, some market sectors are dramatically under-researched and some of the first and second order effects of the market (institutional change and social justice respectively) remain unexamined. In part, these lacunae exist because of the divisions within the field of academic practice. Sociologists, economists and philosophers ask their questions separately and differently and researchers tend to pursue their specialisms within particular sectors of the education system. Also using the term in its broadest sense it is easy to under-estimate the impact and spread of market forces in English education. In particular, the private sector is nibbling away eagerly at various points of education services provision.

English education markets

Sayer (1995, p. 96) makes the point about the term 'market' that: 'people slide unthinkingly between different uses of the term'. This is equally true of analysts, critics and advocates of the market form. Woods (2000, p. 220) makes the similar point that: 'Competition tends to be under-conceptualised in studies and discussions of choice and marketisation in school education, often being used interchangeably with "market." Terms such as "competitor" and "competitive" are called upon to describe relationships and actions as though their meanings are self-evident.' Furthermore, most discussion of education markets still remains at the level of 'abstraction', much less is written about the actual buyers and sellers, labour, constraints and regulations in lived, 'concrete' markets. I would suggest that any comprehensive attempt to review and describe the use of the market form in English education needs to address: competition, supply and demand, producer and consumer behaviour, privatisation and commodification, values and ethics and distributional outcomes. The account below ranges across these concepts with greater or lesser detail and precision.

To begin, four points of clarification. First, *the use of the market form in England is not by any means confined to the education system*. Parallel reforms, with greater or lesser rigour in each case, have been pursued in community services, health (although Labour has unpicked some parts of the market relations inserted here by the Conservatives, the role of GP fund holders as purchasers of hospital services remains), the prison service, the civil service, social housing, community and social care etc. In each case the design and tactics of reform and the market structures created have been different but based upon a common principle; that of avoiding or breaking down monopolies and the introduction of multiple providers. In each case the relative immediacy and nature of the consumer/producer exchange is different, as is, concomitantly the role of the state. In some respects the education market comes closest to a classic market. In the school, FE and HE sectors funding is per capita, budgets, more of less directly, follow choice.[1] In parts of the pre-school market the cash nexus is well established.

One aspect of classic markets which has been pursued with vigour by both Conservative and Labour governments across the public services is the generation and publication of market 'information' as a way of monitoring, comparing and increasing efficiency. That is, both information for providers on costs and for purchasers (sometimes the state, sometimes individual clients) on 'quality'. League tables, performance indicators and output measures abound (see below). However, this 'quality' information is not neutral. It has both intended and unintended consequences. Intended in terms of its steering effects. The Labour government in particular is keen on 'precision targeting' in education. The targets themselves and the publication of results in the form of League tables have very powerful disciplinary and reorganising effects in schools, colleges and universities. Unintended, in as much that there is plenty of evidence of various kinds of 'teaching to the test' activity in schools and schools and colleges compete to attract those students who are most likely to perform well in relation to outcome measures. Thus, paradoxically, the work that 'information' does has negative consequences for some consumers. Over-subscribed schools are reluctant to admit (and quick to exclude) those students unlikely to make a positive contribution to institutional performance or who incur higher than normal costs. For example, Bagley and Woods (1998, p. 781) found that Special Educational Needs (SEN) 'students and their parents are tending to find themselves marginalised and devalued in a competitive environment driven by instrumental values antithetical to their needs and priorities'. (In the USA and perhaps increasingly in the UK, the publication of surgeon's morbidity rates have led some doctors to refuse surgery to some high risk cases (*The Independent*, 7.09.99)). These are examples of what Le Grand and Barlett (1993, p. 214) call 'the problem of cream-skimming'. In other market regimes General Practitioners and social housing managers also have incentives to cream-skim as a way of reducing costs. Clearly in each social market there are implications for the social distribution of access which follow from these effects. Nonetheless, the publication of 'information' is supposed to introduce greater transparency into public organisations and to allow choosers/clients to make judgements about the service or provider which best suits their needs; although this makes very abstract and general assumptions about how choosers make decisions which are not supported by research (see Gewirtz *et al.*, 1995; Ball *et al.*, 2000) (see Chapter 10).

Second, the *market strategies* employed in each area of reform have been mixed. Four main strategies are evident; privatisation, contracting or 'out-sourcing'; finance partnerships; and insertion of direct or surrogate market relations. These categories overlap and inter-relate. In education, such things as school meals services, maintenance and cleaning, and supply teacher provision have been extensively privatised. Direct labour has been replaced by contract labour and in some instances existing levels of pay reduced and conditions of work changed. (The International Labour Organisation is carefully monitoring these effects.) Here schools now act as purchasers and service users. The devolution of budgets has given schools and colleges the freedom to choose among competing suppliers (in some cases including the Local Education Authority (LEA)). The state has abandoned its role here to private exchange relationships. Indeed, education services is now a booming sector of industry with considerable profits being made (see below). School inspections; the running of the parts of two local education authorities (Islington/Cambridge Educational Associates, Hackney/Nord Anglia), with more to come; and the running, so far, of one school (King's Manor, Guildford) have been contracted out to private providers. In the latter case, the contract includes a management fee and performance payments, paid by the LEA, to be divided between the school and the contractor 3Es. In addition, some-where between £1.2 and £1.7 million has been pumped into the school by the LEA and DfEE. Westminster local authority has recently 'out-sourced' its nursery provision, handing it over, amid much parent and union disquiet, to the Buffer Bears chain. Some major players in the 'education services industry' are involved in tendering for and winning these contracts (see below). Here the state or local government act as service clients and monitor contract fulfillment. Harden (1992), in his discussion of the 'Contracting State' suggests that one of the purposes of the use of contracts in public sector services is the pursuit of specific political objectives. He points out that the language of contract has a largely ideological significance.

Finance partnerships, mainly within what is called the Private Finance Initiative (PFI), involve public sector providers in the building and management of schools, hospitals, university plant etc. on a lease-back and management contract basis. Nineteen such deals had been agreed in the schools sector, as of May 2000, with 30 more in the offing. These include £220 m in Glasgow for the refurbishment of all of its 29 secondary schools, £80 m in Birmingham to rebuild 10 schools; and £49 m in Sheffield for capital works in 6 schools. Several PFI schools are already up and running, including those in Enfield, Hillingdon, Dorset and Hull. Again in some of these cases direct labour is replaced by the contractor and some commentators fear that at some point the contract labour may extend beyond catering, cleaning, maintenance, security etc. to the core tasks of teaching, research etc. Cohen (1999) estimates that Britain is committed to £84 billion of spending through the PFI.

Also under this heading of 'partnerships' come the Labour Government's Education Action Zones (EAZs) which were announced in June 1998 as 'the standard bearers in a new crusade uniting business, schools, local education authorities and parents to modernise education in areas of social deprivation' (DfEE, 1998). EAZs were one of New Labour's 'third way' policies – what Giddens (1998, p. 26) describes as 'an attempt to transcend both old style democracy and neoliberalism'. In 1999, the Secretary of State for Education David Blunkett talked about these policies having:

> Got schools and the community and local businesses working together in a way in which market forces and unfettered competition and 'hands-off leave it to the market' never do.
>
> (Speech, North of England Education Conference)

Nonetheless, only one of the first 25 EAZs, Lambeth, in South London, is fully managed by a private company CfBT (more accurately a 'not-for-profit') and active participation by business elsewhere in EAZs is extremely variable, Power and Gewirtz (2001) argue that the actual participation of business representatives in EAZ activities is almost entirely marginal, symbolic and trivial. Even so, the DfEE are very keen to highlight, indeed perhaps exaggerate, the extent of business involvement in its statements and press releases and Gewirtz (1999, p. 150), like Harden in relation to contracts, argues that the role of businesses in EAZs 'may make the privatisation of local school provision more widely acceptable and thus play an important legitimating role'. The significance of such 'incremental legitimation', the shift from the unthinkable, to the possible, to the obvious, should not be under-estimated.

'Business' is also involved in forms of partnership in three other initiatives introduced by the Conservatives and maintained by Labour; CTCs (City Technology Colleges), secondary Specialist schools, and Academies. The latter require a minimum of £50k in sponsorship monies before specialist status and matching funds are forthcoming. The government aims to establish 1,500 by 2006 – half of all secondary schools. Significantly in terms of issues discussed later the social characteristics of the intake of these schools appears to differ slightly from that of their 'comprehensive' counterparts – they admit a smaller proportion of students receiving free schools meal. The Secretary of State for Education has also signaled the intention to establish 200 City Academies along the lines of the US Charter Schools; (by the end of 2004 there are 17 academies open and 42 more in the process of being set up. Sponsors include Bristol City football club, SGI Ltd, a venture capital company, Dixons, HSBC Education Trust, Saga Holidays, InterCity Companies, and a variety of religious organisations and Foundations. Some academies are former CTCs.) Each of these policy initiatives, in different ways, are examples, albeit very limited, of Labour's Third Way. At least that element of the Third Way which breaks with traditional social democratic thinking to reposition 'the state as guarantor, not necessarily provider' (White, 1998, p. 3) nor the financer, of opportunity goods (see below).

There are three contrasting interpretations in play in relation to these 'partnerships'. One, articulated by business and government, represents business involvement as a benign and altruistic commitment to improving education. Another, articulated by many grassroots educators involved in these schemes, stresses that in practice, with a few exceptions, businesses show little real interest. A third, presented by critical analysts of various kinds, like Harden and Gewirtz, argues that these schemes are devices for legitimating greater 'for profit' participation of business in educational provision. As Hatcher (2000, p. 71), puts it 'Education Action Zones are test-beds for future developments in education, including much closer involvement by the private sector in schools'. More dramatically, Monbiot (2000) sees these developments as part of 'the corporate take-over of Britain'.

Increasingly education services are being targeted by business as an area of expansion where considerable profits are to be made (see below). The 'education services industry' as a whole is growing fast 'at impressive rates of 30% per annum' according to the City Finance House Capital Strategies (quoted in *Guardian Education*, 20.6.2000, p. 2). According to the Guardian report, the UK Education and Training Shares Index has since January 1996 significantly out-performed the FTE-SE 100. The smart money is getting into 'education services'.

> In five years time it [private sector management] will be very big. There's a great need for people with proven track records and ideas.
> (Kevin McNeany, Chairman of NordAnglia, quoted in the *Times Education Supplement*, 26.3.99)

The final strategy is the one that has received most attention from critics and researchers. That is *the insertion of competition and choice processes into public sector provision*. Changing the relationships between providers and between users and providers and tying budgets much more closely to patterns of choice within these new relationships. Public sector providers are expected to act like businesses and in a business-like way. These are sometimes called 'quasi-markets'. 'They are "markets" because they replace monopolistic state providers with competitive independent ones. They are "quasi" because they differ from conventional markets in a number of ways' (Le Grand and Barlett, 1993, p. 10). In particular Le Grand and Barlett argue that these are 'quasi-markets' because they are not seeking to maximise profits and their ownership structures are unclear. (As we have seen already these caveats do not apply to all aspects of current education markets.) Such 'quasi-markets', though designed differently, have been inserted into all of the four main education sectors in England – pre-school/nursery, primary/secondary, further and higher education. Although again, there is a different mix of strategies at work in each sector. Furthermore, the policy of market insertion can also be read pursuing 'the general goal of reorganising, maintaining and generalising market exchange relationships' (Offe, 1984, p. 125). Certainly within the UK, a political discourse which privileges 'the private' (in a variety of senses), but particularly in terms of efficiency and quality, is becoming well established.

In many ways the *market-mix* is most dramatic and diverse in the pre-school or 'educare' market. This is a highly segmented and classed market. Very briefly, the day-care nursery 'industry' currently looks something like this: a state sector which caters mainly for socially deprived families; a large number of independent, owner-run, private nurseries, including many Montessori schools; a voluntary sector of 15,500 nurseries, play-groups etc. (most affiliated to the Pre-School

Learning Alliance) – a recent PSLA survey conducted by National Opinion Polls indicated that 20 per cent of these (3.5 k) reported that they were 'threatened with closure'; there are 425,027 places with registered child minders and 110,000 nannies; increasingly state primary schools are opening nursery departments; and, in addition, the existing private chain providers of child care and nursery schooling are expanding fast, new providers are entering the market, and US firms are beginning to make inroads into the UK[2] (see Ball and Vincent, 2000 for more detail).

Two further and related points. One is that like many other markets – energy, transport, agriculture etc. – *education markets are highly regulated*. This does not distinguish them from other kinds of markets. Each of the four education sectors is regulated in a slightly different way. The other is, related to this, that under both the Conservatives and Labour the use of the market, as a form of attrition, discipline and regulation, has not meant the abandonment of other traditional forms of state intervention. Indeed the creation of dispersed market conditions has been accompanied by greater centralisation of control over education and a distinct rise in the scope and number of interventions. There is in effect a dual process involved of decentralisation/centralisation; which drastically reduces the role of local government and local democracy. Whitty, Power and Halpin (1998, p. 35) see such developments as reflecting 'a broader tendency for liberal democracies to develop along the lines of what Gamble (1988) has called the "strong state" and the "free economy"'. The interventions crudely take two main forms. They are either prescriptive or performative.

The former, under Labour, tend to be highly technocratic, based on a black-box, input/output approach to educational planning. The inputs take various forms, most obviously and pertinently such things as '*a greater focus on mental arithmetic*', '*the new literacy hour*', and a '*dedicated numeracy hour*'. There is also the '*strong focus on effective teaching in literacy and numeracy*' in '*improved teacher training*'. Schemes of work are being written for National Curriculum subjects. The Numeracy and Literacy Hours are 'supported' by step-by-step manuals and how-to do-it videos. The National Literacy Scheme development and training work has itself been privatised, and was initially run by a large not-for-profit provider CfBT. These schemes, as indicated already, require individuals and institutions to constantly demonstrate their capacity to perform according to explicit criteria or organisational targets. For schools, these range from setting '*national numeracy targets*' – '*75 per cent of all 11 year-olds to reach level 4 for 2002*' – to the publication of league tables of primary school National Test results and the continuing use of raw GCSE performance scores as the basis for Local League Tables of secondary schools.

Putting all of these elements together some of the complexity, messiness and pervasiveness of education markets in England should be apparent; although there are some common underlying principles at work. Under New Labour, the thrust of marketisation has not diminished and indeed through the notion of partnerships and greater use of contracting the extent and pace of privatisation has increased. However, the emphasis on regulation, performance evaluation, target-setting and direct specification has also increased.

Each of the four education sectors have different market configurations and these configurations have their effects locally and specifically. For the most part, to understand the workings and effects of these education markets we must look to local studies of actual market dynamics. This is somewhat less true of higher education but even here there are 'local' and 'cosmopolitan' institutions and the concentration of student's choices within regions and localities has increased markedly in recent years but so has the development and promotion of 'Borderless Higher Education' in the UK (and elsewhere), as part of an international strategy to increase the numbers of fee-paying overseas students attending UK universities. Education markets develop within specific spatial, social and historical circumstances.

The studies in which I have been involved over a number of years have all been located in the London region. This is a market setting which is contiguous and fiercely competitive. It is also, in all four sectors, a highly segmented market. That is, it is made up of a number of smaller homogeneous markets which respond 'to differing preferences attributable to the desires of consumers' (Wedel and Kamakura, 1998, p. 7). The segmentation is produced by the social and cultural bases of choice, by the constraints of cost, and by forms of selection. The market power of both individual providers and consumers differs considerably. The ability of many of the selective and over-subscribed institutions to 'sell' their services does not depend on the behaviour of other providers. In the school, college and HE sectors, the market hierarchy of institutions produces and articulates with an 'economy of student worth' (Ball *et al.*, 1998). In many localities the result is an increased social polarisation in the state system.[3] That is, a greater separation and concentration of class and ethnic groups in different schools. Lauder *et al.* (1999) report the same outcome in New Zealand; as do Fuller *et al.* (1996) in the US.

In many ways we have as yet no well developed language with which to describe and analyse the 'marketisation' of education. Concrete developments have out-run the scope of our usual conceptual tools. Forms of analysis which were developed in research on state systems of education are no longer adequate. We need to build a new social economics of education; but if it is possible at all, such an enterprise must be able to encompass both the new forms and processes of educational delivery and the changes in values and culture that the dynamics and disciplines of the market bring about. It is to the latter I now move.

A new civility and a new moral economy

Markets, of any kind, are complex phenomena. They are multi-faceted, untidy, often unpredictable and both creative and destructive. Theories of and arguments for the benefits of the market form are diverse, and political support for 'choice and entrepreneurship' comes from a variety of directions. Certainly the application of the market form to the pubic sector in the UK has been driven by an assortment of theoretical and ideological commitments and projects; none of which translate into policy straightforwardly and directly. Policy is rarely like that. Furthermore, it is important to recognise that political support for and the political effects of the market do not simply rest of simple economism. The market form carries with it a political vision which articulates a very individualistic conception of democracy and citizenship. This is captured very powerfully in Margaret Thatcher's oft quoted dictum: 'There is no such thing as society. There are individual men and women and families' (Woman's Own 31 October 1987). Morrell (1989, p. 17) suggests that this remark 'is an expression of the Hayekian view in epigrammatic form'. Morrell goes on to note that 'Hayek is particularly concerned to argue against the involvement of the Government in the life of the citizen'. As signalled earlier I want to give emphasis to some of the social and political implications of the market for the relationships between Government and the lives of citizens.

> The imagination of civil society was the precondition and product of modernity. And so, just like the challenges associated with modernity, it too could not avoid a most bleak destiny after the initial burst of enthusiasm.
>
> (Tester, 1992, p. 176)

The point about Thatcherite neo-liberalism lies not so much in Margaret Thatcher's denial of the existence of society as in her radical and bleak re-imagining of civil society. This rests upon a re-vivified competitive individualism and a new kind of consumer-citizen – the politics of temptation and self-interest – to which her denial alludes. The disciplines and effects of the market are rooted in a social psychology of 'self-interest, that great engine of material progress, [that] teaches us to respect results, not principles' (Newman, 1984, p. 158). Concomitantly, wealth creation is understood as the final measure of success, as against other qualities or accomplishments, and together these are the basis for a 'highly individualistic form of capitalism' (Heelas and Morris, 1992, p. 3). All of this is rooted in the twin values of risk and responsibility. Marquand (1988) sees the market solution as a broad change from a culture of equitable consumption to one of profitable production or a shift towards what he calls an 'unprincipled society'.

The new market citizenry is animated and articulated by Hayekian conceptions of liberty, 'freedom from' rather than 'freedom to', and the right to choice. 'Consumer democracy' is thus both the means and end in social and economic change. 'Active' choice will ensure a more responsive, efficient public sector and 'release' the 'natural' enterprising and competitive tendencies of citizens, destroying to so-called 'dependency culture' in the process. Replacing the latter with the virtues of self-help and self-responsibility (see Deem *et al.*, 1995, chapter 3). This is constitutive of a new or re-worked moral economy. It brings with it a new set of values and a new ethical framework within which relationships and practices in public sector organisations are re-worked.

The other side of all this, in a sense, for the labourers in these new markets, material and personal interests are intertwined in the competition for resources, security and esteem and the intensification of public professional labour – the changing conditions of and meanings for work.[4] The discretionary power of the professional is dissolved or subordinated. In this respect, in education one key aspect of the 'steering' effects of judgement and comparison is a gearing of academic production and reproduction (research and teaching) to the requirements of national economic competition and the concomitant 'de-socialisation' of educational experience (Ball, 2000). Shore and Wright (1999) describe this situation as an 'audit culture' and see modern audit systems and techniques functioning 'as "political technologies" for introducing neo-liberal systems of power'(p. 558).

Living markets!

Let us look a little more closely now at some of the effects of this new economy as they are realised in lived education markets. Two snapshots from different pieces of research. Our research within the post-16, Further Education marketplace demonstrates some of the destructive force of competitive relations (Macrae *et al.*, 1997; Ball *et al.*, 1999). The 1992 Further and Higher Education Act delivered to the government, via the funding arrangements of the Further Education Funding

Council (FEFC), indirect but decisive control of the growth and cost of the FE sector, through the mechanism of 'convergence' of funding. That is, by standardising and reducing the unit of resource within the sector, by adopting unit-costing on the one hand, and by rationalising sites, through accommodation audits and the Hunter building survey – in order to limit capital expenditure on property and estates. The FEFC regime has required of incorporated institutions that they expand their student numbers by 28 per cent (from 1992/93 to 1996/97) while reducing the level of per capita funding to achieve an annual 'efficiency gain'. In effect institutions must run faster in order to stand still. 'An active expansionist market has been created' (Foskett and Hesketh, 1996, p. 2); but there is an over provision of supply in many localities. By 1995 most incorporated institutions had failed to reach the expansion targets (FEFC, 1995). Some estimates suggest that up to 200 Colleges might close or merge.

The particular local market we studied is urban and 'overlapping'. It can be characterised in a variety of ways, it might well be thought of, as one respondent described it, a 'cut throat' market (Deputy Head of Faculty), or put another way, from the point of view of the providers; 'its grow or die' (Student Counsellor). This 'cut throat' quality, which is generated in part by the proximity of multiple providers, in part by the entry of new players and in good measure by the FE funding regime itself, is evidenced in a variety of ways in the market behaviour of and relationships between providers. This market, like those of commerce, rewards shrewdness rather than principle and privileges the values of competition over 'professional' values.

> Look, its dog eat dog nowadays in (local area). We'll take them on intermedi-ate (GNVQ) courses even if we know they are not up to it because if we don't, someone else will...And we know they will drop off. So we encourage them to transfer routes and we are providing strong pastoral support to ensure that we retain them for a second bite at the apple. We've got to hold our numbers you know (laughs)...
>
> (FE college tutor)

Self-interest predominates and steers decision-making. On the one side, there is the self-interest of consumers who 'choose', and on the other, that of producers aiming to thrive, or at least survive (Gewirtz *et al.*, 1995). As one respondent put it – 'the College cannot afford to take a moral stance' (Deputy Head of Faculty). The 'cut-throat' quality and values of competition increasingly in play in this market encourage and make possible a particular variety of actions and tactics. Various respondents identified new forms of inter-institutional behaviour emerging in the context of market relations. The relations between institutions and the 'frames of meaning' evident in stakeholders' perspectives reflect and embody the intensity and desperation, and uncertainties and vulnerabilities of the post-16 market. Competition produces a new set of social relationships. Generally, as one respon-dent explained: 'because of all this competition institutions are isolated in a way that wasn't the case in the days for example of the ILEA (Inner London Education Authority – abolished by the Conservatives), where there was a lot of networking, there was a lot of co-operation, now there seems to be a sort of suspicion' (Bracebridge College). And part of this is 'Spying' – industrial espionage:

> Oh yes we always spy, we have to I'm afraid (laughing). Yes and quite often peo-ple will go out and find out how they are recruiting and what their recruitment

procedures are like and what their induction procedures are like, what their enrolment procedures are like because it can always be a trying time for students so often people will go along and see what other Colleges are like, see how well they do and see if we can learn anything from them.

(Deputy Head of Faculty)

which ranges from keeping an eye on the activities of competitors, to 'poaching' and direct copying. 'It doesn't matter any longer that the College down the road has always run that course very successfully.'

(Student Counsellor)

The culture of the market works both in and on competing organisations. From the inside, on the one hand, there is the development on new cultures, and the attempt to encourage the commitment of 'workers' to the competitive interests of their school or college or university, that is to instill 'a love of product or a belief in the quality of the services' provided (Willmott, 1992, p. 63). From the outside, the twin and related demands of performance (results or league table position or value-added) and recruitment (income maximisation) discourage rational co-operation between organisations and encourage a de-socialised sense of loyalty which can also mean privileging institutional needs above those of students. On the other hand, ratings and rankings are also deployed to drive institutional 'improvements' by fostering competition between groups or departments internally, team affiliations and older loyalties can be exploited to bring about changes which might otherwise be resisted. Here is Bronwyn, a year 4 teacher quoted in Woods *et al.*'s (1997, p. 69) account of *Restructuring Schools, Reconstructing Teachers*, talking about a forthcoming Ofsted inspection.

> I will cope with it, I will take it on board, I will do all the things I'm meant to do and I'll scrape and bow and I will back the headteacher to the hilt and I will back the school to be hilt. I won't let anybody down. But secretly inside myself I'm very, very angry that we're being made to go through this but I'm not quite sure at whom I'm being angry. It is the Government? Is it the LEA? It must be the Government.

Bronwyn takes on both the responsibility of doing what seems necessary to support her headteacher and her colleagues, while dealing with her anger 'secretly inside'. These judgements take on a life of their own. We are responsible for and to *them*. The second example focuses on the position of the 'student-consumer' in post-compulsory education markets. One of the particular characteristics of the post-compulsory market place in many localities in England is the competition between 11–18 schools attempting to retain students in their Sixth Form (16–18) and Colleges of Further Education seeking to attract the same students into their courses and programmes. Within the new funding and competition framework of post-16 education Colleges of Further Education find themselves 'banned' from visiting 11–18 schools to talk about their courses and brochures from competing institutions are not made available to students in 11–18 schools. FE Colleges accept students onto inappropriate courses in order to maximise recruitment. The tactics of both types of provider offer very pointed examples of the inroads of market ethics and 'the chameleon values of the new economy' (Sennett, 1998, p. 26) into the decision-making and priorities of teachers and managers. In this situation professional responses and market responses are very different. A *professional response* would give priority to the needs and interests of students by providing maximum information upon which to base a choice between 'staying-on' at school or going to College. The decision to restrict access to and dissemination of information about alternative providers and to encourage students to 'stay-on' at school even if this might involve them following courses which they are likely to fail, in order to boost numbers and therefore income, is a *market response.*

> The *Opportunities for Choice* document is vetoed by the Head, is has full page spreads on Colleges of FE. We do not take students to 6th form Colleges but we do take them to Careers 2000. There are limits to the flow of information... The bums on seats argument is used all the time to close down issues. And sometimes we shoot ourselves in the foot. Like I have 23 in my A-level English class and it changes the mode of delivery. We probably contravene the Trades Description Act in what we sell as A-levels. A small number of those students may be should not be there, should not be encouraged to stay on to do those kinds of courses.
>
> (Head of Careers, 11–18 GM school)

The two responses, professional and market, and the values on which they are based and which they foster are summarised in Table 8.1. These represent two largely oppositional conceptions of the nature and purposes of education – but they also relate to more general visions of the nature of society and citizenship. Interestingly aspects of both sides are deployed in different Labour education policies – leaving schools to work through the contradictions created; although some aspects of comprehensive values are now eschewed in Labour's policies. In real terms, the pure forms of these values sets are probably hard, but not impossible, to find in practice. More appropriately there is a continuum of positions and a process of 'values drift' over time which effects most schools. That is, both a discursive shift and shift in practices from left to right (Gewirtz *et al.*, 1993; Gewirtz *et al.*, 1995). Schools (and colleges and universities) start from different positions on the continuum of drift and they move at different rates across it. New 'leadership' or changed circumstances may mean that new values are

Table 8.1 Professional and market values

Professional values	*Market values*
Individual need (schools and students)	Individual performance (schools and students)
Commonality (mixed-ability classes/ open access	(Setting/streaming/selection differentiation/hierarchy/exclusion)
Serves community needs	Attracts 'clients'
Emphasis on resource allocation to those with greatest learning difficulties	Emphasis on resource allocation to the more able
Collectivism (co-operation between schools and students)	Competition (between schools and students)
Broad assessments of worth based upon varieties of academic and social qualities	Narrow assessments of worth based on contributions to performativity
The education of all children is held to be intrinsically of equal worth	The education of children is valued in relation to costs and outcomes

embraced with urgency and alacrity, while other institutions will hold out longer, will have a clearer sense of values integrity or are pushed along only reluctantly and slowly (Ball *et al.*, 1994). For some institutions there particular market position may insulate them from competitive pressures. Nonetheless, it is very difficult to escape entirely from the discursive and financial incentives which drive the movement; although different local contexts and market configurations and existing 'collaborative local relations' (Woods, 2000, p. 236) do effect the pace of movement. As Woods points out 'competition has a dual character, structural and agential, each of which is variable' (p. 236).

Now, again very briefly, I want to visit the other side of the market exchange relationship and consider the perspectives of choosers. This will be a rather cursory look at some complex issues. The use of the market, particularly by middle-class choosers appears to be decisively related to the changing economic and labour market context and a concomitant shift in what (Parkin, 1974) calls the 'rules of exclusion'. In a reworking of Parkin, Brown argues that this economic restructuring is accompanied by changes in the 'rules of exclusion' and the movement from *meritocratic* to *market* rules.

> Meritocratic rules of exclusion are based on the ideology of individual achievement in an 'open' and 'equal' contest...However, meritocratic rules do not assume equality of outcome, only that inequalities are distributed more fairly...The increasing importance of '*market*' rules reflects the political ascendancy of neo-liberalism since the late 1970s in Britain and the United States...The Right were able to claim a moral legitimacy for the market system in education dressed in the language of 'choice', 'freedom', 'competition' and 'standards'.
>
> (Brown, 2000, p. 639)

The implication is that these 'rules' operate ideologically and discursively at both a family and political level within the 'new politics of uncertainty', in particular via the 'virtues' of competitive individualism. Lane (1991, p. 318) citing Deutsch, suggests that 'as a psychological orientation competitiveness embraces' cognitive, motivational and moral aspects. The fears, concerns, perspectives and strategies of social subjects are re-interpolated within a discourse of responsibility and a 'vocabulary and ethics of enterprise' – 'competitiveness, strength, vigour, boldness, outwardness and the urge to succeed' (Rose, 1992) – a new 'style of conduct' in (Weber, 1915/48) terms. There is within this, a move away from what Nagel (1991) calls 'the duality of standpoints' and sees as the basis for practical ethics and moral stability – that is the nexus of equality and partiality – towards the ethics of the 'personal standpoint' – the personal interests and desires of individuals. The egalitarian concerns of the 'impersonal standpoint' are deprecated and obscured. Personal motives are given absolute preference over impersonal values. Within the 'market rules of exclusion' both consumers and producers are 'encouraged', by the rewards and disciplines of 'market forces', and legitimated, by the values of the personal standpoint, in their quest for positional advantage over others. Jonathon (1990, pp. 118–19) makes the important point that: 'We are not all libertarians, and do not all endorse the moral values and political commitments that underpin consumerism. Nonetheless, once legislative change gives schooling a libertarian, consumerist context, the pressure is on parents to behave, in their children's interest, as if they endorsed such values, which that is the case or not'. Within this context cultural, economic, political and social assets of families are mobilised 'to stay ahead of the race' (Brown, 2000, p. 637). One facet of this has been a loss of support among the new middle classes for efforts to democratise education and social policy and the progressive experimentation in educational methods and pedagogies.

Across the public sector, the market is now taken to be the one best way to achieve organisational arrangements and the various insertions of the market, 'the private' and 'business', practically and discursively, as described in the first part of the paper, constantly reinforce this hegemony. The market has 'paradigmatic status' for 'any form of institutional organisation and provision of goods and services' (du Gay, 1991, p. 41). All of this does not simply bring about technical changes in the management of the delivery of educational services – it involves changes in the meaning and experience of education, what it means to be a teacher and a learner. It changes who we are and our relation to what we do, entering into all aspects of our everyday practices and thinking – into the ways that we think about ourselves and our relations to others. It is changing the framework of possibilities within which we act. This is not just a process of reform, it is a process of social and ethical transformation. Without some recognition of and attention within public debate to the insidious work that is being done by the market, in these respects, we may find ourselves living and working in a world made up entirely of contingencies, within which the possibilities of authenticity and meaning in teaching, learning and research are gradually but inexorably erased.

Notes

1 The 5–18 private school system is always of course market driven and competes with parts of the state system and accounts for up to 8 per cent of national enrolments and 30 per cent of enrolments in some London Boroughs. The private sector is itself highly segmented.

2 For example: Asquith Court has 73 nurseries (5 new sites this year) across England, Ireland, Scotland and Wales, plus 10 independent preparatory schools. Teddies has 18 nurseries in London and the south west; Kids Unlimited (KU) has 32 nurseries nationwide, and 2 after school clubs. KU specialise in workplace nurseries and are 'due to have 50 by 2001' (Chain Manager 2). Careshare in Scotland has 10 nurseries and is opening one a year. Buffer Bears which began as a British Rail workplace provider now has 21 nurseries, and now also has a partnership with the Home Office. Child Base Nurseries has 21 sites (see *Small Talk* – June 2000 'In just over 18 months, with the addition of the two Badgers Nurseries, the total places with Child Base would have increased 40 per cent'; www.childbase.com). Jigsaw, also specialising in workplace sites, has 20 nurseries currently, 8 more scheduled and a total of 45 scheduled for the end of 2001. Nord Anglia has 9 nurseries and is 'actively seeking' new sites (*Nursery World*, 11.05.2000). Nord Anglia also runs a chain of language schools, 13 independent schools, does Ofsted Inspections and has a teacher supply business and as noted above recently took over the running of a London LEA. In the 6 months to February 2000 Nord Anglia profits were up 156 per cent and turn over up 11 per cent to £31.2 m. Nord Anglia, according to its Chairman, is keen to take over the running of small primary schools (*Guardian*, 22.06.2000). All the providers compete with the nursery departments of state and private schools. Many are bottom heavy as a result, loosing children to nursery classes and schools at 3+. The National Day Nursery Association's (NDNA) chief executive expressed fears that if this trend continues day nurseries will become 'baby farms'.

3 Although in others segregation has been reduced (see Noden, 2000)

4 The pressures of performativity and performance act in particular and heightened forms on those academic workers who are without tenure or on fixed-term contracts.

References

Bagley, C. and Woods, P. A. (1998). School Choice, Markets and Special Educational Needs. *Disability and Society*, 13(5): 763–83.

Ball, S. J. (1997). 'On the Cusp': Parents Choosing between State and Private Schools. *International Journal of Inclusive Education*, 1(1): 1–17.

Ball, S. J. (2000). Performativities and Fabrications in the Education Economy: Towards the Performative Society. *Australian Educational Researcher*, 27(2): 1–24.

Ball, S. J. and Vincent, C. (2000). *Educare and EduBusiness: the Emergence of an Imperfect and Classed Market in Child Care Services?* BERA Conference, Cardiff.

Ball, S. J., Bowe, R. and Gewirtz, S. (1994). Competitive Schooling: Values, Ethics and Cultural Engineering. *Journal of Curriculum and Supervision*, 9(4): 350–67.

Ball, S. J., Macrae, S. and Maguire, M. M. (1998). Race, Space and the Further Education Marketplace. *Race, Ethnicity and Education*, 1(2): 171–89.

Ball, S. J., Maguire, M. M. and Macrae, S. (1999). Young Lives at Risk in the 'futures' Market: Some Policy Concerns from On-going Research. In F. Coffield (ed.), *Speaking Truth to Power*. Bristol: The Policy Press.

Ball, S. J., Maguire, M. M. and Macrae, S. (2000). *Choice, Pathways and Transitions Post-16: New Youth, New Economies in the Global City*. London: Falmer Press.

Brown, P. (2000). Globalisation of Positional Competition. *Sociology*, 34(4): 633–54.

Cohen, N. (1999). How Britain Mortgaged the Future. *New Statesman*, 18 October.

Deem, R., Brehony, K. and Heath, S. (1995). *Active Citizenship and the Governing of Schools*. Buckingham: Open University Press.

du Gay, P. (1991). Enterprise Culture and the Ideology of Excellence. *New Formations*, 13: 45–61.

Foskett, N. H. and Hesketh, A. J. (1996). *Student Decision-Making and the Post-16 Market Place* (Report of the Post-16 Markets Project). Southampton: Centre for Research in Education Marketing.

Fuller, B., Elmore, R. F. and Orfield, G. (1996). *Who Chooses? Who loses? Culture, Institutions and the Unequal Effects of School Choice*. New York: Teachers College Press.

Gamble, A. (1988). *The Free Economy and the Strong State*. London: Macmillan.

Gewirtz, S. (1999). Education Action Zones: Emblems of the Third Way? In H. Dean and R. Woods (eds), *Social Policy Review 11*. Social Policy Association.

Gewirtz, S., Ball, S. J. and Bowe, R. (1993). Values and Ethics in the Marketplace: The Case of Northwark Park. *International Journal of Sociology of Education*, 3(2): 233–53.

Gewirtz, S., Ball, S. J. and Bowe, R. (1995). *Markets, Choice and Equity in Education*. Buckingham: Open University Press.

Giddens, A. (1998) *The Third Way: The Renewal of Social Democracy*. Cambridge: Polity Press.

Harden, I. (1992). *The Contracting State*. Buckingham: Open University Press.

Hatcher, R. (2000). Profit and Power: Business and Education Action Zones. *Education Review*, 13(1): 71–7.

Heelas, P. and Morris, P. (eds) (1992). *The Values of the Enterprise Culture: The Moral Debate*. London: Routledge.

Jonathan, R. (1990). State Education Service or Prisoner's Dilemma: The Hidden Hand as a Source of Education Policy. *British Journal of Educational Studies*, 38(2): 116–32.

Kenway, J. (1990). Class, Gender and Private Schooling. In D. Dawkins (ed.), *Power and Politics in Education*. Lewes: Falmer Press.

Kenway, J., Bigum, C. and Fitzclarence, L. (1993). Marketing Education in the Post-Modern Age. *Journal of Education Policy*, 8(2): 105–22.

Lane, R. (1991). *The Market Experience*. Cambridge: Cambridge University Press.

Lauder, H., Hughes, D. *et al*. (1999). *Trading in Futures: Why Markets in Education Don't Work*. Buckingham: Open University Press.

Le Grand, J. and Barlett, W. (eds) (1993). *Quasi-Markets and Social Policy*. Basingstoke: Macmillan.

Macrae, S., Maguire, M. and Ball, S. J. (1997). Competition, Choice and Hierarchy in a Post-16 Education and Training Market. In S. Tomlinson (ed.), *Education 14–19: Critical Perspectives*. London: Athlone Press.

Marquand, D. (1988). *The Unprincipled Society: New Demands and Old Politics*. London: Jonathan Cape/Fontana Press.

Monbiot, G. (2000). *Captive State: The Corporate Takeover of Britain*. London: Macmillan.

Morrell, F. (1989). *Children of the Future*. London: Hogarth Press.

Nagel, T. (1991). *Equality and Partiality*. Oxford: Oxford University Press.

Newman, S. (1984). *Liberalism at Wits End*. Ithaca, NY: Cornell University Press.

Noden, P. (2000). Rediscovering the Impact of Marketisation: Dimensions of Social Segregation in England's Secondary School 1994–99. *British Journal of Sociology of Education*, 21(3): 371–90.

Offe, C. (1984). *Contradictions of the Welfare State*. London: Hutchinson.

Parkin, F. (1974). Strategies of Social Closure in Class Formation. In F. Parkin (ed.), *The Social Analysis of Class Structure*. London: Tavistock.

Power, S. and Gewirtz, S. (2001). Reading Education Action Zones. *Journal of Education Policy*, 16(1): 39–51.

Power, S. and Whitty, G. (1998). Market Forces and School Culture. In J. Prosser (ed.), *School Culture*. London: Paul Chapman.

Reay, D., Davies, J., David, M. and Ball, S. J. (2001). Choices of Degree and Degrees of Choice. *Sociology*, 35(4): 855–74.

Rose, N. (1992). Governing the Enterprising Self. In P. Heelas and P. Morris (eds), *The Values of the Enterprise Culture*. London: Routledge.

Sayer, A. (1995). *Radical Political Economy: A Critique*. Oxford: Basil Blackwell.

Sennett, R. (1998). *The Corrosion of Character: The Personal Consequences of Work in the New Capitalism*. New York: W.W. Norton.

Shagen, S., Johnson, F. and Simkin, C. (1996). *Sixth Form Opportunities: Post Compulsory Education in Maintained Schools*. Windsor: NFER/Nelson.

Shore, C. and Wright, S. (1999). Audit Culture and Anthropology: Neo-liberalism in British Higher Education. *The Journal of the Royal Anthropological Institute*, 5(4): 557–75.

Tester, K. (1992). *Civil Society*. London: Routledge.

Vincent, C. and Ball, S. J. (2001). A Market in Love? Choosing Pre-school Child Care. *British Educational Research Journal*, 27(5): 633–51

Weber, M. (1915/48). Religious Rejections of the World and their Directions. In H. H. Gerth and C. Wright Mills (eds), *From Max Weber*. London: Routledge and Kegan Paul.

Wedel, M. and Kamakura, W. A. (1998). *Market Segmentation: Conceptual and Methodological Foundations*. London: Kluwer.

White, S. (1998). *Interpreting the 'Third Way': A Tentative Overview*, Deparment of Political Science, Cambridge, MA: MIT.

Whitty, G., Power, S. and Halpin, D. (1998). *Devolution and Choice in Education*. Buckingham: Open University Press.

Willmott, H. (1992). Postmodernism and Excellence: The De-differentiation of Economy and Culture. *Journal of Organisational Change and Management*, 5(1): 58–68.

Woods, P., Jeffrey, B., Troman, G. and Boyle, M. (1997). *Restructuring Schools, Reconstructing Teachers*. Buckingham, Open University Press.

Woods, P. A. (2000). Varieties and Themes in Producer Engagement: Structure and Agency in the School Public-Market. *British Journal of Sociology of Education*, 21(2): 219–42.

CHAPTER 9

STANDARDS IN EDUCATION
Privatisation, profit and values

This chapter is a re-edited version of three papers: J. Oelkers (ed.), 'Education for profit and standards in education: the ethical role of markets and the private sector in state systems', *Futures of Education II: Essays from an Interdisciplinary Symposium*, Bern: Peter Lang, 2003; J. Oelkers (ed.), 'Market mixes, ethical re-tooling and consumer heroes: education markets in England', *Economy, Public Education and Democracy*, Zurich: Peter Lang, 2003; 'School-based management: new culture and new subjectivity', in *da investigacao as practicas: estudos de natureza educacional*, 2002, 3(1): 59–76

I believe that schools will be putting all their back office services [once mainly supplied by LEAs] into the private sector within a few years ... Everyone will want to earn a reasonable margin.

> (Graham Walker, Head of Arthur Andersen's government services department, quoted in the *Times Education Supplement*, 09.01.98)

The UK Labour Government's Education Action Zones (EAZs) which were announced in June 1998 as 'the standard bearers in a new crusade uniting business, schools, local education authorities and parents to modernise education in areas of social deprivation' (Department of Education and Employment 1998). Michael Barber, then Head of the Standards and Effectiveness Unit, in a speech to the North of England Education Conference described the initiative as 'a great opportunity for the business world to play a direct and central role in the management and leadership of Education Action Zones'. He talked about being impressed with US experiments, referring to the involvement of Procter and Gamble in Cincinnati schools, who 'had halved the money spent on red tape in one school district', and citing a California project sponsored by management consultants Arthur Andersen.

In 2002 Arthur Andersen, one of the world's largest accounting and management consultancy firms became virtually defunct, torn apart by scandal and mal-practice following their involvement in the destruction of Enron financial records and misrepresentation of the accounts of other companies.

> David B. Duncan, the accounting partner in charge of work for Enron Corp., told a jury he feared lawsuits and an inquiry by the Securities and Exchange Commission when he instructed his employees at Arthur Andersen LLP to destroy documents last fall.
>
> (*Washington Post*, 15.05.02, p. E04)

Arthur Andersen's humiliation and the prosecution of several senior employees was quickly followed by the revelation that Worldcom, another Arthur Andersen client, had fabricated its accounts to the extent of $3.9 billion in the 15 months to the end of March 2002. Also, in July 2002 Xerox admitted overstating its profits by $1.4 billion between 1997 and 2000 and making 'improper payments over a period of years' in an effort to push up sales in its Indian offshoot. AOL Time Warner is also having its accounts investigated by the Securities and Exchange Commission, as are Adelphia Communications, Peregrine Systems, Network Associates. KMart, Tyco International, Duke Energy, Global Crossing and Dynegy among others. The executives of software companies Quintus, Unify and Legato are facing charges of accounting fraud, as are the founder and executives of Waste Management, another Arthur Andersen client. The SEC described the latter as charged with 'one of the most egregious accounting frauds we have ever seen' (*Independent on Sunday*, 30.06.02, p. B3). These are examples of the consequences of what is referred to as 'aggressive accounting' and are evidence of what Alan Greenspan, chairman of America's Federal Reserve Bank, has described, without any apparent sense of irony, as the 'infectious greed' that had gripped much of American business.

In this paper I want to consider the implications of Worldcom and Arthur Andersen for education and educational standards. The questions to be addressed here, but not answered, are; what standards do we want from our schools? What are the standards below which we will not let our schools fall? That is, what ethical standards? Do we want companies like Arthur Andersen involved in running or advising or providing services to schools? The argument for private involvement in state schooling is a simple one; that the profit incentive and competition generate forms of practice that improve efficiency and raise performance. Even if that is the case, is that all that comes from private sector participation? What of the cultural and ethical changes that accompany the profit incentive? Should we be worried that a hidden moral curriculum may be transmitted directly or indirectly as a result? In other words, what does the private sector 'teach' in our schools and colleges? Is this part of what Saltman (2000) calls the 'collateral damage' of corporatisation or the 'creative destruction' of capitalism, whereby, in this case, profit incentives and business values destroy service values and professional ethics?

For me, in the context of increasing political enthusiasm for business participation in the public sector, the odd thing, the most disturbing thing, is that these issues are not even being raised or discussed. Are there no special concerns to be addressed about the role of ethics in 'privatised' educational institutions? Not simply, that is the ethics of classroom conduct but the ethical conduct of those who sit in the offices of schools. Perhaps though there is nothing special about education that should raise concerns. Perhaps education can no longer be considered as a separate moral sphere, as any different from politics or the economy. Let us begin from there.

Currently the inter-relationships of state, economy and education in developed countries are particularly tight and take a particular form. Indeed, without wanting to dispense entirely with the important differences between the 'continental' and 'anglo-saxon' versions of this relationship, we are beginning to see the wearing away of nation-state specific policy-making, in the arena of global market competition and human capital development. Specifically, there is an ongoing collapse of the social and economic fields of education into a single, over-riding emphasis on policy-making for economic competitiveness. That is, an increasing neglect or sidelining (other than in rhetoric) of the social purposes of education. Cowen (1996) writes about this as the 'astonishing displacement of "society" within the late modern educational pattern'. Education is increasingly subject to 'the normative assumptions and prescriptions' of 'economism', and 'the kind of "culture" the school is and can be' (Lingard *et al.*, 1998, p. 84), is articulated in its terms. This is now sometimes referred to as 'joined up government', within which skills formation or what Ainley (1999) calls 'learning policy' is the driving and integrating principle. As Green (1996) notes this kind of emphasis within different nation states has resulted, certainly across Europe, in the development of a common policy language which is articulated in government reports.

Within all of this, the state 'acts as a "strategic trader" shaping the direction of the national economy both through investment in key economic sectors and in the development of human capital' (Brown and Lauder, 1996, p. 5) – basic, vocational and higher educations are various forms of such capital development. Along side this, agents of the economy act to influence the state to take responsibility for and bear the costs of its interest in an appropriately prepared workforce. The distribution of this cost bearing varies between countries – at least currently.

Even so, within this generic model, the policy convergences to which I am referring, the relationships between the agents of the economy and education are (or have been) for the most part indirect, relationships are mediated by the state, although such agents may be represented at various points in the infrastructure of educational design and delivery. In other words, there are various *recontextualising fields* (Bernstein 1996) within this general set of relationships and within these fields. Economistic discourses are appropriated and transformed into 'pedagogic discourse' (or messages of dissonance are 'sent back' to the fields of knowledge production within the state or elsewhere). This involves a *de-location and re-location* which typically allows for an 'ideological transformation according to the play of specialised interests among the various positions in the recontextualising field' (Bernstein, 1996, p. 116). The point is, or has been, to keep the educational *in* the vocational. There has been a degree of orderliness in all of this, the relationships involved are institutionalised and the fields are, or were, relatively distinct.

Within English speaking education systems, and increasingly also others these kinds of distinct and tidy relationships and demarcations between the economy, the state and education are breaking down. Recontextualisation is weakening as boundaries between fields become ever more porous. As part of this there is a fundamental reworking of the role of the state in relation to the public sector as a whole. A shift '... from the state as provider to the state as regulator, establishing the conditions under which various internal markets are allowed to operate, and the state as auditor, assessing their outcomes' (Scott, 1995, p. 80) or what Neave (1988) describes as the emergence of 'the new evaluative state'. Increasingly, the state sets the policy goals and a performance and target framework within which providers of different sorts (public, private or voluntary) act as deliverers (see below on the OECD). This is 'steering at a distance' by the 'small state'. The same model and relationships are presented as being the most appropriate structures and roles for organisational management within delivery institutions with a central 'core' for policy, audit and regulation and separate 'service delivery units' (OECD, 1995; Thomson, 1998).

Crucially it is a mis-recognition to see these reform processes and the changing role of the state as simply a strategy of de-regulation, as they are sometimes referred to, they are processes of *re-regulation*. Not the abandonment by the State of its controls but the establishment of a new form of control; what Du Gay (1996) calls 'controlled de-control'. As stressed by the OECD, a new relationship of the State to the public sector is envisaged, especially in 'exploring alternatives to direct public provision' and making service provision 'contestable and competitive' – 'Corporatisation and privatisation are important policy options in this context' OECD, 1995, p. 9). In the UK, these options have been pursued with particular vigour.

First under the Thatcher and Major Conservative governments, and subsequently by Labour in the terms of the 'Third Way', through the use of surrogate or 'quasi-markets'; contracting-out/out-sourcing; privatisation; and various forms of public/private partnership (see Chapter 8), to which I shall return in a moment.

Clearly, also the OECD is not the only multi-lateral agency participating in the construction and dissemination of 'new' models of governance, and new relationships between education and the economy (see also Chapter 5). At the level of global policy the changes in the welfare regimes in many developed and developing countries and the attendant transformation of public sector organisations are part of a process of alignment with the 'inviolate orthodoxy' (Stiglitz, 2002, p. 43) espoused by organisations like the OECD, World Trade Organisation (WTO) and the World Bank and the further opening up of these economies to global capitalist institutions. The World Bank and International Monetary Fund (IMF) in particular are firmly committed to what is sometimes called the Americanisation of the world economy. Their staffs are primarily American, their headquarters are in the US, and most of their funding comes from the US Treasury. 'Building free capital markets into the basic architecture of the world economy had long been, in the words of the US Treasury's (then) Deputy Secretary Lawrence Summers "our most crucial international priority"' (Wade, 2001, p. 125). Joseph Stiglitz, reflecting on his time as Chief Economist at the World Bank, describes major decisions taken by the IMF as 'made on the basis of what seemed a curious blend of ideology and bad economics, dogma that sometimes seemed to be thinly veiling special interests' (p. xiii). Rikowski (2001b) also points out that education is a core element of the WTO agenda and outlines the WTO strategy for opening education up to corporate capital. The forces of globalisation, both economic and political, are antithetical to the social market economics of the welfare state. As John Gray forcefully argues:

> Social democrats in Britain and other European countries who imagine that the social market economics with which they are familiar can be reconciled with a global free market have not understood the new circumstances in which advanced industrial societies find themselves.
>
> Social market economies developed in a particular economic niche. They are bound to be transformed or destroyed by the industrialisation of Asia and the entry into world markets of the post-communist countries.
>
> (Gray, 1999, p. 79)

The changing role of the social democratic state is part of a broader transformation. The shift from responsibility for delivery to responsibility for measurement and audit opens up the possibility of two further policy moves. First, that having shuffled off the role of having responsibility for direct delivery of services, it becomes possible for the state to consider a variety of service, deliverers – public and private. This introduces contestability, and competition between potential deliverers, and involves the use of commercial models of tendering and contracting. Second, it also becomes possible to consider alternative models of funding, and the participation of private funders in the development of the public sector infrastructure. In the UK, what is called, the Private Finance Initiative (or Public Private Partnerships) is an example of this. An example which has attracted the attention of the World Bank as a model for developing countries to emulate.

There are two ends to this change of relationship between state, public sector and private interests. Which brings us to the second aspect of boundary weakening. At one end there are changing conceptions of governance, changing constraints on state effectivity, changing political attitudes to the public sector. At the other end is the eagerness of private providers to become involved in the 'education services industry' (and other public sector services), and that eagerness is based on the potential for profit. This is part of what Offe (1984) calls the dissemination of the commodity form and this in its current phase is part of 'the story of the changing face of capital as it redesigns institutions and people for profit' (Kenway and Bullen, 2001, p. 187). Or as Leys (2001, pp. 3–4) puts it: 'In the search for survival, firms constantly explore ways to break out of the boundaries set by state regulation, including the boundaries that close non-market spheres to commodification and profit-making'. Commodification encompasses both an attention to the naturalisation of changes which are taking place in the everyday life of our production and consumption activities and more general processes of capitalism and its inherent crises and instabilities which underpin the search for new markets, new products and thus new sources of profit. In fetishising commodities, we are denying the primacy of human relationships in the production of value, in effect erasing the social. 'Our understanding of the world shifts from social values created by people, to one which is pre-given' (Shumar, 1997, p. 28) and within which '... everything is viewed in terms of quantities; everything is simply a sum of value realised or hoped for' (Slater and Tonkiss, 2001, p. 162).

In the UK, the 'education services industry' as a whole has been growing fast 'at impressive rates of 30% per annum' according to the City finance house Capital Strategies (quoted in *Guardian Education*, 20.6.00, p. 2). According to the Guardian report, the UK Education and Training Shares Index has since January 1996 significantly out-performed the Financial Times Share Index (FTE-SE 100). Similar spectacular growth in private sector education services is evident in the USA. The smart money is getting into 'education services'.

> In five years time it [private sector management] will be very big. There's a great need for people with proven track records and ideas.
>
> (Kevin McNeany, Chairman of NordAnglia, quoted in the *Times Education Supplement*, 26.03.99)

This is part of the expanding social universe of capital, the 'restless development of capital' (Rikowski, 2001a), if you like. And education is increasingly big business and I mean *big*. Many of the major players in the Education Services Industry are associated with multi-national corporations and venture capitalists.

Ensign is a joint venture of Tribal Group and Group 4. Group 4 runs private prisons and prisoner transport. Ensign bids for contracts to intervene in poorly performing local authorities. Its subsidiary *PPI* does school inspections. Tribal also do Internet based teacher training and information management (see below on ethics). *Serco* founded in 1929 has a turnover of £455 million, it operates public bus systems in Australia, runs various air-traffic control systems around the world, and numerous local authority waste disposal services, and is the UK's largest school Inspection contractor. Through its acquisition of QAA it has consultancy contracts for Walsall and Bradford LEAs. Serco, with Barclay's Bank, the construction company John Laing, Innisfree and 3i investors, is a major share holder in *Octagon Healthcare* which is funding one of the UK's largest PFI schemes, the Norfolk and Norwich Hospital.

Having very crudely sketched this backdrop of changing roles and relationships, and I am fully aware that each and every one of the changes I have adumbrated here require much fuller exposition, I now want to move on to look inside these changing relationships and specifically at some of the implications for education of its 'privatisation'. However, in the sense I am using the term here, it is important not to confuse 'privatisation' with traditional forms of private education – that is, education provided by Trusts, Charities and Church organisations. That confusion is highly misleading when we begin to think about the sorts of models and practices, and relationships which are being imported into state education systems from the commercial sector. It is also the case that when I refer to privatisation I want to extend the term to encompass both the participation of private companies in education service delivery and the use of models of private sector relationships – markets, forms of profit and loss – in and between state-run organisations. The purpose here is to begin to develop a more general understanding of the role of the 'private' in education which might allow us to move beyond the description of individual 'cases' of privatisation; although that remains an important task at this time. That is to say, I want to draw attention to the economic, political, cultural and discursive dimensions of privatisation in education specifically, and the public sector more generally.

Within the UK, four main 'privatisation' strategies are evident; direct privatisation either by 'selling off' or 'buying in' services which were previously provided by the state – teacher supply, school catering or school inspections would be examples; contracting or 'out sourcing', that is the use of private companies to run public sector schools, parts of Local Education Authority (LEA) services, and government programmes (like the National Literacy Scheme); finance partnerships like Private Finance Initiatives (PFI) and Public Private Partnerships (PPP); and the insertion of direct or surrogate market relations into service delivery relationships, between state providers and providers and their clientele – like the use of parental choice and school competition. This latter is what Glenn Rikowski refers to as 'Capitalisation'; that is, 'making public schools/universities into value/commodity producing enterprises' (Rikowski, 2003). They 'become institutionally rearranged on a model of capitalist accumulation' (Shumar, 1997, p. 31). However, these categories increasingly overlap and inter-relate. And I want to complicate things further, as signalled above, by using the term privatisation in another sense and a sense that I want to concentrate on here. That is, to refer to a profound and pervasive cultural/ethical/procedural re-engineering of public provision. Or in other words, the dissemination of the discourse of the private within the system of state education, and some of its effects. In this latter usage of the term, I mean discourse to refer to that which can be said and thought and who it is that can speak and with what authority. Discourses also embody meaning and social relations, they constitute both subjectivity and the flow of power. Discourses gets things done, accomplish real tasks, gather authority (Said, 1986, p. 152).

The discourse of the private inserts itself into the ways in which public sector organisations relate to and deal with their clientele, parents and students. Concomitantly, clients are incited by this discourse to take up consumerist relations with providers. As public sector organisations are required to act in a business-like way they are increasingly indistinguishable in their practices and social relations (internally and externally) from their private counterparts. State and private schools advertise themselves side-by-side in the same commercial publications. Again, as part of a bigger story, these advertisements stand alongside a range of other commercial services for children, and the demarcations between education and entertainment, knowledge and commodities are increasingly blurred (see Kenway and Bullen, 2001). Choice of school for many families is part of a complex series of choices involved in the construction of individual educational trajectories and the production of children as educational subjects. The education market is a diffuse, expanding and sophisticated system of goods, services, experiences and routes – publicly and privately provided. For many parents, educational opportunities are sought for their children through a made-up mix of state and/or private institutions, and paid-for add-ons, like educational toys, parental tasks, tutoring, commercial activities (Tumbletots, Crescendo, StageCoach, Perform etc.), and sources of information and advice (School and Higher Education Guides). Parenting itself is increasingly serious, demanding and professionalised – and is now widely taught by both state agencies and commercial organisations.

I want to reiterate that there is a dual logic in these developments of privatisation in education, and elsewhere in the public sector. There are structural changes in the private/public/state relationship. And cultural/ethical changes in the conduct of public sector 'business'. That is, 'privatisation' plays its part in the formation of dispositions towards the commodity, and the aesthetics of consumption, and competitive self-interest – giving emphasis to the 'personal standpoint' in ethical terms (Nagel, 1991). Privatisation does not simply change how we do things, it also changes how we think about what we do, and how we relate to ourselves and significant others. This is the case both for providers and for consumers. For practitioners or 'service delivery staff', all of this stands over and against the aesthetics of welfare professionalism. The notion of 'service', the investment of the self within practice, and professional judgement related to 'right' decisions, are devalorised.

Taking this further, the ubiquity of the discourse of the private is manifest in another sense. That is, in evidence of the replacement of service ethics with the ethics of competition. What I mean by this is the ways in which the incentives and constraints and the culture and values of privatisation and competition act to rework educational practitioners and consumers of education as ethical subjects. As I have argued before market relations bring into play, and legitimate, a set of ethical practices which can be distinguished from those of welfare professionalism – they constitute a different ethical regime if you like (see Gewirtz, Ball and Bowe, 1993; Ball, 1998; Gewirtz and Ball, 1999; see Chapter 6). Little systematic attention has been paid to this new ethical regime despite an increasing number of examples of the effects of this regime within individual and institutional practices, by both state and private providers.

Let me offer some examples of the ethical regime of privatisation in practice, mostly taken from the UK press – and a similar selection could be culled from the US media – and these are by no means representative of systematic or exhaustive coverage. I have many more examples. In the space available I can only use these examples as illustrations; each one raises a variety of issues and could be discussed at some length. In some cases these illustrations point to the direct importation of private sector sensibilities into the education system.

> 'Disgrace of Training Firm' Contracts continued to be placed with a training firm over four years, even though only four trainees out of 276 gained a qualification.
>
> (*Times Educational Supplement*, FE Focus, 27.07.01)

Tribal Group Ensign withdrew its bid for the education contract in Waltham Forest after it was reported that it had offered payments of £5,000 if the bid was successful to two consultants working for PPI, a private firm recently acquired by Tribal and hired to provide management support in Waltham Forest.

(*Guardian Education*, 26.06.01, p. 3)

One way of thinking about the ethical issues arising here is a kind of blurring. That is a blurring of ethical positions – what is 'right' is no longer clear – related to a blurring of moral spheres, and a consequent tension between being business-like and being concerned about students' needs and interests (see Ball, 1998). For example, Thomas Telford, a City Technology College (Whitty *et al.*, 1993), is clearly a model of good practice for the Labour government, not simply as a high performing school but also in its entrepreneurism. Indeed Thomas Telford makes considerable profits. One way that it does this is by selling to other schools and colleges a curriculum package which in effect offers a way of getting more examination passes for less work. Is this cheating or is it creative thinking?

Schools lured by Short cut to top exam scores

The number of pupils taking vocational ICT exams is due to rocket with teaching materials now being marketed by Thomas Telford and Brooke Weston City Technology Colleges. More than a quarter of secondary schools have bought Thomas Telford's materials, earning the school £3 million. Brook Weston's website flashes up a page which proclaims 'GNVQ ICT Intermediate – 4 GCSEs equivalent'... Alan Smithers, of Liverpool University said: 'Some heads have told me they planned to run this course because of the impact it would have on the league tables'.

(*Times Educational Supplement*, 18.10.01)

Here then, curriculum knowledge is commodified in a very direct sense and furthermore what this reflects and disseminates is a new form of social relations between schools and a new relationship of schools to knowledge, a relationship which is no longer articulated in terms of the public good, and certainly not in terms of knowledge for its own sake. Thomas Telford school is probably the best known example of the taking up of these opportunities (made possible by the 1998 and 2002 Education Acts) and there are a small number of others entering this new school-to-school market. However, these legal developments formalise processes already at work within the education market place. A couple of examples from Further Education:

Oh yes we always spy, we have to I'm afraid (laughing). Yes and quite often people will go out and find out how they are recruiting and what their recruitment procedures are like and what their induction procedures are like, what their enrolment procedures are like because it can always be a trying time for students so often people will go along and see what other Colleges are like, see how well they do and see if we can learn anything from them.

(Deputy Head of Faculty)

which ranges from keeping an eye on the activities of competitors, to 'poaching' and direct copying. It doesn't matter any longer that the College down the road has always run that course very successfully.

(Student Counsellor)

And from School:

> A Deputy Head at Hazlett School explained that without the presence of
> an LEA Advisor and with 'delegated budgets, League Tables – I think people
> in schools now have one eye on recruitment, and you know, the reputation of
> their school against another school. So that if I had something going on as a
> Head of Department, I might be reluctant to share it with the school next door
> because there's a sense that I've got one up on them.'

The Excellence in Cities Co-ordinator (the LEA Officer charged with over-seeing
this government initiative) reported that:

> one Head actually said to me, we're not going to show you a copy of our plans
> and whatever, we're not going to have you stealing our good ideas, and taking
> them round to other schools.

Within such enactments of social and moral relations we are witnessing, I would
suggest, what Richard Sennett calls the 'corrosion of character' – the erosion of
responsibility and trust (Sennett, 1998) – and the antagonism of functionality and
morality (Wittel, 2001, p. 71).[1] Furthermore, all of this is the precondition of the
knowledge economy, or what Lyotard calls 'the merchantilization of knowledge'
(p. 51). Knowledge is no longer legitimated through 'grand narratives of specula-
tion and emancipation' (p. 38) but, rather, in the pragmatics of 'optimization' – the
creation of skills, or of profit, rather than ideals.

What the examples above point to is the beginings of the social dissolution of
public service education. In the context of competitive and contract funding, there
is an individuation of schools *and* of the school workplace – more and more
short term projects, freelancers, consultants, agency-workers, fixed term contracts,
skill-mixes – these new kinds of workers are 'with' and 'for' the organisation,
rather than 'in' it as Wittel (p. 65) puts it. Social ties within educational work
become ephemeral, disposable, serial, fleeting – we live as Bauman terms it in 'the
age of contingency' (Bauman, 1996). This further contributes to the dissolution of
moral obligations and welfare based ethical frameworks.

The Head of Thomas Telford has also indicated that his College is interested in
being involved in the setting up of other new schools, specifically Walsall City
Academy. The Head of Thomas Telford is quoted as saying that this is 'just the
beginning' (*Daily Telegraph*, 22.03.01). Already, 3Es, the non-profit company
which runs Kingshurst CTC has won management contracts to run two state
schools in Surrey. Again, in miniature, we see the restlessness and expansionism of
the 'capitalist spirit'.

One general type of practice which has direct parallels with the private sector
examples with which I began, is what we might call, borrowing from Enron
and Arthur Andersen, 'aggressive accounting' for performance. That is the misrepresentation, fabrication or straightforward distortion of performance figures. As
school and college reputations and budgets and teachers' pay, are increasingly tied
to student 'outcomes' then the relationship between 'profit' and performance is
increasingly susceptible to the temptations of creative accounting.

> 'Fiddling the Figures to get the right results', documents a whole variety of
> 'fiddles' employed routinely by schools to massage various of their perfor-
> mance indicators. A deputy head from London is quoted as saying: 'I dont feel
> any shame about it at all. And that's the truth. Everybody does it'.
>
> (*Guardian*, 11.07.00)

Alert Over dubious test Coaching Tactics

The Qualifications and Curriculum Authority will also beef up rules on test security following a number of high profile cases where headteachers have been accused of cheating.

(Times Educational Supplement, nd)

The Deputy Head's comments here are particularly telling. Indicative perhaps of the ethical changes which are taking place here. He feels no shame – the implication is that the ethical environment is not such that these actions attract criticism or stigma – in part at least because 'everybody does it'. It is commonplace, a now normal way of accommodating to the pressures of performance. But it is not just that logic of the profit incentive is at work here. The UK government also sets an example in 'massaging' its own figures. The rendering of educational processes into metric form, into comparable performances also serves another important function, in that it renders educational processes into a form which is more readily privatised – that is, into a contractable form, into a *form for cost and profit calculation*, into a version of education which can be reduced to a commercial exchange based on output indicators, which can then be monitored and evaluated by the state. The use of metrics, targets, linked to incentives and sanctions, and the constant collection and publication of performance data, embeds instrumentality in everything we do. And in the process, what we do is all to often emptied of all substantive content. Increasingly, we choose and judge our actions in terms of effectivity and appearance. Beliefs and values are no longer important – it is output that counts. Beliefs and values are part of an older, increasingly displaced discourse of public service.

The insertion of competition and the fostering of entrepreneurial behaviour also generates tensions and difficulties in relationships between institutions. There are contradictions between rhetorics of co-operation and the realities of market advantage which seem to come as a surprise to ministers and school inspectors.

Inspectors highlight specialist Failings

Most specialist schools are failing to fulfil the key objective of sharing their advantages with their neighbours, school inspectors say.

(Times Educational Supplement, nd)

Specialist schools are reluctant to share innovations and ideas with other local schools – their competitors for recruitment – preferring to 'co-operate' with more distant schools that are no threat to their competitive edge. There is a certain naiveté by government in the notion that it is possible to pick and choose among private sector values. Competition and business advantage, entrepreneurism does not sit easily with the notion of 'sharing' – unless of course, as above, 'sharing' means selling. Greed one might say is contagious, and as values and incentives change, so do priorities, interests and commitments.

Teachers demand share of Profits

Private firms which take over the running of state schools should give teachers a share of their profits, the National Association of Headteachers said yesterday.

(Guardian, 30.05.01, p. 7)

As noted above, education markets have two sides to them – supply and demand. The values of the market place are increasingly evident among parents attempting to get the school they want for their child – their own competitive edge! (see Ball, 2003, for an extended discussion).

Parents 'cheated' to win assisted places

(*Daily Telegraph*, 2.07.00)

With the competition for places becoming increasingly intense, parents will resort to all sorts of ruses to get their offspring through the gates.

(*Independent*, 22.03.01)

Within the discourse of privatisation parents are expected to act as 'risk managers'; 'committed and opportunistic actions' (Giddens, 1991, p. 132) are required to ensure the best for your child in relation to an increasingly competitive and unpredictable future and resulting dilemmas about how to act for the best. Risk, uncertainty and anxiety, in part produced by the market, are also themselves market opportunities – spaces to be filled – parenting itself is increasingly commercialised, as noted already. In the context of risks and anxiety (obesity, anorexia, unemployment, drugs, child abuse, poor schools, dangerous streets, air pollution, food additives) the prudential parent can no longer take on trust either state services or their own intuitive parenting as adequate in providing the kind of childhood which will ensure their child opportunities, advantages, happiness or well-being. To paraphrase Beck 'In the individualised society' the parent must learn, 'on pain of permanent disadvantage, to conceive of himself or herself as the centre of activity, as the planning office with respect' to the 'biography, abilities, orientations, relationships and so on' of their children (Beck, 1992, p. 55). Where they are possible, such investments in the child can later be realised in terms of social advantage. But, as Beck acknowledges, such conditions of responsibility give rise to a new form of inequality 'the inequality of dealing with insecurity and reflexivity' (p. 98). These conditions call up particular resources and skills which are unevenly distributed across the population and erquire a 'strategic morality' which Beck and Giddens now see as dominating society and social life – in other words 'putting the family first' (Jordan *et al.*, 1994; Ball, 2003).

The culture of the market 'is so organised that incompetence and weakness cannot be compensated for' (Douglas, 1994). Within these new conditions of responsibility, the failings of the child are increasingly blamed on the parents and there is a constant stream of media panics around irresponsible parenting which constitute a highly normative and covertly classed view of parental responsibility – 'cloning the Blairs' as Sharon Gewirtz calls it (Gewirtz, 2001).

Conclusion

The two related points I have been trying to develop in this paper are that 'privatisation' in education is increasingly complex and increasingly totalising and that it inserts a new ethical framework into educational practices of a whole variety of kinds. I have attempted to indicate the ubiquity of 'capital' as a set of lived relations which is increasingly embedded in every day consciousness and routine practices in education – those of teachers, researchers, lecturers, students and parents – 'the omnipresent language and logic of the market' (Saltman, 2000, p. ix). Discursively private participation is quickly becoming established as 'the one best way' to think about the future of public sector delivery. The values of the private sector are celebrated, but selectively, and the translation of values and culture into ethics is barely attended to. Saltman (2000) sees the hegemony of the market and the profit incentive as displacing the struggle over values, which is an essential condition of democracy. What we are seeing here is a kind of collapse of the boundaries between moral spheres, which follows the breakdown of the demarcations between public and private provision and between social and opportunity goods. This is, I have suggested, a threat to the standards in our schools – ethical standards. It raises simple but profound questions about what we want from education *and what we do not*.

Note

1   Although Giddens might see these conditions as the bases for 'active trust'.

References

Ainley, P. (1999). *Learning Policy*. London: Macmillan.
Ball, S. J. (1998). Ethics, Self Interest and the Market Form in Education. In: A. Cribb (ed.) *Markets, Managers and Public Service? Occasional Paper No. 1*. London: Centre for Public Policy Research, King's College London.
Ball, S. J. (2000). *Market Mixes, Ethical Re-tooling and Consumer Heroes: Education Markets in England*. International Symposium 'Economy, Public Education and Democracy'. Monte Verita, Ascona – Centro Stefano Franscini: Switzerland.
Ball, S. J. (2002). *Class Strategies and the Education Market: The Middle Class and Social Advantage*. London: RoutledgeFalmer.
Bauman, Z. (1996). Morality in the Age of Contingency. In: P. Heelas, S. Lash and P. Morris (eds) *Detraditionalization: Critical Reflections on Authority and Identity*. Oxford: Basil Blackwell.
Beck, U. (1992). *Risk Society: Towards a New Modernity*. Newbury Park, CA: Sage.
Bernstein, B. (1996). *Pedagogy Symbolic Control and Identity*. London: Taylor and Francis.
Brown, P. and Lauder, H. (1996). Education, Globalisation and Economic Development. *Journal of Education Policy* 11(1): 1–25.
Cowen, R. (1996). Last Past the Post: Comparative Education, Modernity and Perhaps Post-modernity. *Comparative Education* 32(2): 151–70.
Douglas, M. (1994). *Risk and Blame: Essays in Cultural Theory*. London: Routledge.
Du Gay, P. (1996). *Consumption and Identity at Work*. London: Sage.
Foucault, M. (1974). *The Archaeology of Knowledge*. London: Tavistock.
Gewirtz, S. (1999). Education Action Zones: Emblems of the Third Way? In: H. Dean and R. Woods (eds) *Social Policy Review 11*. London: Social Policy Association.
Gewirtz, S. (2001). Cloning the Blairs: New Labour's Programme for the Re-socialization of Working Class Parents. *Journal of Education Policy* 16(4): 365–78.
Gewirtz, S. and Ball, S. J. (1999). Schools, Cultures and Values: The Impact of the Conservative Education Reforms in the 1980s and 1990s in England. *ESRC Values and Cultures Project Paper*. London: King's College London.
Gewirtz, S., Ball, S. J. and Bowe, R. (1993). Values and Ethics in the Marketplace: The Case of Northwark Park. *International Journal of Sociology of Education* 3(2): 233–53.
Gray, J. (1998). *False Dawn; the Delusions of Global Capitalism*. London: Granta.
Green, A. (1996). *Education, Globalization and the Nation State*. London: University of London, Institute of Education.
Harden, I. (1992). *The Contracting State*. Buckingham: Open University Press.
Hatcher, R. (2000). Profit and Power: Business and Education Action Zones. *Education Review* 13(1): 71–7.
Jordan, B., Redley, M. and James, S. (1994). *Putting the Family First: Identities, Decisions and Citizenship*. London, UCL Press.
Kenway, J. and Bullen, E. (2001). *Consuming Children: Education–Entertainment–Advertising*. Buckingham: Open University Press.

Leys, M. (2001). *Market-Driven Politics*. London: Verso.

Lingard, B., Ladwig, J. and Luke, A. (1998). School Effects in Postmodern Conditions. In: R. Slee, G. Weiner and S. Tomlinson (eds) *School Effectiveness for Whom? Challenges to the School Effectiveness and School Improvement Movements*. London: Falmer.

Lyotard, J.-F. (1984). *The Postmodern Condition: A Report on Knowledge*. Manchester: Manchester University Press.

Monbiot, G. (2000). *Captive State: The Corporate Takeover of Britain*. London: Macmillan.

Nagel, T. (1991). *Equality and Partiality*. Oxford: Oxford University Press.

Neave, G. (1988). On the Cultivation of Quality, Efficiency and Enterprise: An Overview of Recent Trends in Higher Education in Western Europe 1986–88. *European Journal of Education* 23(1–2): 7–23.

Offe, C. (1984). *Contradictions of the Welfare State*. London: Hutchinson.

Organisation for Economic Cooperation and Development (1995). *Governance in Transition: Public Management Reforms in OECD Countries*. Paris: OECD.

Rikowski, G. (2001a). *After the Manuscript Broke Off: Thoughts on Marx, Social Class and Education*. BSA, Sociology of Education Study Group, King's College London.

Rikowski, G. (2001b). *The Battle for Seattle: Its Significance for Education*. London: Tufnell Press.

Rikowski, G. (2003). The Business Takeover of Schools. *Mediaactive: Ideas Knowledge Culture* 1: 91–108.

Said, E. (1986). Foucault and the Imagination of Power. In: D. Hoy (ed.) *Foucault: A Critical Reader*. Oxford: Blackwell.

Saltman, K. J. (2000). *Collateral Damage: Corporatizing Public Schools – A Threat to Democracy*. Lanham, MD: Rowan and Littlefield.

Scott, P. (1995). *The Meanings of Mass Higher Education*. Buckingham: Open University Press.

Sennett, R. (1998). *The Corrosion of Character: The Personal Consequences of Work in the New Capitalism*. New York: W.W. Norton.

Shumar, W. (1997). *College For Sale: A Critique of the Commodification of Higher Education*. London: Falmer Press.

Stiglitz, J. (2002). *Globalization and its Discontents*. London: Penguin Books.

Taylor, A. (1998). 'Courting Business': The Rhetoric and Practices of School-Business Partnerships. *Journal of Education Policy* 13(3): 395–422.

Thomson, P. (1998). Thoroughly Modern Management and a Cruel Accounting: The Effects of Public Sector Reform on Public Education. In: A. Reid (ed.) *Going Public: Essays on the Future of Australian State Education*. Canberra: Australian Education Union – Australian Curriculum Studies Association.

Wade, R. (2001). Showdown at the World Bank. *New Left Review* 7(second series): 124–37.

White, S. (1998). *Interpreting the 'Third Way': A Tentative Overview*. Cambridge, MA: Dept of Political science, MIT.

Whitty, G., Edwards, T. and Gewirtz, S. (1993). *Specialisation and Choice in Urban Education: The City Technology College Experiment*. London: Routledge.

Wittel, A. (2001). Towards a Network Sociality. *Theory, Culture and Society* 18(6): 51–76.

CHAPTER 10

THE TEACHER'S SOUL AND THE TERRORS OF PERFORMATIVITY

Journal of Education Policy, 2003, 18(2): 215–28

In a recent newspaper article addressing the increasingly dominant role of numbers and statistics in modern society, David Boyle (*The Observer Review* 14.01.01, p. 1) made a simple but telling point: 'We take our collective pulse 24 hours a day with the use of statistics. We understand life that way, though somehow the more figures we use, the more the great truths seem to slip through our fingers. Despite all that numerical control, we feel as ignorant of the answers to the big questions as ever.

Education Reform is spreading across the globe, as in Levin's (1998) terms, like 'a policy epidemic'. An unstable, uneven but apparently unstoppable flood of closely inter-related reform ideas is permeating and reorienting education systems in diverse social and political locations which have very different histories. This epidemic is 'carried' by powerful agents, like the World Bank and the OECD; it appeals to politicians of diverse persuasions; and is becoming thoroughly embedded in the 'assumptive worlds' of many academic educators (see Ball, 2001). The novelty of this epidemic of reform is that is does not simply change what we, as educators, scholars and researchers do, it changes who we are.[1]

In various guises the key elements of the education reform 'package' – and it is applied with equal vigour to schools, colleges and universities – are embedded in three interrelated *policy technologies*; the market, managerialism and performativity. These elements have different degrees of emphasis in different national and local settings but they are closely inter-dependent in the processes of reform. When employed together these technologies offer a politically attractive alternative to the state-centred, public welfare tradition of educational provision. They are set over and against the older policy technologies of professionalism and bureaucracy. In more general terms the new technologies of reform play an important part in aligning public sector organisations with the methods, culture and ethical system of the private sector. The distinctiveness of the public sector is diminished. Indeed such alignments create the preconditions for various forms of 'privatisation' and 'commodification' of core public services.

Policy technologies involve the calculated deployment of techniques and artefacts to organise human forces and capabilities into functioning networks of power. Various disparate elements are inter-related within these technologies; involving architectural forms, functional texts and procedures, relations of hierarchy, strategies of motivation and mechanisms of reformation or therapy.

When deployed together the new technologies produce what the OECD (1995) calls 'a devolved environment' which 'requires a shift by central management bodies toward setting the overall framework rather than micromanaging...and changes in attitudes and behaviour on both sides' (p. 74). The changing roles of the central management agencies in this new environment rest, as the OECD put it, on 'monitoring systems' and the 'production of information' (p. 75). It is with these aspects of reform, monitoring systems and the production of information, that I am primarily concerned in this paper. They engender what Lyotard (1984) calls the terrors of performativity.

What do I mean by performativity? Performativity is a technology, a culture and a mode of regulation that employs judgements, comparisons and displays as means of incentive, control, attrition and change – based on rewards and sanctions (both material and symbolic). The performances (of individual subjects or organisations) serve as measures of productivity or output, or displays of 'quality', or 'moments' of promotion or inspection. As such they stand for, encapsulate or represent the worth, quality or value of an individual or organisation within a field of judgement. The issue of who controls the field of judgement is crucial. One key aspect of the current educational reform movement may be seen as struggles over the control of the field of judgement and its values (see *Guardian Education*, 9.01.01, extracts quoted below). Who is it that determines what is to count as a valuable, effective or satisfactory performance and what measures or indicators are considered valid? Typically, at least in the UK, these struggles are currently highly individualised as teachers, as ethical subjects, find their values challenged or displaced by the terrors of performativity. Some ephemeral examples:

> What happened to my creativity? What happened to my professional integrity? What happened to the fun in teaching and learning? What Happened?
>
> (G. E. Johnson)

> I find myself thinking that the only way I can save my sanity, my health and my relationship with my future husband is to leave the profession. I don't know what else I could do, having wanted to teach all my life, but I feel I am being forced out, forced to choose between a life and teaching.
>
> (Name supplied)

> I was a primary school teacher for 22 years but left in 1996 because I was not prepared to sacrifice the children for the glory of politicians and their business plans for education.
>
> (Christopher Draper)

> It's as though children are mere nuts and bolts on some distant production line, and it angers me to see them treated so clinically in their most sensitive and formative years.
>
> (Roma Oxford)

The ground of such struggles is often highly personal. Expressed in the lexicons of belief and commitment, service and even love, and of mental health and emotional well-being. The struggles are often internalised and set the care of the self against duty to others.

Despite all of this the technology of performativity appears as misleadingly objective and hyper-rational. Central to its functioning is the translation of complex social processes and events into simple figures or categories of judgement. What I want to attempt here is to 'get behind' the objective facade of this aspect of public sector reform and its technical rationalities of reform to examine the subjectivities of change and changing subjectivities which are threatened or required or brought about by performativity. I shall argue that the policy technologies of education reform are not simply vehicles for the technical and structural change of organisations but are also mechanisms for reforming teachers (scholars and researchers) and for changing what it means to be a teacher, the technologies of reform produce new kinds of teacher subjects. Such reform changes – our 'social identity' (Bernstein, 1996, p. 73). That is, education reform brings about change in 'our subjective existence and our relations one with another' (Rose, 1989, p. ix). This is the struggle over the teacher's soul. Thus, I am concerned with our sense of who we are as teachers in our relations with students and colleagues. My focus will be primarily upon performativity but I shall also refer at times to the other policy technologies of reform identified above.

The appearance of freedom in a 'devolved environment'

The scope and complexity of the reform agenda is breath-taking. It relates markets to management, to performativity, to changes in the nature of the State in a policy discourse, as noted already, which foregrounds 'devolving authority' and 'providing flexibility' (OECD, 1995, p. 29). The reforms are thus presented as giving 'managers and organisations greater freedom in operational decisions and remove unnecessary constraints in financial and human resource management' (p. 29). However, crucially it is a mis-recognition to see these reform processes as simply a strategy of de-regulation, they are processes of *re-regulation*. Not the abandonment by the State of its controls but the establishment of a new form of control; what Du Gay (1996) calls 'controlled de-control' and indeed a new kind of state. In this way, the state also provides a new general mode of less visible regulation, a much more 'hands-off', self-regulating regulation. This is a new 'regulative ensemble' (Aglietta, 1979, p. 101) which is an improvised mix of physical, textual and moral elements which 'make it possible to govern in an "advanced liberal" way' (Rose, 1996, p. 58). Within this ensemble, teachers are represented and encouraged to think about themselves as individuals who calculate about themselves, 'add value' to themselves, improve their productivity, strive for excellence, live an existence of calculation. They are 'enterprising subjects', who live their lives as 'an enterprise of the self' (Rose, 1989) – as 'neo-liberal professionals'. As Bernstein (1996, p. 169) puts it 'contract replaces covenant' or putting it another way value replaces values – commitment and service are of dubious worth within the new policy regime.

Policy technologies

As I have indicated, my particular focus here is not primarily upon structures and procedures, but upon the re-forming of relationships and subjectivities, and the forms of new or re-invented discipline to which this gives rise. Within each of the policy technologies of reform there are embedded and required new identities, new forms of interaction and new values. What it means to teach and what it means to be a teacher (a researcher, an academic) are subtly but decisively changed in the processes of reform.

Table 10.1 gives some indications of the sorts of discursive interventions that the new policy technologies of education reform bring into play; it is not exhaustive. Throughout the installation of these technologies into public service organisations, the use of new language to describe roles and relationships is important, the reformed

Table 10.1 Discursive interventions into the public sector

	Market	Management	Performance
Subject positions	Consumers, Producers, entrepreneur	Manager(s) (managed) Team	Appraisee, comparitor, competitor
Discipline	Competition, survival, income maximisation	Efficiency/ effectiveness Corporate culture	Productivity, targets achievement, comparison
Values	Competition, institutional interests	'What works'	The performative worth of individuals fabrication

educational organisations are now 'peopled' by human resources which need to be managed; learning is re-rendered as a 'cost-effective policy outcomes'; achievement is a set of 'productivity targets' etc. To be relevant, up-to-date, we need to talk about ourselves and others, and think about our actions and relationships in new ways. New roles and subjectivities are produced as teachers are re-worked as producers/providers, educational entrepreneurs, and managers and are subject to regular appraisal and review and performance comparisons. We learn to talk about ourselves and our relationships, our purposes and motivations in these new ways. The new vocabulary of performance renders old ways of thinking and relating dated or redundant or even obstructive. We must become adept at presenting and representing ourselves with this new vocabulary and its prescribed signifiers and the possibilities of being 'otherwise' to or within it are extremely limited (as the teachers quoted above and below found). This speaking of the vocabularies of reform texts is, as my colleague Louise Morley describes it, a form of ventriloquism.

Furthermore, new ethical systems are introduced within the new regulative ensemble, based upon institutional self-interest, pragmatics and performative worth. This involves 'the ideological co-optation of the moral and ethical consciousness of the teachers' (Smyth *et al.*, 2000, p. 86). The reform technologies play their part in 'making us up' differently from before by providing new modes of description for what we do and new possibilities for action. This re-making can be enhancing and empowering for some (but this has to be set over and against the potential for 'inauthenticity'; see below). The ethics of competition and performance are very different from the older ethics of professional judgement and co-operation. A new basis for ethical decision-making and moral judgement is erected by the 'incentives' of performance. Teachers are 'deprofessionalised' and 'reprofessionalised' (Seddon, 1997). There is 'the possibility of a triumphant self of becoming a new kind of professional or of entry into the ever expanding ranks of the executors of quality. We learn that we can become more than we were and be better than others – we can be 'outstanding', 'successful', 'above the average'. All of this involves, in one way or another, 'intensive work on the self' (Dean, 1995, p. 581). This is work which some caught up in the struggle over what is means to be a teacher are unwilling to undertake (again see *Guardian Education*, 9.01.01).

The installation of the new culture of competitive performativity involves the use of a combination of devolution, targets and incentives to bring about new forms of sociality and new institutional forms. In education, the impact of such ideas is evident in the myriad of 'institutional devolution' and 'site-based management' initiatives being introduced in public sector organisations around the world.

These institutions are encouraged to make themselves different from one another, to stand out, to 'improve' themselves. In effect they are to take responsibility for transforming themselves and disciplining themselves and their employees; in the same way 'employees are simultaneously required, individually and collectively, to recognise and *take responsibility for* the relationship between the security of their employment and their contribution to the competitiveness of the goods and services they produce' (Willmott, 1993, p. 522). Organisation cooperation and older forms of collective relations among workers are replaced by performative competition.

Thus, the work of the manager, the new hero of educational reform, involves instilling the attitude and culture within which workers feel themselves accountable and at the same time committed or personally invested in the organisation. These new managers, in part at least beneficiaries of reform, are the 'technicians of trans-formation' (May, 1994, p. 619), or what Foucault calls 'technicians of behaviour', their task 'to produce bodies that are docile and capable' (Foucault, 1979a, p. 294). In Bernsteinian terms, these new invisible pedagogies of management, realised through appraisals, performance reviews and forms of performance-related pay, 'open up' more of the managed to control. The weaker frames of new managerial-ism enable a greater range of the workers' behaviour and emotional life to be made public (Bernstein, 1971, p. 65).

The act of teaching and the subjectivity of the teacher are both profoundly changed within the new management panopticism (of quality and excellence) and the new forms of entrepreneurial control (through marketing and competition). Two apparently conflicting effects are achieved; both an increasing individualisa-tion, including the destruction of solidarities based upon a common professional identity and Trade Union affiliation, as against the construction of new forms of institutional affiliation and 'community', based upon corporate culture. This involves a re-working of the relationships between individual commitment and action in the organisation.

Again such developments are deeply paradoxical. On the one hand, they are frequently presented as a move away from 'low-trust', centralised, forms of employee control. Managerial responsibilities are delegated, initiative and problem-solving are highly valued. On the other hand, new forms of very immediate surveillance and self-monitoring are put in place; e.g. appraisal systems, target-setting, output comparisons. Troman's (2000, p. 349) recent case-study work in UK primary schools found 'low-trust' to be in the ascendant in most of those studied, together with a proliferation of formal 'security-seeking' tactics, with resultant physical and emotional damage to teachers and high levels of 'existential anxiety and dread' (see also Chadbourne and Ingvarson, 1998).

The struggle over visibility

As noted already, in the language of the OECD, at the centre of the reform of the public sector are 'monitoring systems' and the 'production of information' (p. 75). It is the data-base, the appraisal meeting, the annual review, report writing, the regular publication of results and promotion applications, inspections and peer reviews that are mechanics of performativity. The teacher, researcher, academic are subject to a myriad of judgements, measures, comparisons and targets. Information is collected continuously, recorded and published – often in the form of League Tables, and performance is also monitored eventfully by peer reviews, site visits and inspections. Within all this there is a high degree of uncertainty and instability. A sense of being constantly judged in different ways, by different means, according to different criteria, through different agents and agencies. There is a flow of changing demands, expectations and indicators that makes us continually accountable and constantly recorded. We become ontologically insecure: unsure whether we are doing enough, doing the right thing, doing as much as others, or as well as others, constantly looking to improve, to be better, to be excellent. And yet it is not always very clear what is expected of us. Indeed, Shore and Wright (1999, p. 569) argue, in relation to UK Higher Education systems of accountability, that there is an undeclared policy 'to keep systems volatile, slippery and opaque'. Not infrequently, the requirements of such systems bring into being unhelpful or indeed damaging practices, which nonetheless satisfy performance requirements. Organisations will do whatever is necessary to excel or to survive. In other words, these policy technologies have the 'capacity to re-shape in their own image the organisations they monitor' (Shore and Wright, 1999, p. 570).

Increasingly, our day-to-day practice is flooded with a baffling array of figures, indicators, comparisons and forms of competition. Within all this the contentments of stability are increasingly elusive, purposes are made contradictory, motivations become blurred and self-worth is uncertain. We are unsure what aspects of our work are valued and how to prioritise our efforts. We become uncertain about the reasons for our actions. Are we doing this because it is important, because we believe in it, because it is worthwhile? Or is it being done ultimately because it will be measured or compared? It will make us look good! Do we know we are good at what we do, even if performance indicators tell us different? Do we value who we are able to be, who we are becoming in the labyrinth of performativity? Again much of this reflexivity is internalised. These things become matters of self-doubt and personal anxiety rather than public debate. Discussing teachers' anxieties about their ability to cope with the multiple demands on their time quoting Mandy, who says of her colleagues:

> they're not coping very well, I think alot of teachers blame themselves. It depends how confident you are I suppose, and if you know what you are capable of. I think a lot of people even subconsciously stop doing things to make it easier for themselves.
>
> (Smith *et al.*, 2000)

Constant doubts about which judgements may be in play at any point mean that any and all comparisons and requirements to perform have to be attended to. Selection and prioritisation becomes impossible and as a result work and it pressures intensify. In these ways 'the capacities, conduct, statuses and duties of individuals are problematized and worked on' (Dean, 1995, p. 565).

It follows then that these technologies have an emotional status dimension, as well as the appearance of rationality and objectivity. Thus, our responses to the flow of performance information can engender individual feelings of pride, guilt, shame and envy. Let me quote an English primary school teacher who appears in Jeffrey and Woods' (1998), powerful, moving and terrifying book *Testing Teachers* which deals with the UK regime of School Inspections [which may be an extreme case] and examines 'teachers experience of the inspections as a conflict of values, a colonisation of their lives, and de-professionalisation of their role' (back cover).

> I don't have the job satisfaction now I once had working with young kids because I feel every time I do something intuitive I just feel guilty about it. 'Is this right; am I doing this the right way; does this cover what I am supposed to be

covering: should I be doing something else: should I be more structured; should I have this in place; should I have done this?' You start to query everything you are doing – there's a kind of guilt in teaching at the moment. I don't know if that's particularly related to Ofsted [Office for Standards in Education, the agency responsible for the Inspection of Schools in England] but of course it's multiplied by the fact that Ofsted is coming in because you get in a panic that you won't be able to justify yourself when they finally arrive.

(p. 118)

Here then is guilt, uncertainty, instability and the emergence of a new subjectivity.[2] What Bernstein (2000, p. 1942) calls 'mechanisms of introjection' whereby 'the identity finds its core in its place in an organisation of knowledge and practice' are here being threatened by or replaced by 'mechanisms of *projection*', that is an 'identity is a reflection of external contingencies' (Bernstein, 2000, p. 1942).

Furthermore, the work of performativity produces what Lyotard calls *the law of contradiction*. This contradiction arises between intensification – as an increase in the volume of first order activities (direct engagement with students, research, curriculum development) required by the demands of perfomativity – and the 'costs' in terms of time and energy of second order activities that is the work of performance monitoring and management. The increases in effort and time spent on core tasks are off-set by increases in effort and time devoted to accounting for task work or erecting monitoring systems, collecting performative data and attending to the management of institutional 'impressions'. As a number of commentators have pointed out, acquiring the performative information necessary for perfect control, 'consumes so much energy that it drastically reduces the energy available for making improvement inputs' (Elliott, 1996, p. 15; see also Blackmore and Sachs, 1997). Survival and competitive advantage in the economy of education rests equally upon the energy of first order activities and the energy of second order activities (see below on *fabrications*) – producing the potential for what Blackmore and Sachs (1997) call 'institutional schizophrenia'.

There are other 'costs', as indicated already – personal and psychological. A kind of *values schizophrenia* is experienced by individual teachers where commitment, judgement and authenticity within practice are sacrificed for impression and performance. Here there is a potential 'splitting' between the teachers own judgements about 'good practice' and students 'needs' and the rigours of performance (see Bronwyn below). I can illustrate this again quoting teachers from Jeffrey and Woods (1998, p. 160) study of UK primary school Inspections. Veronica, talked about resenting 'what I've done. I've never compromised before and I feel ashamed. It's like licking their boots'; and Diane talked about a lost of respect for herself.

My first reaction was 'I'm not going to play the game', but I am and they know I am. I don't respect myself for it; my own self respect goes down. Why aren't I making a stand? Why aren't I saying, 'I know I can teach; say what you want to say', and so I lose my own self-respect. I know who I am; know why I teach, and I don't like it: I don't like them doing this, and that's sad, isn't it?

There are indications here of the particular performativity – the management of performance – which is 'called up' by Inspection. What is produced is a spectacle, or game-playing, or cynical compliance, or what we might see as an 'enacted fantasy' (Butler, 1990), which is there simply to be seen and judged – a fabrication, as I refer to it below. And as the teacher also hints the heavy sense of inauthenticity in all this may well be appreciated as much by the Inspectors as the inspected; Diane is 'playing the game' and 'they know I am'. The teacher that is inspected here is not Diane. It is someone that Diane knows the Inspectors want to see and the sort of teacher that is hailed and rewarded by educational reform and 'school improvement'. Being this 'other' teacher creates 'costs' to the self and sets up personal, ontological dilemmas for Diane. Her identity is called into question. Cloe, another teacher in Jeffery and Woods study explained:

> You are only seen as effective as a teacher by what you manage to put into children's brains so they can regurgitate in an examination situation. Now that's not very satisfying to one's life...My age group came into teaching on a tide of education for all...But I dont care any more. I think that's why I haven't found my self because I do in fact care...I dont feel that I'm working with the children, I'm working at the children and it's not a very pleasant experience...
>
> (p. 131)

Again Cloe is having real problems in thinking of herself as the kind of teacher who simply produces performances – of her own and by her children. This is not 'who she is' and in the heat and noise of reform she cannot 'find herself'. Her commitments to and purposes for teaching her reasons for becoming and being a teacher have no place. Her relations with children are changed by reform, are *at* them rather than *with* them. These relations seem to her to be inauthentic. What Smyth *et al.* (2000, p. 140) call the 'primacy of caring relations in work with pupils and colleagues' has no place in the hard world of performativity. The discursive resources which made Cloe an effective teacher in her own eyes have been made redundant. Like the performative institution the 'reformed teacher' is conceived of as simply responsive to external requirements and specified targets; and to paraphrase Bernstein (1996, p. 73), we can ask; 'If the identity produced by [performativity] is socially "empty," how does the actor recognise him/herself and others?'. This is exactly Cloe's problem. Cloe's story is a not uncommon one in the UK as the regime of performativity drives increasing numbers of teachers out of the education system (as above). Writing in a language of extremes, of conflict, a 56-year old, 30-year veteran, Head of Drama, accounted for his reluctant decision to leave teaching in a recent article, in this way:

> Education has traditionally been about freedom. But there is no freedom any more. It's gone. Initiative and resourcefulness are banned. Every school has become part of the gulag.
>
> (*Guardian Education*, 09.01.01)

Again the alienation of self is linked to the displacement of individual qualities, mechanisms of introjection, by responsiveness, external contingencies, the requirements of performativity. The result, inauthentic practice and relationships. Teachers are no longer encouraged to have a rationale for practice, an account of themselves in terms of a relationship to the meaningfulness of what they do, but are required to produce measurable and 'improving' outputs and performances, what is important is *what works*. As another of Jeffery and Woods' teachers put it:

> I never get the chance to think of my philosophy any more, my beliefs. I know what I believe but I never really put them into words any more. Isn't your philosophy more important than how many people get their sums right?
>
> (Bronwyn)

This structural and individual schizophrenia of values and purposes, and the potential for inauthenticity and meaninglessness is increasingly an everyday experience for us all. The activities of the new technical intelligentsia, of management, drive performativity into the day-to-day practices of teachers and into the social relations between teachers. They make management, ubiquitous, invisible, inescapable – part of and embedded in everything we do. Increasingly, we choose and judge our actions and they are judged by others on the basis of their contribution to organisational performance, rendered in terms of measurable outputs. Beliefs are no longer important – it is output that counts. Beliefs are part of an older, increasingly displaced discourse. Put another way, teachers like Bronwyn are seeking to hold onto knowledges about themselves which diverge from prevailing categories. These are now seen, in Foucault's terms, as 'knowledges inadequate to their task...naive knowledges...disqualified knowledges' (Foucault, 1980, pp. 81–2). A new kind of teacher and new kinds of knowledges are 'called up' by educational reform – a teacher who can maximise performance, who can set aside irrelevant principles, or out-moded social commitments, for whom excellence and improvement are the driving force of their practice. Under a regime of performativity 'identity depends on the facility for projecting discursive organisation/practices themselves driven by external contingencies' (Bernstein, 2000, p. 1942).

Embedded in almost all of the examples I have quoted are a set of dualisms or tensions. Tensions between belief and representation. On the one hand, teachers are concerned that what they do will not be captured by or valued within the metrics of accountability and, on the other, that these metrics will distort their practice. Alongside this is a further tension, indicated already, between metric performances and authentic and purposeful relationships.[3] Again this goes to the heart of what it means to teach. A Special Needs Teacher quoted by Sikes (2001) feels that her[4] work is especially vulnerable to misrepresentation and distortion, again meaninglessness, and/or non-representation.

> I know that they've made all sorts of noises about acknowledging the sort of work that we do, and so on and so forth but, on one level, that almost makes the whole thing meaningless. It's certainly patronising in my view. Because we can work and work with a kid and at the end of the period of time, what it is, a lesson, a week, a month, a term, a year, years, whatever, there's no discernible change...so much about teaching is about relationships and there's something pathological about managing relationships; I think there is anyway. And what sorts of things can you measure? By and large things that don't matter – and I think that is particularly true of some of the kids that people I know work with.[5]

The other problem for teachers like this working within a performative culture, is that their sphere of activity if unlikely to attract investment from performance managers. That is to say, if this teacher's school managers wanted to extract increases in performance as measured against external targets or competitive averages they would be unlikely to 'invest' in work with children with special needs where the margins for improved performance are limited.[6] In the hard logic of a performance culture an organisation will only spend money where measurable returns are likely to be achieved. This is the conclusion of the research by Gray *et al.* (1999); that performance management is most likely to encourage a search for tactical improvements which result in short term improvements.[7] In this way performativity not only engenders cynicism but has social consequences arising from the distribution effort and investment.

Crucially then, these new forms of regulation have both a social and interpersonal dimension. They are folded into complex institutional, team, group and communal relations and penetrate our mundane day-to-day interactions in such a way that the interplay of their collegial and disciplinary aspects become very murky indeed. Both the interactions and relations between colleagues and those between teachers and students are affected. In terms of the former there are pressures on individuals, formalised by appraisals, annual reviews and data bases, to make their contribution to the performativity of the unit. In this there is a real possibility that authentic social relations are replaced by judgemental relations wherein persons are valued for their productivity alone. Their value as a person is eradicated. This contributes to a general 'emptying out' of social relationships, which are left 'flat' and 'deficient in effect' (Lash and Urry, 1994, p. 15). Again performance has no room for caring. These are not simply things done to us, as in previous regimes of power. These are things that we do to ourselves and to others. What we see here is a particular set of 'practices through which we act upon ourselves and one another in order to make us particular kinds of being' (Rose, 1992, p. 161).

Even so, while we may not be expected to care about each other we are expected to 'care' *about* our performances and the performances of our team and our organisation and to make our contribution to the construction of convincing institutional spectacles and 'outputs'. We are expected to be passionate about excellence. And our performances and those of our organisation cannot be constructed without 'care'. Presentation, 'front', impressions 'given' and 'given off' must be carefully crafted and managed. They are part of the currency and substance of performance. As individuals and organisational actors, our performances must be constructed or fabricated with artifice and with an eye to the competition. These things cannot be left to chance either in relation to the publication of performance indicators, the response to official judgements of quality, or the choices of clients and consumers. The term fabrication seems to capture the sense of deliberation involved here, sometimes involving 'bought-in' professional support, and the specificity or purposefulness of the intended effects and the almost inevitable element of cynical compliance inherent in making up responses to performativity.

Fabrications

The fabrications that organisations (and individuals) produce are based upon one, or some, of a possible range of representations or versions of the organisation or person (see Ball, 2000 for an extended discussion). These versions are written into existence in performative texts. They involve the use and re-use of the right signifiers. Complex organisations like schools and universities are multifaceted and diverse, indeed they are sometimes contested and often contradictory. Within a performative regime it is likely, however, that the choice of those representations which are to be privileged and cultivated will be 'informed' or driven by the priorities, constraints and climate set by the policy environment – examination results, retention, racial equality, social participation. Performativity is promiscuous. Fabrications are versions of an organisation (or person) which does not exist – they are not 'outside the truth' but neither do they render simply true or direct accounts – they are produced purposefully in order 'to be accountable'. Truthfulness is not the point – the point is their effectiveness, both in the market or for Inspection or appraisal, and in the 'work' they do 'on' and 'in' the organisation – their transformational and disciplinary impact. That is to say: 'To be audited, an organisation must actively transform itself into an auditable commodity' (Shore and Wright, 1999, p. 570). To put it another way: 'Colonisation through audit fosters "pathologies of creative compliance" in the form of gamesmanship around an indicator culture' (Elliott, 2001, p. 202). Significantly (Gray *et al.*, 1999) also quote a headteacher who describes his use of tactical improvements as 'the improvement game'. Diane, the teacher quoted earlier, also uses this metaphor. Fabrications conceal as much as they reveal. They are ways of presenting ourselves within particular registers of meaning, within a particular economy of meaning in which only certain possibilities of being have value.

However, such fabrications are deeply paradoxical. In one sense organisational fabrications are a way of eluding or deflecting direct surveillance they provide a facade of calculation between the organisation and its environment. However, in another sense, the work of fabricating the organisation requires submission to the rigours of performativity and the disciplines of competition. There is a surplus of meaning in such exercises. A surplus which spills over into the everyday life of the organisation. Fabrications are both resistance *and* capitulation. They are a betrayal even, a giving up of claims to authenticity and commitment, an investment in plasticity, as the teachers quoted earlier indicate.

> the generalisation of an enterprise form to all forms of conduct may of itself serve to incapacitate an organisation's ability to pursue its preferred projects by redefining its identity and hence what the nature of its project actually is.
>
> (Du Gay, 1996, p. 190).

Crucially, acts of fabrication and the fabrications themselves become embedded in and are reproduced by systems of recording and reporting on practice. They also work to exclude other things which do not 'fit' into what is intended to be represented or conveyed. They may be reactive or defensive or satisfising, as suggested above, or innovative and proactive or differentiating. They must render the organisation into a recognisable rationality which is underpinned by 'robust procedures', punctuated by 'best practice' and always 'improving', always looks for 'what works'.

There is a second paradox which arises here. Technologies and calculations which appear to make public sector organisations more transparent may actually result in making them more opaque, as representational artefacts are increasingly constructed with great deliberation and sophistication. This arises in part from the gamesmanship noted above, from 'creative accountancy' and on occasion from more straightforward misrepresentation or 'cheating' as teachers and principals find themselves under pressure to perform or 'improve' in a competitive environment.

Within all this, organisations in different market positions are likely to arrive at different forms of strategic response. Those on a weak 'market' or performance position may well submit to becoming *what ever it seems necessary to become* in order to survive. Performance improvements may become the only basis for decision-making. The heart of the educational project is gouged out and left empty. Authenticity is replaced entirely by plasticity. The organisation becomes an 'auditable commodity'. For others, in a stronger 'market' or performance position, the impact of performativity may be different; either forms of complacency or reinforcement and/or the possibility of retaining commitment to non-performative values and practices. Elite institutions are best places to evade the judgements of the 'technicians of transformation'.

Increasingly public sector institutions are also required to construct a variety of formal textual accounts of ourselves in the form of development plans, strategic documents, sets of objectives etc. (as are individuals in the form of annual reviews and appraisals). Symbolism is as important as substance here. Such texts symbolise and 'stand for' the corporate consensus of the institution, and indeed these exercises in institutional extrapolation can also work as a means of manufacturing consensus – the focusing of activities around an 'agreed' set of priorities (Ball, 1997). They provide a touchstone of shared endeavour which displaces or subsumes differences, disagreements and value divergencies. Again while fabrications are at their most obvious in the form of major events, glossy publications, and formal plans, they are also part of day-to-day social relations and practices and the routine selection and manipulation of data (see Ball, 1997 for examples) and the selection of effort. The ethical practices of teachers and managers are a second order casualty in all of this. Effectivity rather than honesty is most valued in a performative regime.

The performative society

It is not that performativity gets in the way of 'real' academic work or 'proper' learning, it is a vehicle for changing what academic work and learning are! At the heart of Lyotard's thesis is his argument that the commodification of knowledge is a key characteristic of what he calls 'the postmodern condition'. This involves not simply a different evaluation of knowledge but fundamental changes in the relationships between the learner, learning and knowledge, resulting in 'a thorough exteriorization of knowledge' (1984, p. 4). Knowledge and knowledge relations, including the relationships between learners, are de-socialised. It is this externalisation and de-socialisation that the teachers quoted early are struggling with and against.

Underlying this is the dissemination of 'marketness' (Robertson, 1996) or the enterprise form as the master narrative defining and constraining the whole variety of relationships within and between the state, civil society and the economy. As the OECD explain it 'Reform must also address other aspects of the performance of the public sector, including its wider role in the economy and in society generally. Pushing current reforms further, monitoring and evaluating progress, and managing the evolving role of the state must remain broad priorities' (1995, p. 89).

Within the public sector, the process of 'exteriorisation' also involves a profound shift in the nature of the relationship between workers and their work – 'service' commitments no longer have value or meaning and professional judgement is subordinated to the requirements of performativity and marketing – although I have noted the element of 'cynical compliance' in play in the processes of individual and institutional fabrication. This is part of a larger process of 'ethical retooling' in the public sector which is replacing client 'need' and professional judgement with commercial decision-making. The space for the operation of autonomous ethical codes based in a shared moral language is colonised or closed down. This thus plays its part in what Sennett (1998) calls the 'corrosion of character' and what Power (1994) terms a 'regress of mistrust'. The policy technologies of market, management and performativity leave no space for an autonomous or collective ethical self. These technologies have potentially profound consequences for the nature of teaching and learning and for the inner-life of the teacher. They 'are not simply instruments but a frame in which questions of who we are or what we would like to become emerge' (Dean, 1995, p. 581).

Notes

1   This paper is the third iteration of a series on performativity (Ball, 2000 and 2001). This version draws on but develops the previous ones. This version has also been re-worked from papers given at national conferences in Argentina, Finland and Portugal.

2   Subjectivity is:

> patterns by which experiential and emotional contexts, feelings, images and memories are organised to form one's self image, one's sense of self and others, and our possibilities of existence.
>
> (De Lauretis, 1986, p. 5)

3   Although as various commentators have pointed out, it is not impossible to conceive of a system of benign or progressive metrics, related to reducing social inequalities for example. The question is whether the form and substance of performativity can be separated out. I have my doubts.

4   It is almost certainly not by chance that almost all of the teachers quoted in this paper are women. The gendered nature of educational reform and of performative technologies and its encounters with a gendered teacher professionalism and discourses of commitment and care needs further attention – 'New educational structures and modes of regulation must therefore be assessed in order to expose their gendered manifestations' (Dillabough, 1999, p. 390). It is also important to begin to situate Inspectorial gazes within broader feminist analyses of 'the gaze'.

5   Of course, the other aspect of this sort of talk is the issue of teachers' expectations and the way in which for some children relationships can become a substitute for performance.

6   As Lazear (2001), among others, notes, there are also distributional effects to be attended to here.

7   Unless that is a complex metric is designed to target these low margin areas: see for example Lavy's (2001) account of teachers' performance incentive tournaments in Israel.

References

Aglietta, M. (1979) *A Theory of Capitalist Regulation: The US Experience* (London: New Left Books).

Ball, S. J. (1997) Good school/bad school, *British Journal of Sociology of Education*, 18(3), 317–36.

Ball, S. J. (2000) Performativities and fabrications in the education economy: towards the performative society, *Australian Educational Researcher*, 17(3), 1–24.

Ball, S. J. (2001) Grandes politicas, un mundo pequeno. Introduccion a una perspectiva internacional en las politicas educativas, in M. Andrada, M. Narodowski and M. Nores (eds), *Nuevas Tendencias en Politicas Educativas: Alternativas para la Escuela Publica* (Buenos Aires: Granica).

Bauman, Z. (1992) *Mortality, Immortality and Other Life Strategies* (Stanford, CA: Stanford University Press).

Bernstein, B. (1971) On the classification and framing of educational knowledge, in M. F. D. Young (ed.), *Knowledge and Control* (London: Collier-Macmillan).

Bernstein, B. (1996) *Pedagogy Symbolic Control and Identity* (London: Taylor and Francis).

Bernstein, B. (2000) Official knowledge and pedagogic identities: the politics of recontextualising, in S. J. Ball (ed.), *The Sociology of Education: Major Themes* (London: RoutledgeFalmer).

Blackmore, J. and Sachs, J. (1997) *Worried, Weary and Just Plain Worn Out: Gender, Restructuring and the Psychic Economy of Higher Education*. Paper presented at the AARE Annual Conference (Brisbane).

Broadfoot, P. (1998) Quality standards and control in higher education: what price life-long learning, *International Studies in Sociology of Education*, 8(2), 155–79.

Butler, J. (1990) *Gender Trouble* (London: Routledge).

Cerny, P. (1997) Paradoxes of the competition state: the dynamics of political globalisation, *Government and Opposition*, 32(2), 251–74.

Chadbourne, R. and Ingvarson, L. (1998) Self-managing schools and professional community: the professional recognition program in Victoria's schools of the future, *The Australian Educational Researcher*, 25(2), 61–94.

Dean, M. (1995) Governing the unemployed self in an active society, *Economy and Society*, 24(4), 559–83.

Du Gay, P. (1996) *Consumption and Identity at Work* (London: Sage).

Elliott, J. (1996) *Quality Assurance, the Educational Standards Debate, and the Commodification of Educational Research*. Paper presented at the BERA Annual Conference (University of Lancaster).

Elliott, J. (2001) Characteristics of performative cultures: their central paradoxes and limitations as resources of educational reform, in D. Gleeson and C. Husbands (eds), *The Performing School* (London, RoutledgeFalmer).

Foucault, M. (1977) *Discipline and Punish* (New York: Pantheon Press).

Foucault, M. (1979a) *Discipline and Punish* (Harmondsworth: Peregrine).

Foucault, M. (1979b) On Governmentality, *Ideology and Consciousness*, 6(1), 5–22.

Foucault, M. (1980) *Power/Knowledge* (Harlow: Longman).

Gewirtz, S. and Ball, S. J. (1999) Schools, cultures and values: the impact of the conservative education reforms in the 1980s and 1990s in England (*ESRC Values and Cultures project paper, King's College London*).

Gewirtz, S., Ball, S. J. and Bowe, R. (1995) *Markets, Choice and Equity in Education* (Buckingham: Open University Press).

Giddens, A. (1991) *Modernity and Self-Identity* (Cambridge: Polity).

Gray, J., Hopkins, D., Reynolds, D., Wilcox, B., Farrel, S. and Jesson, D. (1999) *Improving Schools: Performance and Potential* (Buckingham: Open University Press).

Jeffrey, B. and Woods, P. (1998) *Testing Teachers: The Effect of School Inspections on Primary Teachers* (London: Falmer Press).

Lash, S. and Urry, J. (1994) *Economies of Signs and Space* (London: Sage).

Lavy, V. (2001) Evaluating the effect of teachers' performance incentives on pupil achievement. Unpublished paper (Jerusalem: Hebrew University of Jerusalem).

Lazear, E. P. (2001) Paying teachers for performance: incentives and selection. Unpublished paper (Hoover Institution and Graduate School of Business, Stanford University).

Levin, B. (1998) An epidemic of education policy: what can we learn for each other? *Comparative Education*, 34(2), 131–42.

Lyotard, J.-F. (1984) *The Postmodern Condition: A Report on Knowledge* (Vol. 10) (Manchester: Manchester University Press).

OECD (1995) *Governance in Transition: Public Management Reforms in OECD Countries* (Paris: Organisation for Economic Co-operation and Development).

Peters, T. and Waterman, R. (1982) *In Search of Excellence* (London: Harper Row).

Power, M. (1994) *The Audit Explosion* (London: Demos).

Robertson, S. (1996) Markets and teacher professionalism: a political economy analysis, *Melbourne Studies in Education*, 37(2), 23–39.

Rose, N. (1989) *Governing the Soul: The Shaping of the Private Self* (London: Routledge).

Rose, N. (1992) Governing the enterprising self, in P. Heelas and P. Morris (eds), *The Values of the Enterprise Culture* (London: Routledge).

Rose, N. (1996) Governing 'advanced' liberal democracies, in A. Barry, T. Osborne and N. Rose (eds), *Foucault and Political Reason: Liberalism, Neo-liberalism and Rationalities of Government* (London: UCL Press).

Seddon, T. (1997) Markets and the English: rethinking educational restructuring as institutional design, *British Journal of Sociology of Education*, 18(2), 165–86.

Sennett, R. (1998) *The Corrosion of Character: The Personal Consequences of Work in the New Capitalism* (New York: W.W. Norton).

Shore, C. and Wright, S. (1999) Audit culture and anthropology: neo-liberalism in British Higher Education, *The Journal of the Royal Anthropological Institute*, 5(4), 557–75.

Sikes, P. (2001) Teachers' lives and teaching performance, in D. Gleeson and C. Husbands (eds), *The Performing School: Managing Teaching and Learning in a Performance Culture* (London: RoutledgeFalmer).

Smyth, J., Dow, A., Hattam, R., Reid, A. and Shacklock, G. (2000) *Teachers' Work in a Globalising Economy* (London: Falmer Press).

Troman, G. (2000) Teacher stress in the low-trust society, *British Journal of Sociology of Education*, 21(3), 331–53.

Willmott, H. (1992) Postmodernism and excellence: the de-differentiation of economy and culture, *Journal of Organisational Change and Management*, 5(1), 58–68.

Willmott, H. (1993) Strength is ignorance; slavery is freedom: managing culture in modern organizations, *Journal of Management Studies*, 30(4), 215–52.

SOCIAL CLASS AND EDUCATION POLICY

Introduction

Part 3 focuses on the other main preoccupation within my policy sociology work – social class. The papers examine the interface between social class and education policy or how class works on and through policy. The main vehicle of class differentiation and class advantage which is addressed and examined is 'the market' – that is the use of possibilities of choice by parents to manage and control, to some extent, the educational experiences and careers of their children. The concepts developed by Pierre Bourdieu – habitus, disposition, field and distinction – are the key analytical resources in these papers which explore 'choice-making' and the use of capital and other resources by parents in relation to secondary schools (Chapters 11 and 13), post-compulsory education (Chapter 12), and higher education (Chapter 14) (and more recent work has focused on childcare (Ball *et al.*, 2004)). The *Social Justice* paper (Chapter 13) concentrates on the middle classes and considers the dilemmas experienced within this class between a commitment to the interests of the family, as against the public good – the relationships between private principles and social identity. Attention to the middle classes in education allows for an understanding of class relations and class reproduction in education in terms of privilege, rather than deficit, and the ways in which policies themselves are classed. This analysis lays out the groundwork for ongoing work on class fractions, and their different engagements with state and private schooling. The *Ethnic Choosing* paper (Chapter 14) intercuts class with race, and explores how ethnic and class identities play their part within educational choice-making. And the *Grapevine* paper (Chapter 15) explores how information flows around and inflects choice. These papers also inter-related with the themes and issues in the previous section; the re-working of the possibilities of citizenship; the increasing 'privatisation' of education services, and the changing ethical environment (Haydon, 2004) within which choices are made. As Bourdieu and Boltanski (2000, p. 917) put it: 'The education market has become one of the most important loci of class struggle'. Education itself is changed by all this. It becomes in Larabee's (1997) words 'an arena for zero-sum competition filled with self-interested actors seeking opportunities' (p. xx). One way of thinking about the patterns and interactions involved here, between families, educational institutions and state policies, is that we are witnessing a 'managed' (re)convergence between the ideologies, interests and resources of the middle class and the ideologies, interests and resource requirements that are embedded in educational policies. Furthermore, we might see this as giving rise to, or as part of, some sort of mutual conditioning. On the one hand, there is 'the role of politics and the actions of the state in shaping individual and family decision-making processes' (Devine, 1997, p. 39). Class perspectives have to be understood as they are articulated from within changing discourse and policy regimes. In particular here within the discursive framework of 'the market society' and 'the aesthetic of consumption' (Bauman, 1998). On the other hand, the middle classes and their political representatives are strategic agents in the advocacy of the political changes I outline. Choice policies and the reassurances of performativity and accountability in the current socio-economic context, are an effective response to the interest anxieties of the middle class. Current policies in play provide the middle class with the means to exercise power in various educational settings.

Most of the papers in this part have multiple authorship, although I was the lead author in each case, rather than just alphabetically the first author. I could have sought similar pieces which were single-authored but to do so would involve the erasure of an absolutely fundamental aspect of my practice as an academic researcher and writer – collaboration and teamwork. I have been extremely lucky in having worked with a number of wonderful colleagues from whom I have learned and continue to learn about how to think sociologically and do research. Teams are usually safe places within which to try out ideas, get feedback on writing, and make mistakes, and places in which to argue and to challenge one another. Some of what emerges is difficult to pin down to the mind of one person and there are different ways in which people contribute to the development of a good idea. Teamwork also involves divisions of labour – I certainly did not conduct all of the interviews quoted in these papers, but I did do some. The papers in this section draw upon a sequence of seven Economic and Social Research Council (ESRC) funded research projects. Paper 11 is based on data from a study of secondary school 'markets' and parental choices of schools within these. This research was undertaken with Richard Bowe and Sharon Gewirtz. The paper outlines the idea of 'circuits of schooling' which has been taken further in work by Butler with Robson (2003) and (Lauder *et al.*, 1999). Paper 15, written with Carol Vincent, also uses data from this study to explore the form and use of 'information' in education markets. Paper 12 draws on data and ideas from two studies of post-16 education and training markets and the trajectories of a group of 59 young people through these. These studies were done with Meg Maguire and Sheila Macrae. Paper 13 written with Diane Reay and Miriam David focuses on a minority-ethnic, sub-sample from a study of families and students choosing among higher-education institutions. The final two papers are synthetic analyses which address general issues arising from the relationship between choice and class in education markets. These papers deploy data from all of the studies refered to above as well as work recently completed with Carol Vincent on middle-class families' choice of child care (e.g. Vincent *et al.*, 2004).

References

Ball, S. J., C. Vincent, S. Kemp and S. Pietikainen (2004). 'Middle class fractions, childcare and the "relational" and "normative" aspects of class practices'. *The Sociological Review* 52: 478–502.

Bauman, Z. (1998). *Work Consumerism and the New Poor.* Buckingham, Open University Press.

Bourdieu, P. and L. Boltanski (2000). Changes in the Social Structure and Changes in the Demand for Education. In *Sociology of Education: Major themes.* Vol 2. S. J. Ball (ed.). London, RoutledgeFalmer.

Butler, T. and G. Robson (2003). *London Calling: The Middle Classes and the Remaking of Inner London.* Oxford, Berg.

Devine, F. (1997). *Privilege, Power and the Reproduction of Advantage.* British Sociological Association Annual Conference, University of York, 7–10 April.

Haydon, G. (2004). 'Values Education: sustaining the ethical environment'. *Journal of Moral Education* 33(2): 116–29.

Larabee, D. (1997). *How to Succeed in School without really Learning: The Credentials Race in American Education.* New Haven, CT, Yale University Press.

Lauder, H., S. Hughes, S. Waslander, M. Thrupp, R. Strathdee, I. Simiyu, A. Dupuis, J. McGlinn and J. Hamlin (1999). *Trading in Futures: Why Markets in Education Don't Work.* Buckingham, Open University Press.

Vincent, C., S. J. Ball and S. Kemp (2004). 'The social geography of childcare: making up the middle-class child'. *British Journal of Sociology of Education* 25(2): 229–44.

CHAPTER 11

CIRCUITS OF SCHOOLING
A sociological exploration of parental choice of school in social class contexts[1]

S. Ball, R. Bowe and S. Gewirtz, 'Circuits of Schooling: A sociological exploration of parental choice of school in social class contexts', *The Sociological Review*, 1995, 43(1): 52–78

Parental choice of school is one of the main platforms of government education policy and is the centre piece of the *Parents Charter*. But sociological understanding of choice and choice-making is woefully underdeveloped. This paper draws on an ESRC study of market forces in education to explore social class variation in choice of school in one specific locality. The complexity of choice-making is portrayed using data from interviews with parents and it is argued that middle-class parents are taking full advantage of 'the market' to sustain or re-assert their class advantages.

Introduction

This paper two purposes. One is substantive; to present an account of class related patterns of schooling in the context of the new 'market' in education. The other is theoretical; to move beyond the simple empiricism of much parental choice research and begin to develop a conceptual system within which parental choice can be analysed sociologically. Thus the paper is an attempt to break from the abstract and de-contextualised forms of analysis which currently predominate in research on parental choice of school.

The paper draws upon a set of 70 in-depth, loosely-structured interviews with parents of year 6 children in the throes of choosing a secondary school. The interviews were conducted in late 1991 and early 1992. A sub-set of those interviews (16) are quoted from below. The data relate primarily to three adjacent LEAS – Riverway, Westway and Northwark.[2] The social class categorization employed (working-class and middle-class) is derived from a composite of parents' occupations and education and housing – equivocal class have been excluded from the class-related generalisations and tendencies.[3] This is a first analytical forary into our parental data.

The extracts from interviews quoted below are more than usually in adequate in what they can convey, they are very much ripped out of context and lose impact and effect as a result. Choice making is typically accounted for by parents is terms of long narratives or a complex social calculus of compromises and constraints. The quotations are representative examples only – to provide a sense of things (see Gewirtz *et al.*, 1992). Both presences and absences in the data are important to our argument, what is said and what is not said by families in different class groups. And it is important to stress that we are trying to convey a sense of the dynamic between wants and constraints, values and deprivations – this is not intended to be either a one sided social pathology or a one sided structural deprivation argument.

The circuits

Research on parental choice in the Greater London area provides the opportunity to examine the workings of a complex school market system. This is a system which in many respects pre-dates the 1988 Education Act. Competition between schools here is not new and neither is the willingness of some parents to explore to the full the possibilities of choice available to them. But these processes have been given decisive new edge and greater impetus by the provisions of the 1988 Act. In particular our data point up the interplay between social class, cultural capital and choice within the differentiated circuits of schooling in this market system. This analysis is related to our general argument that while there maybe certain general principles of choice and market relations, the dynamics of choice and relations are local and specific. The principles have to be related to local conditions, possibilities and histories.

Across the three LEAs and adjacent areas in which this research in situated there are three clear circuits of schooling which relate differently to choice, class and space. (Different groups of parents 'plug into' each of the circuits and each circuit empowers its students differenttly in terms of life chances.) First, there is a circuit of local, community, comprehensive schools (A) which recruit the major-ity of their students from their immediate locality, have highly localised reputations and which have policies and structures which relate to a comprehensive school identity. They are oriented to fairly definite locales, which is in Giddens' terms a 'physical region involved as the setting of interaction, having definite boundaries which help to concentrate interaction in one way or another' (1984, p. 375). Some newly 'opted-out', Grant Maintained schools (GMS), at present part of this circuit, may be beginning to move between this and the next category. Second, there are cosmopolitan, high-profile, elite, maintained schools (B) which recruit some or often many of their students from outside of their immediate locale, which have reputations which extend well beyond their home LEAs, some of which are (overtly) selective, i.e. grammer schools, others of which have 'pseudo-selective' or limited catchment criteria. These schools are usually considerably oversubscribed.

Third, there is the 'local' system of day, independent schools (C). These are schools which in effect compete with the maintained sector and which provide alternatives or possibilities for parents who also make a choice to maintained schools; although of course they also attract parents who are interested exclusively in the private sector. There is also a fourth parallel but separate circuit of Catholic schools (D), which has its own hierarchy, pattern of competition and spatial struc-ture. We have little to say about the fourth circuit here.

The schools in each of these categories which fall into the remit of our study and which are regularly mentioned by parents in interview are listed below. Most of these schools are referred to in the extacts from data quoted later.

(A) Trumpton, Milton, St Ignatious (D), Oak Glade, Martineau, Ramsay Macdonald, Corpus Christi, Parsons, Overbury, Flightpath, Parkside, Gorse, Blenheim, Lymetheorpe and Goddard.

(B) Suchard Grammar, Princess Elizabeth Arthur Lucas, Flecther, Hutton, Pankhurst, the City Technology College (CTC), Nancy Astor Girls, Florence Nightingale, Cardinal Heenan (D).
(C) Trinity, Camberwick High, Madeley High, Harrod.

Several of the schools in the B circuit are typically considered together by middle class parents when it comes to choosing a secondary school. They are perceived as being schools 'of a kind', although their differences are also understood. They are often considered alongside the C circuit. The A circuit schools are less often considered by the middle-class parents we interviewed and then usually only for reasons of propinquity or special interest (e.g. single sex schooling) or as fallbacks in case other choices are unsuccessful.

> We went to Martineau (single sex girls), Pendry, Camberwick High and Madeley High and Princess Elizabeth. We went to the CTC, but it wasn't quite...it's actually having an open day next week. Trumpton I didn't go to though. I had been going to because I felt I ought to being as it was on the doorstep...I wasn't really interested and at the same time felt I ought to go, but it didn't work out.
>
> (Mrs K)

> She's down for Pendry but we'd actually prefer her to go to Princess Elizabeth. Lisa is more academic than Robert, although she is also quite aristic, she is an all rounder, she loves the sciences, she's good at maths, though she's not been on it...
>
> (Mrs Q)

> We applied to two independents, Camberwick High and Madeley High, and to the CTC college and to Princess Elizabeth. I really wanted her to go to one of the independents dents, you know, the results were that much better... and then Princess Elizabeth...she didn't get in there...and then CTC and Northwark schools were bottom of the list.
>
> (Mrs D)

However, the boundary between A and B is not absolute and fixed and there are borderline schools. And the arrival of the CTC, which 'opened for business' in September 1991, has 'disturbed' local system, as it is intended to do. Similarly some families in a sense also hover on the borderline or move between circuits, particularly between B and C, the cosmopolitan state and private schools.

> We're going to have a look at the CTC college...but that worries me because I feel that in a way it's like a guinea pig school...you don't know how it's going to work out, and I worry about Lisa being one of the first, in case it doesn't work out. But we're going to go and have a look, I'm, not shutting my mind to the possibilities of CTC.
>
> (Mrs G)

> Martineau for a while when they first amalgamated they didn't have a good reputation, and I suppose it was all the...a settling down period and all that sort of thing but I've heard some good reports from that recently, and that's an all girls school. And for Sara I do like the idea of all girls...a single sex school for girls.
>
> (Mrs G)

> We had a look at Milton and thought that was probably the best of...I mean I didn't go to Trumpton school, but I've been past there at lunchtime and I didn't like what I saw, so decided that that definitely wasn't to be looked at.

If he had not been successful in choosing the CTC, then we were going to pay for him, because we didn't consider anything else.

(Mrs M)

Very much, he came and looked at Pendry and he liked it a lot, and he came and looked at CTC and liked it even better, so the choice came down to Pendry and CTC and we were rather hopeful that CTC would come up trumps, which it did.

(Mrs M)

We've come from a family where the tradition has been for the boys to go to the local grammar school, which is now an independent school. So brothers, uncles, cousins are all there and have been there. So there was a very strong inclination for the first son to go to the independent school, Harrod, do you know it...and if he failed that, my only other, or our only other consideration was a local church school...out of the LEA, because I wouldn't consider Parsons. It had a very bad reputation and had had for many years and...it would not have been my choice.

(Mrs R)

Despite the element of tautology we refer to those families who engage with the education market in this strategic fashion as 'cosmopolitans' and those who make a deliberate choice for their neighbourhood schools as 'locals'. Emprically the former are likely to be middle class, but not all middle-class families are market strategists and some working-class although there are one or two middle-class examples. Nonetheless exceptions are exceptions; the pattern of class-related orientations to choice in the whole data set is strong. Altogether middle-class 'choosers' are much more active in the education marketplace (see also Echols *et al.*, 1990; Moore, 1990; and Blank, 1990 for similar findings).

Historical reputations have a key role in sustaining the circuits outlined above, at least for 'cosmopolitan' parents. *The point is that these reputations (or the existence of this circuit of schools) are not apparent to other 'local choosers'*. This knowledge of the system is part of the cultural capital that immediately separates out many middle-class parents (see Gewitz *et al.*, 1992) and orients them differently to school choice. But also many working class parents want and value different things from their schools, localness is often a value in its own right. The priorities and possibilities of choice are significantly different for middle-class and working-class choosers. Choice fits into their lives and life-plans in very different ways. Different class strategies of reproduction are involved, as we shall see.

Working class 'locals'

In the case of the working class respondents choice of secondary school was a contingent decision rather than an open one. Ideas about school were often subordinated to consideration of the constraints of family and locality; '...we find individual consciousness, language and social identity interacting in a dialectical fashion with the immediate social context of people's lives' (Dickens, 1990, p. 11). As Dickens also notes: 'According to Bourdieu, working class ways of life remain largely organised around the "practical order" of simply getting by' (p. 17). Thus, 'choice' of school fits into the practicalities of 'getting by' rather than into some grander social agenda of 'new, rarer and more distinct goods' (Bourdieu, 1984, p. 247). School has to be 'fitted' into a set of constraints and exceptions related to work roles, family roles, the sexual division of labour and the demands of household organisation. And the material and cultural aspects of this are difficult to separate. For our middle-class respondents, it was much more common to find family roles and household organisation being accommodated to school. But it is not simply a matter of education being of less importance for working class families, our interviewees were very concerned that their children get a good education. Rather the competing pressures of work and family life made certain possibilities difficult or impossible to contemplate and others seem obvious and appropriate. Choice of school as 'embedded' in a complex pattern of family demands and structural limitations. This is not a matter of cultural deficit but rather pragmatic accommodation.

Among our working-class respondents social reproduction takes on a more immediate quality, it is more closely tied to a sense of locale and community, of which the family is a co-extensive part. The local school is in Cremin's (1976) terms part of a 'functional community', it is chosen positively for this reason. That is to say, reproduction is defined and constrained and achieved within a spatial framework. Family life, and things such as school choice, are played out within, and over and against, a space and time budget. As Harvey (1989) suggests spatial practices 'take on their meanings under specific social relations of class, gender, community, ethnicity, or race and get "used up" or "worked over" in the course of social action' (p. 223). For the working-class choosers space and family organisation were very often the key elements in choice-making.

> They catch the bus...there's a few children that go to the school, they live in the other road...in the morning, my parents...they take them, because they have to go that way, they go past the school at half past eight, so they take them...then they come home on their own or I go and pick them up...if I'm picking Ian up, I'll pick them up as well. But I think you have to think of that now...where they go.
>
> (Mrs E)

> 20 past 3...the other one finishes at half past three...so you Know what I mean...she [Mrs W] has to fetch him first, the other one makes his way home...he's a bit sensible...and then she has to run down to go and fetch the one at Gorse school, you see...by the time ...the other one has to wait...out there till their mum comes back home...so...makes it very difficult for her. I'll appreciate it if they go to the same school. It's easier for her and for the boys...at least...because...the reason that's true...the education that he's doing...when the second one will go there...Yes, they went to Windsor Primary and then to Parsons, then I bought this house...it's about four years now...so we decided to move here...the nearest school...would be handy more for my wife than to run back to.
>
> (Mr W)

> Too far. I mean...it's not...I mean, supposing something was to happen, god forbid, that means I would have to go miles to get her, do you know what I mean or...get any of the children. I'd rather have a quick way of getting there, you know...
>
> (Mrs H)

> Really only because her brother goes there and its local as well, cos she'll have to pick up her sister as well, so she's got to have something local...Because

my husband really wanted him to go to Crawford Park, because he'd come from there, but we thought it was too far for him to go...that we wanted something really local and by having Trumpton, like my husband said, they can all go there, because it's a mixed school, which is good.

(Mrs N)

Here space, travel and family organisation are tightly tied into the choice of school. In transport studies, activity analysis research, which 'examines interdependencies within the household in respect of the scheduling and time-space constraints placed upon individual household members' (Grieco *et al.*, 1991, p. 1), suggests that 'household organisation lies at the heart of the understanding of travel behaviour' (p. 4). Among lowincome households on time-constrained budgets, the limitations of private and public transport play a key role in a whole range of decision-making. And, as above, these constraints and the forms of household organisation which develop as a result are particular associated 'with the gender roles of women' (Grieco, 1991, p. 4). 'Women in many such households are able to meet their daily domestic responsibilities and to respond to crises only by "borrowing" time and other resources from other houses (principally kin) in their social network' (Grieco and Pearson, 1991, p. 4). Where transport deprivation leads to the social isolation and segregation of particular social groups in particular localities social enclaves are created. The existence of such enclaves reinforces the importance of *the local* and the need for complex intra and inter-household dependencies. Research has also related the existence of enclaves to informational dynamics and local information structures (Weimann, 1982). Our work on parents' knowledge about schools underlines this. These patterns and processes of time and space management and the existence of social enclaves and social networks are of prime importance in understanding school choice making for certain class groups. And such an analysis begins to point up the important interrelationships between market schooling and the other deregulation policies of the current UK government; like transport, housing, health, social welfare and employment training (Carlen *et al.*, 1992).

The information networks of local choosers are limited in scope but nonetheless rich and useful. These network themselves are indicative of the relationship between local schools, families and community.

Well Parsons...my sister in law's children go to Flightpath and each one has done very very well. I've known children to go to Parsons and they haven't done well.

(Mrs H)

Time and space are important in the analysis of choice in another, related, sense. The schooling of children of these working-class families is not normally related to long range planning, it is not about other places and other times but very much about the here and now. Parental aspirations are often vague and typically limited by the wants and needs of the children themselves. (We return to this below.) Thomas and Dennison (1991) in a questionnaire study of inner-city students found 60 per cent reporting that *they* had made the decision about secondary school choice and both Thomas and Dennison (1991) and Coldron and Boulton (1991) found the 'happiness' of their children to be major organising principle in parents' approach to choice of school. It is not about who they might become but who they are. Now in traditional terms this might be interpreted as working class short-termism, as against the deferred gratification of the middle-classes, but alternatively we might see these differences in relation to conceptions of or use of space (and place) and time, that is as the relationship between locality and moral careers (Dickens, 1990).

> but we always said that they could choose the school they wanted to go do...so...she was quite adamant that she was going to Flightpath, she wanted to go there...we went to the open evening...and that's where she wanted to go and so we left it, I mean we just let them choose, even though it's probably not our choice, but it's not us that's got to go.
>
> (Mrs E)

> Yes, yes. I hadn't forced her. I'd never force a child into going somewhere where they didn't want to go, you know.
>
> (Mrs H)

Again we might see this in relation to horizons; time horizons and the imagination of time. The middle-class 'cosmopolitan' families are more likely to 'imagine' their children as dentists or accountants or artists, at university, in the sixth form; whereas the working-class, 'locals' will 'wait and see' they are less likely to speculate about the future of their offspring.

> I'm not educated and I'd really like them to be a bit more than me. I don't expect them to be miracle workers but I expect them to have a decent education...just pass their exams really, I mean I wouldn't be disappointed if they didn't, but I don't tell them that...I wouldn't force them to go on sixth form, but I mean my son at the moment is talking about staying on to the sixth form, but you don't know until it comes to it really.
>
> (Mrs N)

Again though these limited horizons may be in good part a matter of confidence and knowledge. By virtue of their own experiences cosmopolitan parents are more likely to be able to envisage their child in yet to be realised contexts. Again this may be a question of imagination (see below). Thus, in terms of 'getting by' the working-class parents were more likely to start with priorities related to family (or the child's preferences) or propinquity whereas middle-class parents typically started with finding the right school as their priority. But these perceptual differences are related to differences in 'Finite time resources and the "friction of distance" (measured in time or cost taken to overcome it) (which) constrain daily movement' (Harvey, 1989, p. 211). The distribution of 'time-space biographies' is class related – and in this way 'the organisation of space can indeed define relationships between people, activities, things, and concepts' (p. 216). Access to a car, the pattern of bus, tube and train routes, the local transport timetables, the pattern of busy roads and open spaces and the physical location of schools all affect the possibility and the perception of choice. To reiterate, what the interviews reveal are differences both in the ability (or willingness) to overcome 'the friction of distance' and perceptual differnces in spatial horizons. These differences have specific implications for the construction of futures for children. 'Spatial and temporal practices, in any society, abound in subtleties and complexities. Since they are so closely implicated in processes of reproduction and transformation of social relations' (p. 218). In part these horizons (and the complex relationship of space to distance) relate what Harvey calls the 'representations of space' to 'spaces of representation' or imagination; particularly in the latter 'unfamiliarity' and 'spaces of fear' are important.

> *Mrs H:*   She'd go...across the crossing...
> *RB:*   Through the Park?
> *Mrs H:*   Oh no, she wont' go through the park, definitely not...there's a pathway...it goes all the way round, past the library...and then under that footway bridge...then round the corner. She's been taught...she don't go in parks...no way.

The closeness of a school is an important value (as well as practicality) for many parents and will be a major priority or limitation in the making of choices. Most working-class respondents were clearly reticent about choosing schools for their children that would involve them in lengthy travel and reticence is not unrelated to the availability of public transport; although in a number of cases 'closeness' meant within walking distance.

> I think Parsons school is too far away. I mean I know you can get the bus, but...I mean there's a zebra crossing across the road, which you can cross and it's just about 15 minutes, 20 minutes walk...
>
> (Mrs H)

> Mainly because it's one of the easiest to get to for him, by bus...and it's just one bus...and it as the easiest one to get to.
>
> (Mrs G)

But while some working-class families distance and locality is almost the only significant factor in choice for others space is interwoven with other factors. There is a trade-off between this and other concerns.

> I considered Pankhurst girl's school, that's across the road...but I went to an all girls school, and I think it's a good idea for them to mix, and as her brother goes to Overbury we just straight away said Overbury.
>
> (Mrs J)

> Yes, I did see them exam results and my sister...she lives in...and her daughter and son have been in that school...and secondly...the education of that school and the principal...it's very strict, you know...like the kids, if they're not in uniform or they haven't done their homework, things like that, if they muck about...they'll be told off and at the end of the day they're not so...know all the time misbehaving in the school, things like that.
>
> (Mr W)

And while middle-class choosers appeared more confident about their use of space and their children's ability to manage travel and less constrained by unfamiliarity they were still often concerned about distance;

> We did think a little bit, not for very long, about Lockmere, mainly because a colleague at my school, her husband was the deputy head, and she always considered that it was sort of 100 per cent better than our school, but again...I'm not sure that I really wanted them to travel sort of an hour or so a day...morning and night...not with homework and dark evenings so really it entered our head but then quickly went out again.
>
> (Mr P)

Actually Princess Elizabeth is not really that far away. I didn't feel it was...well it is a bit of a distance, it's a tube journey, but it's only three stops on the tube, and for one reason or another, it has quite a good reputation. Though I don't like to take too much notice of reputations, but...she liked the idea of it...

(Mrs K)

I couldn't put a figure on my radius because it was fairly flexible, because it wasn't just a circle...we also took into account the ease of transport...so perhaps...a school over in Westing wouldn't be possible because the transport would be difficult...but Pendry wouldn't be too bad because it's one bus...it's a long walk but then it's one bus ride to Pendry...so the radius changed depending on the transport arrangements.

(Mrs D)

Some middle-class parents went to considerable lengths to make distance possible and safe for their children. But the point is for many middle class parents travel and distance emerge as contingent factors not priority or determinate ones.

when Robert came home from Fletcher on the first day, what I did was...I didn't actually stand at the bus stop with him, cos he would have felt a bit silly, but I followed the bus on my bicycle behind and checked everything was okay, and watched him get off the bus, and met him at home. So summing up it's not a major consideration but obviously you have to take it into account.

(Mr Q)

we'd have to for the first couple of years be fetching her and taking her, then obviously with both of us working, we'd have to reconsider it. But it's an easy enough journey, which was something I looked at, it's not just the distance, but do they travel in unlit parks or have to go under bridges or alleyways...its something I take into consideration.

(Mrs Q)

The complexities of 'choice', and the term must be used with care, for the working-class parents reported here are created by the intersection of the values and constraints of locality. There are vestiges apparent here of the 'localism' which Clarke (1979, p. 240) refers to as 'a pervasive mode of working class culture'. But there are also a set of frictions and limitation and fears and concerns which tie working class students to their local schools.

Middle-class 'cosmopolitans'

The cosmopolitans sometimes 'touch base' with the local system (A) but often express doubts (or different ambivalences) about these schools

Yes. I don't know whether it was just the impression, but it seemed there were more boys there than girls, I don't know what the split is. But...it appeared quite a liberal sort of school...but a parent last year spoke to me, whose sons went there and she was full of praise of Milton.

(Mrs K)

The use of the term liberal is significant here (see below).

Obviously the nearest is Trumpton school. I suppose living very near to the school it's quite off putting, I didn't look at the school...when my daughter was changing. In fact she had just come out of hospital and we didn't drag her around so many of the schools, but I did take Alex to see Trumpton and we were very very impressed with the school. I couldn't see him there but I was very impressed with what they had to offer there.

(Mrs K)

Through the interviews it is clear that the priorities of the cosmopolitan choosers are both more educationally specific and longer term than the working-class respondents. Nonetheless, some parents who are primarily oriented to the maintained/elite circuit (B) are willing to consider the local/comprehensives (A), while other are oriented exclusively to the B circuit. Some of the latter are making a deliberate choice out of the local, comprehensive system, particularly in the case of Northwark LEA. This is partly based on an historic antipathy to Northwark (ex-Inner London Education Authority (ILEA)) schools – an interesting class-related perception that the ILEA was engaged in social engineering not in the interests of aspiring middle-class parents.

We only went to Pendry for Robert...yes, that was the only one we went to for Robert, I just refused point blank to consider the schools in Northwark...It was very soon after the change as well, and things like that and I thought they wouldn't have had time to settle down anyway.

(Mrs Q)

Oh yes, my neighbour across the road has three daughters who've done very well, they're taking A levels at Trumpton school...so yes, I mean we did speak to other people locally...I was just going to say that a lot of people...particularly...that I've found parents very locally here, tended to send their children out of LEA anyway, unless they were very very worried about their travelling at eleven.

(Mrs B)

The exact opposite seems to be the case in Riverway, the LEA system is well perceived on the whole. For many Riverway parents, the Riverway schools have many of the qualities of those schools sought after by aspiring parents elsewhere. They can be pretty confident about *who their child will go to school with*, and about the long-range outcomes of choice.

I suspect all schools in Riverway are not really that different, and I do not believe they're going to go to one school and get into oxford and go to another school...and get no GCSEs. I really don't believe that round here...it's terribly easy to get absolutely bogged down in it all, and I think to some extent I'm falling into that trap at the moment.

(Mrs L)

Nonetheless, even in Riverway there are still some 'markers' of comprehensivism – like mixed-ability grouping and teaching schemes like SMILE mathematics – which are regarded with suspicion by middle-class parents and there is still a large private sector in Riverway, plenty of parents are not content to choose state schools. (More than 20 per cent of secondary age children in Riverway are in the independent sector.)

Overbury we just didn't like that much really. I think I didn't like the way they taught their maths. They all sort of taught out of books. It wasn't set until after two years, they were very late in setting in the subjects...

(Mrs L)

Reputation and image are key to understanding the position of the elite schools and for individual parents general reputations are often supported by first hand reports. The middle-class respondents were likely to refer to multiple sources of information relating to the reputations and practices of the schools they were considering and those they had dismissed.

> I like the idea of uniform, and I must admit...Pendry in the summer with the girls in their cycling shorts, so long as they're blue...I think they could be stricter on the uniform...but children are happy there and things like that, whereas at Corpus Christi, one friend of mine had sent three of her children there and her third child she pulled out after two terms, because the bullying was getting so bad, and they haven't got a strict policy on how to deal with it, and yet at Pendry it's something that comes up at least every week in assembly...how verbal bullying and physical bullying will not be tolerated...it's an infringement of each other's rights and...you know, they wouldn't like it done to them and...it's something that they act on, they don't just pay lip service to...they actually act on it. I mean verbal bullying I think in a way is worse than physical because it's something that's very hard to prove, and very very upsetting for the children.
>
> (Mrs Q)

> some classes have 35...I Just can't understand how teachers can cope, I find it hard coping with two. And they're mine. I couldn't cope with 35 of someone else's. But also at Princess Elizabeth's they have an HMI report which they photocopied and distributed to the parents, and one of the things that the inspectors found there was the attitude of the staff and the girls towards each other, was very caring and very supportive.
>
> (Mrs Q)

> it happened over a period of time somehow...you sort of hear things from people, but at the same time you want to make up your own mind...I knew one family whose daughter's probably in the third year now at Pendry, who had been to Trumpton for a year, but didn't like it at all, and he'd changed her in the second year...I'd also heard from one or two other parents that it had quite a good reputation. We also had an evening session with Mr Allison, the headmaster at St Josephs (primary), he organised a chat...going through various local schools...here and there giving his opinion but...um...it's hard to sort of remember everything, it seemed a very busy time.
>
> (Mrs K)

Also in some cases the reputation of a school has some specificity, that is they are perceived to have or not to have some particular strength or quality; eg Cricket at Lucas, Art and pastoral care at Pendry, technology at the CTC. Aspects of reputation interact with other choice concerns.

> That was one of the bad points really. There is a family who have four daughters and their youngest one is going there this year, Nicki could have travelled with them. But it would have been quite time consuming really, I wasn't very keen. The music didn't seem quite as strong as some of the other schools either.
>
> (Mrs K)

These market niches appear to be matters of marginal academic or curricular difference between schools rather than indicators of significantly different kinds of education (except perhaps at the CTC). But they are part of the 'matching' of the specific qualities or needs of children to the specific qualities or programmes of schools. This was of great importance to middle-class choosers but rarely mentioned by working-class ones. This is part of what Slaughter and Schnieder (1986) call 'holistic' choosing, the parents are concerned with the 'configuration of education' (Cremin, 1976) on offer in any institution. The size of the school can often play an important role here.

> I suppose from first looking at the school, they are dressed immaculately, and that's a very important thing as far as we're concerned. The discipline was always very good there, and I feel that they are secure, in a disciplined school. Also at that time I was very much looking for an extension of St Josephs... I don't know if it's easy to explain...it's...trying to find somewhere where she's been happy for the last seven years, that was important to me. Because Florence Nightingale was on a split site...again that was important to us, because it made it into a very small girls church school, and that's really what we wanted for her, and she was very happy...I mean she was happy there, but she just wasn't able to work, lots of distractions.
>
> (Mrs B)

> Milton, we went to Milton as well actually, yes...We were quite impressed by chatting to some of the teachers, they seemed very dedicated in what they were trying to do, but I felt the size of the school and...it seemed a bit daunting...
>
> (Mrs M)

> I don't think she took too much notice of what her friends were doing...her best friend isn't going to the same school, and...she's happy with Lady Margarets, she liked it, she liked the feeling of the small school...I was a bit unsure about the lack of options possibly, that there is in a smaller school, but I feel it suits her better.
>
> (Mrs K)

Futhermore, some middle-class parents were aware of established patterns of transfer from certain primaries to particular secondaries, almost a preparatory school system related to the secondary circuits. Thus, for cosmopolitan parents the choice of primary school is often the first of several strategic decisions involved in the careful construction of their child's school career. And the primary Headteacher often plays a key role in influencing or deflecting parental choices and in providing crucial 'access' and application information. For example, knowing which schools only consider 'first choices' is extremely important. Some of the cosmopolitan schools also have difficult or obscure system of entry, which are 'known' to the cosmopolitan parents. They are also often aware of the problem of over subscription.

> We looked at Martineau, in fact because she had just come out of hospital I had missed the open day...and...they didn't seem very keen to accommodate us at any other time, whereas Nancy Astor Girls welcomed us with open arms, even the second time around. I mean they're always very over subscribed. It's a very happy school.

Such parents are often able to employ forms of direct contact and negotiation which can be vital in accessing these schools (see Gewirtz *et al.*, 1992). This is where cultural capital plays a crucial role, knowing how to approach, present, mount a case, maintain pressure, make an impact, be remembered (Edwards *et al.*, 1989, p. 215 make a similar point).

> Well we went to see her because ... originally we were thinking of Lisa doing the scholarship and we were thinking of getting in a tutor because ... we realised that you have to approach these tests in a certain way and things like that ... which ordinary school I don't think prepares you for. And then a friend of mine said to me ... oh I know someone who is an educational consultant and if you pay ... if you go to see her, basically she gives you advice on what your child would need tutoring on, if she did, what schools would be suitable, she's independent ... and so rather than sort of paying out for tutors for across the board education, go and have a look to see what Lisa would actually need if she went for a scholarship. And then when we went she recommended a couple of schools, which she thought would be suitable for Lisa, and which Lisa would probably get into ... and ... what was it, it was only maths that she needed help on really ...
>
> (Mrs Q)

> I'd like to talk to him ... (Lisa's primary Head) I'd just like to say to him, Princess Elizabeth want two referees ... one is fine from the head teacher, but they want another one. All her extra curricular activities are associated with the school, so we can't actually give another one, I'd just like to ring him up and say; 'look, is this a problem with Princess Elizabeth?'; because he obviously knows the head teacher there pretty well.
>
> (Mr Q)

> Both schools were terribly over-subscribed. Florence Nightingale didn't make a big sort of fuss about joining the school, they just said that ... obviously if you fill the criteria do apply to the school. We were refused entry initially and then about 48 hours after, we had a place at the school.
>
> (Mrs B)

> I got Corine to agree to my phoning up on the Wednesday, to see if she could go and have another look, and any fears that she had had over it, hopefully dispelled, because she'd obviously got something in her mind about it. But they were ever so kind, and we had the admission secretary who showed us round on a personalised tour, the day before we had to accept or reject the offer and she was shown round with a friend of hers who had been at St Josephs and had moved to the Madelay High junior school ...
>
> (Mrs D)

In terms of image, the iconography of the parents own schooling often plays a part in perception and in choice, they want this for their children. The image of a school is also conveyed powerfully through its students. Clearly, as noted already, part of choosing and not choosing is concerned with who your child will go to school with.

> He loves his computer and all that kind of thing ... yes, that was a sort of ... that was a feature in our choice, but it wasn't the over-riding one. What we were looking for was a good, safe school for him to go to, and we particularly wanted a uniform because I didn't want to get into this ... £80 pair of trainers thing ... which I think ... it's hard not to if you go to a school that

doesn't have a uniform. And the thought that there were only going to be 300 children at this new CTC because they've only been open two years, I thought would be wonderful for Simon because he's at a small school now, and he would transfer to a small school and start and build up... which...he'd get his foot in the door with not so many children then. We thought maybe that would be ideal, touch wood.

(Mrs M)

In this respect for those families oriented to particular 'markers' of image the local school can come off badly because they can see too much of it; for example, the students leaving school.

Well they come out and I mean the uniform thing. They actually look not badly turned out but girls of 13 and 14 were wearing make up to school...then their manner was sometimes very aggressive...and their language was foul...and Princess Elizabeth I've seen girls coming out of there before, and I've always been impressed, and certainly was their manner and their attitude on the night of the parents' evening.

(Mrs Q)

We had a look at Milton and thought that was probably the best of...I mean I didn't go to Trumpton school, but I've been past there at lunchtime and I didn't like what I saw, so decided that that definitely wasn't to be looked at.

(Mrs M)

Examination production is a crucial part of the reputation of the elite/maintained schools, but this is not the exclusive or even primary basis for parental choice. There is a package of cultural indicators and class advantage embedded in these schools, including 'feeling of the atmosphere' which is fundamental to choice making. 'I don't really know what it was, it's more a sort of feeling of the atmosphere and...what sort of options there are after school, that sort of thing' (Mrs K). The parents are making a choice for the whole package, they do not want an examination factory; although they recognise the relationship between recruitment, atmosphere and performance. Quality and ethos rather than academic variety seem to be the concerns of the strategic choosers (Sosniak and Ethington, 1992). They are concerned much more with what Bernstein calls the expressive order of the school, ie, the complex of behaviour and activities in the school which are to do with conduct, character and manner. This expressive order is the medium for the recontextualisation of the student's out-of-school-life and is often 'a formalization, crystallisation, even idealisation, of an image of conduct, character and manner reflected by some, but not all, groups in the wider society' (Bernstein, 1975, pp. 30, 38 and 49). There are relationships here with Maddaus' (1990) and Slaughter and Schnieder's (1986) research in the United States. Both studies found that school ethos and climate were of greater primary importance to parents in their choice of school than were indicators of academic achievement, which were secondary considerations.

I mean somebody said to me, I hated Blenheim, it was just like a grammar school. Well that wouldn't put me off, because it was just like a grammar school necessarily, if I liked the school.

(Mrs L)

Thus, the perception and labelling of schools within these different circuits often seems to be directly class/culturally related.

> Clifford (Mr Q) went to Northwark boys, and I think that was one of the better schools in the area...and then they changed that and they amalgamated with Crawford Park, which one, the distance, two the fact that it's in the middle of an estate is something I'm not overkeen on, I think that school should be in separate environments.
>
> (Mrs Q)

> We have a school very near here called Trumpton, and the acid test that I use, and it's probably not a very good one, other than their academic records, is to stand outside the school and have a look at the kids coming out and see how they behave and how they dress and that...and I did that at a number of schools in the borough and none of them were suitable. It's a sad fact that Pendry, being in a predominantly middle class area, does tend to have a more supportive PTA, the kids are better encouraged at home, it's generally a better school academically than what was on offer round here...
>
> (Mr Q)

> It was the first choice for the Riverway school...although Arthur Lucas was the first choice, overall...so I think...when we actually went to Arthur Lucas...because...again it's a very small school, and the boys are beautifully dressed, which is unusual to find, and the academic side of things, as well as the musical side of things are very much for us...the sports side of things...I think they do play cricket, again that was another factor for us, among the other things, but it just sort of pieced the whole jigsaw together. A complete picture.
>
> (Mrs B)

Again, the iconography of traditional, selective schooling are valued where as markers of comprehensivism, like mixed-ability, non-uniform are also reasons for avoidance.

> And another thing I was pleased to learn about was that there is still an element of streaming in the school. They don't have mixed ability classes for the main subjects, for the core curriculum.
>
> (Mr Q)

> I think the other major factor for us was the fact that they do set them at Arthur Lucas, as they do at Coombe, and we haven't found this to be the case with any other school. And they are set within the first two weeks of starting the school.
>
> (Mrs B)

> Because I don't think mixed ability works when they change school...I think that was a great problem at Florence Nightingale.
>
> (Mrs B)

> We were a little bit disappointed in the sense that...I'd been to an old fashioned grammar school, in the sixties, where it was blazers and caps and berets and things like this and very strict discipline and so on, and so did my husband. We were a bit upset when we went to the parents' evening, or the prospective parents' evening, and they said well we are actually phasing blazers out.
>
> (Mr P)

As part of all this the fact that certain schools are more difficult to gain admission to is significant in itself; this serves as some sort of surrogate guarantee of quality. But also, particularly, as a mechanism of social exclusion, selection provides an assurance of continuity and to some extent commonality.

Further, the middle-class cosmopolitan choices are often based, in contrast to the working-class choices on long-range expectations about a child's education and/or career.

> But I think Lisa is the kind of child as well...I think she'd do what she had to do to get by, whereas at Princess Elizabeth they give that extra bit of encouragement and she needs that, and also they can stay on to do A levels there, whereas Robert isn't intending to do A levels, he wants to go on to art college.
>
> (Mrs Q)

> all through his junior school he's wanted to go on to art college and do something in fashion or design or...something in. the arts, definitely. I mean when he does change his mind it's...he wants to be a screen writer, or wants to be a director, but it's always in the arts...
>
> (Mrs Q)

> Results are an important part, yes, because without qualifications you don't have much of a chance in...and also my daughter is reasonably bright, and I didn't want her secondary school to be wasted. You know, if she's got the ability at eleven, then I don't want it to be killed in secondary school...for her not to achieve her potential.
>
> (Mrs D)

Again here the keynote is complexity. The political simplicities of *The Parents Charter* and the simplicities of some of the existing parental choice research (see Bowe *et al.*, 1994) simply do not capture the messiness, compromise and doubt which infuse the process of choosing a school.

Discussion: complexities of choice

The 1988 Act has enhanced competition between schools and between parents and in particular it has raised the stakes for success and failure in the market place (for schools and parents). In all this, we argue, certain sorts of choices and concerns are privileged, in a variety of ways, and certain parents have advantages in and through choice. (But these data also point up the mismatch between crude government notions of choice-making and the complexities of parents actual choice-making – parents' choice-making is humanistic rather then technological – as noted also by Adler *et al.*, 1987, p. 134). Parents are oriented culturally and materially differently towards the education market. They expect different thing from it. Some see it as a market and others do not.

What we are describing here was an already highly complex and differentiated system of school – with hierarchy, specialisms, selection, and over-subscription all present. Within this system space, distance and transport all play a part in making some schools more 'get-at-able' then others. History and reputation make some school more desirable to some choosers. Schools are more are less well placed in spatial terms and so are families. Patterns of choice are generated both by choice preferences and opportunities and capacities. Thus in making choices, reputation and desirability are played off against other factors, like distance, and like matching.

For some parents it is not the general characteristics of the school that are important but the specific match or fit between the school and their child. For working-class parents the child's wishes are more often decisive but family organisation is a constraint. For middle-class parents family organisation seems to be less of a constraint but child's input in to the choice process in more limited. The individualisation of choice is different in each case. In all ways noted above the market is strongly related to social class differences. There are two distinct discourses of choice in evidence. A working-class discourse dominated by the practical and the immediate and a middle class discourse dominated by the ideal and advantageous.

We want now to attempt to 'place' to education market sociologically in more general terms by applying to it an analysis developed in relation to a somewhat different but related set of changes by Bourdieu and Boltanski. In Bourdieu and Boltanski's (1979, p. 197) language the use of the market by 'cosmopolitan', middle class families, as outlined above, is a particular strategy of reproduction. That is, a strategy by which members of classes or class fractions 'tend, consciously or unconsciously, to maintain or improve their position in the structure of class relations' (p. 198). In our case, three factor 'trigger' or provide for the increased emphasis on strategic choice within the middle-class families reported here. First, there is the steady inflation of academic qualifications and their correlative devaluation. Second, and related, is the increased democratisation of schooling, by comprehensivisation. Both of these pose threats to the maintenance of class advantage by reducing educational differentiation and by changing patterns of access to higher education and the labour market. Third, is the new possibilities offered in and by the policies of school specialisation and increasing selection and choice within a market framework, being pursued by the Conservative government. That is to say, the middle-classes here are making the most of the new opportunities which these policies offer to reestablish their historic economic advantages or newly achieved status position. Or, in other words, changes in educational opportunity have 'compelled the classes and class fractions whose reproduction was chiefly or exclusively assured by the school to increase their investments in order to maintain the relative scarcity of their qualifications and, in consequence, their position in the class structure' (Bourdieu and Boltanski, 1979, p. 220). All of this might be taken as a perverse example of the arguments made by Halsey *et al.*, (1980). They suggest that educational growth, at least initially, tended to increase inequality because new opportunities are taken up first and disproportionately by the middle-classes. Further, they argued that in relation to inequality, 'scarcity of places was the crucial factor' (p. 217). The market is a new 'opportunity' for the middle classes, particularly related in its operation to the conversion of their habitus; and its infrastructure of 'desire', is driven by patterns of scarcity. It must also be noted that all of these factors are set within a context of financial retrenchment in education and general economic depression and unemployment. In relation to both, relative educational advantage takes on added significance. What is important here then is the 'utilisation of the specific powers of the educational system as an instrument of reproduction' (Bourdieu and Boltanski, 1979, p. 205). Furthermore, within the education marketplace this 'mechanism of class transmission' is 'doubly hidden'; it is obscured first of all by the continuing assumptions about the neutrality of patterns of achievement in education, and second, by assumptions about the neutrality of the market itself and by the model and distribution of the 'good parent' upon which it trades. The working-class families are also engaged in a process of social reproduction; but their 'use' of the school system is driven by a different set of purposes, values and objectives. Their utilisation of the specific powers of the education system is accommodative rather than strategic.

The market orientations of the cosmopolitan, middle-class families quoted involve the reinvestment of cultural capital for a return of education capital.

> The educational market thus becomes one of the most important loci of the class struggle...Strategies of reconversion are nothing but the sum of the actions and reactions by which each group tries to maintain or change its position in the social structure or, more precisely, to maintain its position by changing...the reproduction of the class structure operates through a *translation* of the distribution of academic qualifications held by each class or section of a class...which can conserve the *ordinal ranking* of the different classes...
> (Bourdieu and Boltanski, 1979, p. 220–1)

While this analysis of the role and functioning of the market in education undoubtedly needs further test and development it begins to bring policy, agency, class relations and social structure together in a powerful way. It allows us to see the link between the ideological and structural aspects of a public service market and the reproduction of class relations and relative economic advantage. These are the beginnings of a sociological analysis of parental choice.

Notes

1   This paper is an edited version of a presentation to the 1992 British Educational Research Association Annual Conference. It draws upon the work of an ESRC funded research study of market forces in education; award number R000 232858.
2   Northwark is an inner, metropolitan area with a Conservative controlled council. It has a diverse ethnic and socio-economic population; although over the past ten years there has been a steady process of gentrification. The housing stock ranges from detached mansions to council high-rise. It is an ex-ILEA education authority. Riverway and Westway are outer metropolitan areas. Riverway is predominantly middle/upper middle class and has a Social Democrat controlled council. The housing stock is dominated by terraced, semi-detached and detached Victorian and Edwardian villas. There is a large tract of parkland and many social amenities. This is primarily a residential/commuter area. Westway, especially in the southern area covered by our research, is predominantly working class. And there is a large, well-established south Asian community. The housing stock is dominated by 1950s urban sprawl and 1960s low and high-rise council housing. Local employment is provided by light industry and international transport facilities.
3   Data was collected in each interview on both parents' occupations, both parents' educational careers and qualifications, and housing status (ownership, council rented, housing association rented). Using a simple Registrar General's classification of occupations, a categorisation of educational careers into those terminated at the end of compulsory schooling and those with further education and qualifications (using both parents in each case) and housing status – a middle class/working class division was arrived at. Contrary to our expectations all but a few families could be straightforwardly allocated in this way. However, in further analysis we intend to employ a more sensitive classification of class fractions.

References

Adler, M., Petch, R. and Tweedie, J. (1989), *Parental Choice and Educational Policy*, Edinburgh: Edinburgh University Press.
Bernstein, B. (1975), *Class, Codes and Control, Vol. 3*, London: Routledge.
Blank, R. (1990), 'Educational effects of magnet high schools', in Clune, W. and Witte, J. (eds), *Choice and Control in American Education: Volume 2*, Lewes: Falmer Press.
Bourdieu, P. (1984), *Distinction: Social Critique of the Judgement of Taste*, Cambridge, MA: Harvard University Press.

Bourdieu, B. and Boltanski, L. (1979), 'Changes in social structure and changes in the demand for education', in *Information Sur Les Sciences Sociales XII*, 5 October: 61–113.

Bowe, R., Gewirtz, S. and Ball, S. J. (1994), 'Captured by the discourse? Issues and concerns in researching "parental choice"', *British Journal of Sociology of Education*, 15(1): 63–78.

Carlen, P., Gleeson, D. and Wardhaugh, J. (1992), *Truancy: The Politics of Compulsory Schooling*, Buckingham: Open University Press.

Clarke, J. (1979), 'Capital and culture: the post–war working class revisited', in Clarke, J., Critcher, C. and Johnson, R. (eds), *Working Class Culture*, London: Hutchinson.

Coldron, J. and Boulton, P. (1991), ' "Happiness" as a criterion of parents' choice of school', *Journal of Education Policy*, 6(2): 169–78.

Cremin, L. A. (1979), *Public Education*, New York: Basic Books.

Dickens, P. (1990), *Urban Sociology: Society, Locality and Human Nature*, Hemel Hempstead: Harvester/Wheatsheaf.

Echols, F., McPherson, S. and Wilms, J. (1990), 'Parental choice in Scotland', *Journal of Education Policy*, 5(3): 207–22.

Edwards, T., Fitz, J. and Whitty, G. (1989), *The State and Private Education: an Evaluation of the Assisted Places Scheme*, Lewes: Falmer Press.

Gewirtz, S., Ball, S. J. and Bowe, R. (1992), 'Parents, privilege and the education market place', *Research Papers in Education*, 9(1): 3–29.

Giddens, A. (1984), *The Constitution of Society*, Oxford: Polity Press.

Grieco, M. (1991), *Low Income Families and Inter-Household Dependency: The Implications for Transport Policy and Planning*, Oxford University Transport Studies Unit.

Grieco, M. and Pearson, M. (1991), *Spatial Mobility Begins at Home? Rethinking Inter-Household Organisation*, Oxford University Transport Studies Unit.

Grieco, M., Jones, P. and Polack, J. (1991), *Time to Make the Connection*, Oxford University Transport Studies Unit.

Halse, A. H., Heath, A. and Ridge, J. (1980), *Origins and Destinations*, Oxford: Clarendon.

Harvey, D. (1989), *The Condition of Post Modernity*, Oxford, Blackwell.

Maddaus, J. (1990), 'Parental choice of school: what parents think and do', in Cazden, C. B. (ed.), *Review of Research in Education*, 16, Washington, DC: AREA.

Moore, D. (1990), 'Voice and choice in Chicago', in Clune, W. and Witte, J. (eds), *Control and Choice in American Education: Volume 2*, Lewes: Falmer Press.

Slaughter, D. T. and Schnieder, B. L. J. (1986), *Newcomers: Blacks in Private Schools*, Evanston, IL: Northwestern University.

Sosniak, L. A. and Ethington, C. A. (1992), 'When public school "choice" is not academic: findings from the National Education Longitudinal Study of 1988', *Educational Evaluation and Policy Analysis*, 14(1): 35–52.

Thomas, A. and Dennison, B. (1991), 'Parental or pupil choice – Who really decides in urban schools?', *Educational Management and Administration*, 19(4): 243–9.

Weimann, G. (1982), 'On the importance of marginality: one more step in the two way flow of information', *American Sociological Review*, 47: 764–73.

CHAPTER 12

SPACE, WORK AND THE 'NEW URBAN ECONOMIES'

S. J. Ball, M. Maguire and S. Macrae, 'Space, work and the "New Urban Economics" ', *Journal of Youth Studies*, 2000, 3(3): 279–300

> Patterns in the circulation of surplus value are changing but they have not altered the fact that cities...are founded upon the exploitation of the many by the few.
>
> (Harvey, 1973, p. 314)

Introduction

The intentions of this paper are essentially very modest; although its scope is broad. Drawing upon our research on 'post-adolescence' (Macrae *et al.*, 1997a,b), we present three very different 'socioscapes' that separate and stratify the young people in our cohort sample.[1] Socioscapes are 'networks of social relations of very different intensity, spanning widely different territorial extents...' (Albrow, 1997, p. 51). We want to illustrate how three young people; Michael, Wayne and Rachel, are embedded differently within in their locality – Northwark, an inner suburb of London – within London more generally, and within global 'spaces'. In this respect and others, the lives of these young people are shaped in the relationship between a set of structural and material limits and possibilities and various individual factors. That is to say, their different 'opportunity structures' (Roberts, 1968) are in part self-made, constructed out of perceptions and assessments of risk and need and personal efficacy but are also framed by 'real geographies of social action' (Harvey, 1989, p. 355). Thus, we want to highlight the reflexive individualism of these young people – the creative manipulation of 'seemingly contingent geographical circumstances' (Harvey, 1993, p. 294) – but at the same time underline the continuing importance of classed, 'raced' and gendered inequalities in London. We shall also point up the spatial complexity of these inequalities (Ball, 1998; Ball *et al.*, 1998). As Harvey argues those with the capacity to 'transcend space... command it as a resource. Those who lack such a skill are likely to be trapped by space' (Harvey, 1973, p. 82). In looking at the different ways in which these young people address the question 'How shall I live?' (Giddens, 1991, p. 271) our analysis indicates one manifestation of and aspect of what Roberts *et al.* (1994) refer to as 'structured individualisation'.

We try to understand the 'choices' of post-adolescence as part of the much more encompassing construction of individual social identities and the different possibilities for such construction. We deploy a dual epistemology. On the one hand, 'identit[ies] need[s] to be understood as something created in response to a set of circumstances' (Tsolidis, 1996, p. 276), and as forged out of categories of perception and acquired dispositions. On the other, they are the product of the logic of individuality (Grossberg, 1996, p. 97). That is the individual is both 'cause and effect', 'both subject and subjected'. We must also take on board the very difficult possibility that, 'it may be that subjectivity as a value necessary for life is also unequally distributed' (Grossberg, 1996, p. 99).

In a way somewhat like Los Angeles in the USA, London plays a key paradigmatic, but largely unacknowledged, role in UK social theorising. The particularities of London as a global city[2] are often taken to stand for trends or patterns that can be spoken of and applied generally to all of the United Kingdom. Local and regional idiosyncrasies are easily ignored. Here we want to acknowledge the specificity of London and the particular 'opportunities' it offers for new kinds of work for young people. London is a contradictory space in many senses. It consists of several interpenetrating economies – old and new, varieties of ethnoscapes,[3] and changing patterns of opportunity and constraint. Crucially in the 1990s:

> The expanding sectors of employment differ from the contracting sectors in several important respects. In particular they have a much lower proportion of male jobs and fewer jobs open to workers lacking formal qualifications (except in private consumer services...). These growing sectors are short of the skilled and supervisory manual jobs on which males lacking school-level qualifications have traditionally relied to provide more secure and reasonably paid jobs.
>
> (Gordon and Sassen, 1992, p. 110)

Having considered and experimented with a variety of forms of presentation for our analysis we have chosen to offer a set of three individual narratives which represent very different kinds of engagement with a new kind of London/city 'economy' (or economies). These economies are each, in somewhat different ways, essentially 'youthful'. In a very general sense they are part of a well-established process of the commodification of youth. They are also 'the other side of the city story' – the other side of de-industrialisation. They may be particular to 'global cities' like London, but will be reflected, perhaps on a smaller scale, in many other western, urban settings. These economies are founded on the exploitation of 'fashion and music' as commodities in an economy of youth. They could also be described as economies of appearance and experience, of leisure and pleasure, as hedonistic economies. They have their own socioscapes and are internally diverse. They have different local and global dimensions.[4] In terms of the workforce, in large part what we are seeing here is the emergence of what Crompton (1998) calls a new 'service-proletariat'. However, to reiterate, the young people we present are themselves located differently within these economies. There are in these economies what Lash and Urry (1994, p. 143) call 'reflexive winners' and 'reflexive losers'; the latter are adrift in 'the wilder zones of the disorganized capitalist socioscape'.

One of the key and peculiar aspects of these 'new' economies is the particular role of the performativity of the worker and the skills of presentation or what Warhurst *et al.* (1999) call 'aesthetic labour'; 'the embodied capacities and attributes of those to be employed or are employed (p. 3). The blurring in effect of the worker and the work – the creation of unified identities around work roles; in the examples offered in this paper there are: model, hairdresser and DJ. Hochschild

(1979) makes the point that 'within service organisations, employees expend emotional labour. Their work is a mix of mental, manual and emotional labour' (Lash and Urry, 1994, p. 202). These organisations require a 'commodification of feeling' (Hochschild, 1979, p. 569). To an extent, the workers offer performances or are engaged in what Leidner (1993) calls 'interactive service work'. These 'new' economies are also themselves a part of the process of restructuring and re-spatialising the urban landscape, offering 'a multitude of public places for experiences of excitement, pleasure, entertainment, recreation, dining, dreaming and consuming' (Falk and Campbell, 1997, p. 127). These 'new' economies are also pre-eminently 'risky' enterprises. The movements of fashion and taste create an inherent instability and uncertainty which condition the identities, values and 'planning' of the young workers who service and represent these economies in practice and which encourages a sense of detachment.

In part the 'new' economies we touch upon here depend upon and underpin forms of sub-employment and underemployment or 'flexibility' as it is called, and as noted already, play their part in the development of a polarised 'dual-economy'. 'The new employment structure continues to offer job opportunities to the unqualified, but preponderantly within unstable sectors of employment, presenting recurring risks of unemployment and economic marginalization' (Gordon and Sassen, 1992, p. 127). Such employment is double-edged: 'Surplus or discontented workers find other jobs more readily within the metropolitan region than they would elsewhere, while employers have less need to hang on to these workers' (p. 107).[5] These 'new' economies are also often 'feminised'.[6] Service employment accounts for two-thirds or more of total employment in the USA and Europe 'and often 85 per cent or so of female employment' (Lash and Urry, 1994, p. 213). More recent figures, from the DfEE web site reports that service work now accounts for 75 per cent of total employment in the UK; although the service sector is of course very diverse. Nonetheless, many accounts of urban economies appear to neglect these new forms of cultural production or personal service in their concentration upon either more traditional forms as the paradigm for economic analysis or their fascination with information technology as the basis of an alternative 'knowledge economy'.

Many of the young people in our research cohort, like Michael, Wayne and Rachel (see below) are moving through new forms of work in sectors of the labour market which are concerned with the commodification of style. We might think of these young people as 'new style workers'; working upon themselves and for others in the fetishisation of image and the marketing of experience. There is a peculiar fusion of identity work involved here – a self-imaging process. Also the young people we present here are making the most, of what Bettis calls 'liminality'. The *liminal state* of the students, 'one without a defined status or future in the world of work' (Bettis, 1996, p. 106), reflects and is produced by the liminal state of the urban economy. That is, a post-modern urban complexity: 'the fragmentation, loss of community, and de-industrialisation of cities, along with the post-industrial plethora of images, focus on consumption, and changes in types of employment' (p. 107).[7]

The new urban, post-industrial labour markets engender both opportunity and risk – while excluding some 'others' altogether. They are also, as noted above, increasingly important proportions of overall urban and national economic activity in western societies. They have their own internal hierarchies and structures. Modelling, DJing and hair styling each offer some potential for a 'glossy future' or they may equally well produce low-wage, serial, sub-employment. Luck, tenacity and talent are important but 'success' also depends on who you are and who you know – differently distributed forms of 'capital'. Warhurst *et al.* (1999, p. 10) make the point that: 'Aesthetic labour is most apparent at the level of "physical appearance" '. Essentially our point is that London, and other global cities are characterised by a plethora of service/style outlets; from fast food bars, cafes and restaurants, cyber-cafes, haircutters, fashion retailers, clothes manufacturers to specialist music/night time venues. These are staffed by young people and target young people. They offer new kinds of employment but entail new kinds of risk and new kinds of discrimination.

A great deal of research on education and work in the UK still, despite the efforts of such as the Birmingham school, seeks to unify, essentialise and construct 'youth' as a deviant stage. Thus, much of the work on adolescence focuses on social problems such as drug use, teenage motherhood and delinquency (Lees, 1993). Even the class and ethnic analyses of the 1970s and 1980s, with their emphases on 'spectacles' of 'deviant' working class youth culture, on 'lads' rather than 'earoles', which celebrated 'the savage chauvinism of male youth culture' (Lees, 1993, p. 4) may be misleading in their sense of unicity. That is they fail to reflect the diversity of youthful 'socioscapes' to be found in the context of the global city – they are insensitive to time and space discrepancies.

Currently we are struggling with the challenge of trying to make sense of and write about the lives of an extremely diverse cohort of young Londoners; some of whom are refugees, parents, university students; some live with their families, others their single parent, yet others have their own accommodation. They come from a wide range of class/'race' positions and are evenly divided, male and female. In what follows we want to explore a set of three of the narratives or 'time-space biographies' (Hagerstrand, 1975) from this cohort; those of Michael, Wayne and Rachel.[8]

Michael

Michael is white, his mother is a single parent and does not work, he has a younger brother and sister, he is gay. He is a gentle and polite young man, always well-dressed. He has highlights in his hair and is of slim, medium build. He lives with his family in a flat in a 1950s block of local authority owned flats. He attended a Pupil Referral Unit (PRU) for most of his last two years of compulsory schooling and has few formal qualifications (3 GCSE passes, 1 A–C grade). Michael finished his school career at the PRU as a result of being bullied in his secondary school and refusing to return. He feels that he was not supported by his secondary school. His area of 'career' interest is very clear and long-standing.

> I have been thinking about it since I was eleven. My mum used to make clothes and everything and I used to help her. I just had an interest in clothes. I knitted a cardigan, and jeans, loads of clothes I made myself...I am interested in Art as well and I started putting together an art portfolio and I'll take it to College and show them what I am doing...I like doing my hair. I like anything to do with fashion, I like jewellery, clothes, hair.

Michael's vocational commitments are very much bound up with his identity, who he is, how he looks. He wears his interests on his sleeve, literally. He is making himself up, so to speak, through the clothes he makes, through his hair style.

On leaving school Michael's initial plan was to attend College to do a Fashion and Design course. He found most of the courses he wanted to do were only available to 18 year olds and would be expensive, so although he was offered several places including the London College of Fashion, he decided to train and work in Hairdressing until he was 18. 'It went on for ages, I didn't know what I was doing...I was really stressed about it. I had a word with my mum and we talked about it and we decided that I was going to stay working until I am 18...and then I'll go to College'. He was already working in a salon three days a week while at the PRU but through a Hairdressing Journal found a better paid job with 'on the job' (Network) Training. 'Its five days a week and I go to the (Hair) College as well in Oxford Street...I get about £80–90 a week plus £5–15 a day in tips'. Michael sees the job and especially the (Hair) College course as a way of making 'lots of contacts. I have got a lot of phone numbers already which is really exciting. So I am building up for the future all the time'. So, what is important is who you know and not just what you know.

In many ways this is contradictory. Michael is aware that formal education on its own is not sufficient and is networking himself into/across/between a new community into which he 'fits' well. Yet at the same time he needs a course or some formal training. The skill is to make the two work in tandem; if he doesn't 'know' people, maybe he will become trapped in a form of trading down – working in a local salon, not 'up west' in the heart of the global city. He sees his future in fashion design. 'When I've done the College course I'll be able to design clothes'. His *imagined future* and his route to that future are clear and continually in sight. But Michael finds the 'realism' of work more demanding than he had anticipated. 'I knew it was going to be hard. It is a bit harder than I realised it would be, You are more independent...I knew but I didn't really know'. He has to come to grips with being responsible for himself and for others; 'It is different'.

> When you're at school or whatever, you're sort of protected...It's not real life...I still have dreams and that but you begin to see that the one's you had earlier were just that, just dreams. You have to be more grown up, more mature...I try to act grown up but I often don't feel it.

While all this is more difficult than school, in other ways it is easier. 'Its easier because the people that I mix with and work with and whatever are people like me'; and this illustrates just how his new identity is being constructed through the blurring of the job and the role. 'People like me' was a phrase Michael repeated. He had felt out of place at secondary school 'because there is too many different sorts of people all together'.

With independence there are new freedoms. 'You get to meet a lot more people...You can stay out all night, all weekend, go to parties, I can choose me own clothes'. Altogether Michael has a sense of moving towards his goal. 'I am more settled. I know where I am going, I know how I am getting there or what ever. I have got my life planned out now'. What was a split, disrupted, unfulfilled identity is now more coherent – it makes sense. Within his work and study environments, Michael feels affirmed.

After a few months in his training placement he moved again, this time to a salon in the West End. 'It was all so slow. I thought I'll be here for years and I'll still not be a proper hairdresser'. But while he enjoyed the new location 'it got really busy straight away, they didn't have much time to train me...I was like working hard and not getting proper pay because I was a junior stylist but I wasn't getting trained'. He moved again to another central London salon. 'I had a friend and he was a hairdresser...I didn't bother telling him I was training...and they were hunting for people to come and work for them...so I was nervous at first there but I knew what I was doing'. Michael now works two days a week 'I get £100 per day' and attends a north London College three days a week. Interestingly, he chose the College because:

> Well it looks nice, it is like trendy and has really like modern ideas and decor and the people are like nice and helpful and it is really just like the sort of place I would want to go with the things I want to do and whatever. Its my sort of place.

A nice example of the ascendancy of style over content! Michael has found an institutional habitus in which he feels comfortable. He is now saving to do a Certificate in Fashion course at a prestigious London Fashion College 'it lasts about a year and they give you the basics and everything' and his ambition to become a fashion designer is firming up:

> I would like to go and work for a big shop...Christian Dior or something like that...I would probably be starting off just like helping other fashion designers, caring materials and stuff like that...most people start that way and just build themselves up...you just learn things from watching people and meeting people.

The steps between where he is and where he wants to be are filling-in, becoming clearer.

> If I can't do that I will probably go on and do like another five years at college...and get a degree or something there...as long as I feel I am learning things I don't mind how go I take or what I do...I know it can take years...people who are very successful in big fashion houses...have just started like me and worked up. You just need flair, hard work and a bit of luck.

And this final sentence clearly illustrates the way in which individualisation projects (Beck, 1992), coupled with class-mobility dreams (Walkerdine, 1997), are firmly embedded in the narratives which the young people tell themselves.

Much of Michael's social life in clubs, bars and restaurants mirrors and reinforces his interest in fashion.

> There's one called Legends and we go there on a Thursday night...and we are always nervous about getting in...they only let gorgeous people in...most of the time I drink vodka and cranberry juice...me and my friend are going away this year to the Dominican Republic [...] I like Prada, Gucci, I bought a pair of Patrick Cox shoes just before Christmas £250...I wear these like jeans, they are like printed newspaper, I got them and the jacket to match, the trousers are like £407 and the top for £208 something like that [...] I go to the gym a lot, I spend a lot of money at the gym. I spend a lot of money going out, socialising...

But he continues to live at home and is invested heavily in his family and in particular in his relationships with his mother.

> I pay her at the end of the month, I pay her so much rent and the I help out with the bills and put some money towards the telephone bill and I give my

sister pocket money and stuff...I've taken my mum to the theatre...out to dinner things like that...I took her shopping at the West End as well for her birthday, splash out a bit...I take my Mum to places that my Dad should be taking her to...We do family things take my sister out...

Nonetheless: 'We argue about lots of things, we argue about money, she also knows that I am gay...she doesn't really accept it...she does most of the time'. When asked to envisage life in five years time Michael was clear about one thing: 'if I do leave home my mum will come with me...I eventually want to have a big, nice house, I don't want to have children...so instead of the children I will have my mum'.

Michael's post-adolescence and his transition into working life is a combination of planning and experimentation. He is very strongly personally invested in his 'working life'. His interests, his fantasies about the future, his leisure and life style and social relationships are tightly bound together in his emerging identity. He is accomplishing an identity, even perhaps making a project of himself in a positive and highly motivated fashion.

> I don't really think about my relationships, I am now, whatever, but if they happen, they happen, if they don't, they don't. It is just, I will concentrate on my work and everything more than anything else and just enjoy myself as I go along...

Michael's socioscape is extensive, his work and social life takes him far and wide across the city, involving him in a variety of social networks. His College is in north London, he works, shops and goes to clubs in the West End, but he continues to live at home.

Wayne

Wayne is white, he wants to be a music engineer/producer, his father works as a freelance DJ and van driver, his mother drives for 'Meals on Wheels'; the state-managed service which brings hot meals to senior citizens doors. Wayne lives with his parents in a local authority flat in a post-war housing estate. He gained no qualifications at all while he was at school. In his first interview while still at school he talked vaguely of 'going to College' but could not identify a course he wanted to do. His mum: '...wants me to go to College'. Wayne had a sense of what he would like to be but he saw little chance at that time of getting from where he was to where he would like to be.

> I want to be a studio engineer for music and she said [careers officer] that I would need to get quite high grades for that. That is when she said to me that I would need something else to back me up just in case...Well, my back up plans are, I'm not sure. If I had to stay on here [at school] then I would, but I wouldn't really want to...I try not to think about it that much, not during school anyway. No, just like now and again I think I get worried.

Talking about his friends Wayne explained:

> Most people you know they have been in school for so many years they just want to get on with their lives now, they've had enough of sitting in

classrooms, they're bored, they just want to get a job and some money...they want a fresh start, a job, a new life, not more writing and learning things that nobody cares about...

Significantly, 'learning things that nobody cares about' encapsulates the redundancy of formal education in Wayne's world. There was no 'choice' for him and little of relevance to his 'real' social world in what was presented in the formal school curriculum. Essentially, Wayne has had enough, his learning identity is exhausted, indeed his identity as a learner may be in Weil's (1982) sense 'inhibiting' even 'destructive' (p. 223). There may also be intimations here of a kind of identity formation that Wexler (1992) calls 'defensive compensation'. Wayne sees no future for himself in formal education, at least for the time being. Evans and Hienz (1994, p. 10) suggest that:

> in cases where individual decision-making about training and employment does not lead to a balance between personal preferences and job requirements, identity development is precariously limited, because one's ambitions and orientations cannot be carried through in the work context.

In the same way, if your interests are with aspects of the 'new' economies of youth, as in Wayne's case with music and music-related technologies, and these are not reflected in the formal offer of education and training in an accessible manner, then you have to look elsewhere – perhaps to the sort of personal networks and social grapevine which Michael is busy developing, or just rely on luck and happenstance.

Again there are indications here of what Bettis calls the liminal state: 'If students perceive a lack of certainty or predictability in their lives...envisioning their future lives is a gamble' (Bettis, 1996, p. 13). Wayne did rather half-heartedly explore the possibility of a College course and had a vague sense of what was out there.

W: I have rung up a few but I can't remember what ones, but they said you have to ring back at another time, because the time I get back from school it is a bit late, so I suppose I will probably have to take a day off school and do it.

S: So you haven't got any information from the Colleges yet. Have you seen any College brochures?

W: Well it was from other people who had sent off for them and I lent them and had look at them...if I do look through (the local paper), I look through it quickly and I haven't seen anything.

S: So you haven't seen anything. What about College Open Evenings?

W: I haven't been to any yet.

Little of this information seemed relevant to Wayne. The substance of most Careers teaching at school had passed him by. As was the case with many other students, he could remember little of the advice or guidance proffered. Nonetheless, he is aware of the landscape of possibilities in post-16 education and training. He has been exposed to some preparation although little has seemingly been remembered.

S: You have the City and Guilds lessons, don't you. What sorts of things go on there as far as Careers are concerned?

W: He just gives us sheets and that just things like that, and tells us to read the question, write about it, what do you think.

S: So do you get any sort of information from him about what you might do next year?

W: Yes I suppose a bit yes.

S: Can you think about anything you have done?

W: (Long pause). No not really.

S: Did you get a copy of this little booklet called *Choices*? (Careers options in the local area for post 16's). Was it any good, can you remember?

W: I can't really remember...I know the Careers Officer told me there was a few that I could go on but I can't really remember. Some people might do 'A' levels and GVQs or something. We spoke about them in City and Guilds but I can't really remember that much about them.

S: Yes, now if I said to you what Colleges could you go to, what Colleges could you name?

W: I can't really remember.

This also points up some of the subtleties and difficulties of ethnographic research. We had pre-specified our research concerns ('choices' made by young people in the urban post-compulsory education and training market). We had also constructed a set of topics to explore in the interviews. Thus, 'of course, we influenced what they said by the questions we asked and the ways we asked them' (Hodkinson, 1999, p. 562). Talking about an irrelevant experience which is not part of any horizon for action (school and post-compulsory college) might well just precipitate an 'I don't remember' response.

Wayne's responses indicate that he is aware of the 'normal' post-compulsory route of college and is caught up in this to a degree – after all, school has been pushing this message for some considerable time. All of our cohort have been socialised to recognise the importance of formal qualifications – even if some of them are unlikely to gain any. So it is not surprising that Wayne attempts to produce himself in this manner, in the way he is supposed to – a partial attempt to maintain self-esteem in the interview context. It was however evident throughout the series of interviews that Wayne's locus of interest lay elsewhere, outside of school, outside of formal training, outside of mainstream careers and job markets. And when he talked about this, the response was focused, informed and involved.

S: So let us just think about this sound engineer business. How long have you thinking about that?

W: Years.

S: So what has attracted you to that?

W: My dad is a DJ. He plays music, I am as well, I suppose that is why, and I know a few people who make records and things like that...I have been in there helping like and it is just something that I have always wanted to do...When I was about eleven or something he just got the equipment and just started off. He goes to all different clubs and he gets paid for that...I have played at a few clubs before, three times that my dad has actually done with friends and I just wanted to go into sound engineering to do it, because that is what like most of the other people the bigger names, that is what most of them do, that is how they get well known...DJ he just plays the music. I think I could do that because I've seen my dad do it and it looks easy.

By the time of his second interview his focus (in the interview at least) had shifted towards an interest in 'on the job' training (Network Training). But Wayne was still 'thinking about' rather than committed to this path.

W: You need qualifications and you wouldn't you probably wouldn't get that if you just had a job.
S: Why do you think qualifications are important, Wayne?
W: I'm not sure but I don't think, I think you will just get a rubbish job that won't go anywhere if you don't have qualifications.

Network Training seemed to offer the right balance between getting a qualification of some kind and gaining some 'experience' without the rigours of more 'writing and thinking and being bored'. In all this Wayne's 'learner identity' appears fragile, 'used up' rather than thoroughly alienated. However, Rees *et al.* (1997, p. 493) make the important point that: 'Learning identities are not simply the product of formal education...they also emerge in relation to informal learning opportunities, with rather different implications for the evaluation of alternative courses of action'. As we shall see, Wayne is looking at post-16 routes as means to get to where he wants to be. His parents are presented as supportive rather than directive.

> I was thinking of doing a network training but we haven't found much out about that yet...I don't know I just thought about going to College then I thought about going to the Sixth Form and I wasn't too sure about that and then I thought of doing a network training...I didn't read about it but people have been speaking about it again and I thought I might like that and then I found the stuff at home so I had a little look...quite a few of my friends want to do it yes...because like me they've had enough of school and that...I don't know, I think it gives you more experience than College, rather than sitting there being taught all over again you can actually go and do it and move about and do things not just writing and thinking and being bored. My mum sent off for a few things and that from Colleges, but I think I told you about that before. Anyway it wasn't really what I wanted, and after I found out about network, I just wanted to go and do network. [my parents] think it is a good idea. My mum just says whatever I want then do it. [my dad] is the same, he doesn't say much.

The one constant in Wayne's general uncertainty about life after school remained his interest in music production and DJing. He saw Network Training as a possible 'way into the business', in part an investment in the development of social capital. As with Michael, 'who you know' is an important part of Wayne's career trajectory. Perhaps this all points towards a wide range of networks and contemporary urban grapevines.

> I don't know, I suppose I could always try and get other work as being a producer or something like that, because like through my dad, my dad knows a few other people and that, that do all that professionally and make their own records so I could just go to them with what like I have done or whatever, network training or whatever and just see what they think.

For Wayne his involvement in music and the 'club scene' could be seen as a way of beginning to replace or rebuild social networks and characteristic trajectories which had been eradicated by the 'economic restructuring' of the 1980s. His introduction into these social networks is through his family and a kind of apprenticeship into the 'family business'. These represent an 'opportunity to develop a different conception of [his]...abilities from that gained for formal education' (Rees *et al.*, 1997, p. 493).

Eighteen months on from leaving school Wayne had done one year of a College Studio Engineering course but then dropped out because the course 'was rubbish' and 'was more electronics than there was engineering' and 'I was only in the studio for about a month'. He then worked with 'a uncle's mate' installing fitted-kitchens but found this interfering with his increasing involvement in DJing. 'I was playing at the Lyceum at the Friday and a couple of stands on Saturday' and 'doing the Internet on a Saturday afternoon as well, so I thought, sod it'. He now spends three days a week working for his father's Internet radio station, without pay. This involves 'on air' work but Wayne commented that 'when I was at school I wasn't too interested in computers. And then, like, as soon as I started doing this with my dad I have learnt a lot about computers, I can even type now'.

Wayne continues to live at home but does not contribute to the family finances, although his mother wants him to pay rent 'I had an argument with my mum last night, she said I have got to. But I'll cross my fingers' and 'my mum was always saying to me, you should have a job but now she understands, now I am playing out a little bit more'.[9] 'I told her that I would help around the house but I don't'. Arguing with your Mum about money and work seems one of those 'normal' things of family life for our young people, as Michael put it: 'We had some arguments and stuff like that, she just, we still have arguments, she is just being my mum'.

Wayne sees his future firmly in DJing. 'I suppose I am quite happy where I am, for now, in two years I would like to be playing out somewhere bigger'. But he does not rule out the possibility 'when it comes to five years' of 'going back and doing a course'. Wayne appears to have developed or rebuilt a sense of personal self-esteem and efficacy which was undermined through his school career. In some ways it could be argued that in-school discourses which stress normative patterns of 'exam qualifications as achievement' have masked or silenced any alternatives. He says 'I don't know how to describe myself, I don't think I am stupid'. He is making a career and an identity in what is literally a 'twilight world' of cash-in-hand activities, £60–70 for an hours work; clubs open and close and 'the DJ world is about who you know', loose networks and fragile reputations. But this is where he feels at ease, competent, engaged. It may well be that the risk involved in performance is part of this 'high' – the excitement/risk is based on personal skill, hard work and maybe a bit of luck too! 'I get bored with things really easy, music I never get bored, music changes all the time do you know what I mean, especially drum and base it changes all the time'.

Wayne is perhaps an archetype of the Giddensian 'self-reflective identity'. He manages and in some ways thrives in a liminal world somewhere between work and unemployment, adolescence and adulthood, independence and living at home, it's 'too cushy at home'. He is self-employed but not paying tax. He does not 'sign on' (for state welfare benefits) and the Job Centre has nothing he is interested in. There is perhaps something here of Erikson's concept of youth as a moratorium, a period of experimentation. 'I suppose at some point I am having to get some kind of job but not yet though'.

Rachel

Rachel lives with her family in their large, semi-detached Victorian villa. She is white, slim, tall and very attractive. She is always socially at ease. She was spoken about by several of her school peers as the 'golden girl' of the school. She was admired and encouraged by her teachers and as well as her exceptional academic record was gifted at sports and dancing. Both her parents are university graduates; her mother a Trades Union official, her father an Architect. Her older brother is studying languages at University.

The question of Rachel going on to University was never in doubt. But it was clear to Rachel that she would not be staying on at Northwark Park School post-16 and she took very seriously the process of choosing another institution for her A-levels. Moving into post compulsory education was going to be path of a predetermined route towards professional, high-status, employment. Rachel wanted a distinctive pathway which would reflect and enhance her personal capacities and offer advantages in the competition for Higher Education places. Indeed, her family and teachers expected nothing less than this for her. 'You want a challenge…like a good college that is difficult to get into. That's why I have been looking at the sort of best colleges round this way'. Even in her final compulsory year of school, when she was still fifteen, she was beginning to research and think about her university and course options and again she was aiming high. Her *imagined future* is extensive and carefully planned. Her spatial horizons are also already broad. She is looking for something which will mark her out as superior.

> I have been looking at Universities, I have looked at lots and I want to go somewhere where it is difficult, that only takes the best, where the grades are highest. I am ambitious and I want to do well. That is another reason I don't really want to stay here because it is not really a sixth form for the ambitious. If I did Medicine I would love to go to Edinburgh because they have study and work opportunities in America, Australia the Far East and Europe and apart from sport that is like my second love is like to go and travel…

Rachel achieved some outstanding results in her national examinations at 16 (10 GCSEs at grades A–C) and eventually chose the well-thought-of Riverway Tertiary College at which to study A-level Biology, Chemistry and English. In the 'economy of student worth' Rachel was a highly desirable commodity. 'I just walked in on enrolment day…they saw my results and they just went like blonk, blonk, and put me in the tutor group and there you go, you are in…'. Rachel soon settled in at Riverway, although she found it rather daunting to begin with. Several students in her tutor group had previously attended private schools and 'were just so confident'. Nonetheless, she was elected as student representative; which: 'will look good on my UCAS form (UK Application scheme for university admission). I got in the netball first team, so I'm doing alright. I'm in the drama club and the netball team and met loads of like really friendly people there too…'. Rachel is fully aware of what sorts of activities lend a high degree of social cachet, credibility and personal integrity in relation to making application to prestigious Universities. Alongside her College course, Rachel also worked part-time to finance her social life. Her parents paid for her travel to College each month but she paid for most of her other 'necessities'. She worked for Tesco's supermarket 12 hours a week during GCSEs and 16 hours during A-levels. During this time she was 'promoted'.

Throughout Rachel's final year at Northwark Park and first year of A-levels it had remained her ambition to study medicine at university. However, after visiting some hospitals and a spell of work experience at a teaching hospital (undertaken because 'it would look good on my UCAS form and show that I was serious about my choices') she changed her mind.

> I felt that most of the doctors were very good, but they were very narrow-minded...I feel like its no point in giving people medicines when you're not addressing the problem in the first place and I feel that if I do Human sciences first I will have a much more broader understanding of that when...if I do go on to medicine...

Somewhat by chance Rachel came across a course in Human Sciences at Cambridge: 'I read the thing and I was like wow, hallelujah, just tell me what to do. So that's what I've applied to do'. She also applied to and was interviewed for a course in Psychology and Neuro-Science at Manchester. Rachel was very aware of the complex balancing of choices, offers and grades involved in maximising her final chances and had carefully researched and thought through her options.

> I really want Imperial to give me a low offer, which I don't know if they will...Because in their prospectus it says, 'Ranging from A, B, B, to B, B, C' and if they give me B, B, C then if I don't get into Cambridge, that'll be my first choice, because it's the course I want to do. Like I said I've got problems with the Sussex one, and they're the three Universities that do this course.

She was interviewed for the Cambridge course and 'was the only person there who went to a state school, the only one'. The interview took place over two days and she described the first day as 'a total disaster' but on the second day 'I had that private school bit of arrogance, the second time, because I didn't care...I thought well I'll go down fighting, and that is what I did and I got offered a place'. However, also looming large in this particular 'choice' equation was the matter of Rachel's current boyfriend, who she met during her work experience.

> I am now going out with a lawyer and its a big coup because he's very, very old...30...[another kind of time horizon!]...I started going out with him because I found him fascinating and I like his mind.

Rachel's parents were unhappy about her relationship and this led to a series of family squabbles, to escape from which she began spending more and more time at his house. In their first year together they holidayed in Turkey and after finishing her A-levels booked to go to California. Rachel continued working in Tesco's to earn as much as she could before University began. As it turned out her A-levels grades were a disappointment to her, an A, B and C. Not good enough for the Cambridge course. After receiving her results she spent most of the day ringing round various universities without success. She found the experience extremely stressful. Only one other possibility emerged.

> I couldn't think straight, I was in a panic and you've got to move fast if you're going to get something good and it's not fair in a way, it's such a scramble. But you can't think straight and people tell you things on the phone and you're just, oh right, and you just accept it and I know I couldn't get in where I wanted but I wasn't like thinking, because I was so gutted. They had already offered me a place for next year when they turned me down for this year, they said I had got a place next year, that was definite...I was quite gutted in

a way because if I had put them as my first choice I probably would have got in. I would have been going somewhere, it was like a big risk to put Cambridge down and I took the risk and I ended up with nothing. When I hadn't done badly and I got nothing. Imagine, all that work, all the horrors of the Cambridge interview and I got through all that and ended up with nothing.

Her failure to get into Cambridge was a major blow and while she remained confident in her abilities, at the same time she was seeing herself as a 'second chancer', someone who had just missed that point of distinction.

If I did re-takes and got three As, and applied again Cambridge wouldn't take me. They wouldn't take people who have got re-takes, realistically. They don't need second chancers, they have enough clever people to choose from first time round, so no, I wouldn't take second chancers, if I was Cambridge. I am not prepared to do re-takes because I did well enough. I know I did well enough and I am not prepared to do it just to go to Cambridge...I know I can do it and I don't need to prove myself to anyone.

She considered other possibilities, and with the help of a friend of her mother, through the 'clearing' scheme, found a place at Sussex but decided against it. Interestingly and importantly, her reason for the refusal of a place, after her initial rush and panic was (still) based on her desire to access a high prestige and distinctive university. Her rejection was based on aspects of class-taste and desire for distinction and advantage.

I thought if I go there I will regret it because it feels like it is second rate and I didn't want to take something just for the sake, just because I hadn't planned the year out and I could so easily have said, okay, I'll go to Sussex, but it wouldn't have been the right decision for me.

Rachel decided to take a 'gap year' and work full-time for Tesco's where she was offered the post of Assistant Manager of Customer Services. She had also begun some modelling assignments and had appeared on some television advertisements. 'I don't know whether I want it [the Tesco's promotion], because I have just signed a modelling contract over the summer holiday'. At the same time she was intending to leave her family home and move in with her boyfriend. He, along with his parents, was putting gentle pressure on Rachel to start a family. But in interviews she remained adamant that she would not consider having children until she had finished her first degree. 'I have to live my life because, if I don't, he knows I would resent him'. Her *imagined future* partly as a result of her failure to get into Cambridge, partly because of her relationship with Paul was now less certain. But she saw herself as having a number of possibilities and life choices ahead.

I don't know, I haven't decided yet, I don't know. I might do medicine then, or I might have a family and do a part-time degree or part-time masters or I could train to be a teacher, I don't know, I could do anything I want. I think I will have loads of choices. I will wait until it happens because my course is so broad in my first year it is like I am going to do so many different areas of Science that interest me, biological sciences and psychology and stuff like that [...] If I like it so much I could go into research, anything.

In the meantime her modelling work offered some entirely different possibilities. Rachel explained.

> They pick you up from your house in a car and they drive you there, you have your make up done, you put on whatever they ask you to wear and then you just stand in front of the camera...she phoned me up and she went, the producers on the show really liked you, they would like to book you again but it would be much easier if you go and sign with an agency, go and see this agency, I really recommend them, they are quite small so they have time to look after their models really well...We went along, they were really interested, they said, yes we will definitely book you...they looked me in the face and they were like, you actually would probably sell very well in Japan. If you go to Japan we give you £10,000 to go to Japan for six weeks and that is your money, out of that you have to pay for your air fare and your accommodation and you pay for your test shots once you are there. So the first time you go you will probably only come back with about three grand, but next time...you will probably come home with about fifteen grand, and I am sitting there going...I could buy a car, I was sitting there thinking all of this.

Rachel continues to set the 'risks' and possibilities of modelling against the security of her Tesco's job.

> I could go to castings every day for a whole week and not get a job. It is like you go along and you take your book and they basically just stare at you and decide whether they are going to employ you [...] because I have only got four photos...I shouldn't be going to castings. The job is ten days in Spain and it is worth £2,000...I will go to this, but there is no guarantee I have got the job. It is highly unlikely because it is the first ever one I have been to [...] So Tesco's has to take priority because I need so much money to live and I know what I'm getting there.

But all this is an interim. It is just one of a range of choices which Rachel has at her disposal right now. At the same time she is forward thinking and has other intentions and ambitions.

> but I don't want to be a model. It is different for the others because that is what they want to do. Like the agency know that I want to go to University and they said, there is no way that we would stop you going, we reckon that it is better that you go because this isn't going to last forever.

While in many ways Rachel remains buoyant and clear headed about her options and her future, she also feels that her failure to get to Cambridge and the stresses and strains surrounding that has changed her. Her idea that for her, anything was possible has been deflated. Failure is a relative thing. She now feels:

> older than I was...like before...I thought I could do anything I wanted, I thought I could fly, everything I touched worked out, now I am a bit more cautious, not so sure. I am tired more tired than I ever have been...I am, at the end of the day a bit gutted that I didn't get into University this year. I feel as if I've aged, sometimes I feel really old and that's funny.

In many ways Rachel epitomises many of the clichés of late modern London life but clichés which are more often associated with 'thirtysomethings' rather than teenagers. She has a stable relationship and a job. She has left her family home and has already travelled widely. Modelling offers contacts with the worlds of television, fashion and publishing and the possibility of more travel. She expects to spend two or three months travelling at the end of her 'gap year'. In a sense her life is already being lived in a global 'socioscape'. Her friendships also span a range of ages and contexts – from boyfriend and his colleagues to her immediate College and school peers – and her future horizons stretch considerably ahead and involve a complex of education, work and domestic possibilities.[10]

Rachel's narrative is also a good example of the 'partial rupture' which now characterises some forms of class reproduction in global cities. In a society where more and more, higher education is a mass rather than an elite experience, middle-class people have to obtain their certification from top-rated institutions to assure the reproduction of their class advantages. In a risk society class reproduction may be increasingly less inevitable. Rachel is aware of this and she takes 'risks' to attain distinction, to gain a place at the 'best' university. But she misses her mark. As much work on youth transitions in the UK has indicated (Furlong and Cartmel, 1997; Hodkinson *et al.*, 1996), changes in the traditional labour market coupled with speed of change have heightened senses of risk, even for those with excellent academic credentials. 'Processes which appear stable and predictable on an objective level may involve greater subjective risk and uncertainty' (Furlong and Cartmel, 1997, p. 37). Rachel wants 'the best' and wants to be 'the best'. While an academic version of this is 'on hold' she can excel in other ways.

Discussion

Compared with Michael and Rachel, Wayne's world is a local one rather than a London one and a static rather than a mobile one. His socioscape is much more narrowly drawn, set between the clubs he plays-out at and his work for the Internet radio station (admittedly with its own kind of global possibilities). His social networks are also set within the immediate framework of his DJing. A good deal of time is spent at home with his 'decks' and his music collection. He 'gets by' financially and the future is currently postponed. He survives on his sub-employment and with a good degree of continuing dependency on his parents. He is very much 'embedded' in his locality and his home. His limited acquisition of the formal markers of adulthood contrasts starkly with the lifestyles and responsibilities of Rachel's and Michael's 'grown up' worlds.

For Michael, Wayne and Rachel, in different ways, their work in the new, urban, service economies of fashion and music involve them in an investment of self that is presentational, performative and embodied. It requires them to 'work on themselves', most obviously for Michael and Rachel, as increasingly part of a more general 'life of style'. In these three narratives, the boundaries between the social life/self and work life/self are unclear. They overlap, they become blurred, they construct and constitute identity. Here too, the new kinds of employment/sub-employment in the new economies are also evident – Wayne's cash in hand, Rachel's sense of risk in a modelling 'career', against her supermarket job and a higher education, Michael's daily wage and movement from salon to salon.

Two questions, at least, could be asked about our presentation and analysis. First, are these just old 'class stories'? What has changed? We hope that our account of the 'new economies', new forms of 'post-adolescence' and new spatial differences is an obvious and adequate response to that. At the same time, old inequalities have not disappeared but neither are they the same. What is important as Savage and Bulter (1995, p. 347) argue is to explore 'continuity and change simultaneously'. Second, does the presentation of a 'set' of contrasting 'time-space biographies' work? Our response to that is that we are attempting to capture and illustrative the complexity of contemporary, urban inequalities within and across the lives and identities of young people. Differences and inequalities are multi-faceted and are played out and develop and compound over time. The biographies and 'sets' are a means, a device, for analysing and presenting this.

In retelling the unfolding stories of three young people in our research cohort we inevitably run the risk of drawing primary attention to individual differences, in which: 'The individual himself or herself becomes the reproduction unit of the social in the lifeworld' (Beck, 1992, p. 90). This may work to displace or disguise some of the older and persistent continuities of disadvantage, as signalled by the class backgrounds of the three. Despite living in the same locality, each of the three young people works within different and stratified horizons and time-spans[11] – Wayne – local, Michael – urban, Rachel – global. Their accounts of their 'choices' and decisions in the London education and labour markets, point up the different 'opportunity structures' which frame these 'choices' and the different 'futures' and identities towards which they are struggling. The relationship between opportunity and education is different in each case and related to different 'learner identities'. In effect, 'these people inhabit co-existing social spheres, coeval and overlapping in space, but with fundamentally different horizons and time-spans' (Albrow, 1997, p. 47). The material, social class differences between them are reflected in and compounded by time-space inequalities. Michael's and Rachel's social relations are increasingly disembedded from local contexts of action.

> We therefore need to conceptualize contemporary local social relations in relation to a concept of time-space social stratification [...] Time-space social stratification is the frame within which inequalities of access to resources and life chances are contained today which are more acute than any which prevailed during the period of class-based industrial society'.
>
> (Albrow, 1997, p. 54)

Notes

1   This paper draws on our study of the post compulsory experiences of a cohort of young people from an inner London comprehensive school, Northwark Park and the nearby PRU. PRUs provide education and support for young people who cannot attend mainstream school; they may be school phobic, they may have been permanently excluded from schooling etc...We have been tracking a group of 59 students (42 from the school and 17 from the PRU) from their last year of compulsory schooling through three additional years of post-16 education, training and social relations. The cohort was deliberately chosen for its diversity i.e. 'race', class and gender as well as post-16 'careers'. Our local market extends over an inner-city/suburban setting based around the Northwark area of London (see Gewirtz, 1995) and is defined in terms of the expressed interests and choices of this cohort of year 11 young people. This local, lived market encompasses several different, small LEAs that organise their schools' provision in different ways. The main players in the market for our young people are two 11–18 secondary schools, 5 FE colleges, a tertiary college, a denominational sixth form college and two TECs. Three other FE colleges, another sixth form college, and an 11–18 denominational school impinge upon the margins of this market. We have engaged with and interviewed the main groups of actors in this market; providers, that is those offering education,

training or employment; intermediaries, that is those offering advice or support, including teachers, careers officers and parents; and consumers or choosers, that is the young people themselves and their families. (See final report to ESRC of phase one of the study for further details.)

Our study is small-scale, intensive, multi-dimensional and longitudinal. As indicated above, our data are based upon contacts initiated with a group of Year 11 students in 1995. Our original sample, all year 11 students, was 110 : 81 from the comprehensive school and 29 PRU. From this cohort of students a smaller group was selected for in-depth study. This sub-sample was constituted to represent the range of Northwark Park students in terms of sex, social class, academic attainment, 'ethnicity' and destinations and routes from school to work and includes some young people who had already opted out of formal education. They were interviewed once in each of the Spring and Summer terms of Year 11 and at some point in their first year post-16 and again at some point in the second and third. The research was funded by two end-on ESRC grants. The research was initially designed to examine the dynamics of one, urban, Post-16 education market but over time the research has evolved to focus more generally on what McDonald (1999) calls 'struggles for subjectivity' – that is the relationship between new experiences of selfhood and new patterns of social life.

2 Crucially and particularly in relation to our concerns here, global cities are denoted by a very distinct 'dualist pattern of employment change, of a growth of professional-managerial jobs on the one hand, and of a large McDonaldized workforce on the other. The former in part produces the latter' (Lash and Urry, 1994, p. 196). Sassen (1991) describes global cities as 'sites for (1) the production of specialized services needed by complex organizations for running spatially dispersed networks of factories, offices and services outlets; and (2) the production of financial innovations and the making of markets, both central to the internationalization and expansion of the financial industry' (p. 5). But as Harloe and Fainstein (1992, p. 245) warn there is 'no simple division between' global cities and 'other cities' .

3 The landscape of persons and moving groups in the global city (Appadurai, 1992, p. 585).

4 What is also interesting is the degree to which cyberspace/the web enables space itself to be transcended. In relation to the commodification of youth, the net is critical in terms of the disemination/globalisation of cultural forms which fuel the construction of youth-style commodification; the 'new' youth economies.

5 However, Turok and Edge (1999) make the point that, the cities share of national employment in the UK actually fell between 1993 and 1996, and that there is a sizeable 'jobs gap' in the major cities between the number of people who want work and the number of jobs available.

6 In the late 1980s UK employment in bars, cafes, restaurants and hotels increased by nearly thirty percent (Riseborough, 1993, p. 35). At the same time, retailing was 'imaged' as a 'leading edge' sector in Britain's 'new' service economy (Du Gay, 1996, p. 96). Bates (1993, p. 72) has also noted the rise and rise of the power of the world of fashion which offers a tantalising set of space-dreams and escape routes which frequently result in a 'trading down' to fashion retailing or high street hair cutting. These, with sport and music, constitute what we refer to as the 'new' youth economies.

7 Liminality is a 'synergistic concept in that characteristics of the macro- and micro-worlds play off each other' (p. 108). Thus, 'the concept of liminality addresses the uncertainty in which these students exist, both in their daily lives and in the economic and social context of the city and society in which they reside' (pp. 110–11).

8 Our various attempts at analysis and interpretation have been continually confronted by the obdurate diversity of our data. That diversity refers to both the variety of trajectories and positions occupied by the young people in the study as well as the range of data, over time and across topics, amassed for each of the young people. The accounts generated are 'complex narrative achievements' (MacLure, 1995, p. 16). We have also interviewed a sub-sample of their parents. The interviews have branched out from work and education choices in the first instance, to cover family lives, relationships, sexuality, finance, health, religion, politics, leisure, music, drugs etc. Our analysis has been in Glaser and Strauss' (1967) terms 'ever-developing' (p. 32); the 'joint collection, coding and analysis of data is the underlying operation' (p. 41). As the outcome of this process,

much of our recent writing has been based upon 'analytic' 'sets' of young people. This is a device we have adopted as a way of representing, analysing and interpreting data. It seems to work. It blends fairly detailed narratives with a degree of conceptual focus. That means that the narratives are selective in relation to points of comparison and contrast between the young people in each set. The stories in each case are not complete or exhaustive but focused around themes and points of comparison. Each set addresses a range of issues via patterns of similarity and difference identified in the narratives elicited from the young people. Thus, the emphasis is upon themes which are picked up within and between the sets. This allows us to do some conceptual development work and to generate theoretical descriptions. One of the tasks we have set ourselves is to find and develop a 'language of description' for representing and interpreting this diversity of lives. This language draws on existing theory, other research and our own home-grown conceptualisation work – which rests upon the disciplines of data coding (Strauss, 1987). Each of the sets provides the opportunity to highlight specific concepts and specific life-experiences but we are not suggesting that the groupings are mutually exclusive in this way or that the allocation of young people to the sets is simple or absolute. There are some themes and concepts which are generic and recur and some of the distinctions between young people are very fine indeed. The presentation is thus heuristic, a tropic device which has weaknesses as well as strengths. We want to achieve a kind of analysis which is subtle and flexible. That is to say, the groupings of young people, as represented in the sets are not intended to essentialise them. To be absolutely clear, the sets are not categories or types. Indeed, they are very much a retreat from such a style of analysis.

Michael, Wayne and Rachel were selected here to highlight issues related to space, new economies and post-adolescence. See Ball *et al.* (2000)

9 'Playing out' refers to Djing in public venues as opposed to in the home or among friends.

10 We might also read Rachel's story differently. As a very specifically gendered experience, hemmed in by the gendering expectations of various 'significant' others – university, co-habitation, motherhood, modelling and customer relations at Sainsbury's are a telling, perhaps over-determining ensemble. However, Rachel's story like the others is unfinished and open-ended.

11 People can reside in one place and have their meaningful social relations almost entirely outside it across the globe – this means that people use the locality as site and resource for social activities in widely differing ways according to the extension of their sociosphere (Albrow, 1997, p. 53).

References

Albrow, M. (1997). Travelling Beyond Local Cultures: Socioscapes in a Global City. In *Living the Global City: Globalization as Local Process* (ed.) J. Eade. London, Routledge.

Ball, S. J. (1998). *It's Becoming a Habitus: Identities, Youth Transitions and Socio-economic Change*. BERA Annual conference, Queens University, Belfast.

Ball, S. J., M. Maguire and S. Macrae (1998). 'Race, Space and the Further Education marketplace'. *Race, Ethnicity and Education* 1(2): 171–89.

Ball, S. J., M. Maguire and S. Macrae (2000). *Choice, Pathways and Transitions Post-16: New Youth, New Economies in the Global City*. London, Falmer Press.

Beck, U. (1992). *Risk Society: Towards a New Modernity*. Newbury Park, CA, Sage.

Bettis, P. J. (1996). Urban Students, Liminality, and the Postindustrial Context. *Sociology of Education* 69: 105–25.

Crompton, R. (1998). *Class and Stratification: An Introduction to Current Debates*. Oxford, Polity Press.

Falk, P. and C. Campbell (eds) (1997). *The Shopping Experience*. London, Sage.

Furlong, A. and F. Cartmel (1997). *Young People and Social Change: Individualisation and Risk in Late Modernity*. Buckingham, Open University Press.

Gewirtz, S., S. J. Ball and R. Bowe (1995). *Markets, Choice and Equity in Education*. Buckingham, Open University Press.

Giddens, A. (1991). *Modernity and Self-Identity*. Cambridge, Polity.

Glaser, B. G. and A. L. Strauss (1967). *The Discovery of Grounded Theory*. London, Weidendeld and Nicholson.

Gordon, I. and S. Sassen (1992). Restructuring the Urban Labour Markets. In *Divided Cities: New York and London in the Contemporary World* (eds) S. S. Fainstein, I. Gordon and M. Harloe. Oxford, Blackwell.

Grossberg, L. (1996). Identity and Cultural Studies – is That All There Is? In *Questions of Cultural Identity* (eds) S. Hall and P. du Gay. London, Sage.

Harloe, M. and S. Fainstein (1992). Conclusion: the Divided Cities. In *Divided Cities: New York and London in the Contemporary World* (eds) S. S. Fainstein, I. Gordon and M. Harloe. Oxford, Blackwell.

Harvey, D. (1973). *Social Justice and the City*. London, Edward Arnold.

Harvey, D. (1989). *The Condition of Postmodernity*. Oxford, Basil Blackwell.

Harvey, D. (1993). From Space to Place and Back Again: Reflections on the Condition of Postmodernity. In *Mapping the Futures: Local Cultures, Global Change* (ed.) J. Bird. London, Routledge.

Hochschild, A. R. (1979). Emotion Work, Feeling Rules and Social Structure. *American Journal of Sociology* 85(3): 551–75.

Hodkinson, P. (1999). The Origins of a Theory of Career Decision-making: A Case Study of Hermeneutical Research. *British Educational Research Journal* 24(5): 557–72.

Hodkinson, P., A. C. Sparkes and H. Hodkinson (1996). *Triumphs and Tears: Young People, Markets and the Transition from School to Work*. London, David Fulton.

Lash, S. and J. Urry (1994). *Economies of Signs and Space*. London, Sage.

Lees, S. (1993). *Sugar and Spice. Sexuality and Adolescent Girls*. London, Penguin Books.

Leidner, R. (1993). *Fast Food, Fast Talk: Service Work and the Routinization of Everyday Life*. Berkeley, CA, University of California Press.

McDonald, K. (1999). *Struggles for Subjectivity: Identity, Action and Youth Experience*. Cambridge, Cambridge University Press.

MacLure, M. (1995). Telling Transitions: Boundary Work in Narratives of Becoming an Action Researcher, CARE, University of East Anglia.

Macrae, S., M. Maguire and S. J. Ball (1997a). Competition, Choice and Hierarchy in a Post-16 Education and Training Market. In *Education 14–19: Critical Perspectives* (ed.) S. Tomlinson. London, Athlone Press.

Macrae, S., M. Maguire and S. J. Ball (1997b). Whose 'Learning Society'? A Tentative Deconstruction. *Journal of Education Policy* 12(6): 499–510.

Rees, G., R. Fevre, J. Furlong and S. Gorard (1997). History, Place and the Learning Society: Towards a Sociology of Lifetime Learning. *Journal of Education Policy* 12(6): 485–98.

Roberts, K. (1968). The Entry into Employment: An Approach Towards a General Theory. *Sociological Review* 16: 165–84.

Roberts, K. (1993). Career Trajectories and the Mirage of Increased Social Mobility. In *Youth and Inequality* (eds) I. Bates and G. Riseborough. Buckingham, Open University Press.

Roberts, K., S. C. Clark and C. Wallace (1994). Flexibility and Individualism: A Comparison of Transitions into Employment in England and Germany. *Sociology* 28(1): 31–54.

Sassen, S. (1991). *The Global City*. Princeton, NJ, Princeton University Press.

Savage, M. and T. Butler (1995) Assets and the Middle Classes in Contemporary Britain. In *Social Change and the Middle Classes* (eds) T. Butler and M. Savage. London, UCL Press.

Strauss, A. (1987). *Qualitative Data Analysis for Social Scientists*. New York, Cambridge University Press.

Tsolidis, G. (1996). Feminist Theorisations of Identity and Difference. *British Journal of Sociology of Education* 17(3): 267–77.

Turok, I. and N. Edge (1999). *The Jobs Gap in Britain's Cities: Employment Loss and Labour Market Consequences*. Oxford, The Polity Press.

Walkerdine, V. (1997). *Daddy's Girl. Young Girls and Popular Culture*. Basingstoke and London, Macmillan Press.

Warhurst, C., D. Nickson, A. Witz and A.-M. Cullen (1999). Aesthetic Labour in Interactive Service Work: Some Case Study Evidence From the 'New' Glasgow. *Services Industries Journal* 21(3): 279–301.

Wexler, P. (1992). *Becoming Somebody: Toward a Social Psychology of School*. London, Falmer Press.

CHAPTER 13

SOCIAL JUSTICE IN THE HEAD
Are we all libertarians now?

C. Vincent (ed.), *Social Justice, Identity and Education*,
London: RoutledgeFalmer, 2003

Issues of social justice are normally conceived of and dealt with in terms of the effects of policies or institutional practices or the application of abstract principles. Individuals are typically only brought into play as the bearers or perpetrators of injustice – as racists for example – or as the victims of injustice. Here I want to position individuals somewhat differently. I want to look at middle-class parents as the bearers of principles of justice and as actors producing aggregate social effects through the playing out of the relationships between their principles and their actions. Within this I shall consider the way in which principles and actions are, for some, part of a 'liberal' social identity – a way they think about themselves and present themselves to others, that is their relation to the social world. At points my deliberations touch upon some well-worn debates around the issues of liberalism and communitarianism (Kymlicka, 1989).

This paper is drawn from a broader and more general analysis of the strategies of middle-class families in the education market place (Ball, 2003). It is also a greatly attenuated version of a more extended discussion of the values, principles and actions of parents in this context. Here the emphasis is upon discussion rather than data, but some extracts from interviews and case-studies of two families are deployed to ground and illustrate aspects of the discussion.

Overwhelmingly, the existing literature on parents and school choice either excludes consideration of values and principles altogether, or relegates these to a subordinate role. In a sense this is one of a number of ways in which this literature is 'captured by the discourse' (Bowe *et al.*, 1994) it seeks to explain. Both advocates of choice and choice theories tend to rely on narrow rational and utilitarian conceptualisations of the chooser and choice researchers tend to take these on board in an unreflexive way. Goldthorpe's (1982) work is one example where pre-eminence is given to calculation, and Hatcher (1998) subjects this to telling criticism. Altogether little attention is given to values in research into choice, and this is part of a more general neglect of the ethical dimensions of social arrangements like the market within social research Bottery (1992) being a notable exception. Morgan's (1989, p. 29) point, bears re-iteration, that an over-emphasis on rational calculation can lead to a 'diminishment of our moral understanding of human agency'. As Jordan *et al.* (1994, p. 4) suggest, the 'denizen of the marketplace – homo economicus is somewhat emaciated'. Attention to the role of values and principles in real decision-making settings almost inevitably disturbs the neat simplicities of homo economicus.

The personal aims, interests and desires of individuals are, as Nagel (1991, p. 14) puts it, 'the raw material from which ethics begins'. This paper works with some of that raw material and is about the ethics of the education market place as enacted through the principles and practices of middle-class families as they attempt to realise their desires for their children in the immediate and for the future. In previous works I began to explore how the education market 'calls up' and legitimates a certain sort of ethics in the practices and perspectives of education providers (Ball, 1997, 1998; Ball *et al.*, 1997). I argued that a shift is 'taking place in schools and colleges from... "professional" values or the values of "professional community"' (Grace, 1995) to the values of the market (see also Gewirtz *et al.*, 1993). That is, where there is competition to recruit, non-market values and professional ethics are being de-valued and displaced by the 'need' to 'sell' schools and colleges and make and manage 'image' in the competitive education marketplace. The discourses of policy which animate and infuse the market work to provide a climate of legitimation and vocabulary of motives which make new ways of action thinkable, possible and acceptable and 'old' ways seem less appropriate. Thus, within the educational context, the pedagogy of the market 'teaches' and disseminates 'a new morality' (Ball, 1998). One part of this shift, I suggest, is the articulation of a market ontology producing new kinds of moral subjects and changing the ways in 'which we think ourselves, the criteria and norms we use to judge ourselves' (Rose, 1992, p. 161). The result may be 'an attenuated creature' (Cohen, 1992, p. 183). This paper asks just how attenuated that market creature might be.

However, the education market does not invent or import an entirely new values system rather it draws upon classical liberal views underpinned by political and economic individualism. These individualisms hail and celebrate independent and rational beings 'who are the sole generators of their own wants and preferences and the best judges of their own interests' (Lukes, 1974, p. 79). Choice then is a key concept in the political articulation of these beings. These values both interrupt the fragile discourse of welfare, wherein the state represents collective interests, supports universalism and manages politics to support all members of the citizen-community, and reaffirms the deeply entrenched tenets of bourgeois individualism which had predominated in UK society before the welfare state. These values are given new impetus and a new kind of discursive validity within our contemporary 'market society' – 'the horizon within which more and more people live ever-larger parts of their lives' (Slater and Tonkiss, 2001, p. 203). This market society entails '...the privatist dissipation of normative self-obligations and institutional ties' and displays 'unmistakable tendencies towards social closure' (Berking, 1966, p. 190). Thus, 'social protectionism' presents itself 'as a promising strategy in the competitive struggle for material and symbolic advantage – all of these phenomena conjure up the image of a society whose assets in solidarity and legitimacy are exhausted' (Berking, 1966, p. 190). Bourdieu addresses these changes in a rather oblique way when he refers to a transformation in the mode of social reproduction, which means that 'scholastic errors tend to count more than moral errors, with academic anxiety, previously a more male concern, replacing ethical anxiety' (1986, p. 369).

However, the ethics of the market are not, as I hope to show, hegemonic. They are contested or struggled over 'in the head' or at least in some heads, in the 'profound complexity and disparity' (Cohen, 1992, p. 184) of what Cohen calls 'empirical pragmatics' (p. 183). Here I want to extend my previous examination to focus on the 'consumer' in the education market. Here in particular, the decision-making related to choice between state and private schooling provides a rich nexus of personal conflicts within which ethical positions are formulated or tested in relation to practice. This draws attention to the themes of individualism, responsibility and guilt, and in relation to these the contradictory role of the middle-class collectivity, what Jordan *et al.* (1994, p. 77) call the 'microcommunities of mutual commitment' – the 'other side' of privatism.

There are, embedded in the literatures on class and on choice, two distinct themes; one which portrays middle-class families as, sui generis, decidedly self-interested and calculating, the other, reinforcing this, points up the various effects and consequences of the market ethic as contributing to the destruction of collective social relations and commitments. In other words, the generation of a 'consumer ethic' which 'produces consumers who are isolated' and therefore 'untrammelled by the constraints and brakes imposed by collective memories and expectations' (Bourdieu, 1986, p. 371). This literature is supported more generally by recent work on individuation within high modernity (e.g. Giddens, 1991; Beck *et al.*, 1994).

Nonetheless, I suggest this is only half of the story, the individualism of the school consumer is, in particular locations, mediated and encouraged through collective and familial memories and expectations. I will explore this further. I want also to consider how it is that middle-class families 'prioritise their commitments to others, how they reconcile conflicting demands arising from these priorities, and the extent to which they recognise the wider social relevance of their actions'? (Jordan *et al.*, 1994, p. 4). Jordan *et al.* (p. 12) drawing on their interviews with middle-class families are unequivocal, they find that 'when there was a clash between their political principles and the best interests of their children, they should put the family first'. The picture here is not quite so clear cut, and perhaps the simplest and best position from which to start, is Pahl and Wallace's (1985, p. 106) point that family choices and strategies may well be invested with 'a mixture of rationalities'.

I suggest that strategies of social closure are both informed and driven by a degree of reflexive knowingness but also firmly shaped by the dispositions and practical sense and inventions of habitus. The question is, whether that knowingness extends to an awareness of the effects and consequences of their actions, or should we simply accept the dictum offered by Dreyfus and Rabinow (1983, p. 189) that 'people know what they do; they frequently know why they do what they do: but [very often] they don't know what what they do does'. In the simplest, and may be on this occasion, the most useful sense, we need to slip away from the binary, either or position. That is, it is neither the case that middle-class families are cynical individualists who recognise that they contribute to and indeed are motivated by, the creation of social inequalities; nor they are merely trying to do the best for their own children and have no real sense that their individual actions might have larger social consequences. Rather, that we all act within unclear and contradictory values systems which are complexly and unevenly related to our social practices. Our ethics are situated and realised within a variety of material and discursive contexts. In other words, 'We see things from here' as Nagel (1991, p. 10) puts it, from an individual point of view, or more appropriately for our purposes, from the point of view of the family. Set over and against this is the challenge of seeing that what is true for us is also 'true of others' (p. 10). The problem of recognising others as ourselves. Class and race identities rip across this possibility. Running through the processes of schooling and choice for middle-class families is a strong sense of boundaries between 'us' and 'others' – a sense of 'other' families as not 'normal', as not intelligible in terms of 'our' values, attitudes and behaviour. The whole point is that these others are not easily recognisable or understood, what is there for 'us' does not seem to be true for 'them'. Nonetheless, principles have their part to play within the liberal social identities which these families claim for themselves. They are people who have concerns about the general social good. Within all of this, in making decisions about the schooling of their children, the families represented here are engaged in complex cobbling together of public and private values, all a part of what van Zanten and Veleda (2001) call 'ethical brico-lage'. Although the value of 'putting the family first', in one way or another, remains the centrepiece of this decision-making. In philosophical and common-sensical terms, this is all very proper. Morally parents have a right, even a duty perhaps, to do their best to get an adequate education for their children. Action taken to benefit a child is not strictly self-interested. We are not required to treat our intimates in the same ways as we treat or think about others. These are 'sound motives' (McLaughlin, 1994). In philosophical terms there are actions we are entitled to take even though they may not lead to the best of all possible overall outcomes. It would be difficult to lead a normal life otherwise. However, clearly for some parents their concerns go beyond adequacy to a commitment to achieve maximal positional advantage for their child. This is not easy to defend on moral grounds, particularly as it involves an explicit awareness of and in effect a con-doning of inequalities of provision. However, Jonathan (1989, p. 334) does sug-gest that arguments can be made that parents have a duty to secure the interests of their child 'even (or especially) in circumstances where they are in competition with the interests of children in general'.[1] There is a further difficulty enmeshed in all of this; that is, how do we know what is the best for the child? Is it simply what parents say it is? Is best, a singular notion? In particular is what is best now the same as what might be best for their child in the future? This is the basis of deferred gratification. It also raises the question of the child's role in deciding what is in his/her best interests. All of this means that within the interviews considered here, the parents are frequently engaged in sophisticated processes of re-working, recovery and post-hoc legitimation of a tenuous liberal social identity. Let us see!

I want to run three arguments together here. First, that middle-class values priv-ilege certain sorts of selfish, or at least short-sighted individualism. Second, that the market feeds and exacerbates this to produce 'attenuated beings'. Third, nei-ther of the previous are adequate in all cases to account for the complex, situated values which are involved in decision-making about schooling. In effect this is a story that can be told in more than one way – more or less sympathetically or cyn-ically. Should I emphasise the complexity of contradictory value systems and the dilemmas of love as against the social good or the use of post-hoc rationalisations to legitimate selfish behaviour? At times my tone, and my analytic stance is ambiguous, and not unintentionally so.

Choosing schools

The dilemmas and values within school choice are pointed up particularly well, particularly sharply, as I have suggested above, when it comes to choosing between state and private schools. I will use this as a focus for the major part of this paper. I shall employ two different presentational and interpretational devices in the chapter to 'get at', illustrate and develop the issues adumbrated above. First, I will pick out some aspects from an heuristic model or map of choice which attends specifically to values issues. I will then work through two 'case studies' of values and choice – the Wilkinsons and the Simpsons.

I want to propose a map which will allow us to look at the ethical dilemmas of choice in an orderly way. This map is drawn from and based upon the analysis of parents' accounts of their choice-making. It is a dynamic relational model, the elements are not free-standing categories, they are interacting dimensions in the empirical pragmatics of choice. Only rarely does one element predominate, more typically they interplay to produce analytic complexity and individual doubt and confusion. However, there are particular interpretational difficulties embedded in this kind of analysis and discussion, more than is usually the case when working with qualitative data. How far can we accept these accounts and the motives and rationales presented at face value? To what extent can we read-off or read-into these accounts value rationalities? Indeed to what extent are these respondents ever themselves clear of the reasons for their choices when values are set in relation to other sorts of more practical concerns? What I would suggest here is that rather than seeing the examination of values-in-use as indictments or critical accounts of individuals or families, they are regarded as different possible 'types' of decision-making; although, as we shall see there are some examples where the role of values in relation to choice seems absolutely clear cut. Also the narratives vary in the extent of reflexivity that they display.

While some aspects of the map may seem straightforward, overall I want to stress the messiness and the difficulties which are involved in plotting the work done by values rather than come to any clear cut resolutions. I take a more equivocal position than do Jordan *et al.* (1994, p. 141), who make the point in their study that in the context of choice of school 'the concept of "putting the family first" was most explicitly deployed'.

For the moment I want to concentrate on just one aspect of the map that is the way in which the families' principles are 'situated'.

As Jordan *et al.* (1994, p. 146) found the 'carefully reasoned' accounts of choice offered by parents work as 'generalised guidelines, and that actual decisions are often taken in the wake of events or developments that are inherently unpredictable'. Even these parents do not intend to be taken by surprise. There are very few examples of clear cut, once and for all, principles at work in these parents' accounts. Mrs Brown (see below) believes 'passionately' in comprehensive education. Nonetheless, she also recognises that not all comprehensives are the same and that therefore not just any comprehensive will do for her children. School choice is a social mechanism which enables her to put her commitments into practice. Generally, choice is one way of retaining middle-class commitment to the state sector. Principles, like those of Mrs Brown are thus 'situated' in a particular way within policy. And in stark contrast to other parents, even if the academic progress of her children is not what she would wish, she sees other social benefits of a comprehensive schooling. On the whole, parents' expectations of schools are primarily utilitarian although issues of social mixing, the relationships between school and the 'real world', are of importance for a small minority of parents:

> really that's a lot to do with my politics and my husband's politics, that I passionately believe in comprehensive education, or in state education ... and I think it holds a lot of very good things for children, I wouldn't want them to be closeted away from the real world, I'd rather they went out and saw ... what life was really like for a lot of people ... and understood it. I can see there are faults in it, I think the first two years at the school they wasted their time ... both of my two elder ones. They back pedalled a lot ... and they didn't get on with work, but I still wouldn't change my mind, I still would want them to go to a comprehensive school, even knowing that ... when it came to the time to send Toby there ... knowing that he would probably back

pedal for a couple of years, I still saw advantages we well had two things very strongly on our mind, one was we wanted co-ed for him, because again three sons…and so I do believe that boys benefit from being taught alongside girls…and we both very strongly believe in comprehensive education, so we wanted a comprehensive school…co-educational school. And there wasn't an awful lot of choice in Northwark in those days. There was a school which in fact was nearer to us, which now I probably would have sent them to, because it's changing, it's getting a good reputation, it has a strong head, and its reputation is improving a lot, but in those days it was a pretty grim place, with a lot of fights outside the school and…a not very attractive building, so that was off the list. I think we looked at an all boys school, just so that we didn't make our decision without at least having looked at something else, and that absolutely horrified me, it was just like a seething bed of aggression, I didn't like it at all.

There is a further dimension to this situated aspect of principles and values. Principles are situated in relation to the realisation of the comprehensive ideal, as parents saw it. That is, there were a number of parents for whom comprehensive education would be a real choice, in the best possible of all schooling worlds. That is, if comprehensives were what they were 'supposed to be'; although what they are supposed to be was not always clear. And whether if they were what they were 'supposed to be' they would be comprehensive is also unclear. Part of this non-realisation is brought out by the existence of the private sector and its creaming-off of other children like their own, thus creating a social and academic mix in the comprehensive school which is deemed unacceptable. Here we can see some glimpses of a link between individual choices and a more general social good. Here principles are suspended until circumstances change. They do not come into play because the circumstances in which they would or should operate do not pertain. Here government policy towards private schools creates a situation which discourages choice of state school, but the effects of policy arise from the aggregate of individual choices.

Principles are situated in a second sense. As several of the parents' made clear, it was possible to take up particular principled stances towards the schooling of their child, given the sorts of schools available to them in their locality, and in relation to the 'sort' of child involved. Some respondents were frank enough to indicate that their principles might not have operated in the same way in a different locality; 'the effects of our actions are altered by the context and because we ourselves are transformed by our place in it' (Nagel, 1991, p. 17). This is also linked in some of the accounts to the targeting of a particular locality when house-hunting. This is the point often made by critics of allocative school systems – that some parents can use their financial capital to 'choose' a state school by buying a house in the catchment area of their preferred school.

we knew about Overbury secondary school obviously because it's just across the road from here, so you can't actually miss it…it was something that we had sort of thought about, but neither of the boys had even started school then, they were only 3 and 18 months when we came here.. and we had thought probably then that they would go on to St Botolph's and then after St Botolph's, that's when we thought…that's when we might go private, if we went private. And from here there are quite a lot of private schools, so we thought we're sort of getting the best of both worlds really.

(Mrs Smith)

As it turned out, as Mr Smith explained, choosing a state school from where he lives was 'easy', dilemmas of principle are avoided. He also suggests that the costs of a mortgage can be seen as an alternative to the costs of private schooling. This is a useful reminder of the argument made by Savage *et al.* (1992, p. 59) that 'property costs...are becoming more integrally tied to processes of middle-class formation. We suggest that increasing numbers of the middle-class can draw upon both property and cultural assets'.

> St Vincent's, is a very odd area, cos what happens is...people move into it, and then they start to have children...they like the local schools, and then you find that where they might have moved out they tend to stay and really only move within the area, to stay within the state sector because they either find that they've got a large mortgage so they can't afford to pay the fees...for private education or they want to support state education and actually it's very easy if you live here. You know it's easy to really support state education because if you look at the results they're pretty good...and having said that...the type of parents that live in Riverway and Tideway...they should be good. I mean I think everybody that I know have got a degree...

Values and principles are situated in a third sense. That is, values systems are constructed, or influenced, or inflected within families, social networks and local communities. They become part of the taken for granted response to decisions, what people like us, in this place, do. This is where collectivity comes back in, and is a basis for the values of individualism, the putting of the family first. These social contexts constitute a moral community within which the necessity of an attitude, toward family, schooling and parenting, is formed and maintained. Specific versions of the good parent circulate within this community which both provide a repertoire of meanings through which to account for actions and operate to constrain or judge those actions.

> that's the way it is here...everybody who can afford to sends their children to independent schools, especially in this particular part of the borough.
>
> (Mr Curry)

> from the way the family operates it will probably be the line of least resistance which is...if we can afford it then you go to Alleyns as well...yes, I mean...or we will afford it somehow and he will go to Alleyns as well...
>
> (Mrs Laidlaw)

As a model of good parenting, the actions of the Blairs (Gewirtz, 2001) would suggest that paying for private tutoring to underwrite your child's school performance (*Evening Standard*, 4.07.02, pp. 1 and 5) is what good parents do. This was certainly the norm in Riverway.

Primary school events and social activities and the school-gate network of mothers, together with children's own reporting back to parents, are all influential in establishing a sense of normal trajectories for children like 'ours' and appropriate choices for parents like 'us'. Norms and expectations circulate through networks of talk, and specifically questions and comparisons related to choice-making. Norms and expectations become embedded over time in the parental cultures of particular primary schools, making some choices obvious and others perverse; although in London many primary schools would have a mix of such cultures.

The Wilkinsons and the Simpsons

I now want to take a slightly different analytical tack and get even closer to the work of 'ethical bricolage' by taking two families as case studies of choice and ethics in practice. Now you might well wonder why it is that both these case studies are of families who end up choosing state schools rather than private. There are two main reasons. First, they serve particularly well to illustrate the complexity and dilemmas of choice. Second, in contrast to the majority of private school choosers they go beyond the obviousness of choice in their narratives. First there are the Wilkinsons and then the Simpsons. Mr Wilkinson is a senior civil servant and Mrs Wilkinson is a teacher in a private secondary school, they both attended grammar schools and a high status University, they have three sons, at the time of interview aged 3, 7 and 11.

The Wilkinsons started out thinking about their children's schooling in terms of sending them to private school. However, Mr Wilkinson presents two 'reasons' for eventually choosing state schools for all three sons. The first reason displays careful rational calculation, in the literally sense. The costs are too high, at least that is the opportunity costs. Nonetheless, the Wilkinsons' thinking displays strategic care. The family's material capital will be deployed to fund an educative infrastructure within the home and to provide back-ups and interventions in order to assure success and insure against failure.

> A long time ago we put Toby's name down for St Peter's school...because St Peter's is the local school...a private school, of very high standard...very very expensive, and when we had two children we wondered whether to put the second one down and when it was the possibility of three boys going to a private school, because if you add the fees up, and income...we could just about afford it, but when we had three, we realised that we had no intention of sending them, we would be spending a fortune, and we do have a reasonable mean a stretch in terms of other things...so on the basis of finance we thought it would need to be a pretty special school that would require us to give up as much as we would have to give up; and in terms of making any financial decision you should look at what else you could buy with that same amount of money...and we decided that we could do more for our children by spending on computers and books and...other resources at home, and if necessary later on...buy coaching and remedial teaching, if that was necessary...than by committing to the private system from the start...and so we didn't take up the invitation from St Peter's to send Toby along for the tests at age seven, and we've no intention of trying at age 13. So that would be the first reason.

The Wilkinsons' second reason for choosing the state sector is articulated in a different discourse and Mr Wilkinson displays a considerable degree of reflexivity in relation to the 'strength' of the family's principles. There are two related elements to these principles. One, identified previously, expresses a belief in educating their children in a setting which reflects the social diversity of the world at large. This includes a rejection of single-sex education and the studied traditionalism of a grammar school. Neither are considered relevant to 'today's' world. The other indicates a link between the family's choice and the general social consequences of choice. This was not common in the data set as a whole. Here what is acknowledged is the 'creaming' effect in the state sector which results from the choice of private school.

The issue of diversity or mix crops up again below and has an interesting and rather complicated relationship to the issues of boundary and closure which also run through my more general analysis of middle-class strategies. If I can indulge for a moment at least in the safe simplicities of binarism, the families who are referred to in this paper display either one of two tendencies, a preference for absolute or relative closure. In other words, they draw the social boundaries of schooling in different places, on different sides of the state/private boundary. For some, the absolute division of private from state schooling is inescapably necessary. For others, like the Wilkinsons, a more fuzzy social division somewhere inside the state system is acceptable but will require careful vigilance and policing, and sometimes pressure to maintain.

> The second reason for not going for private education was really on a matter of principle...everybody's principles I think have a certain degree of strength, and I'm not sure how strong ours would ultimately be, my wife has taught for 10 years in the private sector, and she therefore has an awareness of what qualities there are in a private school as distinct from the qualities you get in a state school...and we all have to live our lives in a world with a mixture of all sorts of other societies around us...with other people in society around us...and I think that's probably what...on a matter of principle...would persuade us not to use a private school now...and because we see in this area how much quality is already being deprived of the comprehensive schools, by the number of children who are driven off each day to the private schools around, and we would prefer not to contribute to that, but to bring up our children in something which represents a small slice of the world that they're going to have to live...I had forgotten what it was like in an all boys school, and when I got there I remembered what it was like in an all boys school, and for the reasons I gave in not choosing private education, I don't actually think you get a cross section of society...in a single sex school, and I would like Toby to grow up in a society which was peopled almost equally by women, and so the last thing to do is to cut all his experience of the opposite sex out...during his school years. That was...I think one of my reasons for rejecting Tiffins [grammar]. The other reason was that it was just so old fashioned. It reminded me of what education was like 25 years ago. I don't want to put Toby through that, I want to put Toby through the education of today...I'm sure that education has to be very different today than it was when I was at school.

While the Wilkinsons knew what they would be getting in the private sector they were much less sure about 'quality' within the state sector. They believed that having chosen to remain in the state sector, they would have to take choice of a particular school very seriously indeed. They ended up comparing between two comprehensive schools and somewhat less seriously a state grammar school and developed a checklist of indicators they considered important. These mainly concerned the quality of teaching and the subjects and activities on offer, in effect both the instrumental and expressive order. What they end up with is a messy calculus of issues, of very different sorts, both 'big' and 'small', more or less important, resting on both instrumental and expressive values. For example, the Wilkinsons, unlike other families, are not willing to send their sons long distances to find the 'right' school. Like the working-class families reported in Gewirtz *et al.* (1995) the idea of the school being an extension of the local community is important to them. They are also impressed by the traditional connotations of Latin being offered, although do not see this as something of direct relevance to their son, opportunities for sport, and, in contrast, the modern connotations of IT provision:

> we also have set down a checklist I suppose, because we found it very difficult to make a final decision as to which school to opt for. The quality of the staff is a very difficult thing to judge, but I think is actually one of the critical things...how much the teachers are going to stimulate the children to want to learn...and...in every subject it's quite difficult because there are so many subjects that you can't start to get a grasp of...so we .. have...at both Fletcher and at Chiswick...been to the open evening when you can go round and look at the school facilities...talk to the staff, talk about how teaching is done in particular subjects, and we've also been on a tour of the schools... looking at the schools in normal working hours. So we've been looking primarily for the quality of the teaching and the choice of subjects offered and taught. So one of the factors for example that makes Chiswick particularly interesting is that they offer a slightly wider choice of subjects that are taught, they don't for example...group all the humanities together quite as much as they do at Fletcher...They offer the option of doing Latin should a child want to do that. Toby probably won't want to do that but nevertheless it's nice to be in a school where you know that that choice is available. Another factor which has influenced us is the quality of the IT equipment on display and the IT which is apparently used in teaching. The reason for this is that we believe that schools which are using IT in this way are more likely to be up to date with other aspects of teaching too, so that we would judge those schools to be up to date, reflecting the current requirements and understanding about subjects taught...Another factor I think is the sports facilities...in particular because Toby loves playing football and neither Sarah nor I were at all sporty when we were at school...and we want to encourage him to be what we weren't, because when you come to be part of a team in any organisation, I think it's extremely valuable that you've been part of a team in some sort of sporting activity; so we've been very keen to encourage Toby in that, and so we've looked at sports facilities...but not only sports facilities, but the encouragement of children to take part, and so therefore we've been impressed by the range of clubs, extra curricular activities, the sorts of things that children can opt into. So I think those were the key things that we were looking for. Another thing that's very important to us...is that the school should be accessible to where we live...in some ways I rather regret that there is a choice of school at all...because we've sent Toby and Jacob to the local primary school, because it's the nearest school and because we felt it would offer a satisfactory service. There's an awful lot of time and energy wasted in bussing children to schools that are some distance away... both in the private sector and in the state sector, and so what we were looking for was a school to which Toby could walk, a school at which other people would be going from this neighbourhood to that school...in other words a neighbourhood or a community school, and that's why we haven't looked at schools further away from us in this borough, even though they might offer a perfectly adequate product. And in some ways we realised that that could leave us vulnerable, because we know nothing about the other schools in the borough and should we fail to get Toby into Fletcher, we would have no basis on which to judge whether what we were being offered was at all satisfactory.

The Wilkinsons were also influenced by things they did not expect to find, that is impressions which they accumulated during their visits to schools. The effects of how the schools looked, as well as how they presented themselves – impressions 'given' and 'given off'. The third and final source of choice data is the 'objective' cold knowledge provided by school results. Here the Wilkinsons are able to deploy a considerable range of skills and judgements. They see these data as 'requiring' interpretation, both in terms of the intakes of the schools and their current as opposed to previous policies and practices. They also find the schools' own interpretation and presentation of results to be 'confusing'.

> The results and presentation of the school...I haven't mentioned, partly because they require a great deal of interpretation...the way in which the government statistics were recently received gives a good indication. We were quite surprised...well we were not surprised, because we were already aware that the results at Chiswick school are nowhere near as good at the moment as the results at Fletcher school, nevertheless we believe the quality of the teaching there that's being offered there at the bottom of the school and the product when those years come through to taking their exams will be very different from what they have now and that's partly because the school has turned itself around and become very much more successful. And so...in looking at the results...everyone wants to present their results in their best light. In fact the results were presented in an extremely confusing light, and I think it's actually very difficult indeed to judge how effective a school is, and in particular...I think it's difficult because you have no idea what the quality of the intake was that the output should really be compared with, you can't work out the added value. But...we felt with Chiswick that the setting that was available and the choice of subjects...indicated that the school was now much more interested in catering for the more academic pupils...and setting does not take place in Fletcher except in maths and so if we go to Fletcher we won't get quite the same...ability...the feeling that Toby will be taught in a group of children who want to learn. Both Sarah and I are suspicious about mixed ability teaching, which is what the majority of teaching at Fletcher is. And then...I realise I'm adding a number of...supplementary points but...there is a difference that Fletcher is a school that effectively caters for first to fifth years, there is no sixth form. There are no sixth forms in any Riverway schools, but Chiswick school is a school which includes a sixth form and again we felt that that would influence the quality of staff, because with a teacher in the house, we know that staff are more interested in going to schools where there is a sixth form, so that they get a share of the most challenging teaching, as well as the ability to influence children right at the bottom of the school, and perhaps steer them towards the specialisms at the top of the school.[2]

Grouping practices are viewed as being of major significance in providing contexts for 'more academic pupils' those 'who want to learn'. In other words, there are lines to be drawn within social diversity and there are limits to community and social mixing. These are not matters of principle in the general sense, they are not seen as such by the Wilkinsons. These are matters of necessity, which make choice of a state school possible. What this highlights is the way in which different things become issues of principle for different families, and the different points at which principles give way to practicalities or the embedded values involved in putting the family first. This also indicates something of the effectiveness or accuracy of

New Labour's opinion testing; although it is difficult to know to what extent the government's overt commitment to setting reflects or moulds opinion.

The Simpsons are a 'mixed' couple in the sense that Mrs Simpson is a public sector professional, a speech therapist, and her husband a private sector professional, a civil engineer, who had been made redundant a couple of weeks prior to the interview. Both parents had been privately schooled. Neither enjoyed or rated very highly their own school experience.

> He didn't enjoy his education at all, he didn't think it was a very good education. I went to an all girls private day school and didn't enjoy my education at all, either. Having said that we both went to university so, if you like it gave us whatever that required. But I felt that my education was very unchallenging...very very unchallenging, very dull, and I had so much to learn when I left school and went to college. I had to learn to live...

Again here the private system is seen as unworldly, as not offering a proper preparation for the 'real' world. For the Simpsons this real world is a social world. For parents who choose private school, it is often because it *does* prepare their children for the 'real' world. But this real world is an economic or utilitarian one. The Simpsons also have a clear cut principled position toward private schooling. But they also recognise the tension between public principles and private pragmatics and did look at and consider private primary schools. They found these schools inappropriate for their son. Like almost all of the parents interviewed, proper, serious choice-making and being a good parent meant considering, for their child, all possible options, including private schools. Mrs Simpson also points up a set of tensions between an educational, child-centred and principled decision-making ensemble and a more socially instrumental set of concerns. There are compromises to be made on either side. Either choosing the guarantees offered by the private sector but forms of teaching and learning inappropriate to the child, or going for state school which is deemed more appropriate, in a variety of ways, but which does not offer the same guarantees:

> both of us are very pro state schools. And I have a lot of problems philosophically with even coping with the fact that independent schools exist. I do feel that every child has the right to a good education, and I really don't think you should get it just because you've got more money than Joe Bloggs next door. Having said that, when it comes to your child, we did go and have a look...we looked at actually at every level, we looked at the infant level and did not like at all what they were doing, it was far too heavy...far too formal...and then we looked at junior school level and felt that Shavell was better actually than any of the private schools we went to look at...depending on what you're wanting. If you want them to go to Westminster you have to send them to a prep school, but that's not what we wanted anyway. Ridley particularly is the sort of child...who doesn't necessarily go down that formal road...he learns in a very erratic sense...and there was no room for that sort of ingenuity and individuality I felt, within the prep school system...you either did A, B and C and you came out with D or you didn't make it. So I felt that that would actually totally inhibit him. And we did go and have a look at Hampton grammar, which is the independent...but in fact...the only reason I would have really considered it was because of ensuring...if you like, like an insurance policy, that if he went there, he was very likely to come out with

good results. And I suppose when you send your child to a comprehensive, which is not the system that we knew as children, you have less of a guarantee. However, I would have found it very difficult to make that decision, given my own thoughts about state education, and all of that.

Bernstein's analysis of the new middle classes suggests that these tensions, dilemmas and contradictions are representative of the structural ambiguities embedded in the positioning and perspectives of the new middle class. He says: 'The contemporary new middle class is unique, for in the socialisation of its young [there is ?] a sharp and penetrating contradiction between a subjective personal identity and an objective privatized identity; between the release of the person and the hierarchy of class' (1990, p. 136). This is also a further aspect of individualism and what Jordan *et al.* (1994, p. 94) refer to as 'the discourses of a developmental self'. While perhaps not an ideal – typical new middle-class woman, Mrs Simpson seems very aware of this contradiction and she chooses release rather than hierarchy. She chooses between the particularities of her child and the trajectory of advantages offered by private schooling. However, the alignments between principles, person and advantage differ from case to case, as we have seen.

The son's own preferences play a key role here but are set over and against the expectations and pressures of the extended family. Choice of state school involves taking a stand against norms strongly embedded within history and practices of the family. Brantlinger *et al.* (1996, p. 589) suggest that when it comes to the relationship between liberal principles and practice that mothers' role as 'status maintainers' put them 'in a contradictory or dissonant position'. In other words, mothers are frequently at the focal point of responsibility for ensuring both the well-being of their children and the reproduction through education and through the children of the social and class position of the family. In some circumstances, personal principles, the child's interests and the expectations of the extended family may be mis-aligned.

> He said he'd pay us back his pocket money every week, if we promised him we wouldn't send him to an all boys school where you pay fees, and that rather clinched the deal. Also I said would he like to take the exam just in case, now maybe that was just a reassurance for me to say, well alright, he would have a place in grammar school, he's bright enough for that, but we turned it down... and he said, if I don't want to go there, I don't think I'm going to be trying terribly hard in the exam, so I might fail, so I can't see any point in sitting it... and I'm really not sorry. But equally, because he's in contact with both my brother's children, and my husband's children [from a previous marriage] are both at independent schools, both very expensive independent schools... and so we very much had to strike out on our own... and to put this whole conversation in context... it has caused me a huge amount of personal anguish... going down the road that we go, and we've come under huge pressure from parents and in-laws and the rest of the family. And a lot of persuasion that we ought to be sending our children to private school...

In contrast to the Wilkinsons, the Simpsons' account does not touch upon the more general social consequences of their decisions. Their principles come across as primarily abstract and personal rather than grounded in any strong sense of a common good. Even so, though different, neither of these families are simply 'unencumbered', asocial individuals, nor entirely 'separate self-contained, motivated by the pursuit of private desires' (Sandel, 1982 quoted in Martin and Vincent, 1999). There are some faint glimpses here of what Rikowski (2001) calls 'the class struggle within the human' or the *psychology of class* (p. 15) a 'clash of forces and drives' which recur 'in and through our everyday lives' (p. 15).

So what?

So what, if anything, can we conclude from this examination of the values and principles of the middle class. I have tried to avoid a one-sidedly grim picture, a dystopic view of a more general de-socialisation and de-moralisation of society (Fevre, 2000). I have not sought to over-emphasise the role of bourgeois individualism and ignore the growth of what Berking (1966) calls solidary individualism.[3] Berking puts forward a balanced view, wherein the tendencies of individualisation in modern society also involve 'learning, at all levels of social intercourse, to deal with paradoxical demands on one's behaviour, controlling one's affects without ceasing to be, natural, utilising the chances offered by an increasing informalisation without casting conventions to the winds, demanding authenticity, and steering clear of the constraints of depersonalisation' (p. 195). In fact, this is a reasonable rendition of the sorts of tensions and dilemmas of 'between-ness' that I want to capture as a common, although not universal element of the perspectives and orientations of these families. They feel responsible for their children but still recognise themselves as living in a complex and diverse social world, within and towards which they also have some sort of responsibility. Although again it is tempting to want to produce a binary here – a separation between those more clearly typified by bourgeois individualism and those who might be said to be solidary individualists. These are not simply calculating, uncaring people. But they are very desperate to do the best for their children. They typically work within and make decisions in a mass of contradictions which set pragmatism and love against principles and the impersonal standpoint. Nonetheless, the outcomes of these decisions may give some support to Goldthorpe's conception of the service class as 'essentially conservative in outlook' (1982, p. 180).

It is not the individual choices of particular families that create social divisions and inequalities, it is the aggregate, the pattern of choices, the hidden hand of class thinking, if you like, the repetition of certain decisions, views, perspectives and actions – that is, what Bourdieu would call 'a system of dispositions to a certain practice... the regularity of modes of practice' (1990, p. 79). Where dilemmas are recognised, these dilemmas capture 'the dialectic between alternative views, values, beliefs in persons and in society' (Berlak and Berlak, 1981, p. 124), but what we see is a particular 'pattern of resolution' (p. 132), or 'dominant modes of resolution' (p. 133). Certainly these families see themselves as autonomous decision-makers in a contradictory but all too 'real' world, their sense of a responsibility, and an uncertain future looms large. This sometimes means having to privilege 'necessary' interests over public principles. When it comes down to it 'commitments to the welfare of others... were not part of the respondents' primary accountability' (Jordan *et al.*, 1994, p. 197) putting the family first was. Then again we must also realise that people, and circumstances change. These are not fixed moral subjects and as Kymlicka (1989, p. 11) suggests 'we may regret our decisions even when things have gone as planned'. I have tried to present the case that impersonal values do play a part in school choice for the middle class, that these are not simply attenuated individuals, and indeed there are some families for whom principle is more important than simple advantage. This is not a simple story of self-loathing. Nonetheless, the material presented and discussed here does confirm Jordan's account of the predominance of the 'personal standpoint'. Where it exists, the support of these families for or willingness to trust their children to comprehensive education rests upon being able to find comprehensive settings in which certain kinds of social relations and forms of distinction are available to them. For others, the risks to their child or the imperatives of social advantage make any kind of comprehensive education unthinkable. Ethical considerations do impinge upon the calculus of school choice but are subordinated to both calculation and the values of individualism. That is to say, most families regard the choice between public and private school as having ethical connotations but principles are not adequate in themselves as guides to action. 'Without any ill-will toward others, the logic of their choices must always tend towards giving their offspring a headstart...' (Jordan *et al.*, 1994, p. 222). Nonetheless, these risks are also 'felt' and articulated in terms of safety, the child's physical and emotional well-being. The risks and concerns here are reinforced by media discourses around child safety issues and the apparent rise in serious incidents of bullying.

A final point on the 'social arrangements' of the education market and social justice. Nagel argues that political theories and the 'social arrangements' to which they give rise require of us a particular kind of relation between the personal and impersonal standpoints. He goes on to assert that 'I believe that any political theory that merits respect has to offer us an escape from the self-protective blocking out of the importance of others... (Nagel, 1991, p. 19). Neither choice theory specifically nor Thatcherite social theory more generally pass Nagel's test of being worthy of respect. However, what Nagel had not anticipated or taken account of is the reinvention of political theories and social arrangements which operate in such a way as to 'externalize the demands of the personal standpoint' (p. 5), rather than the impersonal. The current approach to the management of the public sector in the UK and increasingly elsewhere does take up what Cohen (1992, p. 183) calls a Thatcherite theory, or rather the colonising legacy of the 'discourse of Thatcherism' (Phillips, 1996, p. 236), and its 'assumption of a grotesquely simplistic notion of causality' with a 'depiction of the individual whose self-direction has been beaten into dust by the reflex hammer of self-gratification', as Cohen (1992, p. 183)[4] picturesquely puts it. In classical liberal terms, this is the rejection of any conception of a public good over and above the sum of individual ends. The values and incentives of market policies give legitimation and impetus to certain actions and values and inhibit and de-legitimise others. The material conditions of the late modern, global economy also play their part in generating certain 'necessities' and making other things seem dangerous or frivolous. In other words, values only ever partly float-free of their social context.

Nonetheless, embedded within these situated pragmatics there are several of the essential features of classical liberalism. In particular the central issue here is that of choice, but choice has a variety of functions within liberalism. It is not simply a matter of the exercise of political rights but is also key to the articulation or production of identity. The idea, as Bauman (1993, p. 4) puts it, is of individuals with 'identities not-yet-given' which in their construction over time involve the making of choices. This is very much to the fore in the relationship between parents' commitments to their child and their commitments to the principle of school choice. That is, some parents seem to believe that they can only enable their child to realise personhood by exercising their freedom to choose an exclusive educational environment, and that their child's particular selfhood might not be realised elsewhere. As against this, other parents choose to expose their children to social diversity as part of their self-formation and perhaps in a sense extend for them the possibilities of choice; although the point is that for some parents, some choices may not be welcome. However, as I have suggested and tried to demonstrate, these notions of the choice of what is good for the child are themselves embedded in social attachments and communal values. Here the liberal 'asocial self' is socially validated. For some parents these attachments produce or reinforce a coherence between private principles and social identity (Sandel, 1982) which are given further credibility by dominant political models, as noted above. They are clear about what it means to be a good parent. For others however, things are not so clear cut and they find themselves torn between very different sorts of social identities and values, and thus confront the possibility of being a 'good parent and a bad citizen' (White, 1994, p. 83). For these parents the distinction between public and private spheres, between individualism and communitarianism, is not clear-cut. Politics, identity and social justice (in the head, and in effect) are tightly bound and beset by tensions in these messy knots of values and perhaps we are not all libertarians, yet!

Notes

1 She goes on to assert that 'this places society in general – or its policy-making representatives – in a considerable dilemma' (p. 334).
2 There is an interesting difference in register and tone between Mr Wilkinson's highly rational dissection of school choice making and the more emotional accounts provided by most respondent mothers.
3 Williams (1959, p. 325) defines bourgeoisie individualism as resting on 'an idea of society as a neutral area within which each individual is free to pursue his own development and his own advantage as a natural right'.
4 On the other hand, Crewe (1989) reflecting on a analysis of the British Social Attitudes Survey concludes that the 'Thatcher crusade for values change' has failed.

References

Ball, S. J. (1997) 'Markets, equity and values in education', in R. Pring and G. Walford (eds) *Affirming the Comprehensive Ideal*, London: Falmer.
Ball, S. J. (1998) 'Ethics, self interest and the market form in education', in A. Cribb (ed.) *Markets, Managers and Public Service? Occasional Paper No. 1*, London, Centre for Public Policy Research: King's College London.
Ball, S. J. (2003) *Class Strategies and the Education Market: The Middle Class and Social Advantage*, London: RoutledgeFalmer.
Ball, S. J., M. Maguire and S. Macrae (1997) *The Post-16 Education Market: Ethics, Interests and Survival*, BERA Annual Conference: University of York.
Bauman, Z. (1993) *Postmodern Ethics*, Oxford: Blackwell.
Beck, U., A. Giddens and S. Lash (1994) *Reflexive Modernization: Politics, Tradition and Aesthetics in the Modern Social Order*, Oxford: Polity Press.
Berking, H. (1966) 'Solidary individualism: the moral impact of cultural modernisation in late modernity', in C. Lash, B. Szersynski and B. Wynne (eds) *Risk, Environment and Modernity: Towards a New Ecology*, London: Sage.
Berlak, A. and H. Berlak (1981) *Dilemmas of Schooling: Teaching and Social Change*, London: Methuen.
Bernstein, B. (1990) *The Structuring of Pedagogic Discourse*, London: Routledge.
Bottery, M. (1992) *The Ethics of Educational Management*, London: Cassell.
Bourdieu, P. (1986) *Distinction: A Social Critique of the Judgement of Taste*, London: Routledge.
Bowe, R., S. J. Ball and S. Gerwitz (1994) 'Captured by the discourse? Issues and concerns in researching "Parental Choice"', *British Journal of Sociology of Education* 15(1): 63–78.

Brantlinger, E., M. Majd-Jabbari and S. L. Guskin (1996) 'Self-interest and liberal educational discourse: how ideology works for middle-class mothers', *American Educational Research Journal* 33: 571–97.

Cohen, A. P. (1992) 'A personal right to identity: a polemic on the self in the enterprise culture', in P. Heelas and P. Morris (eds) *The Values of the Enterprise Culture*, London: Routledge.

Dreyfus, H. L. and P. Rabinow (1983) *Michel Foucault: Beyond Structuralism and Hermeneutics*, Chicago, IL: University of Chicago Press.

Fevre, R. W. (2000) *The Demoralization of Western Culture: Social Theory and the Dilemmas of Modern Living*, London: Continuum.

Gewirtz, S. (2001) 'Cloning the Blairs: new labour's programme for the re-socialization of working class parents', *Journal of Education Policy* 16(4): 365–78.

Gewirtz, S., S. J. Ball and R. Bowe (1993) 'Values and ethics in the marketplace: the case of Northwark Park', *International Journal of Sociology of Education* 3(2): 233–53.

Gewirtz, S., S. J. Ball and R. Bowe (1995) *Markets, Choice and Equity in Education*, Buckingham: Open University Press.

Giddens, A. (1991) *Modernity and Self-Identity*, Cambridge: Polity.

Goldthorpe, J. (1982) 'On the service class, its formation and future', in A. Giddens and G. Mackenzie (eds) *Classes and the Division of Labour: Essays in Honour of Ilya Neustadt*, Cambridge: Cambrdige University Press.

Grace, G. (1995) *School Leadership: Beyond Education Management: An Essay in Policy Scholarship*, London: Falmer.

Hatcher, R. (1998) 'Class differentiation in education: rational choices?', *British Journal of Sociology of Education* 19(1): 5–24.

Jonathan, R. (1989) 'Choice and control in education: parents' rights, individual liberties and social justice', *British Journal of Eduational Studies* 37(4): 321–38.

Jordan, B., M. Redley and R. James (1994) *Putting the Family First: Identities, Decisions and Citizenship*, London: UCL Press.

Kymlicka, W. (1989) *Liberalism, Community and Culture*, Oxford: Clarendon.

Lukes, S. (1974) *Power: A Radical View*, London: MacMillan.

McLaughlin, T. (1994) 'The scope of parents' educational rights', in M. J. Halstead (ed.) *Parental Choice and Education: Principles, Policy and Practice*, London: Kogan Page.

Martin, J. and C. Vincent (1999) 'Parental voice: an exploration', *International Studies in Sociology of Education* 9(2): 231–52.

Morgan, D. (1989) 'Strategies and sociologists: a comment on crow', *Sociology* 23(1): 25–9.

Nagel, T. (1991) *Equality and Partiality*, Oxford: Oxford University Press.

Pahl, R. E. and C. D. Wallace (1985) 'Forms of work and privatisation on the Isle of Sheppey', in B. Roberts, R. Finnegan and D. Gallie (eds) *New Approaches to Economic Life*, Manchester: Manchester University Press.

Phillips, L. (1996) 'Rhetoric and the spread of the discourse of Thatcherism', *Discourse and Society* 7(2): 209–41.

Rikowski, G. (2001) *After the Manuscript Broke Off: Thoughts on Marx, Social Class and Education*, paper presented at the BSA, Sociology of Education Study Group, King's College London.

Rose, N. (1992) 'Governing the enterprising self', in P. Heelas and P. Morris (eds) *The Values of the Enterprise Culture*, London: Routledge.

Sandel, M. (1982) *Liberalism and the Limits of Justice*, Cambridge: Cambridge University Press.

Savage, M., J. Barlow, P. Dickens and T. Fielding (1992) *Property, Bureaucracy and Culture: Middle Class Formation in Contemporary Britain*, London: Routledge.

Slater, D. and F. Tonkiss (2001) *Market Society*, Cambridge: Polity Press.

van Zanten, A. and C. Veleda (2001) 'Contexts locaux et strategies scolaires: clivages et interactions entre classes et classes moyennes danes la peripherie urbaine', *Revue du Centre de recherche en education* 20: 57–87.

White, P. (1994) 'Parental choice and education for citizenship', in M. Halstead (ed.) *Parental Choice and Education: Principles, Policy and Practice*, London: Kogan Page.

CHAPTER 14

'ETHNIC CHOOSING'
Minority ethnic students, social class and higher education choice

S. J. Ball, D. Reay and M. David, '"Ethnic Choosing": Minority ethnic students, social class and higher education choice', *Race Ethnicity and Education*, 2003, 5(4): 333–57

> In this universe of continuity, the work of construction and observation is able to (relatively) isolate homogeneous set of individuals characterized by sets of properties that are statistically and 'socio-logically' interrelated, in other words, groups separated by differences.
>
> (Bourdieu, 1986, p. 259)

The New Labour government in the UK now seems determined to take the issue of working class and minority ethnic participation in Higher Education very seriously. Announcements in February 2001 outlined a variety of policy tactics designed to drive up the overall participation rates of 'non-tradition' students or 'students from poorer backgrounds' and to increase the proportions of such students, or more precisely some of these, in high status Universities. That is 'bright students from poorer backgrounds', as they are referred to. The under-stated backdrop to this is a recognition of the significant status and reputational (and material) differences between Universities and, apparently, the intention to leave such differences untouched while attempting to change the distribution of types of students across the different institutions. Indeed, one of the possible side-effects of the new policies is an exacerbation of some aspects of difference as the 'bright students from poorer backgrounds' are 'creamed-off' by the 'old' (pre-1992) universities. This is all a part of New Labour's commitment to the creation of a meritocractic education system.

However, although as we suggest, there is an implicit recognition of differences between universities and between university intakes within these policy initiatives, there is no sense of an awareness of the processes of performance, choice and selection which produce intake differences.[1] Nor is there any reference to the outcome differences between universities, and the implications of these for students from 'poorer' or minority ethnic backgrounds. Brian Ramsden, Chief Executive of HESA, argued some time ago that the definition of participation needs to be changed to take account of 'outcomes' and total 'involvement' in HE (see Coffield and Vignoles, 1997). Our data does not address issues related to university selection; although we can illuminate some aspects of the processes which produce differences in performance (Reay *et al.*, 2001a). Here we will examine processes of student choice of University, related specifically to minority-ethnic students. There is a solid body of literature which addresses the issue of patterns HE access for 'minority' students (e.g. Taylor, 1992; Modood and Shiner, 1994; Abbasi, 1998; Modood and Acland, 1998) and a small amount of work on 'minority' students

Table 14.1 Ethnicity and gender of the 'minority' sub-sample

Ethnicity	Male	Female	Total
Bengali	1	2	3
Bangladeshi	3	1	4
Sri Lankan	1	1	2
Indian	5		5
Pakistani		1	1
African-Carribean		1	1
Nigerian	2	3	5
Ghanan		1	1
Ugandan		1	1
Philipino		1	1
Chinese	3	1	4
Jordianian	1		1
Algerian	1		1
Iranian	2	1	3
Guyanese		1	1
Black British	4	4	8
Mixed-race	2	5	7
Jewish	5	11	16
Total	30	35	65

experience of HE (e.g. Bird, 1996; Osler, 1999) but almost nothing has been written on how 'minority' students choose among HEIs.

This paper is based upon a close analysis of interviews with a sub-sample of students from London-based, ESRC funded study of Higher Education (HE) choice. This sub-sample consists of 65 Minority Ethnic ('minority')[2] students, including 16 Jewish students, 35 female and 30 male, from the total of 120 who were interviewed in the study. The backgrounds, identities and class positions of the minority students are very diverse – see Table 14.1. The interviews elicited educational career histories from the students and a narrative account of their choice of higher education institutions. Specific questions were asked about information used, support received, constraints etc. In addition to the students, 15 intermediaries and 40 parents were interviewed and 502 students completed a questionnaire. A small number of careers advice interviews, HE application preparation sessions, Oxbridge application advice sessions and meetings for parents on HE choice were observed.

Our study is focused upon two cohorts of student 'choosers', their parents and various intermediaries (careers teachers, sixth form tutors etc.) in 6 educational institutions; an 11–18 mixed comprehensive with a large minority ethnic, working class intake (Crieghton Community School (CCS)) and a comprehensive sixth form consortium which serves a socially diverse community (Maitland Union (MU)), a tertiary college with a very large A-level population (Riverway College (RC)), an FE College which runs HE Access courses (Fennister FE College (FFEC)), and two prestigious private schools, one single-sex boys (Cosmopolitan Boys (CB)), one single-sex girls (Hemsley Girls (HG)). All of the institutions are in or close to London. Our research is institutionally located in this way so that we are able to explore the effects of individual, familial and institutional influences and processes in choice-making (Table 14.2).

Two things must be made very clear from the outset. First, what we refer to here as 'ethnic choosing' is situated within a variety of other criteria, constraints,

Table 14.2 Interview data by school

School	Interviews		
	Student	Intermediary	Parent
CB	12	1	4
HG	15	2	10
MU	33	4	14
RC	26	3	8
CCS	11	1	4
FFC	23	4	40

concerns and possibilities of choice, many of which are articulated or experienced by other students. Ethnicity, on its own does not explain or account for the choices of minority ethnic students. Second and concomitantly, any generalisations about the 'minority' students in our sample are very dangerous. Differences among the 'minority' students in terms of social class and 'educational inheritance' are clearly important and these differences are played out in applications and admissions to HE. This point is one of the main themes of this paper. As Madood and Shiner (1994, p. 4) warn: 'It is...not appropriate to speak of a White-ethnic minority divide'. Minority ethnic, as we shall see, is a very diverse analytic category. In some respects therefore this provides a vehicle for discussion of some general and generic issues about choice but it is also the case that there are some aspects of choice that are specific to or particularly bear upon minority ethnic students. That is, the nature of or criteria for choice combine in particular ways for some 'minority' students. In relation to our research as a whole then this paper attempts to put ethnicity in context. In the table above and the extracts quoted below, with two exceptions, the ethnicities attributed to the students are those used by the students themselves.

The London setting for the research is, as we shall see, important in the concerns, experiences and perceptions of the students. They view the world of HE from a London perspective and this is particularly important in relation to issues related to the 'ethnic mix' of HE institutions. It is worth noting that 45 per cent of Britain's 'minority' population live in Greater London compared with 10 per cent of the White population (Equal Opportunities Commission, 1994) and that 20 per cent of the London population are identified by the Office of National Statistics (1997) as members of 'minority' groups; 22 per cent of the population of London were born outside of the UK. Of course, the actual distribution of these groups within London is very uneven. For example, in 1994 23 per cent of the population of Tower Hamlets and 45 per cent of Brent were of minority ethnicities compared with less than 5 per cent in Richmond.[3] Furthermore, 40 per cent of all minority ethnic HE students are in London HEIs, mainly in the 'new' universities.

We want to begin by constructing two contrasting ideal-types of 'minority' chooser. In the spirit of the disclaimers above many facets of the types are evident across our sample as a whole.[4] The ideal-types work as a set of simple binaries and have all the crudities and drawbacks of such a formulation but here they are intended to set up a base-line or framework for further, more nuanced discussion later in the paper. They should not be mistaken for descriptive categories. They are in Weber's terms hypothetical selections, a step away from reality. A few students certainly do fit fairly neatly into one or the other but that is not the point or purpose here.[5]

Table 14.3 Ideal types of HE chooser

Contingent choosers	Embedded choosers
Finance is a key concern and constraint	Finance is not an issue
Choice uses minimal information	Choice is based on extensive and diverse sources of information
Choice is distant or 'unreal'	Choice is part of a cultural script, a 'normal biography'
Few variables are called up	A diverse array of variables are deployed
Choice is general/abstract	Choice is specialist/detailed
Minimal support (social capital) is used	Extensive support (social capital) is mobilised
Ethnic mix is an active variable in choosing	Ethnic mix is marginal or irrelevant to choice
Choosing is short term and weakly linked to 'imagined futures' – part of an incomplete or incoherent narrative	Choosing is long term and often relates to vivid and extensive 'imagined futures' – part of a coherent and planned narrative
First-time choosers with no family tradition of HE	'Followers' embedded in a 'deep grammar of aspiration' which makes HE normal and necessary
Narrowly defined socioscapes and spatial horizons – choices are 'local'/ distance is a friction	Broad socioscapes and social horizons – choices are 'national'/ distance is not an issue
Parents as 'onlookers' or 'weak framers'/mothers may give practical support[a]	Parents as 'strong framers' and active participants in choice

Note
a See Project paper 6, On families and choice-making.

For want of better terms or markers the two types are referred to as *contingent* and *embedded* choosers. These may also be thought of as two different discourses of choice. The social conditions of choice for each type are different. Some of the major differences are summarised in Table 14.3. It is important to bear in mind however that this is not a stark and total antithesis, after all the students reported here are all wanting/intending to go on to Higher Education, with varying degrees of enthusiasm. The similarities between them must be borne in mind as well as the differences.

It is now important to explain and illustrate these differences. In each case data from a small number of students are deployed to illustrate the types. The illustrations are used in this way to indicate the complexity of choosing in the interrelationships among the characteristics of the types. These illustrations 'stand for' the patterns identified within the whole sub-sample. Later we will begin to muddy some of these neat but crude distinctions and further data will be referred to.

The contingent chooser

The contingent chooser is typically a first generation applicant to HE whose parents were educated outside of the UK. Their parents are working class and have low incomes. The student can expect little financial support from them in choice-making or in funding HE itself; although there may well be emotional support and high levels of encouragement and expectation within the family for the achievement of credentials.[6] Mothers sometimes figure large in giving practical support and encouragement.[7] But expectations are 'generic' and sometimes unrealistic and weakly linked to 'real' imagined futures. HE becomes a break or hiatus in family and personal narratives. The decision to apply for HE or the realisation of HE as a possible next step is 'recent' – made at the end of GCSEs or during A-level courses. HE and 'getting a degree' are general categories; neither family not student have much sense of the different kinds and statuses of higher educations on offer or what HE study will be like: 'the new system with its fuzzy classifications and blurred edges encourages and entertains...aspirations that are themselves blurred and fuzzy' (Bourdieu and Passeron, 1979, p. 91) and not surprisingly 'faulty perceptions... are encouraged by the anarchic profusion of courses' (p. 92). The status distinctions between 'old' and 'new' universities is either not recognised or not seen as significant. The processes of information gathering and choice are mostly left to the student, who often will act on the basis of very limited information. There is a high reliance on a few 'significant others' for 'hot knowledge' – that is first or second hand recommendations or warnings related to specific institutions based on some kind of 'direct' experience (Ball and Vincent, 1998) – but contingent choosers end up relying more heavily on 'cold knowledge' (guides, prospectuses and websites etc.) than their embedded counterparts. Their social capital is of limited relevance here. The student and family have fewer direct links to higher education experiences and in many instances none. At this point they are 'condemned to experience [the culture of HE] as unreal' (Bourdieu and Passeron, 1979, p. 53). Subjects rather than 'courses' are discussed and distinctions between institutions does not operate at the level of differences in course structures or content or teaching strategy. Visits to institutions or attendance at 'open days' are rare.[8] Contingent choosers 'might be described as working on the surface structure of choice, because their programmes of perception rest upon a basic unfamiliarity with particular aspects' (Gewirtz *et al.*, 1995, p. 47) of HE. Spatial horizons of action are limited; partly for reasons of cost and partly as a result of concerns about ethnic fit and ethnic mix and the possibility of confronting racism. Institutions which offer an ethnic mix, with good numbers of the students' own ethnicity but no predominant group, are favoured. Leaving London or leaving home is rarely an option for these students; although some would be keen to do so if circumstances allowed. Madood and Shiner (1994, p. 38) note that a disproportionate number of 'minority' students make applications to their home regions (as does Taylor, 1992). Family and community relationships are positively valued and local choices also reflect this. Staying at home may also be a factor which off-sets the potential isolation reported by 'minority' students in some HEIs (see Bird, 1996; Taylor, 1992, p. 369 also makes this point).

Let us look at some data to illustrate and 'fill out' some of this general description. The vignettes presented below were chosen to illustrate variety within the types rather than a simple commonality.

Jamaal came to the UK from Bangladesh when he was six. He has seven brothers and two sisters and his family are mainly involved in restaurant work. He attends Crieghton Community. He 'cant remember' his parents giving him any educational advice, 'I think they were more worried about my elder brothers getting jobs'. None of his family had stayed on at school to do A-levels. When choosing his A-levels he first had in mind a job in aeronautical engineering but then switched to medicine and chose physics, chemistry and maths. He explained 'in my family you're seen to do really really well if your son becomes a doctor'. But he 'couldn't really handle' physics and dropped it in favour of sociology; 'it was one of my other friends...he said it was really interesting'. Jamaal is now hoping to do social science at University. 'I haven't got any plans, I just want to get a degree and see what happens later on in social science, I'm really interested in international relations but I don't know'. His UCAS choices were Westminster, East London, Luton, Middlesex, Guildhall and North London. He would have liked to have had the option to apply outside of the London area but practical constraints made this impossible. There were four main factors underlying this selection.

> It was mainly, you know, where I can have contact with my relatives and so on...It has to do with my family but also my friends. Also obviously I wanted to stay in London and obviously the predicted grades were also a factor. And also the financial aspect...but I wanted to go outside London if I could.

Jamaal admitted knowing 'not much' about the places he had chosen; 'I just looked up the prospectuses and that's about it'. But he does have 'a lot of friends who are in different universities'. The points offers made by the different institutions are now a prime consideration in Jamaal's thinking but this is weighed against other factors – like the possibility of confronting racism and his preference for an institution with a high proportion of Asian and Muslim students.

> Luton asked me for 16 points too but the thing is with Luton, it is a very racist area, so that has put me off. Now I know I dont really want to go there...There's been recent headlines in the news and also my friends there have experienced racism. One of my friends transferred from Luton to Sussex [and] Asian families are generally close-knit, so they stick together so I'd want to go somewhere where there were other Asian students...Most of the universities that I have chosen have Islamic Societies, I mean that would be an indicator that they dont discriminate and stuff.

Cassie is dual heritage. Her mother is a mature entrant to teaching and her father a social worker; both graduates of the University of North London. Her parents are separated and she lives with her mother. She is doing GNVQ courses at Maitland Union and wants to do a degree in business management with 'the idea of getting into hotel work. I would like to manage a hotel'. This came from 'my aunt, she worked as a maid in a hotel, and she used to tell the stories about famous people and stuff...and I like to travel...and you get to meet a lot of new people'. It was 'mum' who suggested business management. 'We were talking about it and she said it might be best' but 'she didn't mind, she said if that was what I wanted to do then that was alright'. Cassie wants to go to HE outside London 'but not too far' and 'got the UCAS book and rung up loads of universities and looked at the entry requirements and stuff'. She also looked on the UCAS website but has not visited any of her choices. Her mum is 'looking forward to me moving out...but she said I could stay if I want to'.

She applied to Chester, Suffolk, Southampton and North London. She had put Oxford Brookes but they changed their GNVQ requirement to a distinction and so 'I couldn't go there any more'. She 'had heard from my uncle's partner that it was a good university...'. Her first choice is now Chester 'They've got a good night life there and the university looks really nice' and 'I would prefer to be right in the city centre rather than tucked up in some village in the middle of nowhere'. She believes that it is only two and a half hours from London. Her mum and dad will both help with costs and 'I hope to find a part time job'. Cassie wants a 'place of my own, my own space...and experience what life is like'. Her mother does not mind where she goes 'as long as I go to university I suppose'. Cassie's friend Carrie has also chosen Chester and that was a key factor, they wanted to be together but 'We did talk about it being White [Laughs]'. Mum and Dad said:

> I should got to an area that is like mixed. And has got like a whole kind of different, lots of people of all different races...and that if you're mixed race that's the best thing to do...Carrie wanted to go to Wales and that was not a place for me...there's quite a lot of mainly White people there, so I thought it would be quite boring...

Cassie found choosing and making her application quite stressful and relied on 'mum mainly...I was very hard'.

Adeibe's parents are from Algeria. His father is a radio engineer and his mother a nursery worker. He attends the Maitland Union consortium. When he was young he wanted to work on television and 'be famous' but he had 'never' talked to his parents about what he might do when he finished school. Careers Advisers had suggested computer design but he 'wanted to do something with science' and his family [despite his 'never'] 'said that would be best for me'. He chose A-level Biology, Design Technology and Maths. When confronted with a UCAS application Adeibe had to decide what he wanted to do. His family 'helped me pick a university' and 'my mum phoned up for me to different universities'. He did not visit any universities or attend the HE Fair but also made some phone calls and used the UCAS web-site. He did not find school 'really helpful...they didn't give me any ideas where I should apply'. He did not discuss his choice with teachers or friends but 'my mum helped me alot'. He had no other advice; 'I dont really know anyone who has been to uni apart from a friend of my dad'. 'I wanted to do something in science with sports...I just went through and picked the ones that I liked' from a list of 'about thirty' within his 18 point target range. Mum 'wanted me to do what I thought best [but] she helped me finalise universities'. Adeibe wanted 'somewhere in a big city' but not 'too far' and 'easy to get to' and 'cheaper' than London, and the social life 'was one of my main things' although his mother did not think this important. He selected Bristol, Nottingham, UCL, Hertfordshire and Greenwich. He 'wasn't bothered about league tables', but did look at them, or about 'old' and 'new' universities. He also did not look at social or ethnic mix; he 'didn't know about that'. Nottingham is his first choice, he has been to the city a couple of times; 'It has a nice feel about it'. His dad will 'set up a fund' to help pay for University but 'I will have to work' and take out a loan. He has not thought about what jobs he might do after university.

Shamina is Bengali. She has a brother who is an accountant and went to Westminster University. She started thinking about A-levels while at Saturday school and discussed it with her family. She attends Crieghton Community. She chose A-level Media Studies and Sociology and is predicted two Cs. Her parents were 'really happy' that she decided to stay on and said that 'you have to basically do A-levels and go on to a degree if you want the chance of a good job...I was born in this country and went through the whole education system here, so because of that they want me to go to further education and study at University'. Shamina was unsure of what course to apply for, she 'was confused about what to do'. She thought about social policy and 'read up a bit about that'. Her 'sister-in-law does social policy and management at Guildhall...and she was telling me its really good stuff' but 'I want to do something else, something to do with crime' and law...so then I came up with criminology'. Guided by her teacher she decided on Criminology and Social Policy combined. But as for university again 'she was confused', like her friends 'we were all finding it too hard to choose'. Prospectuses 'didn't tell you everything you needed to know' but she also looked at some University websites. Eventually 'I was in a rush and panicking' and 'I put Kingston, Middlesex, South Bank, Westminster, East London and Thames Valley, all London basically because I wanted to study in London...I didn't want to go outside London. Its quiet to me, not busy, I dont like it'. But this is also to do with finances 'because living at home would be much cheaper...because you don't need to pay for the rent and food'. She also looked at UCL but 'they wanted too many points'. Middlesex is Shamina's first choice, although she has not been there and her knowledge of the university is rather thin; 'my friend went there already and said it's a really nice place, they have all the facilities there to do with her course'. Again 'hot knowledge' and personal recommendations are highly valued when available. Her brother said Westminster was 'good, but at the end of the day it's up to me'. A friend is also going to Middlesex 'but if I have to go somewhere where there is no one I know I'd still go'. Travelling is not an issue, although Shamina is a little vague about where Kingston is 'but I think I can manage them all'. As to costs her parents say 'we will help you as much as we can...We will be beside you' but she will need to work part-time and take out a loan.

The priorities and position of, and the 'unreality' of HE for the contingent chooser are epitomised by Sheila, a black British young women who lives independently in a hostel and is dependent upon welfare benefits. City University is her first choice. She was asked why.

> I dont even know anything about the University. I've read the prospectus and the way media and sociology are described it sounded really great and its in the city and it will be beneficial economically, I think, because I spent so much money to get to college and its nearer than Brunel. Brunel is miles out!

Contingent choosers know little about the institutions they choose, even their first choice universities. Choosing is a process involving the balance of practical constraints with a limited number of positive criteria. These criteria are primarily extrinsic, all 'extravagances' are excluded (Bourdieu, 1990b, p. 56). The frictions and vagaries of distance impinge firmly upon choice. Despite the cosmopolitan experiences of these young people and links with family across the world their actual 'socioscapes',[9] or 'real geographies of social action' (Harvey, 1989, p. 355), are relatively compressed or foreshortened. They inhabit very different 'time-space biographies' (Hagerstrand, 1975) from those of the embedded choosers.

The embedded chooser

The embedded chooser has parents who attended university and often other relatives and friends with experience of university, but not necessarily in the UK. University attendance is a well-established and expected route beyond school, part of a 'normal biography' (Du Bois-Reymond, 1998). Such students are subject to subtle and 'diffuse incitements' (Bourdieu and Passeron, 1979, p. 20) to further study. To not go on to HE is virtually unthinkable and certainly unacceptable to parents. Thus, the singularity of individual dispositions are positioned firmly 'within the class and its trajectory' (Bourdieu, 1990b, p. 60). University is often linked to particular career trajectories and entry into prestigious professions or highly paid commercial occupations. Career aspirations are often long standing and vividly imagined, part of a coherent and connected personal narrative. They are common-sensical and self-evident. The family are able to mobilise various forms of support and information for the student; like arranging work experience or discussions with people in target occupations. Parents are directly involved in choice-making, for instance in making visits to Universities and commenting on UCAS application forms. Types of information used in choice-making are diverse and value is given to both 'hot' and 'cold' knowledge. League Table positions being a significant example of the latter. The nature of courses as well as institutions are attended to. Cost is not an issue and is either taken for granted or openly discussed and settled by parents. The type and status of University attended is important but location is a secondary issue. It is expected that if necessary, the student will move out of the family home and away from London to get the 'right' course and the 'right' institution. Such students approach HE choice with confidence and certainty. At this point at least they are in many respects akin to Bourdieu and Passeron's (1979, p. 53) 'bourgeois students', 'who make higher education an experience into which enter no problems more serious than those they put there'. Some of these choosers would prefer institutions that are ethnically mixed but do not expect to find a problem with racism in HE settings. Again, some illustrations will put further flesh onto this outline.

Sarah's parents come from Ghana and they both attended Manchester University, her older brother is also at Manchester doing Materials Science. Her sister is reading Economics at Coventry. Her father is a lecturer in bio-chemistry and her mother a midwife. She attends Creighton Community. 'My parents have always told us – you are all going to university...so it has always been sort of automatic for me...Its not like I had the choice'. But Sarah wants 'to go to University anyway and I've heard too much about how good it is'. From watching *LA Law* Sarah decided she wanted to be a lawyer and 'my dad showed me a few things in the encyclopaedia and helped me find stuff about it'. She asked her Careers Advisers which would be the 'best' universities for law. 'They said those with the "best reputation" were Cambridge, Oxford, Manchester, Bristol and Warwick but that every single university that teaches law is good' and 'they told me to look at the universities that have a lot of people getting jobs after they finished their degree...'. She became 'quite firm about the ones I wanted to go to' and again 'my dad had already told me alot of stuff'. She perused prospectuses, used the CD-rom of the UCAS and attended the HE Fair and 'learned a lot about the universities in the way they presented themselves'. She also went with a school trip to the Manchester universities. Her reaction to the universities was very different. At Manchester 'the first thing they spoke about to us was education, they talked about the course...showed us the libraries and stuff, it was really good' Manchester Metropolitan 'was such a contrast' they were shown a video of 'the social life and we saw people drinking...and then they took us to the gyms and that...It put me off'.

Sarah is predicted Two Cs and a D. 'So I thought to myself. I've no chance of Oxford or Cambridge, although those are the best places to go to, lets get real...so I applied to Manchester Met...Sussex, Leeds, Leeds Met, Cheltenham and Thames Valley.' She plans to visit Sussex and Swansea and 'ask my dad to come'. She has a conditional offer from Sussex her first choice, three Bs. And she does not 'mind at all whether its a city or not. It just depends where I can get in'. She is fed up with London and 'I wanted to get away, I wanted to be independent. I dont want my family around, you know...[and] they would have preferred me to go away and experience being away from the family'. Her parents were helpful with the UCAS form 'my dad found a few mistakes...they were very helpful. They'd been through it with my brother and sister'. She did look at the League

Tables but says that they 'might tell you which ones are successful but it depends on what kind of person you are because I could go to a top university and absolutely hate it...it didn't really affect my choice'. The ethnic makeup of the universities did interest Sarah.

> I did read about the African Caribbean societies and the Asian societies and all the different things they do, and I know there are quite a few people, a few black people and Asian people who do go to Sussex and Manchester Met and stuff like that and that was important that they had those sorts of societies there. It 'means you know you're not going to be the only black person there. So I know the population is predominately White in Sussex, but even then that didn't effect me really, because I thought as long as there are some black people there, and there are some Asian people there, and Chinese people there, whatever, I don't mind because I prefer to be somewhere where there is different cultures. And so I did make sure that there was a mix yes....

Sarah's parents will 'be able to help contribute' to the costs of HE but 'there are so many things they could do with their money, more important than bailing me out'. Both her brother and sister worked their way through university 'and they seem quite all right' and 'I'll borrow the money. I'm determined to get a law degree. And if I'm in debt I'll pay it somehow'. She has discussed university with friends as well as family and has begun to develop a sense of some of the 'real' demands and possibilities involved.

> Simon, my friend has gone to Imperial, and I've spoken to him a lot about stuff like that, my friend has gone to Liverpool University to do a medicine degree, she got two As and a B, so she knows a lot about that. My other friend went to Bristol, so I do have quite a few friends who have been to university, and some who started university a year ago. You know, in London, so I have spoken to them a lot about university.

Sarah explained that the course she took was more important to her than the University and she preferred 'the modern way of teaching things'.

Navid came to the UK from Iran when he was six. His father is a lawyer. One sister did accountancy at South Bank. The other is doing medicine at Manchester. He attends Cosmopolitan Boys School. HE has always been on the cards. 'It is just the culture I am from, it is expected. No one usually drops out, in Iran, where I am from, it is sort of expected of you. Not really expected, as in there's pressure put on you, but sort of something you don't think about – oh well, I'll drop it at sixteen, it's not really an option'. None of his family or family friends have not gone to University. Here we see habitus as predisposition 'without any calculation' (Bourdieu, 1990b, p. 53) at work. '...your parents sort of expect you to do well, in a way, and so you have that responsibility, and you sort of just work towards it. And I always knew that I was going to be a scientist, so it wasn't a problem to me, I was looking forward to A-levels actually...the decision of my going into A-levels wasn't a decision. It was what shall I study at A-level'. Navid developed high expectations for himself which reflected the culture of his private school. 'When we were looking at A-levels and everything, loads of people were doing four A-levels and going to Oxford and Cambridge, and I made myself a sort of promise that I would want to do four A-levels, it doesn't matter what I did, I just wanted to put pressure on myself and see if I could cope. And to this day I have regretted that

I didn't apply to Oxbridge.' But he wants to become a dentist and explained that 'King's and Bristol are the Oxbridge of Dentistry'. His choice of career was backed up with considerable research and embedded in an unusually vivid sense of what such work would and could entail.

> so many people I talk to go – oh, a dentist, that just 'means you have to look at peoples' mouths all day. But if you just take it a step beyond that, when you look at what it actually is, it is a stable job, it is connected with the sciences, and there is a wide variety of things you can get into. I was quite interested in medicine before, but then I sort of, the surgical side of medicine, the extreme, extensive surgery, I just do not find interesting. So I sort of, I looked at the career options I had and dentistry seemed ideal... they asked me at one of my interviews, what type of thing do you want to go post graduate in? And I said – well, definitely not maxi-filial surgery. And they said – why? And I said it was just something that just doesn't appeal to me. I prefer to be in contact with the patient and have a relationship with them, rather than to anaesthetise them and just perform surgery on them.

He saw this as an interesting and sensible decision. 'I had the opportunity to go off and do something which I also enjoy and which will get me some money and make a stable life for myself.' Navid's choice narrative offers a particularly coherent and highly organised account of his educational career in relation to his expectations of a future work career. All of this is very 'real'. Even more so in that Navid embeds his decisions within an extensive social network. He discussed his choice with:

> Dr Anderson (Head of 6th form), especially, and Mr Rumsey, because he used to be a teacher and we are quite close... I asked them alot of questions, they guided me, but I think the most influential people were, I've got quite alot of dentist friends. People who have come from Sweden and people who have graduated here, and the person I did my work shadowing with... in summer I usually go to Iran to visit all the family, and I worked with an orthodontist and that was quite revealing... my mum's cousin owns the clinic...

He also discussed his HE with his GP. 'He said don't not go to King's, its too good an opportunity to miss.' His view of the high reputation of dentistry at King's was well researched. 'I know at least seven or eight people who have studied either medicine or dentistry at King's.' There is a considerable body of social capital in play here. And he was also secure in the notion that he would be comfortable at King's. 'I think there will be people who will suit my social interests....' Like other private school students Navid displays the predispositions of a habitus 'pre-adapted' to such a milieu (Bourdieu, 1990b, p. 61) and a strategy without 'strategic design' (Bourdieu, 1990a, p. 108). There is a sense here of what Bourdieu (1990a, p. 108) calls 'ontological complicity'. In all this Navid's parents provided a strong frame of expectation; 'if I said of was going to drop out after A-levels I think they would have something to say about that'; but were expected as being 'hands-off' in relation to choice; 'I dont think my dad has influenced any of us in our choices... They shouldn't really interfere.' Navid had no interest in the presence of other Iranian students. Indeed he disavows any cultural commonality (see later); 'I am not culturally towards Iranian, actually I am quite the reverse'; but he did express a preference for a location with 'cultural mix'; 'it sort of makes me feel better that I know people from different cultures...'.

More that anything else the 'minority' students in the private schools reflect the values, choices and concerns of their school peers. The private school students share identities, attitudes and actions. 'Minority' students like Navid are able to deploy as a resource, what could be termed 'transnational cultural capital', forms of legitimate knowledge that have efficacy within the field of HE in the UK.

Lena is Black British with a South African mother with an art foundation qualification and Ghanaian father with an engineering degree from Ghana. She attends the MU consortium. All her education has been in the UK and she described herself as 'totally academic'. She got 9 A stars and an A at GCSE. Her career choice, for sometime, had been between Law and medicine, but she did work experience at the Law Centre 'and really hated that...It was so boring...just paperwork'. Her parents 'support me, they said – you can do what-ever you want basically'. She did more work experience in GPs surgeries and 'really liked that'. Her form teacher's brother, a doctor, helped organise the place-ments. In year 12 she 'was asked by some teachers if I wanted to apply for sort of Oxbridge and I said no then...'. The reasons were simple; 'I want to stay in London, I want to stay at home in Camden, and at the time I liked Imperial and UCL. That's where I wanted to go.' She 'knows GPs who teach there, one at Imperial and one at UCL, and they both recommended...'. Again, in various ways, Lena's choice has become very vivid for her and is embedded in a stock of social capital on which she can draw for information, access, sponsorship and support. She does voluntary work in a local hospital one afternoon a week. Despite her deciding against Oxbridge the school kept up 'lots of pressure' and 'so I applied to Cambridge as well'; although her mother was not keen 'she said you know the debt I would be in by the end of it would be so high. That it would be financially much better to live at home'. One of Lena's teachers, whose daughter was reading medicine at Cambridge arranged for the girls to meet. From this and her other contacts and work experience she acquired a good grasp of the different degree and training structures for medicine and could compare the different courses in some detail. She then first visited Oxford with two friends and a teacher who had been a student there, and then went with three friends to see Cambridge; 'we arranged to visit a few colleges'. The facility of all this is again in contrast to the laboured and distant choices of the contingent choosers. Lena applied to New Hall 'It was impressive', but she was under-whelmed by Cambridge itself 'It was just a little town'. As to the other students she was aware that 'they are sort of middle class' but 'didn't really mind that' although her two friends were 'put off' by 'the posh people who will look down on me'. Here we see the limits of 'onto-logical complicity' and the natural milieu of HE made unnatural. Lena is made aware of the 'sense of one's place' and the 'sense of the place of others' (Bourdieu, 1990a, p. 113). (The issue of class fractioning among the embedded choosers merits further exploration.) She attended three interviews and took a test and 'thought it was brilliant' and says she was 'seduced by the ivory towers stuff'. She was not offered a place and was also turned down by the Royal Free and is now waiting to hear from UCL and Imperial. Her mum 'is pleased, she didn't want me to go'. The UCL interview day was full of familiar faces 'rejects from Cambridge' but 'more talkative, a bit more friendly'. She is now less worried about costs 'I've decided I'm just gonna go for it and take out loans...And so I am going to stay at home and that will reduce it a bit, I've got a Sunday job, so that will help a little more'.

Wing is Chinese and attends Riverway College. She was born in the UK, her par-ents come from Hong Kong, they own and run their own shop. None on her family 'has ever been to university'. Her interests are in Business Studies and economics and she is good at maths. She already has a sense of a future for herself linking the here and now to a foreseeable work life. 'I wanted to go into like the financial sector. When I've done a degree in economics...maybe after I get my degree, work for a company and go aboard for a bit, if I could go to America and come back and stuff.' She was not sure what university but 'I wanted to go to a good university...depending how well I do in my A-levels'. She is already 'hoping to do an extra year and get a Masters degree'. She sought advice from the brother of a friend who 'went into economics and he's like got a job in it and everything. So he was really aware of which universities are quite well know for having good economic departments'. Wing checked in the subject league tables 'not looking in the overall tables, but the subject' and in addition 'my economics teacher was telling me'. The careers office 'didn't really help me'. Again specialist, first hand advice is better than second hand and general. From this LSE and Bristol emerged, although Cambridge was top of the League Table. Wing had two interviews with the Riverway College Oxbridge advisers, but 'I dont think my grades would be good enough'. She also consulted *Which University*? Which was helpful because as well as the subject 'its about the place, the city...'. The courses appeared 'quite similar'. Wing has offers for 5 of her UCAS choices 'all kind of quite high actually' but is still waiting on LSE, her first choice. 'I think its the best place and also I want to stay in London...because I want to go into the financial sector and London is the main city.' She went to the LSE Open Day and 'Its quite nice I liked it, its very city like. Its not like a university as you imagine...'. It is interesting that Wing had 'imagined' what a university would be like. Leeds is her insurance place – 'a few of my friends have been up there and loved it'. She will go to the Open Day. All of her choices are for city Universities 'I want to stay in a city...I didn't really fancy going to the country side'. A part of this is to do with ethnic mix and a concern about racism in the 'White highlands':

> London is quite mixed so that doesn't affect me much at the moment, but I do worry about when I go far away to a different city and they might be all White and they might have protests against other colours. Because you see in London you don't really have much racism but I know that there is racism in other places that aren't so mixed.

Even so she would not stay 'just because I want to stay, it is more the better university I would go to'. Her parents 'would prefer me to stay at home' and they have been saving to help her financially; 'they will support me anyway. I think they have kind of got the financial means to do so'. But they do not know the English education system; 'So it is just like I am by myself.' For Wing the social capital deployed by other embedded choosers is not so readily to hand and has to be worked at with a degree of 'strategic design'. She has to improvise.

Ethnic mix

As indicated already a number of the 'minority' students interviewed, took the ethnic mix of the universities they considered applying to into account in their decision-making. Of the 65 'minority' student transcripts analysed; 25 students indicated ethnic mix as a factor they had taken into account; 34 stated that this was not a concern or made no mention of it; the remaining 4 made vague references to 'mix'. State and private and school-age and mature students were all represented among those for whom ethnic mix was an issue and students from the full range of 'minority' ethnicities were included. However, overall the FE and

CCS students, those from mainly working-class backgrounds, were more likely to identify ethnic mix as a concern (11) than the private or MU or RC students. The RC students seemed least concerned (2). To reiterate, ethnic mix was one among a variety of *choice criteria* in play but could be a decisive factor in *not* considering certain universities, or types of universities or areas of the country as possible choices. The relevance of ethnic mix within choice in turn begs questions about the nature of ethnic identity. For all but two or three students it would probably be accurate to say that their ethnic identity, as displayed or called-up in the choice of HE, is as Modood *et al.* (1994, p. 119) argue 'a plastic and changing badge of membership' which is located 'in a wider set of linked identities' (p. 117):

> ethnic identities are not simply 'given' or fixed over time. The field of ethnic minority identities in Britain indeed displays the context-dependent and to some extent interest-dependent characteristics of identity.
>
> (Modood *et al.*, 1994, p. 6)

Choice was for some students, in part, about sustaining aspects of their ethnic identity or having this identity valued and defended or at least not having to defend or assert the value of their identity. Some HE contexts were seen as more tolerant of difference, or perhaps more accurately these were contexts where difference and diversity were 'normal'. Settings of diversity potentially offer an escape from essentialism, from fixity and allow for the possibility of play across a variety of identities; the making and re-making of identity. Nonetheless, as Gillborn (1995) points out fluidity can in fact fix very quickly. In contrast there are those contexts – where particular ethnicities predominate – in which either identity becomes fixed in relation to the prevailing norm (what ever that might be) or in which there is a strong possibility of being positioned as 'other'. In other words, there are, or appear to these students to be, different possibilities for identity in different sorts of settings and concomitantly different risks of marginalisation.[10] Candice, who is 'dual heritage/black British', from the MU consortium, was wary of Warwick on these grounds.

> I'm very conscious that the attraction for me of staying in London is the racial mix you get at even some of the top universities, you know, that one of the main reasons for choosing London would be my racial background. I did notice how White Warwick was and that did make me feel a bit uncomfortable, like I was an outsider.

Amrit, a Bengali student from CCS, made the same point.

> I don't care if there are lots of different ethnic backgrounds and stuff, people from different ethnic backgrounds, that doesn't bother me. As long as it is mixed with all sorts of people there, not just White... I'd want it to be all mixed but I can get along with anyone, basically, the colour or what race they are, that doesn't bother me.

Deborah, from CCS, whose parents are Nigerian, picks up the other aspect of this in her contrast between 'mix' and 'swamping'.

> My friend, who is Nigerian. I think basically there is a lot more Nigerians that go there [Oxford Brookes], than say, Leeds or whatever. You know, how you get one ethnic minority dominating another, in comparison to another place,

and she goes, I mean, she didn't say it was swamped with Nigerians, but she said that you do get quite a lot. You could probably pick out seven or eight Nigerian students, you know, every day or something like that.

When asked if this was important to her she went on to say: 'I wasn't really too bothered about that. It was really nice to know, yeah, there are Nigerian students there, so I liked that about it but it doesn't really matter'. What seemed to be of issue for almost all of these students, to different degrees of significance, was mix or diversity rather than the presence of significant numbers of others of the same ethnicity as themselves. The latter would have the potential effect of foregrounding ethnic identity as against other dimensions of identity (cf. the experience of Amma, Chapter 3; Ball *et al.*, 2000). Diversity offers the potential, as these students see it, of backgrounding ethnicity.

For the White students we interviewed, ethnic mix was not a concern, at least not one that they shared with us, either in positive or negative terms (with two exceptions – see below). There was certainly no indication of anything like an ethnic identity at work in relation to choice-making. Although mix could have been an issue if, what were described below as 'ethnic universities' were being considered. The question of social mix, when it did elicit a response from White students was interpreted either in terms of social class or more vaguely, but also perhaps class related, in terms of the intelligence and interests of other students.[11] This may be no surprise. This 'absence' has its own significance. Various researchers and commentators have noted:

> the identity of White culture is 'absent' in a number of senses, both political and subjective... An identity based on power never has to develop consciousness of itself as responsible, it has no sense of its limits except as those are perceived in opposition to other.
>
> (Pajackowska and Young, 1992, p. 202)

Nonetheless, it would be difficult to see all the White students in our sample as inhabiting 'an identity based on power' within the field of HE choice. Social class remains as a major fault line in patterns of HE participation (see Ball *et al.*, 2002). Only two students articulated an awareness of White ethnicity. Both represent interesting confirmation of Pajackowska and Young's point. Simon, a private school student, described his school as 'almost run' by the Jews 'with the Asians' and opined that 'you almost feel like a minority being White'. He was 'looking forward' to going to University (York) 'to experience being in the majority'. Within the context of almost feeling like a minority Simon has developed a consciousness of himself as White. The only mention of the negative connotations of the ethnic mix of universities, made by a White student, Lucy, was a reference to 'swamping' and not dissimilar to Simon's concern.

> To be honest I don't like to feel swamped, that I'm on my own sort of. Like I wouldn't like to be where its mostly Black. I'm a bit worried about King's my mum said one of their colleges is down in Brixton and I don't want to feel scared. Do you know what I mean? I'm not racist but I want a mix that's not all black like here. I don't want to be outnumbered.

The other references to the impact of minority ethnic representation in Universities came from two minority ethnic students who were worried either about the predominance of certain minority ethnic groups in particular institutions (as above) or the status implications of having a degree from an 'ethnic university'. Annas, a mature student, who is Jordanian, explained that:

> I applied for South Bank University, my personal opinion, I think it is good in computing, but it has the reputation somehow of being an ethnic university and I think that is not good for getting jobs afterwards.

And Candice, commented that:

> and everyone just everyone said dont apply to North London. Its a fact of life as a black person that you're going to be judged harshly there's no point in making life more difficult for yourself by going somewhere everyone sees as no good if you dont have to. It wasn't just school all my friends and my mum's friends said 'just dont do it'. Also I met someone at the University of East London who said it was virtually impossible, really really difficult to get into law as a black female from an old Poly. You are just automatically going to be seen as second rate.

Let us look more closely at some of the comments made about 'ethnic mix'. A number of examples are quoted in the vignettes above, these and others are discussed below. We could think about the responses of the 'minority' students as falling into three rough and ready categories. Those who are 'de-racialised' choosers, for whom ethnic mix is not part of their thinking about university choice; those who are 'race aware', who have 'thought about' ethnic mix but for whom this is not a major factor in their choices; and those, a small minority, who are 'race active', for whom ethnic mix is a significant factor, among others, in choice-making. Sheila, who is Black British and from MU, is a good example of being 'race aware':

> I would say that using this school as an example, there aren't a lot of black people in this school. And I think I've got on quite well despite that. It doesn't bother me. I am not one of those people that sit there and think – oh, I'm black and there's all these White people around me. I just get on with it basically. It doesn't bother me, as long as I don't face any kind of discrimination, which I haven't faced in this school. Everyone just accepts you as you are, do you know what I mean? So I just get on with it. I don't think it's going to be a problem.

Elizabeth and Navid quoted earlier would also fit here. In contrast Temi (Nigerian CCS) and Hinal (Indian CB) represent aspects of the 'race active' category. Temi has a view that racism is more likely to be experienced in particular locations – the White highlands – and this is transmitted via grapevine knowledge.

> DR: And you talked about, your brother was saying Kent's not a good university because it is very White. Is that an issue in relation to the other universities?
>
> T: Not really because I've mostly applied to universities that have a mix of different cultures. I think Middlesex, Guildhall, they're quite mixed. Brighton he did say it was quite a few White people, mostly White people but not racist like Kent. Anyway I am used to that kind of area, I used to be down there...

Hinal had lived in Newcastle and was clear from his experience there that he would not consider choosing a provincial University and wanted to stay in London.

> Well, we had a lot of like, dad's friends and my friends were there, but I suppose, this kind of sounds really hard to say, but some people were quite racist in the neighbourhood. And in fact, we actually went there to see the old house, and my brother was driving and we stopped the car to let these people walk past, and they shouted out racist slurs, and this was in our neighbourhood, where we used to live, so when I am driving through that place, or my brother's driving, but it just occurred to me that I wouldn't want to stay there again.

Jamaal, who was presented earlier is a clearer example. His Islamic identity and sense of community was a key aspect of his HE applications. Laura, Cassie, Helen and Wing, and in a different way Candice and Annas, all quoted earlier are 'race active'. In contrast Sabrina, an Iranian young woman (MU) did not see 'mix' or racism as issues for her: 'university is sort of where mature people go, I dont think they would be like that!' (cf. Osler, 1999). Navid, Kurram (Bangladeshi RC) and Vishal (Indian RC) in stronger terms, evince a desire to escape their ethnic peers and distance themselves from an identity which is predicated or mainly founded upon their ethnicity. They are perhaps, in Cote's (1996) terms, 'dis-investing' in one sort of identity capital and 're-investing' in another sort, or as Beck (1992) would put it, they are making their biographies into a reflexive project. Kurram and then Vishal explained:

> I dont hardly have any Asian friends at all, because I've kept it that way. Not because I dont like them, but I prefer not to be in such a big Asian group. Because I just dont like it.
>   That's the main point in coming here (RC), really, to get away from, because like, where I live, mostly Asians. So I thought I'd come here to get a different view of life. It's been a good experience...It makes me think I wouldn't mind [what University] because I think I'll make friends with different sorts of people...

Furthermore, even those 'minority' students who are either 'race active' or 'race aware' still see ethnic mix as only one factor among several in their decision making and a number of these end up selecting and then deciding to attend institutions which are predominantly White. This is a reminder of the dangers of a uni-focused analysis. While ethnicity may be a significant feature in the HE choices of some minority students, it is not necessarily crucial or predominant for most. It does not tell us everything we need to know about choice. Nonetheless, it would be a useful exercise to follow-up these different perceptions and concerns and choices in relation to patterns of degree completion (see Bird, 1996; Osler, 1999).

Another variation of 'race active' choosing occurs in the decision-making of some of the Jewish students in our sample; although only 4 of the 16 Jewish students viewed their Jewishness as having a bearing upon their choice of University. For these 4, the existence of a significant Jewish student community at University was an attraction; for 3 of the 4 this meant as Helen, from Hemsley Girls school put it, 'a good Jewish social life'. Lydia, from Riverway College, selected all her UCAS choices by combining League Table rankings of Law departments with the guide to campus life provided by the Union of Jewish students. Even here though things are not straightforward. Lydia avoided Manchester because, as she put it: 'its full of Becky's'. She put Nottingham as her first choice. However, as in the case of other 'minority' students, ethnic identity for Jewish students was plastic, changing, inter-linked and context dependent. Anne, another Hemsley student, explained: 'I quite like it when there's a mix...Because I'm reform. I dont go to a Shul or any-thing like that. I just, I just am Jewish. I don't really do anything'. Alexandra, who taught Jewish Studies to young children, also from Hemsley, explained that 'my parents want me to apply to Leeds, its got a very high Jewish population and my parents are keen on that' but went on to say 'Its not that important, its not the deciding factor'. But exactly as in other ethnic groups there were other Jewish students for whom their own ethnicity was unimportant to them in their sense of themselves and their choice-making.

Discussion: ethnicity, class and class fractions

As should be clear by now, the differences which were evident among the 'minority' students in our study cannot be conveyed adequately without reference to social class. Essentially the 'contingent'/'embedded' division is class-based. For those rep-resented here as 'contingent choosers' the decision to attend university and obtain a degree has a specific 'class meaning', in addition to, and interwoven with its impli-cations for ethnic identity. Giddens' (Beck *et al.*, 1994, p. 74) representation of choice as 'obviously something to do with colonising the future in relation to the past...', is very apt here. For contingent choosers, going to university involves them becoming a person different from the rest their family and many of their peers, in eschewing a 'normal biography' and at the same time risking a sense of feeling themselves 'out of place'; even if they 'fulfil the conditions that the space tacitly requires of its occupants' (Bourdieu, 1999b, p. 128). As Bourdieu and Passerson put it in a much earlier study: 'to want to be, and to want to choose one's identity, is, first of all, to refuse to be what one has not chosen to be' (1979, p. 38). This is equally true of ethnic and class aspects of identity for the 'minority' working-class students in this study; although for a small minority of these students their choice of HE is framed by an attempt to retain a 'fixed' ethnic identity. It is equally apparent that some others are working upon themselves to disentangle themselves from an ethnic identity and a sense of ethnic community. Whether this is always possible is another matter. Some minority ethnic students, particularly those from working-class backgrounds risk 'alienation' and isolation (see Bird, 1996), much in the way described by Jackson and Marsden (1962). However, this is not simply a matter of existential discomfort. Ozga and Sukhnandan (1998, p. 321), in a study of HE non-completers, relate non-completion to 'lack of preparedness for university life – inadequate sources of information and unrealistic expectations and compatibility of choice'. That is 'the degree of match between students and their choice of institution and course' (p. 322). First generation choosers without appropriate cultural capital or relevant social capital may easily find themselves in the 'wrong' place or in the 'wrong' course with all the risks of drop-out that that brings into play. Indeed, half of the ten UK Universities with the highest drop-out rates also have high propor-tions of minority ethnic students (HEFCE figures). Some of the choices made by some of the 'contingent' choosers were haphazard to say the least. Moogan *et al.* (1999) also make the point that being able to draw upon direct, word of mouth, 'experience qualities' in decision-making about HE is a 'risk reducing strategy'. As we have seen access to such 'grapevine knowledge' is unevenly distributed, so too are the time and resources available to commit to information and knowledge gath-ering and accessing professional support structures and expertise and such support was differently available in the institutions in our study. Alongside these personal and social dimensions of choice, for many contingent choosers, the direct financial costs and opportunity costs of HE study are a considerable burden. Hesketh (1999) found that working-class students were least happy about and least likely to take out a loan. Typically such students are required to live at home, minimise the costs of travel and work part-time during term time. This not only creates a different kind of HE experience but again produces risks in terms of course performance and completion.

In contrast to all this, as noted already, the 'embedded' students are moving into a class setting in which they feel comfortable; although it may be that some over-estimate the racial tolerance and social mixing within university settings (Osler, 1999). Going to HE is a natural progression, part of a well-established 'normal biography'. Cultural and social capital are in good supply and make the process of choosing into a vivid experience that is set in relation to longer-term planning and expectations. Costs are not an issue, working in term time is not expected, and is often actively discouraged by parents. Moving away from home is seen by many as part of the experience of HE and these students were the only ones to talk about 'extra-curricula' activities at University. They know what to expect and what opportunities they might take advantage of. But class is an issue here in another sense. For middle-class minority ethnic students from state schools, like some of their White peers, Oxbridge is class-different. It is 'posh', it is 'private school'. They do not feel comfortable there as they do in other university settings.

Choice is both inappropriate but useful as a conceptualisation of the decision-making processes examined here. Inappropriate because of its tendency to emphasise individual preferences but useful in reminding us that this decision-making is a set of practices – the key point is that we must retain the link between constraint and volition (James, 1996), and between dispositions and possibilities. Related to this kind of view of choice, Beck (1992, p. 131) makes the argument that:

> Class differences and family connections are not really annulled in the course of individualisation processes. Rather, they recede into the background relative to the newly emerging 'center' of the biographical life plan...from knowing one's 'class' position one can no longer determine one's personal outlook, relations, family position, social and political ideas or identity.

In relation to university choice, he is both right and wrong. Right in so far as indicated already 'contingent' choosers are planning a biography that involves a kind of break with family and class, and in some cases, ethnic background, although, on the other hand, many of them end up staying at home. Wrong in as much that class still has a great deal to tell us about outlook, relations and identity (see also Reay *et al.*, 2001a,b) particularly in relation to the continuities of life-planning and strategies of closure (Ball *et al.*, 2002) which were evident among the 'embedded' choosers.[12] Increasingly, the relevant questions about ethnicity and class in relation to HE are not just about; who goes? but also; who goes where? and why?

Notes

1 That is, apart from concerns about the 'elitism' of some 'old' universities. In part, New Labour's recent set of initiatives to adddress issues of uneven social participation in HE was sparked and framed by the experiences of a single student, Laura Spence. High achieving Laura, daughter of middle-class parents from Tyneside became a cause celebre

when her application to Magdalen College, Oxford was rejected and she ended up studying at Harvard supported by a full scholarship. Gordon Brown, New Labour's high profile Chancellor of the Exchequer, condemned Oxford's selection procedures as elitist. Gordon Brown described Magdalen College's rejection of Laura's application 'scandalous' and involving 'an interview system more reminiscent of the old boy network and the school tie than genuine justice in our system'. Laura and Oxford's procedures became headline news in the UK and indeed around the world for several weeks.

2 The terminology used in the paper to describe the individual students draws upon their preferred nomenclature. We are very aware that categories of ethnicity are socially constructed and contested and change frequently (see Mason, 2000; Bonnett and Carrington, 2000). The generic shorthand 'minority' is used here to refer to all the Jewish, dual-heritage and non-white students in our sample. It is recognised nonetheless that 'minority' is as much a statement of power relations as it is a statistical observation; although here, as will be seen, these power relations are immensely complex. As is evident in the discussion in the paper the salience of ethnicity as a component of social identity varies considerably across the sub-sample. We are also very much aware of the problemmatic constitution of 'minority' here. The 'minority' subject is 'irretrievably heterogenous' (Spivak, 1993, p. 79). Or to look at it another way 'White' itself is neither unitary nor unproblemmatic (Bird, 1996, p. 97). Welsh, Scottish, Irish, Hungarian, Polish, German are just some of the 'identities' not included here but represented in our full sample. The point is that the lines of demarcation could have been drawn differently. Nonetheless, we would suggest that, given the nature of our findings, the overall thrust of the arguments in the paper would not have been altered significantly.

3 These statistics are taken from 1991 census data which did not include a Jewish report category.

4 As explained below the differences here are strongly class-related and differentiate working-class from middle-class students across our sample as a whole. The concern with ethnic mix is however almost exclusively limited to the minority ethnic students.

5 As a reminder:

> An ideal type is formed by the one-sided accentuation of one or more points of view and by the synthesis of a great many diffuse, discrete, more or less present and occasionally absent concrete individual phenomena, which are arranged according to those one-sidedly emphasised viewpoints into a unified analytical construct.
>
> (Shils and Finch, 1949, p. 90)

6 This can create its own difficulties when parental expectations and young people's interests and talents do not coincide.

7 Parents and mothers in particular were most broadly engaged in support of the lower or 'new' middle-class embedded choosers but least involved among the private school choosers. For the latter, the levels of support and organisation within the schools reduced the necessity for direct practical engagement from parents. As within several other issues identified in the paper, this flags up the significance of class fractional differences within the middle-class.

8 It is worth thinking about this in more than one way. The failure to visit is a problem of cost and organisation and confidence for these students – the private schools and MU organised programmes of visits. But this is also a problem of knowing what to look for. When they do talk about the universities they are interested in it is often in terms of the 'facilities', a concrete but also 'safe' version of the institution – buildings, rooms, equipment. What else is there to 'see'. The maintaining of a 'distance' from the universities may also be in part an issue about knowing how to behave, how to look and act like – embody – a university student – an issue of habitus.

9 Socioscapes are 'networks of social relations of very different intensity, spanning widely different territorial extents...' (Albrow, 1997, p. 51).

10 This is different from the findings of Modood *et al.* (1997) which indicate that in the main those of minority ethnicities who expressed an ethnic preference were more interested in the presence of their own group than the presence of other ethnicities, in relation to schools (pp. 320–23) and nieghbourhood (pp. 189–90). The difference between those findings and ours may well be related to age and context, and social class, as well as to

the location of the research. The arguments put here are intended to be specific in these senses rather than general.

11 Osler (1999, p. 56) reports that the 'minority' students she interviewed found their experiences of exclusion as complex, especially 'when other factors such as social class or gender steretyping come into play'.

12 However, having argued for the centrality of class divisions in HE choice and having established patterns of commonality across ethnicities but within class groups we are not intending to suggest that class commonalities are absolute nor that class 'washes out' ethnic difference. The class experiences of different ethnic groups are likely to be different in terms of 'structures of feeling' and subjectivity and the possibilities of agency. Different kinds of historical relationships to British capitalism and Empire may well produce different textures in the lived experience of class. Our data in neither extensive enough nor finely tuned enough to develop the analysis further in this regard.

References

Abbasi, K. (1998). Is medical school selection discriminatory. *British Medical Journal*, 317, 1097–98.

Ball, S. J. and Vincent, C. (1998). 'I heard it on the grapevine': 'Hot' knowledge and school choice. *British Journal of Sociology of Education*, 19(3), 377–400.

Ball, S. J., Maguire, M. M. and Macrae, S. (2000). *Choice, Pathways and Transitions Post-16: New Youth, New Economies in the Global City*. London: Falmer Press.

Ball, S. J., Davies, J., Reay, D. and David, M. (2002). 'Classification' and 'judgement': social class and the 'cognitive structures' of choice of Higher Education. *British Journal of Sociology of Education*, 23(1), 51–72.

Beck, U. (1992). *Risk Society: Towards a New Modernity*. Newbury Park, CA: Sage.

Beck, U., Giddens, A. and Lash, S. (1994). *Reflexive Modernization: Politics, Tradition and Aesthetics in the Modern Social Order*. Oxford: Polity Press.

Bird, J. (1996). *Black Students and Higher Education*. Buckingham: Open University Press/SRHE.

Bonnett, A. and Carrington, B. (2000). Fitting into categories or falling between them? Rethinking ethnic classifications. *British Journal of Sociology of Education*, 21(4), 487–500.

Bourdieu, P. (1990a). *In Other Words: Essays Towards a Reflexive Sociology*. Cambridge: Polity Press.

Bourdieu, P. (1990b). *The Logic of Practice*. Cambridge: Polity Press.

Bourdieu, P. and Passeron, J.-C. (1979). *The Inheritors: French Students and their Relation to Culture*. London: Chicago University Press.

Coffield, F. and Vignoles, A. (1997). *Widening Participation in Higher Education by Ethic Minorities, Women and Alternative Students* (The National Committee of Inquiry into Higher Education). Newcastle: Department of Education, University of Newcastle.

Cote, J. E. (1996). Sociological perspectives on identity formation: the culture identity link and identity capital. *Journal of Adolescence*, 19, 417–28.

Du Bois-Reymond, M. (1998). 'I don't want to commit myself yet': young people's life concepts. *Journal of Youth Studies*, 1(1), 63–79.

Equal Opportunities Commission (1994). *Black and Ethnic Minority Men and Women in Britain 1994*. Manchester: Equal Opportunities Commission.

Gewirtz, S., Ball, S. J. and Bowe, R. (1995). *Markets, Choice and Equity in Education*. Buckingham: Open University Press.

Gillborn, D. (1995). Racism, identity and modernity: pluralism, moral anti-racism and plastic identity. *International Studies in the Sociology of Education*, 5(1), 92–114.

Hagerstrand, T. (1975). Survival and arena: on the life history of individuals in relation to their geographical environment. In T. Carlstein, D. Parkes and M. Thrift (eds), *Human Activity and Time Geography*, Vol 2. London: Edward Arnold.

Harvey, D. (1989). *The Condition of Postmodernity*. Oxford: Basil Blackwell.

Hesketh, A. J. (1999). Towards an economic sociology of the student financial experience of higher education. *Journal of Education Policy*, 14(4), 385–410.

Jackson, B. and Marsden, D. (1962). *Education and the Working Class*. Harmondsworth: Penguin.

James, D. (1996). *The Home and the University: Habitus and Diversity of Experience in Studentship*. Paper presented at the BERA, Lancaster.

Mason, D. (2000). *Race and Ethnicity in Modern Britain* (2nd edn.). Oxford: Oxford University Press.

Modood, T. and Acland, T. (eds) (1998). *Race and Higher Education*. London: Policy Studies Institute.

Modood, T. and Shiner, M. (1994). *Ethnic Minorities and Higher Education*. London: Policy Studies Institute/UCAS.

Modood, T., Beiston, S. and Virdee, S. (1994). *Changing Ethnic Identities*. London: Policy Studies Institute.

Modood, T. *et al.* (1997). Ethnic Minorities in Britain, London: PSI.

Moogan, Y. J., Baron, S. and Harris, K. (1999). Decision-making behaviour of potential higher education students. *Higher Education Quarterly*, 53(3), 211–28.

Osler, A. (1999). The educational experiences and career aspirations of black and ethnic minority undergraduates. *Race, Ethnicity and Education*, 2(1), 39–58.

Ozga, J. and Sukhnandan, L. (1998). Undergraduate non-completion: developing an explanatory model. *Higher Education Quarterly*, 52(3), 316–33.

Pajackowska, C. and Young, L. (1992). Race, representation and psychoanalysis. In J. Donald and A. Rattansi (eds), *Race, Culture, Difference*. London: Sage.

Reay, D. (2000). 'Its taking me a long time but I'll get there in the end': mature students on access courses and higher education choice. ESRC HE Choice Project Paper 4: CPPR, King's College London.

Reay, D., Davies, J., David, M. and Ball, S. J. (2001a). Choices of degree and degrees of choice. *Sociology*, 35(4), 835–47.

Reay, D., David, M. and Ball, S. J. (2001b). Making a difference: institutional habituses and higher education choice. *Sociological Research Online*, 5(4): http//www.socresonline.org.uk/5/4.reay.html

Shils, E. A. and Finch, H. A. (1949). *Max Weber on the Methodology of the Social Sciences*. Glencoe, IL: The Free Press.

Spivak, G. C. (1993). Can the subaltern speak. In Williams and Chrisman (eds), *Colonial Discourse and Post-Colonial Theory*, Hemel Hempstead: Wheatsheaf Harvester.

Taylor, P. (1992). Ethnic group data and applications to higher education. *Higher Education Quarterly*, 46(4), 359–74.

CHAPTER 15

'I HEARD IT ON THE GRAPEVINE'
'Hot' knowledge and school choice

S. J. Ball and C. Vincent, '"I heard it on the grapevine": "Hot" knowledge and shcool choice', *British Journal of Sociology of Education*, 1998, 19(3): 377–400

Introduction

> the abstract individual of neo-classical economics is not the burdened, worried, haunted, embedded, memory-infested, befriended, kinsperson that stalks the social stage. There are no generalisations one can sensibly make about the socially relevant behaviour of this consumer.
>
> (Warde, 1994, p. 227)

Many studies and accounts of parental choice of school make reference to the crucial role of social networks and informal information gathering and exchange in the processes of deliberation and selection. However, as it turns out, we actually learn little from these studies about the configurations, interactions and influences of these networks and processes – the grapevine. In this paper, we intend to begin to map and analyse the patterns, effects and variations which can be identified in 'grapevining' in a data set of interviews with 172 parents (138 interviews) choosing secondary schools for their children.[1] We are concerned, therefore, with the structure, social relations and dissemination of grapevine knowledge, not with its content. The latter has been examined in some detail in a series of companion pieces to this paper (see, e.g. Gewirtz *et al.*, 1995; Ball *et al.*, 1996; Ball and Gewirtz, 1997; Ball, 1997c; Reay and Ball, 1997). This paper also draws upon a typology of parental school-choosing developed in previous work. The typology consists of *skilled/privileged, semi-skilled*, and *disconnected* choosers. Not the most efficacious terms, perhaps, but they seemed as good as many others we tried and better than most. The first and third types we argue are differentiated strongly but not exclusively by social class, the second is a mixed group. They also represent different sets of values about choice and about schooling. The skilled/privileged have high *inclination to* and *capacity for* choice; the semi-skilled, high inclination and low capacity; the disconnected, low inclination and low capacity, (see Tooley (1997) and Ball and Gewirtz (1997) for a critique and defence of this typology). In the discussion below we explore *both* social class differences *and* concerns which cut across class. Furthermore, some of the properties of the responses discussed relate to gender (or other factors) rather than class differences.

Defining the grapevine

The most striking aspect of the 'grapevine' is its pervasiveness in the data. It is almost impossible to find a transcript where parents do not refer to drawing upon the impressions and experiences of friends, neighbours and relatives in their choice-making. Most deal with this at some length. For example:

> Hearsay has a big effect, a bigger effect possibly than people realise...in the sense that a lot of feedback comes from parents whose children have already started, and that's the only way you can tell...you can go round a school and it looks nice and there's plenty on the wall, but it doesn't mean to say that the school is good, and if parents around said 'oh well my child was unhappy there and I took him away', that's going to influence you, especially if it's somebody's opinion that you respect. I think most parents will admit to going round school a couple of times and listening to the headmaster or headmistress speak...is not enough information.
>
> (Mrs Wallace)
>
> Asking friends I suppose, that was the first thing, asking friends who've got older children, where their children have gone.
>
> (Mrs Totteridge)
>
> Also I talked to the children [already at the school] as well about it. And how they felt and how they were getting on and whether they liked it.
>
> (Mrs Leyton)

These quotations highlight the variety of roles played by informal social networks in school choice-making, and clearly illustrate the potential of such networks to mediate between personal concerns and feelings and public issues. The analysis of such networks reveals what Wellman *et al.* (1988, p. 137) call the 'fuzzy reality' of personal relationships, with all the idiosyncracies, messiness and complexity inherent in relations between friends and family. Wellman *et al.* (1988) and Wellman and Wortley (1990) argue that such networks are crucial to individuals, both in terms of their day-to-day living and also in times of crisis; and for many parents, choice of school is very much a kind of crisis. Social networks influence the way in which people make sense of, take up positions towards, and respond to their surroundings. Networks, produced within the personal domain, can also equip individuals for their engagement with the public sphere. We will demonstrate these effects by focusing here on 'the grapevine', a particular manifestation of social networks, and one which clearly arises from the private realm in order to address the public arena. Local and personal social networks mediate public/private activities like parental choice and are thus crucial in developing an understanding of the practices and meaning of choice.[2] Choice is typically embedded in 'the local' and in the circulation of social myths; 'a myth tells what one should desire...and how to get it...' (Bailey, 1977, p. 4). Attention to the grapevine socially re-embeds choosers and highlights the methodological dangers involved in ripping choices out of context.

In a recent study of the ways in which groups of their inhabitants understand and engage with the northern cities of Manchester and Sheffield, Taylor *et al.* (1996) make the following comment,

> The material landscape evokes both celebration, and fear and anxiety. Through gossip and story-telling it may also come to inform local folk belief and myth...This local culture structure can be understood, following Raymond Williams, as a 'local structure of feeling' that distils a set of local wisdoms and folklore about local place.
>
> (pp. 28, 32)

They continue by arguing that a locality gains its identity from its social, geographic, and demographic specificities which are, in turn, closely tied to the 'local class structure' (Urry, 1981), arising from current and past patterns of employment and production in the area. The reactions, responses to, and under-standings of residents concerning their environment constitute a 'local structure of feeling'. Taylor et al., emphasise that different social groups, different publics, interact with the cities in very different ways, although there are also instances of common understanding and shared perceptions.[3]

Taylor et al., in their application of Williams' (1979) concept of 'structure of feeling' to the field of social geography, use it to explore the relationships between individual understandings of the built environment and the characteristics of the 'material landscape' itself. Their intention is similar to Williams', i.e. 'to simulta-neously posit an interrelationship between areas of individual and general experi-ence, private and public processes and social structures and historical formations' (Elridge and Elridge, 1994, p. 112).

In this light, the grapevine is a collective attempt to make sense of the locality and particular features within it (in this case, schools). It works through and is animated by story-telling, rumour and gossip.

In classic ethnographies, gossip is often presented as destructive and punitive (see, for example, Lantz's (1958) study of Coaltown and West's (1954) study of Plainville). There have indeed been examples in which gossip appears to have played such a role in relation to schools, especially non-traditional, 'progressive' schools (Wright, 1989). The data described here contain many examples of the power of the negative story, the destructive anecdote,

> Interviewer: Why are you so set against Trumpton and Milton?
> Mrs Angus: Terrible schools. I mean I know a lot of parents whose kids go there...and I mean I don't really want her having O-levels in how to sniff glue and roll joints and god knows what, and it seems its all that kids do [there]. They're wild, just wild.

However, such adamant beliefs are in the minority. Even more frequently, there are references not to certainty, but to uncertainty, to an awareness that school reputations are vulnerable to change. The grapevine is fickle and a school which may be 'flavour of the month' (a term used three times in the data) one year may lose its favour in subsequent years.

> I spoke to Damien's teacher when we went to a parent/teachers' evening... and he was amazed at how strong the feeling was against Parsons, because in previous years, it's been automatic for the kids from Windsor [Primary] – because it's so close, Parsons – that they would automatically go there.
> (Mrs Shearer)

In this respect, the grapevine can be characterised in terms of rumour, rather than gossip (although the two are obviously inter-related – see Ball, 1987). Ball describes rumours as being at their most rife 'in the absence of other, more reliable sources of information...It is a way of filling in missing information or explaining the inexplicable. Rumour is a "response to ambiguity" (Shibutani, 1966)' (Ball, 1987, p. 219).

The sense of ambiguity, of wrestling with the inexplicable and obscure, comes over strongly in many of the transcripts. This conveys a sense of bewilderment

Table 15.1 Comparisons between official information
            and grapevine knowledge

Official	Grapevine
Logic	Feel/emotion
Abstract information	Direct knowledge
Evidence	Anecdote
Results	Impressions
Proffered	Experiential

which is experienced by even the most 'skilled' choosers – indeed, sometimes too much knowledge is a bad thing. However, significantly, the grapevine is often seen as *more* reliable than other 'official' sources of information, especially those provided by the schools themselves. The comparisons between grapevine knowledge and official information (Table 15.1) are reflected in a set of inter-related polarities which run through the data. They counterpose formal, public, abstract knowledge with personal, social knowledge. There is a degree of scepticism about the former and a general preference for and sense of greater usefulness about the latter. But the latter are not always digested uncritically.

'Official' knowledge is 'cold' knowledge, normally constructed specifically for public dissemination. The form it takes is abstract – examination results, lists of school activities, outlines of school policies, etc. 'Grapevine' knowledge is 'hot' knowledge, based on affective responses or direct experience. For some parents, personal recommendation is perceived to be far more trustworthy than apparently 'objective' data, an issue to which we return later. Mrs Walsh makes this clear when she talks about examination results.

> They might do it to fool you! No, 1 couldn't work it out really, to be honest, myself...and I'm in the trade. They had all these As and Bs and so many per cent here...oh...but then some of the people that I know who...you know, are Katie's age...they've got brothers and sisters...like Jackie, who teaches with me, her daughter's there and another teacher that teaches at the Wandle...her daughter's there, so...I think well if they've done alright.
>
> (Mrs Walsh)
>
> A lot of people tell me it's very much how you feel about a school...as much as...hard logic, and I tried to think what my child...my child would need.
>
> (Mrs Bond)
>
> I've just heard from various people...again that might be just an emotive reaction...I've no real evidence to back that up...
>
> (Mrs Brent)
>
> I don't know that I would go totally on exam results from schools...it really is part of the children's attitudes and the overall impression, I think.
>
> (Mrs Eastcote)

The grapevine is perceived as particularly acute at delivering information about certain significant topics, particularly those relating to the conduct and demeanour of students.

> Just talking to friends, there was a huge amount of chat went on for about two years beforehand... socially, in the playground... to other staff members, I just talked to anybody, not asking the right questions I suppose... about what exam results were like... so much as... are the children happy, and things like discipline and behaviour in a street... and how they walk from lesson to lesson, how much litter there is in the playground... whether there's any graffiti... the state of the toilets, they're all things I was far more concerned with... than what the examination results were.
>
> (Mrs Southgate)

This emphasis on the welfare aspect of school life derives from a widely expressed parental concern for the 'happiness' of their child at school, an amorphous, though strongly expressed, desire for their general well-being and security (Coldron and Boulton, 1991). Through the grapevine, the under life of the school can, to some extent, be unlocked, and in ways that specifically address issues that parents are especially interested in, but ones that, in their publicity, schools may well choose to ignore. The grapevine is a powerful way in which parents can circumvent professional control over information and the resulting selective public presentation (see Ball, 1997a,b), and gain a sense of the life of the school as experienced directly by the students.

> I feel that each school gets its own reputation, I feel that talking to parents and talking to the children who are already going... like say for example if in any school there is racial harassment or there are some drug problems or things like that happening, then it gets round doesn't it? People talk about it... this is happening in this school and so on... and I mean you get to hear about it as well... how the headmaster or headmistress are dealing with the problem... you know, how tough they are. Or whether they're just pretending that nothing is happening, or they are actually facing the problem and dealing with it, they're actually doing something about it.
>
> (Mrs Kohli)

To talk of 'the' grapevine is, of course, inaccurate. There are many different grapevines and an individual's access to them is structured primarily by class-related factors. Where you live, who you know and what community you belong to are vital determinants of the particular grapevine that is open to you. Clearly this is not simply a spatial issue. One of the strengths of an analytical focus on social networks is that it implicitly questions traditional models of 'community' based on geographical location, by emphasising the totality and extensiveness of an individual's social contacts (Crow and Allan, 1994). Different networks, different grapevines can and do exist within one small locality. Some are loose and amorphous, others tightly knit and firmly bounded. They are constructed within and across localities. They are placed differently in relation to sources of knowledge, are marked by different concerns and priorities, and contain different social resources. Butler (1996), writing about gentrification in Hackney, demonstrates how the 'spatial togetherness' of different social classes and ethnicities which has arisen in some parts of the borough, has not led to any notable decrease in social distance. Middle-class incomers mix with other 'people like us', use particular local facilities but not others, and patronise particular schools, but not others. Grapevines and informal networks derive from and reproduce people's 'cultural scripts' (Dehli, 1996), products of their social location and background. Consider the following two views of Trumpton School.

Trumpton is, or was, I don't know whether it still is, the most popular school...It's got such a good name...the majority of parents automatically send their children there, and of course when they find out their friends are going there, they want to go there.

(Mrs Pallister)

And I always said that I'd never send her to Trumpton really, I don't think it has a very good reputation...and seeing...I suppose working close to it, or in the area...and seeing the children going to school, but I think probably that's unfair, wherever you live, whatever's your local secondary school, it always looks horrendous in a way.

(Mrs Walsh)

Analysing the grapevine

The data suggest three broad sets of parental responses to the grapevine. These are composites with diverse properties in each case. There are some class-related differences between and, in some respects, within the three groups. However, each type of response or reaction is also influenced by a kaleidoscope of other factors, such as personal characteristics, gender, attitudes and availability of friends and neighbours with children, length of time spent living in the locality, general perceptions about the quality of local educational provision and so on.

Suspicion

The first set of responses relate to those parents for whom the affect of the grapevine is fairly minimal, or at least mitigated by the addition of other elements, attitudes or circumstances. This further subdivides into three factors.

First, those parents who try to 'fill out' or contextualise the grapevine by seeking additional sources of knowledge. These are almost all middle-class parents who go to considerable lengths to maximise their market information. This was often a long-term project, with information being collected and stored over a number of years. By doing this, these parents are attempting to locate 'objective' data concerning the schools, and introduce it into their decision-making, thereby exerting some sense of rational control over the process of choosing. They do this either by seeking out sources of 'cold' knowledge – examination results, research findings and/or written information such as school prospectuses – or by trying to widen the number of people they speak to, systematically seeking out 'knowledge-able' parents.

We read the prospectus, got the results of the borough...for the last time they were published, which was the year before...went and looked at all the schools, spoke to teachers in the schools, spoke to other parents, and spoke to my friends who were scattered across the borough and where their children went and what they felt about it.

(Mrs Snaresbrook)

Dee round the corner, a friend of mine, whose husband is a government statistician...did quite a lot of surveys into all the schools, including the independent sector...and Lockmere came out as their first choice, for many reasons... covering the sort of long and short of it, basically, and Overbury came out as their second choice, but as I say... that one because I didn't feel right about it, but that gave me a lot of confidence in the fact that they had studied it quite seriously... I mean these exam results are very hard to actually interpret unless you're really in the know, but Dee worked them out and that's what she came up with, so I took her word for it.

(Mrs Roding)

I sought people out, and spoke to people who aren't close friends of ours but I know have got children at those different schools, and my wife did this too, and... I suppose... perhaps because we know more of them at Blenhiem we got perhaps a slightly stronger positive feedback about Blenhiem... very hard to find anyone who thought there was anything much wrong with it.

(Mr Ife)

I do know a lot of people who have got older children, so the first thing I did was... when I realised... because a note came home from school about the second day of term saying having visits from people representing the different schools... I started ringing round... what did people think of the schools that their children were at... and what were the pluses and the minuses... in fact I got Paul to organise a sort of questionnaire...

(Mrs Bond)

My mother had done a lot of research and cut a lot of articles out and she kept me flooded continually with stuff I'd never have time to find myself... Her views were very much that she thought Alice would do better at an all girls' school.

(Ms Wallace)

Whilst this group of parents are predominantly middle class, the second sub-division comprises a small number of parents, all working class, who appear to reject the grapevine's information. These parents do not, however, seek to replace the grapevine with 'cold' knowledge, but rather rely instead on their own or their child's affective responses

We didn't know the area and we'd heard... like all things... you hear some people say... 'this school is good...' 'no, that school's good...' so in the end we thought we'd wait and see what came, and as it was the very first thing that happened was that Tania's school organised a visit down to Lymethorpe, and the whole class went off for the morning. She came back saying she'd had a very good time.

(Mr Tufnell)

It was a choice of two schools, Parsons and Flightpath... she chose Flightpath and that was it. I mean we didn't go to look at any of them... We weren't really that bothered as I say... because to me, all schools are the same.

(Mr Fairlop)

A lot of people that I spoke to... we know quite a few people... with children who go to Flightpath, and they've all said that their children have done very well... there. All schools have got their bad points, that's what everybody said... which is true... they have... good and bad... but not really... we just visited them and they seemed happy with them so we just let them choose.

Well, you get half the people saying...'oh I wouldn't send my child there'...and then half of them say...'oh it's brilliant,' so you can't make your mind up on that.

(Mrs Everley)

Our neighbours send them to Flightpath from here...so all the children from Mustafa's class...they're going to Flightpath.

(Mrs Ishtar)

For these parents, choice of school is not the anxiety-ridden process it is for some others. One of the reasons that this group is so small is that many parents find themselves caught up in the grapevine almost against their will. There is a strongly class-related aspect to this. Mrs Lancaster, a 'reluctant' middle-class participant in the grapevine, demonstrates a rejection of a different kind. She describes the social pressure she perceives as emanating from her peer group.

Mrs Lancaster: Everybody I speak to seems to have a different view, it's probably best not to speak to anybody
Interviewer: Have you spoken to a lot of different parents?
Mrs L: Yes, I have, only because they've had meetings at the school... Wherever you go, it's quite funny, because I went to the swimming club on Saturday, to fetch Lottie from swimming and I walked in the door and everyone was sitting around waiting for their children round these tables, deep in discussion...a crowd of people...and I walked in the door and someone said, 'oh come on, it's the secondary school discussion again. Come and join in...' Oh no, not again!... I think Riverway [LEA] parents have always been like that. There's always been an enormous amount of discussion, wherever you go...everyone's always talking about it. I think I've been much less like that with the girls [than with the older child] simply because I have the sort of feeling now that in fact it doesn't really make all that much difference, they are as they are...and although obviously the school has some influence on them. I mean I suspect all schools *in Riverway* are not really that different, and I do not believe they're going to go to one school and get into Oxford and go to another school...and get no GCSEs. I really don't believe that *round here*... it's terribly easy to get absolutely bogged down in it all, and I think to some extent I'm falling into that trap at the moment. You should go round and make your decision and I think we will do that...

(Mrs Lancaster, emphasis added)[4]

The third subgroup within the *suspicion* category are those who are excluded from the grapevine, either because of some particularity of their circumstances or because they are from outside the locality. Men, for example, may have more limited access to the grapevine than women. Information mainly flows through relationships between women (David *et al.*, 1994), often focused around primary schools and neighbourhoods. Mothers are seen as primarily responsible for their children's primary education, regardless of whether or not they are in paid employment. Mrs Alperton, for instance, receives her information from:

> Mothers of children who'd perhaps got children in my other children's classes and older ones...it's...Trafalgar's a friendly school...lots of mums know each other socially...and you tend to chat and things like that...
>
> (Mrs Alperton)

One father, a widower (Mr. Butt), found himself because of his gender in a very different position from Mrs Alperton. His access to grapevine knowledge was restricted:

> Interviewer: Did you talk to a lot of different people...when you were going through this process?
> Mr Butt: No. Some...but not very many...it's very much a female led process...in that...discussion making system...so I feel out of it.

Individuals differ in the extent to which they are embedded in their locality. Being part of a geographical community, which includes the local primary school, is an advantage when it comes to accessing grapevine information. One mother (Mrs Ansari, a divorced immigrant from Iran) who had few links with her neighbours, and whose own friends did not have children, describes the difficulty of having no-one from whom she could glean information about schools, or about how to approach schools. By contrast, Mrs Shadwell is firmly and deliberately embedded within the social networks surrounding the school.

> If you're in a school, and you're fairly active within a school, you know parents who've got older children and younger children...The ones who have got older children who are coming to the decision that we've come to now...friends who have got older children have said...you have got to be the one that keeps the finger on the pulse...and one very good way of doing that is if you're on the PTA [Parent–Teacher Association].
>
> (Mrs Shadwell)

Those who are newly arrived in the area do not have a history of local knowledge on which to build, nor easy access to local networks. The Tufnells, quoted earlier, were in this position. Another parent alluded to the way in which some schools targeted parents outside the local area, thereby by-passing their poor local reputations.

> Corpus Christi school has a reputation for violence, again, although I understand it's very well marketed outside the LEA...but people who live here know of the sort of local troubles that go on outside the school, so I wouldn't have considered Corpus either.
>
> (Mrs Fawcett-Majors)

Doubt

The second broad set of responses derive from those parents who rely heavily on the grapevine, but who also question it. These parents share an awareness of the grapevine's fallibility, either as way of judging schools in general and/or as a way of determining which school is right for a particular child. The grapevine becomes one factor amongst many from which choices are made. As Mrs Shadwell suggests below, this use of what could be called 'compounding grounds', provides for greater certainty.

Interviewer:	Did you consider Goddard at all?
Mrs Shadwell:	No.
Int:	Your reasons?
Child:	I didn't like it.[5]
Mrs S:	It hasn't got a very good reputation, although I have heard the head is a very good head...and the journey as well, it's a bit of an awkward journey anyway.

(Mrs Shadwell)

My sister in law's children go to Flightpath and each one has done very very well. I've known children to go to Parsons and they haven't done well... I think Parsons school is too far away.

(Mrs Harper)

In this way, the grapevine has a role in confirming people in their choices.

I've been living here for eight years now, so I know a hell of a lot of the parents round here, so yes, we have done [spoken to other parents about choice of school]. But I didn't...not to make up my own mind really...they helped to make up my mind that Milton and Trumpton was definitely what I didn't want. I mean they helped me along these lines, but not help me to make up my mind what I wanted to choose for her. More just made me feel that I was right not to choose the other two...if anything.

(Mrs Angus)

Similarly, the absence of anything negative heard on the grapevine proves a positive. Mrs Richards puts this very interestingly, 'and I actually decided that there was no reason for him not to go to Parsons'.

The parents in this group are aware of the complexity of making judgements about schools. For most (see note 5), choice is often invested with stress and anxiety, which sometimes induces panic; although this may be a middle-class phenomenon. As noted earlier, Gewirtz *et al.* (1995) refer to the professional middle-class parents who participated in this study as *privileged/skilled* choosers.[6] From the interplay of unclear or contradictory social principles, of diverse aspirations, desires and concerns related to their children and their children's future, and of multiple sources of impression and perception, choosing a school often emerges as a complex and confusing business. In some ways, the more skilled you are the more difficult it is. A good deal of this stress arises from the significance privileged/skilled choosers, especially, invest in the need to choose the 'right' school. But some also stems from the sense that no matter how much information and knowledge are available, it is often unclear, contradictory and inconclusive. Information is at a premium and yet too much information can be confusing and some parents panic or freeze as a result. Toffler (1971, p. 246) refers to the phenomenon of 'over choice' in the market place, where the 'advantages of diversity and individualisation are cancelled by the complexity of the buyer's decision-making process'. Mrs Cole provides a vivid example of this scenario:

Mrs Cole: Yes, it was a school gate nightmare...everybody was kind of
               frantic, it was incredible, and it went on for weeks...
Interviewer: Yes...you said here, panic and confusion.
Mrs C: There was, absolutely, and I think up till then Parsons had been
               flavour of the month, and for some reason it was kind of going
               into a state of decline...in opinions, gossip and hearsay...We
               just actually...I mean...we went hopefully with an open mind
               to all the schools we looked at...there were other people who
               had had Parsons in mind since the child was at infants' school,
               suddenly started...it was not what they wanted any more and
               they just didn't know how to go about...and at one point
               somebody said...if somebody stood at the school gate, with a
               little notice saying...I've decided on this school...they'd all
               go...phew...right...we'll all go there, and I think maybe that
               was partly because all the schools were good.[7]...there wasn't a
               clear...like, that's a good place and that's rubbish, it wasn't
               like that...So in a way it was a good sign, that we had
               the choice of the places to send them to. But it went on for
               weeks...you'd spend several evenings going round the schools,
               you'd go during the day, and you kept bumping into the same
               people...all going...'god...' It was incredible!

                                                              (Mrs Cole)

I kept trying to remain that bit removed to try and see it in a dispassionate
way, but it is difficult...because obviously people do get very passionate
about these things...I mean there are parents at my school...who have
become I think really quite obsessive about the whole thing...

                                                              (Mrs Collier)

In part, this type of intense response is to do with the significance of the
decision for many long-term planning, middle-class parents.

We knew it was coming up...it was like a blight on the horizon...it was, it
was really like a cloud on the horizon, what shall we do, what shall we
do...and we spoke to lots of people, you know, neighbours whose children go
there...neighbours whose children go to private school, and go to school
outside of the LEA, all sorts of...things really. So in a way you're doing
research, for a year, if not more.

                                                              (Mrs Walsh)

The uncertainties of choice seem to feed into a sense of continuing doubt for
some parents – even once the choice is made questions still remain: is the chosen
school the right one?

I thought God you know, if it's going to make him that unhappy to go somewhere else, I don't want to add to problems. So we plumped for Parsons. And
as I say I'm not totally certain that we've done the right thing with my son
but...

                                                              (Mrs Drurie)

The usefulness of grapevine information can vary depending on the extent to which parents consider choosing a school as an abstract decision or a grounded decision in matching the child with the right school. Privileged/skilled choosers, especially, involve themselves in a process of *child-matching*, which Ball has described elsewhere in the following terms:

> They are looking to find a school which will suit the particular proclivities, interests, aspirations and/or personality of their child. For some (objective/ goal-oriented), this is often *the* primary concern and is driven by very precise academic concerns and aspirations related to their child. The matching is based on a specific future/goal orientation. Here the child is often complexly constructed in terms of traits, needs and talents. This in itself complicates choice, especially when combined with 'insider' knowledge of the school system. For others (subjective/person-oriented) the matching is more gener- alised or is related to more immediate concerns about their child's happiness or ability to cope or flourish at school (Coldron and Boulton, 1991) and to more general future possibilities. But in both cases the 'best' school is the 'right' school.
>
> (Ball *et al.*, 1996)

Other parents, elsewhere described as *semi-skilled* choosers (see below) were more concerned with finding a school generally perceived as 'good'. Mrs Bradford's son is likely to attend an academically prestigious, selective school, despite her personal reservations.

> One of his best friends,... his parents were sort of looking around as well at places, because they weren't too keen on sending him to Milton or Trumpton, and they said well have you put him in for Suchard, which I'd never even heard of so...I sort of rushed round and got the application forms about two days before the closing date, and put him in for that...and...he took the exams...I mean basically we were sort of keeping everything open and he did- n't get into the CTC, he didn't get offered a place, so...we said we'd take Milton and then he passed the Suchard exam, and I still hadn't made up my mind whether he would go there or Milton, but after a month or so, it seemed that having passed the exam, he had to go there really. Again, it's still quite a big school, it's 900, it's all boys, which is quite what I didn't want, and it's very academic and very...I mean it's the sort of school I went to...
>
> (Mrs Bradford)

> It was...what's the word...second hand, I hadn't actually visited any of the schools before then, but my next door neighbour's children both go to Lockmere. It used to be the old grammar...which I know has nothing to do really with nowadays, but reputation I still think...and quite a lot of children from Nelson [Primary] have gone there in the last couple of years, so that all mainly looks very favourably upon that school, and I haven't heard any adverse criticism.
>
> (Mrs Westbury)

All the parents in this second broad grouping accepted the grapevine as an important contributory factor to their decision-making. They did differ on the extent to which they were swayed by what they heard. Mrs Alperton describes the difficulties of making an independent decision, until she visited the schools and was then able to bring her own affective response into play.

> I think this time last year...when so many people were going to Lockmere, I thought, perhaps Lockmere probably, and then talking to other people... who spoke just as well of Overbury, I thought oh maybe Overbury. So I wasn't sure at all until I visited the schools. It was very hard...and people had said to me...'how did you choose?'...Before we got this far...a lot of people had said to me...'well you just feel...when you go into a school...', and I didn't really know what they meant until it happened.

Lane (1991) calls markets 'theatres of emotion', and argues that they are 'saturated with emotion, pride and shame and guilt (the emotions that are identity related) anger and aggression: self love...[and]...the approval motive' (p. 58). Choice is not a simple, rational event.

> Of course it's difficult to...disassociate yourself from what you've heard, and because you know it's the flavour of the month school. I kept trying to remain that bit removed to try and see it in a dispassionate way, but it is difficult.
>
> (Mrs Collier)

Once made, the choice of a school remains a highly personal, emotive issue. People want the confirmation of others' agreement. Again, this perhaps reflects the uncertainty many people feel over making their choice.

> We happened to go round Martineau with friends whose daughter was going to go to Trumpton, and they were rather antagonistic towards all other schools, and they wanted all the other schools to be absolutely awful compared to what they'd chosen...you know...your own choice in these matters...and they were convinced the Martineau girls had been chosen for PR. Well, I suppose they had to some extent, but I wouldn't want to go to a school where they didn't put their best people forward...
>
> (Mrs Neville)

> Well we started asking people's advice, because that's the way your normally go about things, and it actually...then we'd go and see a school and think...oh, well this looks quite good, and then it was sort of a personal affront I used to think if someone else criticised the school that you thought was good. So we try now not to say anything.
>
> (Mrs Theydon)

> This is the funny thing, it's quite interesting how people perceive things differently because...when I talked to some of them, no way would they consider Parsons. You know what I mean, it's just how you interpret the feeling of the school, and I got slightly stressed about this because I thought, well...I certainly didn't like Overbury at all, and that's the one everyone seems to choose as their second one...you know, so I was going against what everybody else was thinking was good, so it made you think, gosh, why is it me feeling the opposite? But a friend at school, I actually found out...she actually chose the same selection as I did, and she chose Parsons for the very same

reasons as I did, so she felt the same as me. So it was interesting that we are definitely... because you have to be careful because so many people... you listen to people, and I think this is one of the big problems... so many people make or break that school from reputation, and you must try and overlook what these people tell you because they have no real experience of the school...

(Mrs Rawlings)

There are several interesting points here: the uncertainties involved in going against the grain (Lane's approval motive), doubts about one's own perceptions, the support of someone else's choice. And the problem with reputations: that reputation is not always based on direct knowledge, it is 'pseudo information'.

People have these most amazing attitudes and say... 'oh you couldn't possibly send your child to X'... they've probably never even been inside the building!... I actually find it quite amazing... we did start looking at schools... and the schools have very good sessions as you wander round, and you go in the evening and you go in the day... and it's really quite a revelation... they're not all beating each other up all the time... and lessons are progressing.

(Mrs Neville)

Acceptance

Some people referred to the grapevine as a highly reliable source of information, and certainly more so than information given out by the school, which is seen as packaging, as public relations. Possibly this group of parents are less confident in their ability to decode the school's presentations. In this way they share the characteristics of the group of parents of mixed social class who have been described elsewhere as semi-skilled (Gewirtz *et al.*, 1995). 'The families represented by this sort of chooser have strong inclination but limited capacity to engage "effectively" with the market: their cultural capital is in the wrong currency... These families talk about potential school choice as outsiders, often relying at least in part, on the comments and perceptions of others...' (Gewirtz *et al.*, 1995, pp. 40, 41).

Interviewer: Have you been to any open days or evenings at the school?
Mrs Wapping: No, we didn't go, because we're very aware of the fact that they're selling it... that they're selling a package, and I didn't honestly think it would give a fair view of what the schools are like... so I more or less relied on people who are in the schools... and just observing what goes on around them... what the children are like, how they behave, basically.

We didn't actually go in, but with various enquiries from parents,'cos to be honest that's the only way you get a good picture of what the schools are about. And because I work at present, I know loads of mums locally now.

(Mrs Charing)

'The semi-skilled seek reassurance from those they see to be informed or more authoritative in such matters... Perhaps as a result, rumour and reputation are much more likely to be taken at face value', (Gewirtz *et al.*, 1995, p. 43).

Education professionals and others with 'inside' knowledge of schools are viewed as particularly useful and reliable informants.

Ms Northwood: My sister in law is also in education...and she does disruptive children in schools and has some intimate knowledge of schools...and I also listened to what she had to say, I forgot to say that...

Interviewer: Right, and she suggested that Ramsey McDonald wasn't the best option.

Ms N: That's exactly it, yes.

Um, I think it wasn't a very informed decision...I think it was very likely that his two brothers go to Milton and he knows lots of their friends...that go there, and he goes along to all their Christmas functions and my husband is quite involved in the PTA...so he often goes along and helps with the raffles and things, so he's already involved in Milton school life. He went to see this school with a very good friend of mine who is also a teacher, and I know she was very disappointed in some aspects of what she saw there, she's a very forthright New Zealand lady who would chat about what she though, and I think Tom heard her opinions...and that made him no longer want to go there....I had every confidence in the friend that went there. This is her third child that's going...and she teaches in the secondary sector, and she does in fact know a lot more about it than myself, so I was quite happy to put my decision in her hands...

(Mrs Southgate)

Now somebody else who I knew, who was doing a project there, probably much the same as you're doing, she was involved in looking at several schools right across London and she said she'd never actually been in a school that had an attitude like Parsons...and she said she found it very disturbing, and that...well coming from a professional that put me off...completely...

(Mrs Wapping)

I know one lady who was a dinner lady at Eagleton for half a day and...walked out in disgust and wouldn't go back...I mean that sort of thing does colour your judgement.

(Mrs Flowers)

Peer group pressure is another important motivator, one that appears active in all social groups. This included those parents who were potential customers in the private-school market. A small number of such respondents specifically mentioned that they were aware of 'pressures' emanating from their social community or reference group or from the parents at their child's primary school which encouraged them in the idea that private was the 'right' choice (Ball, 1997c). Lane's (1991) 'approval motive' is also relevant here. This was particularly evident within those primaries that had developed a tradition and reputation for transferring children to the private sector at age 11.

It was followed very quickly on that...that once they started junior school that your problems were not over, that it actually was going to be like this from then on...what you choose and...in an area like this there is pressure on you to look at private education...it's very very strong...25%...I mean it wasn't true of the road we started in. We all trooped to Bleinheim primary but of course as you move up the housing market a bit, you suddenly find yourself terribly...just makes you question...what you're doing it for, who you're doing it for...you know...your standard state education.

(Mrs Harris)

There's also...the other thing which is my favourite...is that such a high proportion of primary children go to...out of the state sector. I think when your children's friends, when their peers...and to a much lesser extent this year but certainly with Beatrice's year...when all my school's bright kids are going into the independent sector, it's very hard when you've got one of the brightest kids, to say you're going to send that child into the state sector because...you're seeing...I mean what was the likelihood of her finding any peers...academically...anyone to spar against at all?

(Mr Tulley)

Many parents feel strongly that it is important to keep their child with children from a similar social group, and this is another concern which socially differentiated grapevines are particularly suited to addressing.

There was a big local estate which quite a few boys were coming from... I mean it's all sort of hearsay really...it's one of those things...concrete evidence...and it's all sort of rumours and hearsay, although one of my friends lived up on that estate and she knew some of the boys there and her son was saying...well I'm not going there...and the ones...from Gorse were going on there and he'd have got to mix with that lot, so a lot of it was on sort of hearsay really...but you sort of have these things in the background, and you wonder about it.

(Mrs Latimer)

Definitions of one's own social group can also contain a racial, or in this case, a racist element.

Interviewer: You said you rejected Gorse. Why was that?
Mrs Newley: Um...I think...because of the Indians, I'm afraid. Sounds horrible, but there are a lot that go there...It's a good school apparently, I've never had a look.

Conversely, Mr. Kumar, a South Asian parent who sent his children to Gorse School, spoke with some wariness of the predominantly white Flightpath School. The phrase 'a bit rough' is probably a euphemism for racist behaviour.

Some time ago we did read in our local paper what sort of school it was...the kids were a bit rough up there sometimes, things like that...I think some action has been taken by the education department...But it had a really bad name.

(Mr Kumar; see also Gewirtz *et al.*, 1995, pp. 49–50)

Conclusion

In an earlier project paper, Bowe *et al.* (1994) described the school-choice process using the metaphor of a 'landscape of choice' to invoke the varied and multilayered contexts in which decisions are made.

> The experience of 'choice' is of a landscape that is neither flat nor unidimensional, nor linear, nor ordered, nor tidy...Information is rarely complete, decisions often seem only to be 'the best that can be done', provisional and fragile. From where you stand aspects of the landscape may be 'out of sight', and moving across the landscape changes the 'way things look'. Decisions are made about the possibilities available on the basis of look, feel and judgement as well as rational reflection...

The metaphor of landscape is an apt one in this context, as the grapevine has both spatial and social aspects to it. That is, its substance is conditioned by where you are and who you know, by the 'material landscape' and 'local structures of feeling' produced by class, culture and routine social practices (Taylor *et al.*, 1996). In the face of what for many parents are the constantly shifting uncertainties of school choice, the grapevine offers some indications, some pointers for the way ahead. Through engagement with the grapevine, parents can feel more firmly embedded in their choice, confirmed in it by the opinions and choices of their friends and relatives.

Suspicion, doubt, acceptance – the three categories of responses to the grapevine which we have outlined in this paper – are not straightforwardly related to social class. Nonetheless, access to particular grapevines is socially structured and patterned. Responses to the grapevine are also influenced by personal characteristics and social considerations, such as the degree to which the parents see their child's primary school companions as an appropriate reference group. Therefore, within the three broad groups, some types of behaviour are more in evidence amongst particular social fractions. Those who are suspicious of the grapevine are either professional middle-class parents who have the cultural capital to seek out extensive and detailed 'cold' knowledge with which to replace, or at least supplement, the grapevine, or a small group of working-class parents who in their perception that there are few significant differences between schools have little use for it. Those who use, but nevertheless doubt, the grapevine are a mixed-class group of privileged/skilled choosers and semi-skilled choosers. For these parents, the grapevine and their awareness of its fallibility and fickleness often add to the anxiety and stress they experience in choosing a school. It is the third group, the acceptors, for whom grapevine knowledge is the most helpful. For these, mainly semi-skilled choosers, the grapevine provides an apparently reliable and comprehensible way of 'decoding' schools, and making a choice grounded in the opinions of other parents like oneself. And it is this, the possibility or promise of making a choice which is socially embedded, which ensures that few parents, whatever their doubts or suspicions, can entirely resist the pull or influence of grapevine knowledge.

In more general terms, we suggest, the role and function of grapevine knowledge can be interpreted and understood in a number of different ways and at different levels of abstraction. For instance, the forms of knowledge and ways of knowing which are displayed in the data may indicate some general characteristics of education policy effects and of social orientations towards 'authoritative knowledge' which are symptomatic of 'the conditions' of late modern society. In particular, the apparent ambivalence towards 'official' information and the sense of distrust and confusion, and lack of self-confidence, in parents' perceptions and understanding of schools are all suggestive of a situated manifestation of the 'crisis of representation'. That is to say, the codes of social discourse which are in play within the education market are unstable; '...the symbolic forms in which cultural value is normally stored are themselves devalued and social signs lose their capacity to provoke or articulate a desired social meaning' (Lee, 1993, p. 162).

As a part of, as well as in response to, this crisis, schools are now carefully, and 'professionally' attending to and 'managing' their image; the relationships between signifier and signified become increasingly slippery in consequence (Ball, 1997b). Parental awareness of this process reduces both trust and the possibilities of certain knowledge. Image, information and sense compete for attention and vie for authenticity.

There is a dual political–economic context to this crisis. The dismantling of the heavily symbolised and distinctive grammar-secondary modern divide is one context. The comprehensive school movement replaced a clear cultural coding of schools, with its 'obvious' relationship to 'cultural profits' and social reproduction, with a system of fuzzy distinctions and complex social purposes (Bourdieu, 1986). However, we want to argue that through the 1970s and early mid-1980s this shift may have been of marginal significance to most parents, although the political 'discourse of derision' did begin to seriously undermine the symbolic value invested in comprehensivism. The private sector continued to operate to provide a stable storage of cultural value for those who wished and were able to have access to those schools. In the late 1980s and early 1990s, three things combined to radically change the 'trading' position of state schooling. One was the introduction of unfettered parental choice – what might be termed 'the politics of temptation' – alongside the development of a new discourse of 'good parenting' which centred upon choice. Being a good parent means taking choice seriously. The second was the move to mass higher education and the subsequent abolition of the binary divide alongside the steady rise in GCSE examination performance. Entry into higher education was becoming more socially diverse and the links to the labour market more competitive as a result. Third was the economic recession with its particular impact on the professions, managers and the 'new class of cultural intermediaries'. Within this context of economic uncertainty, certification inflation and an increasing differentiation and diversity of schools, choice takes on a key role in strategies of social and economic reproduction. Viewed in this light 'choice' is not a form of selfish behaviour that is natural to the human condition (as Hayek, e.g. would have argued), it is a socio-political construct of its times. Jordon *et al.* (1994) develop a similar argument in their study of middle-class families and individualism. They suggest that recession, 'unmanaged congestion', has transformed education back into a positional and 'oligarchic' good and heightened middle-class anxieties about their children's futures.

> In effect, the institutions for 'managed crowding' in the social democratic era were swept away, and the positional economy was again laid open to the effects of individual and household decisions.
>
> (p. 212)

In this respect the grapevine has a dual function. It provides information, however flawed, and it provides a medium of social comparison – with others 'like us' and 'others' not 'like us'. Viewed in this way we can begin to see how choice of school is being subsumed within general class-related strategies of consumption.

> the tendency is for social groups to seek to classify and order their social circumstances and use cultural goods as a means of demarcation, as communicators which establish boundaries between people and build bridges with others.
>
> (Featherstone, 1991, p. 63)

If we accept choice as social comparison then the logic is that social contexts of choice are as or more important than the abstract/objective qualities of goods; 'need is not a need for a particular object as much as it is a "need" for difference (the *desire for social meaning*)' (Baudrillard, 1990, p. 45, emphasis in original).

Within this new situation, we suggest, the removal of traditional markers of cultural value, the discourse of derision, and a general cynicism towards 'official' knowledge leave many choosers facing the 'terror of contingency' (Pfeil, 1988, p. 386) and the sort of 'sense of panic and uncertainty' (Lee, 1993, p. 165) we see in the grapevine data. The half-hearted Conservative Party commitment to a 'grammar school in every town' and the more general encouragement by New Labour for selection and specialisation may be seen as tactics aimed at re-stabilising the sign system and cultural value of schooling. The use of conventional signs and images by some schools, and the development of stable reputations by some schools, or strong relationships between schools and localities, also provide at least some parents with a greater sense of relative certainty about their choice of school. Furthermore, as we see in the project data overall, at a local level there still are vestiges of a meaningful symbolic system of school 'values' (Gewirtz *et al.*, 1995).

Finally, exploration of the uses of grapevine knowledge demonstrates the limitations and distortions of research which rips choice out of social context or desocialises choice-making and treats it as a kind of individual rational calculus. This kind of research with its reliance on checklists and criteria tends to treat all kinds of knowledge as equivalent and simply as more of less important to different individuals. Such research does little more than reproduce and reinforce the abstractly constructed individuals which policy-makers and economists substitute for the 'burdened, worried, haunted, embedded, memory-infested, befriended, kinsperson(s)' (Warde, 1994), we find inhabiting our data.

Appendix

The tables below summarise the social-class data for the 45 families quoted in the text. The tables are organised in relation to the categories discussed in the paper, although we would not want to suggest that the categories are fully watertight. That is to say, a few families display characteristics of different sorts of perspectives towards and involvements in 'grapevines'. However, the majority can be matched to a particular category. In some instances in the paper, families are quoted within the discussion of categories but as counter-points or to establish distinctions; these are marked by an asterisk (*) in the tables.

Table 15A.1 Parents quoted in the general discussion

No	Name	Mother's occupation	Father's occupation	Mother's education	Father's education	Ethnicity	Housing
130	Mr and Mrs Totteridge	Hairdresser 3M	SE antique restorer 3M	Sec to 16	Sec to 16	W	
10	Mr and Mrs Leyton	IIIN	IIIN	Sec mod 16	Sec mod 16	W	
26	Mr and Mrs Shearer	Systems proger II	FreeL model maker IIIM	Gram As + Poly	Gram + app + day release	W	O/O terraced
5	Mrs Brent	Pt teacher Behv/diSTb II	Architect I	Convent TTC	Prep + gram + mature degree	W	O/O detached
19	Mrs Eastcote	Nursery asst IIIN	Kitchen fitting co. owner II	Gram + As + college	Sec mod 15	W	O/O semi-D
44	Mr and Mrs Pallister	House worker	Motor engineer 3M	Sec to 15	Sec to 15	W	133
133	Mrs Kohli	Admin officer, Civil Service 3N	Machine operator 3M	India + comp to 16	India + some HE	A	O/O semi-D

Notes: Hswrker = house worker; pt = part-time; SE = self-employed; As = A-levels; PGCE = post graduate certificate in education; Os = O-levels; gram = grammar school; sec mod = secondary modern; FE = further education; HE = higher education; PG = postgraduate; TT/TTC = teacher training/teacher training college; uni = university; prep = preparatory; comp = comprehensive; app = apprenticeship; W = White; B = Black; A = Asian; O = other; Semi-D = Semi-detached; HA = Housing Association; O/O = owner occupied; hse = house.

Table 15A.2 Maximise: this is an exclusively middle-class category

No	Name	Mother's occupation	Father's occupation	Mother's education	Father's education	Ethnicity	Housing
3	Mrs Roding	Pt sec + estate agent IIIN	Admin accnt w/sale electrics II	Sec mod + coll/office GCEs	Gram + work	W W	O/O town hse
23	Mrs Snarsebrook	LHA speech therapist II	Redundant civil eng II	Uni	Uni	W	O/O semi-D
72	Mr Ife	Primary school tchr II	History lecturer II	Gram + TTC	Public school + PhD	W	O/O
24	Ms Bond	Pt computer proger II	Divorced	Gram + uni	—	W	O/O terraced
96	Mrs Wallace	Financial const + co. director I	Systems analyst consultant II	Boarding + uni + PG	Gram + uni	W	O/O hse
2	Mrs Morden	School secretary IIIN	Boro planning officer I	Tech + uni	Oratory + uni + PG	W	O/O semi-D
33	Mrs Gillespie	Houseworker/ secondy teacher II	Scientific consultant II	Gram + BSc + PGCE	Gram + BSc + Phd	W	O/O semi-D

Notes: Hswrker = house worker; pt = part-time; SE = self-employed; As = A-levels; Os = O-levels; gram = grammar school; sec mod = secondary modern; FE = further education; HE = higher education; PG = postgraduate; TT/TTC = teacher training/teacher training college; uni = university; prep = preparatory; comp = comprehensive; app = apprenticeship; W = White; B = Black; A = Asian; O = other; Semi-D = Semi-detached; HA = Housing Association; O/O = owner occupied; hse = house. PGCE = post graduate certificate in education;

Table 15A.3 Reject: this is an exclusively working-class category

No	Name	Mother's occupation	Father's occupation	Mother's education	Father's education	Ethnicity	Housing
69	Mr Fairlop		Unemployed driver IIIM	Comp	Comp	W	Council hse
35	Mr Tufnell	Separated	Unemployed driver 3M	—	Sec mod 15	W	Council flat
61	Mrs Everley	Sales asst IIIN	Milkman IIIM			W	Council hse
32	Mr and Mrs Ishtar	House worker	Unemployed		Sec mod	A	Council hse
48	Mrs Lancaster *	Coll advice service IIIN	Chartered accountant I	Gram + As	Gram + uni	W	O/O semi-D

Notes: Hswrker = house worker; pt = part-time; SE = self-employed; As = A-levels; PGCE = post graduate certificate in education; Os = O-levels; gram = grammar school; sec mod = secondary modern; FE = further education; HE = higher education; PG = postgraduate; TT/TTC = teacher training/ teacher training college; uni = university; prep = preparatory; comp = comprehensive; app = apprenticeship; W = White; B = Black; A = Asian; O = other; Semi-D = Semi-detached; HA = Housing Association; O/O = owner occupied; hse = house.

Table 15A.4 Excluded: this is a mixed category

No	Name	Mother's occupation	Father's occupation	Mother's education	Father's education	Ethnicity	Housing
52	Mrs Ansari	Beautician IV	Business/ Diplomat IIIN	Iran	Iran	O	Council flat
86	Mr Butt	Widower	Snr Lecturer 1		Sec mod + uni + MSc	W	O/O hse
75	Mrs Fawcett-Majors	Research officer 3N	Grounds man IV	Gram + BA/PGCE	Sec mod 15 + apprentice	W	
18	Mrs Shadwell	House worker	BBC engineer IIIN	Gram school/Os	Sec mod + tech coll	W	O/O semi-D

Notes: Hswrker = house worker; pt = part-time; SE = self-employed; As = A-levels; PGCE = post graduate certificate in education; Os = O-levels; gram = grammar school; sec mod = secondary modern; FE = further education; HE = higher education; PG = postgraduate; TT/TTC = teacher training/teacher training college; uni = university; prep = preparatory; comp = comprehensive; app = apprenticeship; W = White; B = Black; A = Asian; O = other; Semi-D = Semi-detached; HA = Housing Association; O/O = owner occupied; hse = house.

Table 15A.5 Rely but question: this is mainly a middle-class category, one family with an ambiguous class position and two working-class families are included

No	Name	Mother's occupation	Father's occupation	Mother's education	Father's education	Ethnicity	Housing
46	Mrs Harper	Child minder IV	Furniture maker IIIM	Sec to 15	FE	W	Council hse
1	Mrs Cole	Teach. nonAtt Ctr II	Civil sevt II	Gram + Art College	Direct grant + HE	W	O/O
21	Mr and Mrs Collier	Junior teacher II	Redundant charity wker IIIN	Comp + TTC	Sec mod-tech Coll	W	
50	Mrs Walsh	Primary teacher II	Postman IV	Sec mod + TTC/CtEd	Gram	W	O/O terraced
71	Mr and Mrs Drurie	Clerical IIIN		Sec mod 16 GCEs	Sec mod 15	W	O/O bungalow
70	Mrs Bradford	Coll. librarian II	Freelance photogher IIIN	Direct grant boarding Uni + PG	W	W	O/O Terraced
30	Mrs Westbury	H/worker ex DHss Officer IIIN	Video-tape engineer IIIN	Gram/Os + dance school	Gram + HND	W	O/O Semi-D
8	Mrs Alperton	Gardner IV	Admin/ researcher II	Gram + secretarial coll	Gram + HND	W	O/O
67	Mrs Neville	C.Servant computer proger II	Brit Gas services manager II	A-levels	Sec mod + degree + MSc	W	Semi-D O/O terraced
82	Mr and Mrs Theydon	SE systems analyst II	SE advertising 3N	Gram + uni	Gram + uni	W	O/O hse
63	Mrs Richards	Infant school II	Chartered acc I	TTC	University	W	O/O detached
6	Mrs Angus	Mature student/ housewker	Unempld, decorator IIIM	Sec (16)CSEs now doing As	Sec (16)	W	Council flat

Notes: Hswrker = house worker; pt = part-time; SE = self-employed; As = A-levels; PGCE = post graduate certificate in education; Os = O-levels; gram = grammar school; sec mod = secondary modern; FE = further education; HE = higher education; PG = postgraduate; TT/TTC = teacher training/teacher training college; uni = university; prep = preparatory; comp = comprehensive; app = apprenticeship; W = White; B = Black; A = Asian; O = other; Semi-D = Semi-detached; HA = Housing Association; O/O = owner occupied; hse = house.

Table 15A.6 Acceptance: this is a mixed-class category

No	Name	Mother's occupation	Father's occupation	Mother's education	Father's education	Ethnicity	Housing
11	Mrs Wapping	Fulltime mother	Water industry	Sec mod to 16	Sec mod to 16	W	O/O ex-council
4	Mrs Charing	Houseworker	SE builder 3M	Sec mod to 17	Sec mod to 18 + day R1 ONDs	W	O/O terraced
73	Ms Northwood	Pt shop keeper IIIN	Divorced	Catholic Sec mod (15)	—	W	O/O terraced
85	Mrs Southgate	Primary teacher II	SE architect 1	O/O ps + Gram + Cert Ed	Gram + art school	W	O/O hse
92	Mrs Flowers	Home worker	Printer 3M	Sec mod- OLS + civil service	Sec mod nqs	W	O/O hse
13	Mrs Harris	Indpdent Socworker II	Journalist II	Gram + uni	Gram + uni	W	O/O semi-D
105	Mr and Mrs Tulley	Clinical psycholgst 1	Professor of history 1	DG + Oxf + TT + Msc	DG + Oxford + PhD	W	O/O hse
22	Mrs Latimer	Coord commcare grp PT II	Execoff locgovt II	Prep + gram +	Gram + uni	W	O/O terraced
138	Mrs Newley	Assistant buyer 3N	Office worker 3N	Sec to 15	Sec to O levels	W	Rented housing trust
90	Mrs Kumar	Hswrker pattern cutter 3M	Unempled systems analyst 2	Kenya Os Fashion College	India uni + LLB	A	O/O hse

Notes: Hswrker = house worker; pt = part-time; SE = self-employed; As = A-levels; PGCE = post graduate certificate in education; Os = O-levels; gram = grammar school; sec mod = secondary modern; FE = further education; HE = higher education; TT/TTC = teacher training/teacher training college; uni = university; prep = preparatory; comp = comprehensive; app = apprenticeship; W = White; B = Black; A = Asian; O = other; Semi-D = Semi-detached; HA = Housing Association; O/O = owner occupied; hse = house.

Notes

1   ESRC project no. 232858. The paper draws upon one of several re-analyses of the interview data set. The primary data for this particular analysis was identified by a search and sort excercise using a set of key words. This was done independently by Barbara Watson-Powell, to whom we are very grateful. Extracts from 87 of the interviews were thus identified as having relevance to the issue of social knowledge of schools – the grapevine – information about schools obtained from friends, relatives, personal contacts, etc., plus references to reputations, local knowledge, informal knowledge, etc., These extracts were then subject to intensive and axial coding (Strauss, 1987) separately by Vincent and Ball and a set of key categories and concepts were identified. These were then compared, discussed and reworked. The coding was subsequently related back to SES data on the families (see Appendix 1). The reworked categories and concepts form the basis of the paper as it stands. The paper was initially presented at the PERN symposium at the BERA 1996 Conference, University of Lancaster. See Gewirtz *et al.* (1995) for an account of the entire research and details of the schools referred to in the paper. It is only possible to quote directly a tiny proportion of the total data. In fact, 45 families are quoted in the paper.

2   Many studies of choice-making take it out of social context and de-socialise it, thereby reinforcing the ideological representations of competitive individualism.

3   For instance, several groups, children, the elderly, and young women, identify the same parts of the cities as areas they perceive to be unsafe.

4   A small group of middle-class parents apparently share the assertion of the working-class 'rejecters' that all schools are similar (see, especially, the earlier quotes from Mr Fairlop and Mrs Everley). Mrs Lancaster is one of this group, as are Mrs Morden and Mrs Gillespie who say,

> Like this year I know plenty of people that have equally bright children and have chosen all different schools and are quite happy with the choice...
>
> (Mrs Morden)

> Everybody I knew just about had either sent their children to Parsons or Lockmere...and I think they all seemed pretty happy with the choice.
>
> (Mrs Gillespie)

However, these parents live in Riverway Local Education Authority (LEA), and their comments, as Mrs Lancaster makes clear, pertain to the schools *in the locality*. Riverway is a small LEA with a fairly stable and homogeneous middle-class population.

5   There is little direct evidence in this data set of a children's grapevine, although Taylor *et al.* (1996) point to the existence of a more general grapevine amongst children and young people concerning the reputations of different areas of their cities. Stephen Ball's current research into choice in further education clearly reveals a students' grapevine concerning different sites and types of further educational provision (Macrae *et al.*, 1996).

6   Economic, social and cultural capital are all important here. These choosers were able to 'decode' school systems and organisations, to discriminate between schools in terms of policies and practices, to engage with and question (and challenge if necessary) teachers and school managers, to critically evaluate teachers' responses and to collect, scan and interpret various sources of information (Gewirtz *et al.*, 1995, p. 25).

7   Mrs Cole is also referring to schools within Riverway LEA (see note 5). Her reference to changing parental opinions of Parsons School (also noted by Mrs Shearer above) illustrates how schools which appear to occupy a transitory or divergent reputational position incite particular confusion.

References

Bailey, F. (1977) *Morality and Expediency* (Oxford, Basil Blackwell).
Ball, S. (1987) *The Micropolitics of the School* (London, Methuen).
Ball, S. (1997a) Good school/bad school, *British Journal of Sociology of Education*, 18(3), pp. 317–36.

Ball, S. (1997b) Performativity and fragmentation in postmodern schooling, in J. Carter (ed.) *Postmodernity and the Fragmentation of Welfare: A Contemporary Social Policy* (London, Routledge).

Ball, S. J. (1997c) 'On the cusp'; parents choosing between state and private schools, *International Journal of Inclusive Education*, 1(1), pp. 1–17.

Ball, S. J. and Gewirt, S. (1997) Girls and the education market, *Gender and Education*, 9(2), pp. 207–22.

Ball, S. J., Bowe, R. and Gewirtz, S. (1996) School choice, social class and distinction: the realisation of social advantage in education, *Journal of Education Policy*, 11(1), pp. 89–112.

Baudrillard, J. (1990) *Cool Memories* (London, Verso).

Bourdieu, P. (1986) *Distinction: A Social Critique of the Judgement of Taste* (London, Routledge).

Bowe, R., Ball, S. and Gewirtz, S. (1994) Parental choice, consumption and social theory, *British Journal of Educational Studies*, 42(1), pp. 38–52.

Butler, T. (1996) 'People like us': the gentrification of Hackney in the 1980s, in P. Cohen (ed.) *Rising in the East: The Regeneration of East London* (London, Lawrence & Wishart).

Coldron, J. and Boulton, P. (1991) 'Happiness' as a criterion of parents' choice of school, *Journal of Education Policy*, 6(2), pp. 169–78.

Crow, G. and Allan, G. (1994) *Community Life* (London, Harvester Wheatsheaf).

David, M., West, A. and Ribbens, J. (1994) *Mothers' Intuition* (London, Falmer Press).

Dehli, K. (1996) Travelling tales: education reform and parental 'choice' in postmodern times, *Journal of Education Policy*, 11(1), pp. 75–88.

Eldridge, J. and Eldridge, L. (1994) *Raymond Williams: making connections* (London, Routledge).

Featherstone, M. (1991) *Consumer Culture and Postmodernism* (London, Sage).

Gewirtz, S., Ball, S. and Bowe, R. (1995) *Markets, Choice and Equity in Education* (Buckingham, Open University Press).

Jordon, B., Redley, M. and James, S. (1994) *Putting the Family First: Identities, Decisions, and Citizenship* (London, UCL Press).

Kenway, J., Biggum, C. and Fitzclarence, L. (1993) Marketing education in the postmodern age, *Journal of Education Policy*, 8(1), pp. 28–41.

Lane, R. (1991) *The Market Experience* (Cambridge, Cambridge University Press).

Lantz, H. (1958) *People of Coal Town*, (New York, Columbia University Press).

Lee, M. (1993) *Consumer Culture Reborn* (London, Routledge).

Macrae, S., Maguire, M. M. and Ball, S. J. (1996) *The Role of Grapevine Knowledge in Student Decision-making*. Paper presented to the Learning Society Programme conference 'Markets and Choice', Bristol.

Pfeil, F. (1988) Postmodernism as a structure of feeling, in N. Grossberg (ed.) *Marxism and the Interpretation of Culture* (London, Macmillan).

Reay, D. and Ball, S. J. (1997) 'Spoilt for Choice': the working class and educational markets, *Oxford Review of Education*, 23(1), pp. 89–101.

Shibutani, T. (1966) *Improvised News* (Indianapolis, IN, Bobbs-Merril).

Strauss, A. (1987) *Qualitative Data Analysis for Social Scientists* (New York, Cambridge University Press).

Taylor, I., Evas, K. and Fraser, P. (1996) *A Tale of Two Cities* (London, Routledge).

Toffler, A. (1971) *Future Shock* (London, Pan).

Urry, J. (1981) Localities, regions and social class, *International Journal of Urban and Regional Research*, 5, pp. 455–74.

Warde, A. (1994) Consumers, consumption and postfordism, in R. Burrows and P. Hoggert (eds) *Towards a Postfordist Welfare State?* (London, Routledge).

Wellman, B. and Worthley, S. (1990) Different strokes by different folks: community ties and social support, *American Journal of Sociology*, 93(3), pp. 558–88.

Wellman, B., Carrington, P. and Hall, A. (1988) Networks as personal communities, in B. Wellman and S. Berkowitz (eds) *Social Structures: A Network Approach* (Cambridge, Cambridge University Press).

West, J. (1954) *Plainville, USA* (New York, Columbia University Press).

Williams, R. (1979) *Politics and Letters* (London, New Left Books).

Wright, N. (1989) *Assessing Radical Education: A Critical View* (Milton Keynes, Open University Press).

CHAPTER 16

THE RISKS OF SOCIAL REPRODUCTION

The middle class and education markets

London Review of Education, 2003, 1(3): 163–75

'modernity...brings uncertainty to the very mode of existence'.
(Giddens, 1991, p. 102)

Risk is almost an obligatory concept in social theory and analysis these days although it has a plurality of meanings.[1] We live, as some theorists put it, in a 'risk society'. Risk society according to Beck (1998, p. 10) is 'the end of nature and the end of tradition'; and it is 'a society increasingly preoccupied with the future' (Giddens, 1998, p. 27). Risks are diverse and new forms are constantly arising. There is an 'over-production' of risk. We are all effected and Beck suggests: 'Risks display an equalizing effect' (1992, p. 35). We face the brittle uncertainties of individual self-management, as Beck sees it, alone and 'fragmented across (life) phases, space and time' (1997, p. 26). This is a bleak and elemental social world. Concomitantly 'risk monitoring presupposes agency, choice, calculation and responsibility' (Elliott, 2002, p. 298) – both individualisation and reflexivity.

This paper takes a rather different view of risk, as having both collective and divisive dynamics and effects. I offer not so much an alternative view as one that is re-socialised. As Douglas (1994, p. 3) opines 'it is hard to maintain seriously that the perception of risk is private'. The focus here is on the 'mundane' risks attached to the day-to-day processes of social reproduction in middle-class families. I shall re-visit some of the processes involved in the those 'definite social exertions' (Parkin, 1979, p. 63) that middle-class families must make on their own part 'or face the very real prospect of generational decline' (Parkin, 1979, p. 63). I have written at greater length and in more detail about these exertions elsewhere (see Ball, 2003a). Here, I map out some of the social and emotional complexity, for the middle class,[2] of social reproduction in relation to educational institutions and the education of their children. These risks arise from the engagements between the family and the education marketplace, and are embedded in the paradox wherein society becomes structurally more meritocratic but processually less so, as the middle class work harder to maintain their advantages in the new conditions of choice and competition in education (Halsey, 1995). 'People have to take a more active and risk-infused orientation to their relationships and involvements' (Giddens, 1998, p. 28). The paper is peppered with extracts from interviews with middle-class parents. These serve for illustration and discussion.

While Beck and Giddens have written the sociological headlines of the 'risk society', their representations of risk have a number of weaknesses and limitations (see Crook, 1999; Dean, 1999; Elliott, 2002). In particular, 'Beck's approach to risk can be characterised as totalising, realist and relying on a uniform conception of risk' (Dean, 1999, p. 131). Elliott (2002, p. 304) argues that 'Beck fails to adequately consider...that individualization...may directly contribute to, and advance the proliferation of, class inequalities and economic exclusions'. While I would not demur from his realism, Beck's portrayal of risk as an ontological condition of all humans fails to take adequate account either of the social differentiation of risk or of the existence and social consequences of different regimes of risk and risk management. Therefore the discussion here draws to a greater extent on the more nuanced work of Crook (1999), and to a lesser extent Douglas (1994), rather than the 'super-realists' Beck and Giddens. Crook's conceptual framework provides a language for thinking about the relationship between risk regimes and different forms of risk management behaviour. In other words, it creates a theoretical space in which it is possible to think about both the role of the social actor and the role of the state, together.

In an unintended restatement of Parkin's (1979) thesis of class and social closure Erenreich (1990, p. 83) makes the point that the 'barriers that the middle class erected to protect itself make it painfully difficult to reproduce itself'. That is to say, the individualist mode of social reproduction is fraught with difficulties and beset by anxiety and 'the fear of falling'. To put it another way: 'Utterly dependent on market and state, the social fate of the many is becoming the particular fate of each individual' (Berking, 1996, p. 191). The regime of choice, of neo-liberalism, in social policy threatens an equality that was unthinkable within collectivist modes of social reproduction – the risks of choice are, in theory, open to all. As Kemshall (2002, p. 1) argues 'risk, is replacing need as the core principle of social policy formation and welfare delivery'. While the middle class enter the education market with considerable advantages, tangible and otherwise, 'resources to at least attempt to live [the] dream of order' (Crook, 1999, p. 186), there are no guarantees, no certainties of a smooth and uneventful process of social reproduction. This is the paradox of political liberalism. A version of what Giddens (1998, p. 41) calls the 'risk/reward ratio'. Middle-class parents, like all parents, can only do their best – deploy their capitals as strategically as they are able and 'through careful moulding and psychological pressure...predispose each child to retrace the same long road they themselves once took' (Erenreich, 1990, p. 83). In particular, these families rely heavily on 'the domestic transmission of cultural capital' (Bourdieu, 1986b, p. 244). This is very evident, for example, in the way middle-class students have the necessity of Higher Education inculcated into their thinking as something 'automatic', obvious. In other words, social reproduction is a risky business. 'There are fewer and fewer unquestionably given paths of life conduct available' (Berking, 1996, p. 195). This sense of risk in the enterprise of education interplays forcefully with the strong sense of 'responsibility' which is so central to middle-class individualism. 'A key feature of risk in the "risk society" is the meshing of risk, responsibility and prudent choice' (Kemsall, 2002, p. 1).

In effect, risk theorists like Beck and Giddens now see the whole of society and social life as dominated by a kind of strategic morality. 'In the individualised society, the individual must therefore learn, on pain of permanent disadvantage, to conceive of himself or herself as the centre of activity, as the planning office with respect to his or her own biography, abilities, orientations, relationships and so on' (Beck, 1992, p. 55). Risk constantly reinforces a particular kind of individual responsibility and mirrors and 'calls up' the liberal values of the developmental self. Commenting on this Giddens (1998, p. 33) at least nods towards the classed aspects of such strategic morality. He suggests that within 'risk society the middle classes detach themselves from public provision', that they have 'a more active orientation to their lives' and that 'it is not surprising that those who can afford to, opt out of existing welfare systems'. Individual responsibility is increasingly replacing collective assurance against risk. This touches upon the main tenet of my analysis. First, that the construction of an educational career by middle-class parents for their children is denoted by particular kinds of planning and thoughtfulness. Second, that the skills and orientations of, or dispositions for such work have some particularly to the middle class. This gives rise to a new form or perhaps exaggerated form of inequality, that is 'the inequality of dealing with insecurity and reflexivity' (Beck, 1992, p. 98). Douglas (1992, p. 34) goes further and argues that increased risk, or fear of danger, leads to social closure, the strengthening of the 'lines of social division in a community'.

Perversely then, while the market form privileges middle-class families, the sense of risk and uncertainty experienced by the middle classes in relation to social reproduction is almost certainly heightened by the market. There is a constant interplay between risk and control here. That is to say, there is 'risk anxiety inherent in neo-liberal over-production and under control of risk' (Crook, 1999, p. 181). The market has a degree of openness and unplannedness which constantly threatens to overwhelm the orderliness and planning, the futurity, which denotes many middle-class households. 'The more risks, the more decisions and choices that have to be made' (Beck, 1998, p. 10). However, it is often not clear what the right choice is. Choice of child care, of school, of post-compulsory education is often, for middle-class families, a matter of uneasy compromises. Indeed, there is currently a kind of moral panic around schooling and school choice, particularly in metropolitan settings.

Families are expected to take responsibility for choosing and to choose responsibly; although responsible actions may also be opportunistic and detrimental to the interests of others – a 'new moral economy of welfare' (Rodger, 2000, p. 3). Rose (1996, p. 57) goes as far as to suggest that the new advanced liberal regime of choice, the enpowerment of the citizen-consumer, produces a further paradox and is a yet more sophisticated means of government: 'It has become possible to actualize this notion of the actively responsible individual because of the development of a new apparatus that integrates subjects into a moral nexus of identifications and allegiances in the very process in which they appear to act out their most personal choices'. They are drawn into the ontology of the market. Within the regime of choice increasingly the failings of quasi-markets become lodged within the shortcomings of individuals or families rather than with the 'organised irresponsibility; (Beck, 1998) of 'out-moded' bureaucracies. Douglas (1992, p. 321) argues that the culture of the market, of individualism, 'is so organised that incompetence and weakness cannot be compensated for'. For middle-class families there is both too much choice, and thus always a possibility of wrong or unsuccessful choice-making in the education market place, and never enough. Choice of school, and schools chosen both require assiduous and careful attention if the risks of social reproduction are to be minimised and control of the future maximised. When it comes to children, parental responsibility has no limits and indeed seems to be continually expanding. 'Individual agents must become risk monitors and risk calculators' (Crook, 1999, p. 171) who operate within 'the precautionary principle' (Tait and Levidow, 1992) – 'we knew we could get my son into the local school and the question is whether there's something better' (Mr Simpson).

The calculus of uncertainty and choice makes all decision-making reflexively unstable. The concern about getting things wrong is ever present.

> you think of the happiness of your child for the next 5 or 6 years, of course its a big decision, you wonder if you are going to make the right one, cos ok, you can change, but you dont want to unsettle them.
>
> (Mrs Hillerman)

In the changes and contrasts outlined above, two very different forms of risk and risk management are juxtaposed. On the one hand there is the modernist, welfarist, one-fits-all, 'organised risk management' solution of comprehensivism and neighbourhood schooling which is perceived, by large numbers of middle class parents, as engendering the risks of levelling and massification in relation to their projects of social reproduction and differentiation and developmentalism – making the most of the child. The continuing political and media critique of state schooling generally and comprehensive schooling in particular emphasises their dangers, rightly or wrongly, in these respects. On the other, there is the privatised and more open, post-welfare, choice solution – the education market. And again risk is an inherent characteristic of the market form, an essential part of its dynamic, a quality that is celebrated and set over and against the conservatism of bureaucratic systems. The market form rests both on responsibility and resourcefulness and an absence of certainty.

Part of the riskiness of the post-welfare, choice system inheres in the importance of and elusiveness of useful and 'accurate' information. Knowledge is increasingly indeterminate and contingent. Complete and completely reliable information may be an impossibility in human processing institutions and the perceived adequacy or reliability of information available both undermines parents' trust of lay and expert actors and exacerbates anxieties.

Trust/distrust of professional and expert systems

In the education market you can never know enough but often know too much, and within all this it is difficult to know what is important and what is not; 'for the educated middle classes of the advanced societies, at least, risk communications merge with problems of consumption and lifestyle choice in a general information overload that is more likely to provoke anxiety and insecurity than a sense of safety and control' (Crook, 1999, p. 180).

> I'd like to be able to pick up so much more, it's this thing that you can't pick up until to get into the classroom, how good are they? And I don't mean when they're on display, that means you want some kind of independent judgement system...I'd rather have too much than too little...a whole variety, capital rate of spending, floor space of gyms whatever. If we're not too careful we're going to concentrate on one aspect of it that is examination results.
>
> (Mr Christie)

'This overload connects with the arbitrariness and necessary incompleteness of even the most assiduous individual risk calculation' (Crook, 1999, p. 180). Mr Christie's point also highlights what Bourdieu (1986b, p. 253) describes as 'the gratuitous expenditure of time...' involved in ensuring reproduction, here spent on collecting more and more information, which leads to more and more discussion within the family and the family's social network. Distrust, self-interest and the over-supply of information within market societies are a heady and unstable combination. This may be a paradox of reflexive modernisation; on the one hand the idea that information is related to control, and, on the other, the idea that all information is potentially unreliable. Indeed, Douglas (1992, p. 32) suggests that 'knowledge is falling apart' and that 'no one offers us certainty'. In a way that parallels Parkin's analysis, Douglas suggests that the move from 'hierarchy' to 'market' or individualism removes certainty. Thus, another of the paradoxes of choice is that the market itself (applied to schools, as elsewhere) 'undermines the communicative conditions of intersubjective trust' (Berking, 1996, p. 199). Market systems produce a particular genre of communication which is not to be trusted – tradition is displaced by new modes of communication and new forms of 'knowledge' – promotion, advertising and 'aggressive accounting' (Ball, 2003b) for example. The result is, for middle-class parents, a frustration of reason, the lack of a perfect science of choice, of complete, accurate, robust information.

Within neo-liberal, risk regimes, especially in the creation of quasi-markets, the state takes on a role of information and advice provision (see Ball, 2000), for example, in education, through the publication of League Tables, Inspection reports etc. but again there is a paradox. Crook (1999, p. 180) argues that 'the provision of advice and information means, precisely the 'production' and communication of risks in greater numbers'. Somebody is always at the bottom of the League table or below average performance or have a poor Inspection Report. This is the substance of 'scaremongering' as Giddens (1998) calls it. However, it would also be irresponsible for middle class parents to simply leave the collection and provision of information to the state. Responsibility must be played out, taken seriously. 'To rely on the state to deal with the harmful effects of known, calculable and individually manageable risks appears feckless and culpable' (O'Malley, 1996, p. 202). This leads to a collecting, sifting, checking, and re-checking of information, and the use of perceptions, experiences, advertising and hearsay. In a sense, all information is considered but none, or almost none, is trusted.

> Yes, we went to open days in the private sector, we went to Overbury and Tideway open days...the year before we chose for Tim...we went to them the year we chose for Tim...we went round in the day and we also made an individual visit to Tideway...So yes, we must have gone round Tideway four or five times.
>
> (Mrs Mankell)

All information is considered, but not unthinkingly, there is a degree of scepticism about the information required from schools by the state. 'Expert systems' have to be dealt with skilfully. This information does not stand up on its own and has to be supplemented by the immediacy of the visit and direct questioning by the family themselves. There are themes from classical liberalism embedded here; the importance of self-reliance and the concomitant 'suspicion' (Collini, 1979) of the state.

> Yes, especially now that they have little choice but to include exam results and truancy rates and all the rest...I'm fully in favour of public information, so yes, I would say...you know, any organisation, and schools are stupid if they don't...again present themselves as best they can, so if anybody didn't take care of a prospectus I'd wonder what on earth they were up to. The little bits

of paper shoved in the back are usually what we poured over because that was exam results, details about how they split up the curriculum, list of staff and what qualifications they'd got...so it did matter, yes, and we did look very carefully at them...and that was often out of the prospectuses, that we got our kind of hit list of three or four key questions...that we wanted straight answers to...when we visited.

Again considerable time, effort and expense, and skill, are involved. These families have a certain 'distance from the world' (Bourdieu, 1994) that permits planning and reflection, relatively unencumbered by 'material constraints and temporal urgencies' and freed from the 'submission to necessity'.

Your own impressions are important but even they cannot always be trusted. As Crook (1999, p. 175) suggests hyper-reflexive ordering 'operates through networks rather than institutions... It is associated with individualism and the reflexive monitoring of the self'. Normativities and performativities are embedded in 'good parenting'. What the good parent does/is, taking responsibility and the vital contribution of social capital to decision-making are all embedded in social networks.

you visit one school after another, sometimes on consecutive evenings...you don't really get a chance to sit down and think about the school that you've seen, you're just bombarded with information, bits of paper to read, and it's not really long enough to sit down and really think about it, and also if you go and visit a school on one day, they could be having a bad day or you could be having a bad day and you don't really get a true picture of that school. So it was really friends who'd got older children, who felt that they really didn't have long enough to make that decision...plus if we wanted Alex to go privately he would have to be tutored, and it takes about two years really...for them...to get used to the idea of having to sit exams, doing things within a time limit, and they are just taught in a different way in the private sector, so if you really want to do that you've got to give your child a fair chance...so we thought...so we wouldn't feel rushed in our decision that's why we started looking two years ago.

When it comes down to it information may not be enough. Indeed as suggested earlier the more you know the more doubtful you can become. And in this arena of choice, for these parents mistakes, may be 'low probability' but 'high consequence'. Their child's whole future, as they see it, is at stake.

Spatialisation of risk and class – strategies and concerns are localised

Over and against the generalised sense of anxiety which besets the middle class project of social reproduction, it is also important to acknowledge that risks and the perception of risk vary. In education the risks of relative 'failure' or 'drop out' or learning fatigue vary, to some extent, according to the resources available to the family. Some families minimise risk by deploying their economic capital to buy educational advantages in the private system. This is a fairly sure and certain way of doing your best for your children in terms of ensuring a high probability of educational success and social advantage. More of which below. Also some families are able to use economic, social, cultural and emotional capitals at moments of crisis or key moments of transition to ensure access to privileged trajectories or to avert calamity (see Ball, 2003a, chapter 5). Interventions of various kinds are a key tactical device in managing the 'uncertainties' of schooling (see Vincent and Martin, 2002). There is indeed a growth of 'risk services' which can be bought-in to support or prepare the child in the quest for educational success – this is part of the commodification and privatisation of risk (Elliott, 2002). However, the risks, or perceptions of risk, with which we are concerned here, also vary according to where you are, that is, where you live, and who else lives there. Risk is spatialised (Butler and Robson, 2002).

School markets are different in different localities. They differ by virtue of who attends the schools and in terms of the organisation and history of education provision and in relation to local politics. The directing and socialising effects of local social networks also differ in relation to stability and integration. Classes and class fractions are realised in subtley different ways 'in interaction', in participation in the 'lifestyle' of the locality and its social networks. These are different 'spaces of subjectivity'. Class then takes on an emergent, localised quality. There are different engagements between class and locality. Particular classes and class segments are attracted to and are able to afford to live in these localities and within the localities class is realised differently; 'people make choices about where to live that are informed by their sense of "who they are", which, in turn, confers and identity on them' (Butler and Savage, 1995, p. 204). These differences give rise to different local class cultures, infrastructures and histories. There are different sedimentations of class which give rise to what Butler and Robson (2003, p. 21) call different 'narratives of the areas'. In turn these give rise to different 'situated risk logics' as Lupton (1999, p. 6) calls them. Mrs Connelly makes the point very nicely:

> I mean this area, which is St Vincent's [in Riverway], is a very odd area, cos what happens is...people move in...into it, and then they start to have children...they like the local schools, and then you find that where they might have moved out they tend to stay and really only move within the area, to stay within the state sector because they either find that they've got a large mortgage so they can't afford to pay the fees... for private education or they want to support state education and actually it's very easy if you live here. You know it's easy to really support state education because if you look at the results they're pretty good...and having said that...the type of parents that live in Riverway and Tidewell...they should be good. I mean I think everybody that I know have got a degree...so the chances are that our children will go on and at least do A levels, so I think if you're dealing with that type of parent, whether they go privately or state, the results should be good. And there's a lot of those type of people living round here.
>
> I didn't think it was necessary within this area to send her to a private school. The only reason I would even consider an independent school would be is I was living in an area where I felt the schools were appalling.
>
> (Mrs Dexter)

Here, the local schools are seen as a reflection of the locality and of the parents who send their children to them. Depending on circumstances, this can provide a sort of guarantee, an assurance of success, or alternatively it can generate a sense of heightened risk. The school is not represented as an independent variable with qualities of its own separate from its intake. This gives a general indication of the way in which perceptions of schools and perceptions of risk are constructed. The logic of this is that in another setting, as Mrs Dexter says, the evaluation of the state sector, as a whole or locally, might be very different. In this way, the choice between state and private schooling has to be understood as socially located in local class relations. But there are further aspects to the 'class' logic embedded here. For some parents there is a further dimension to choice of state schools. That is the messy tension between affording private education and valuing in principle state education. But for others, irrespective of location, private schooling is always preferable simply because it is not state schooling and because it offers inherent advantages to their child. In all this risk is not a stable category. Rather: 'Risk is a way – or rather a set of different ways of ordering reality' (Dean, 1999, p. 131).

The state sector as a risk

For some parents entrusting their children to the state sector is simply one risk that they are unwilling to take. Mrs Crichton explained, very simply, that she was 'nervous about the state sector' and the 'problem of taking a chance with your child and throwing them into the state sector'. For such parents private schools provide environments and opportunities and forms of provision which are simply not be available, as they see it, to their children from the state sector. Parents like Mrs Crichton regard entering their child in the state sector as putting their child and their child's future *at risk*. Such a position is both moral and strategic. 'the process of decision-making is regarded as a specialised technique for connecting belief, desires and actions' (Devine, 1997, p. 11). Private schools are 'class enclaves' (Teese, 2000) which offer 'long term protections from potential risk in an increasingly uncertain world' (Sedden, 2001, p. 139). As such 'the class project feels like good parenting' (Sedden, 2001, p. 139). Private schools offer a cultural milieu, 'a communicative order of self-recognition' (Teese, 1981, pp. 103–4), which is coherent and undiluted, and constitutes a 'protected enclave for class formation' (Sedden, 2001, p. 134). As Teese (2000) concludes, private schools are fortified sites within diverse school systems which represent class projects and 'renew middle class culture and collectivity in predictable ways across generations' (Sedden, 2001, p. 136). They also work to transform or reinvest economic into cultural capital. In effect these enclaves work to export risk of failure to state schools. They protect and reproduce classed 'communities of destiny'. In effect choosing the private sector, as a response to the risks of the state sector, can be seen as a different, older, form of risk management. That is, what Crook (1999, p. 182) calls 'neo-traditonalism' which can produce 'local solidarities, whether defined by taste, ethnicity, place or other markers that take their significance from a balance of inclusion ("us") and exclusion ("them")'. The private school provides a definitive form of boundary maintenance, of closure. It avoids the possibilities of social 'pollution' which can arise when order and boundaries are breached – indiscriminate mixing can threaten 'ontological insecurities' (Giddens, 1991). Private schooling limits the degree of social mixing to tolerable levels. It is a choice for exclusivity and also for advantage. It is, as Crook suggests, a basis of solidarity, in effect, of 'recognition'. In a sense, it is an enclave in which neo-liberal policies do not operate. The risks threatened by equality through choice can be avoided. And indeed, for some families the private sector has an obviousness to it. It is a non-choice. It is 'an alternative to constant "choice", anxiety and isolation' (Crook, p. 181) and mobilises 'versions of safety and certainty' (p. 182). Choice of private school avoids the 'chronic problematization of the signifier' (Lash, 1994, p. 157) that attends the question of what is a 'good' state school. The private schools are 'instead rooted in shared meanings and routine background practices' (Lash, 1994, p. 159). As Beck (1998, p. 10) puts it: 'Risk society begins where tradition ends...' – private schooling is a reinvention of tradition.

> Everyone I know either went to a grammar school or a private school...so it's something...comprehensive to me is a complete unknown quantity, so therefore it's alarming, only based on ignorance really. And also you do have to handle those...varying degrees, you are not in an environment where everybody wants to work.

Here Mrs Grafton is willing to take the risk of sending her child to state school but she does this reflexively and her language of 'panic' and 'alarm' gives some indication of the emotional underpinnings of the decision-making involved. Rational and affective responses are messily mixed. For Mrs Grafton the comprehensive school is an unknown, and she is anticipating difficulties in 'an environment' where not 'everyone wants to work'. The 'not everyone' is the 'other', those children who are not like mine. These are the risks of social mix, of boundary crossing, of going outside of grid and group (Pakulsi and Waters, 1996, p. 118). Indeed, Douglas suggests that risk works to maintain cultural boundaries (Lupton, 1999, p. 4). Risk is a response to the unknown, the dangerous. It can make us cautious, inward-looking. In the case of schooling, these are risks that have to be managed, 'handled' by the family. Again there is a clear sense of the perspective of reflexivity and planning that underlies the enterprise of education within the family. Indeed, there are glimpses here, and throughout these accounts of what Crook (1999, p. 175) calls 'a hyper-reflexive ordering'. This is particularly evident in the 'over response', the hyper-responsibility, of many middle-class families in their management of the problem of choice. They appear in their own accounts, and indeed may be concerned to want to appear, 'as responsible and calculating prudentialists' (O'Malley, 1996, p. 199).

Anxiety, emotion and class choosing

Obviously, we see various capitals intertwined here. There is an emotional as well as social and material expenditure involved in choice-making. While I do not want to overplay the emotional and psychological aspects of the market behaviour of parents and students, there are constant worries about getting things wrong, about failing the child, about mistaking priorities, about not finding the perfect school or right university; 'the extent of parents' ethical and social responsibility today...is historically unprecedented...The contemporary family is under a pressure to educate' (Beck-Gersheim, 1996, p. 143). The other side of all this is various forms of guilt. Both a personal guilt about letting the child down or in some cases social guilt about choosing private schooling in preference to the state sector (see Ball, 2003c). As one parent put it simply, you make 'judgements about yourself' (Mrs Cornwell).

Again, concerns both about getting it right and doing the right thing are engendered and reinforced within social networks. Indeed, as market theorists, like Hayek, make clear, markets, given their very different 'institutional conditions' (Hindess, 1987), are typically messy places, but also places that rely heavily on appropriate traditions and morality to work 'properly'. Parents, in part, become middle-class moral subjects by learning and acquiring behaviours and attitudes from others in their class setting. In this anxiety can be contagious but panic is offset by deliberation, emotion by rationality: 'we dont just make judgements, we worry, sometimes agonise, about them...' (Kymlicka, 1989, p. 11).

> I did it with my husband... Allan [son] knew that we were looking at schools, because what happens is, in September and October and November, the school is abuzz with manic parents... and that filters right down... we just said we're going to have a look just to see so that when the time comes for you... we don't feel panicked and rushed.
>
> (Mrs Cornwell)

Emotions are also in play in parents' responses to schools. Both negative responses, such as aversion, and positive, such as recognition. This is part of the lived reality of class, its emotional reality, what Reay (1999, p. 90) calls 'the emotive intimacies of class'. Those 'gut feelings' that are a 'primitive' form of class awareness, an identification of and with 'people like us' – 'the taken-for-granted understandings they bring to their relationships with others' (Reay, 1997, p. 226). The sense, as Bourdieu puts it, of being like 'a fish in water'. Such responses are outside the rational, not irrational, but irreducible to a simple calculability.

Futurity

Choice has a history within families and also, and crucially, it has a future. Choice is about getting from the present to a particular kind of class and social location in the future. It is about prediction, imagination and assurance. This is why control is so important and why also risk is ever present. Planning and anxiety go hand-in-hand (Giddens, 1991). The future is now 'more absorbing' but also 'at the same time more opaque' (Giddens, 1998, p. 28). Middle-class ontologies are founded upon incompleteness, they are about becoming, about the developmental self, about making something of yourself, realising yourself, realising your potential. This is an essential feature of a liberal identity – the unfinished self. These parents envisage certain sorts of futures for their children of both a worldly sort and of the person, of character. They see themselves as having the responsibility to make particular futures possible or available through their actions and planning in the here and now. These are possibilities that cannot be taken for granted, but they are 'worth striving for' (Lewis and Maude, 1950, p. 245). Individualism must be tempered by hard work and 'the productive use of time' (Allatt, 1993, p. 153). The future has to be invested in and the future has to be actively 'joined up' to the present. It is important to know what you want to be.[3] Lewis and Maude (1950, p. 288) suggest that the English middle class 'are what they are... because of what they wanted to be'. A good number of the parents are able to say what their child, age 11, wants to be.

> She was crying, saying 'well mummy I dont know what I want to do', but we have actually consciously talked to her about the idea that, if you want to be... let's say... purely for example, a doctor, you've got to spend alot of years in college and training and it takes this long... so we've actually talked to her about it... just so she realises what she's letting herself in for... sometimes it worries her a bit because she's got friends who say 'I want to be this'.
>
> (Mr Pelecanos)

In particular, these parents envisage their choices at 11 for their child as a precursor to, a step towards, their children's entry into Higher Education (HE). These parents work hard to naturalise HE as an obvious future route for their offspring. They are in many cases envisaging their child's educational trajectory in order to position them advantageously in relation to HE entry.

> ours both are above average, not geniuses but both above average... You therefore want to make sure you're going to be able to give them a good education that will allow them to go on and do higher education...
>
> (Mrs Mankell)

> Yes, now definitely... we really really hope that they will stay on beyond 16... somewhere. We really really want them to do Higher Ed... but not saying... it's got to be the route we took, or that it's got to be a particular route... yes.
>
> (Mr Symons)

However, within this, parents seem careful not to appear as 'pushy', a fine line needs to be trod between attentive support and overbearing pressure. The individuality of the child, their developmental self, has to be recognised, at least to some extent as having an autonomy, an unpredictability. But the riskiness of the future also has to be made clear.

> well after secondary school... we'd assume, and I'd be very disappointed if he didn't then go on to sixth form college, that is the sixth form college in Riverway, so that's what he'd do... after secondary school I hope... and then I hope after that, but you never know what might happen... that he'd go to university.
>
> (Mr Parker)

In effect, these parents are seeking to achieve some 'narrative coherence', linking and making consistent the lives of their children with their own. They are also reproducing through their children their tastes, distinctions and world view; although these are related to a set of 'flexible futures, a landscape of possibilities rather than discrete and rigid paths' (Beck-Gersheim, 1996, p. 153). Nonetheless, there are some very clear and fixed markers or way stations on those paths – like HE. Again, we should not over-estimate the newness of this, after all the middle class have always been denoted by an orientation to the future. It is the increased ubiquity and sophistication, and also its technicisation, that is remarkable; '... the pressure of planning and expectation on parents is not only growing quantitatively, but also assuming qualitatively new forms' (Beck-Gersheim, 1996, p. 139). Planning is starting earlier and involves, for some families, the mobilisation or 'buying in' a sophisticated set of preparatory experiences, and guidance, as well as making the best possible use of state support and facilities. All is best represented perhaps in what O'Malley (1996, p. 199) calls 'prudentialism'. This is deeply embedded in the middle-class habitus inflecting perceptions, appreciations and actions in a particular way – the perception of risk and its management. This sense of risk, or of social ordering, is productive, it makes certain things possible. This is constantly reinforced by the state's emphasis of the responsibilities of parenthood, and particularly motherhood (see Vincent 2000, chapter 2).[4] Again, in its role of providing information for parents on school performance, the state encourages them to act as rational and calculative choosers, to make the best choices in the interests of their family, and their future. Within such a regime, the prudent subject will invest carefully in their family's future (O'Malley, 1996, p. 201). Such investments require resources, skills and capitals that are unevenly distributed across the population but with which the middle classes are particularly well endowed. The education market with all its risks is well accommodated to the dispositions and interests of the middle class. Their assiduous engagement with choice, their use of their capitals, their particular sense of responsibility, all contribute to their social reproduction and the assurance of their social advantages.

Notes

1   This is a revised and restructured version of a chapter from Ball (2003a).
2   The families upon which the paper is based all 'fall within what Goldthorpe (2000) calls the "service class" '; possessors of 'delegated authority' and 'specialised knowledges'. The 'sample' is draw from four research studies of educational and child care choice (see Ball, 2003a) for details.
3   There is a tension here between 'becoming' and 'wanting' – the source of a great deal of contemporary fiction.
4   Or as Walkerdine *et al.* (2001, p. 175) starkly put it 'the bourgeois subject is feminine'.

References

Allatt, P. (1993). Becoming Privileged. In I. Bates and G. Riseborough (eds) *Youth and Inequality*. Buckingham, Open University Press.
Ball, S. J. (2000). Performativities and Fabrications in the Education Economy: Towards the Performative Society. *Australian Educational Researcher* 27(2): 1–24.
Ball, S. J. (2003a). *Class Strategies and the Education Market: The Middle Class and Social Advantage*. London, RoutledgeFalmer.
Ball, S. J. (2003b). Education for Profit and Standards in Education: The Ethical Role of Markets and the Private Sector in State Systems. In J. Oelkers and E. Berner (eds) *Democracy, Education and Market*. Zurich, Lang.
Ball, S. J. (2003c). Social Justice in the Head: Are We All Libertarians Now? In C. Vincent (ed.) *Social Justice, Identity and Education*. London, RoutledgeFalmer.
Beck, U. (1992). *Risk Society: Towards a New Modernity*. Newbury Park, CA, Sage.
Beck, U. (1997). *The Reinvention of Politics*. Cambridge, Polity Press.
Beck, U. (1998) Politics of Risk Society. In J. Franklin (ed.) *The Politics of Risk Society*. Cambridge, Polity Press.
Beck-Gernsheim, E. (1996). Life as a Planning Project. In C. Lash, B. Szersynski and B. Wynne (eds) *Risk, Environment and Modernity*. London, Sage.
Berking, H. (1996). Solidary Individualism: The Moral Impact of Cultural Modernisation in Late Modernity. In C. Lash, B. Szersynski and B. Wynne (eds) *Risk, Environment and Modernity: Towards a New Ecology*. London, Sage.
Bourdieu, P. (1986). Forms of Capital. In J. Richardson (ed.) *Handbook of Theory and Research for the Sociology of Education*. New York, Greenwood Press.
Butler, T. and G. Robson (2002). Social Capital, Gentrification and Neighbourhood Change in London: A Comparison of Three South London Neighbourhoods. *Urban Studies* 38: 2145–62.
Butler, T. and G. Robson (2003). Plotting the Middle Classes in London: Gentrification and Circuits of Eduation in London. *Housing Studies* 18(1): 5–28.
Butler, T. and M. Savage (eds) (1995). *Social Change and the Middle Classes*. London, UCL Press.
Collini, S. (1979). *Liberalism and Sociology: L. T. Hobhouse and Political Argument in England 1880–1914*. Cambridge, Cambridge University Press.
Crook, S. (1999). Ordering Risks. In D. Lupton. (ed.) *Risk and Sociocultural Theory: New Directions and Perspectives*. Cambridge, Cambridge University Press.

Dean, M. (1999). Risk, Calculable and Incalculable. In D. Lupton. (ed.) *Risk and Sociocultural Theory: New Directions and Perspectives*. Cambridge, Cambridge University Press.

Devine, F. (1997). *Privilege, Power and the Reproduction of Advantage*. British Sociological Association Annual Conference, University of York, 7–10 April.

Douglas, M. (1992). *Risk and Blame: Essays in Cultural Theory*. London, Routledge.

Ehrenreich, B. (1989). *Fear of Failing: The Inner life of the Middle Class*. New York, Pantheon.

Elliott, A. (2002). Beck's Sociology of Risk: A Critical Assessment, *Sociology* 36(2): 293–315.

Giddens, A. (1991). *Modernity and Self-Identity*. Cambridge, Polity.

Giddens, A. (1998). Risk Society: The Context of British Politics. In J. Franklin (ed.) *The Politics of Risk Society*. Cambridge, Polity Press.

Halsey, A. H. (1995). *Change in British Society (4th edition)*. Oxford, Oxford University Press.

Hindess, B. (1987). *Freedom, Equality and the Market: Arguments on Social Policy*. London, Tavistock.

Kemshal, H. (1992). *Risk, Social Policy and Welfare*. Buckingham, Open University Press.

Kymlicka, W. (1989). *Liberalism, Community and Culture*. Oxford, Clarendon Press.

Lash, S. (1994). Reflexivity and its Doubles. In U. Beck, T. Giddens and S. Lash (eds) *Reflexive Modernization: Politics, Tradition and Aesthetics in the Modern Social Order*. Cambridge, Polity Press.

Lewis, R. and A. Maude (1950). *The English Middle Classes*. London, Phoenix House.

Lupton, D., (ed.) (1999). *Risk and Sociocultural Theory: New Directions and Perspectives*. Cambridge, Cambridge University Press.

O'Malley, P. (1996). Risk and Responsibility. In A. Barry, T. Osborne and N. Rose (eds) *Foucault and Political Reason: Liberalism, Neo-liberalism and Rationalities of Government*. London, UCL Press.

Pakulski, J. and M. Waters (1996). *The Death of Class*. London, Sage.

Parkin, F. (1979). *Marxism and Class Theory: A Bourgeois Critique*. London, Tavistock.

Power, S., Edwards, T., Whitty G. and V. Wigfall (2002). *Education and the Middle Class*. London, RoutledgeFalmer.

Reay, D. (1997). The Double-bind of the 'Working-class' Feminist Academic: The Failure of Success or the Success of Failure? In C. Zmroczek and P. Mahony (eds) *Class Matters: Working Class Women's Perspectives of Social Class*. London, Taylor & Francis.

Reay, D. (1999). Class Acts: Educational Involvement and Psycho-sociological Class Processes. *Feminism and Psychology* 9(1): 89–106.

Rodger, J. (2000). *From a Welfare State to a Welfare Society: The Changing Context of Social Policy in a Postmodern Era*. Basingstoke, Macmillan.

Rose, N. (1996). Governing 'Advanced' Liberal Democracies. In A. Barry, T. Osborne and N. Rose (eds) *Foucault and Political Reason: Liberalism, Neo-liberalism and Rationalities of Government*. London, UCL Press.

Sedden, T. (2001). Revisiting Inequality and Education; a Reminder of Class; a Retrieval of Politics; a Rethinking of Governance. *Melbourne Studies in Education* 42(2): 131–44.

Tait, E. J. (1992). Proactive and Reactive Approaches to Risk Regulation: The Case of Biotechnology. *Futures* 24, 219–31.

Teese, R. (2000). *Academic Success and Social Power: Examinations and Inequality*. Melbourne, Melbourne University Press.

Vincent, C. (2000). *Including parents? Education, Citizenship and Parental Agency*. Buckingham, Open University Press.

Vincent, C. and J. Martin (2002). Class, Culture and Agency. *Discourse* 23(1): 109–28.

EPILOGUE

Much remains to be done and I continue to work within the three fields outlined in the papers above; the development of an 'effective policy analysis', an analysis of policy events, of the relational changes which underpin them; the application of such an analysis to education policy and specifically to the 'privatisation' of public education and its effects on social justice and on what it means to be educated; and continuing attempts to understand the particular role of social class in all this – and the different educational ontologies of upper, middle- and working-class families.

BIBLIOGRAPHY

Books

Authored

(1981) Ball, S. J. *Beachside Comprehensive: A Case Study of Secondary Schooling*, Cambridge, Cambridge University Press.

(1984) Ball, S. J. '*Participant observation*', *international encyclopedia of education: research and studies*, Oxford, Pergamon Press.

(1986) Ball, S. J. *Sociology in Focus – Education*, London, Longmans.

(1987) Ball, S. J. *The Micro-Politics of the School: Towards a Theory of School Organization, London*, Methuen. London, Routledge (SCSE annual book prize 'Best book on education').

(1990) Ball, S. J. *Politics and Policymaking in Education: Explorations in Policy Sociology*, London, Routledge (republished in Chinese 2003 East China Normal University Press).

(1992) Bowe, R. and Ball, S. J. with Gold, A. *Reforming Education and Changing Schools: Case Studies in Policy Sociology*, London, Routledge.

(1994) Ball, S. J. *Education Reform: A Critical and Post-Structural Approach*, Buckingham, Open University Press (republished in Chinese 2003 East China Normal University Press).

(1995) Gewirtz, S., Ball, S. J. and Bowe, R. *Markets Choice and Equity in Education*, Buckingham, Open University Press.

(1996) Radnor, H. and Ball, S. J. *Local Education Authorities: Accountability and Control*, Stoke-on-Trent, Trentham Books.

(2000) Ball, S. J., Maguire, M. M. and Macrae, S. *Choices, Pathways and Transitions Post-16: New Youth, New Economies in the Global City*, London, RoutledgeFalmer.

(2003) Ball, S. J. *Class Strategies and the Education Market: The Middle Class and Social Advantage*, London, RoutledgeFalmer.

Edited

(1984) Ball S. J. (ed.) *Comprehensive Schooling: A Reader*, Lewes, Falmer Press.

(1984) Goodson, I. F. and Ball, S. J. (eds) *Defining the Curriculum: Histories and Ethnographies*, Lewes, Falmer Press.

(1985) Ball, S. J. and Goodson, I. F. (eds) *Teachers' Lives and Careers*, Lewes, Falmer Press.

(1988) Green, T. and Ball, S. J. (eds) *Inequality and Progress in Comprehensive Education: A Reconsideration for the 1980s*, London, Routledge.

(1989) Ball, S. J. and Larsson, S. (eds) *The Struggle for Democratic Education: Equality and Participation in Sweden*, Lewes, Falmer Press.

(1990) Ball, S. J. (ed.) *Foucault and Education*, London, Routledge (also published in Spanish; (1993) *Foucault y la educacion*, Madrid Paideia/Morata; Polish (1994) *Foucault i Edukacja*, Kracow, Impuls. and Japanese (1999)).

(2000) Ball, S. J. (ed.) *Sociology of Education: Major Themes. Vol.1 Theories and Methods; Vol. 2 Inequalities and Oppressions; Vol. 3 Institutions and Processes; Vol. 4 Politics and Policies*, London, RoutledgeFalmer.
(2003) Ball, S. J., Fischman, G. and Gvirtz, S. (eds) *Crisis and Hope: The Educational Hopscotch of Latin America*, New York, Routledge.
(2003) Tamboukou, M. and Ball, S. J. (eds) *Dangerous Encounters: Genealogy and Ethnography*, New York, Peter Lang.
(2004) Ball, S. J. (ed.) *The RoutledgeFalmer Reader in Sociology of Education*, London, RoutledgeFalmer.

Published articles in refereed journals

(1980) Ball, S. J. 'Mixed-ability teaching: the worksheet method', *British Journal of Educational Technology*, January–February, 22(1).
(1981) Ball, S. J. 'Continuity and conflict in comprehensive schooling', *New Universities Quarterly*, 35(2).
(1981) Ball, S. J. 'Doing teaching: a phenomenological analysis of teacher–pupil relations', *Reflections: Essays in Phenomenology*, 2(1), 54–69.
(1981) Ball, S. J. 'The sociology of education in developing societies: a review essay', *British Journal of Sociology of Education*, 2(3), 301–13.
(1982) Ball, S. J. 'A reply to torode', *Reflections: Essays in Phenomenology*, 3(1), 30–3.
(1982) Ball, S. J. 'Competition and conflict in the teaching of English: a socio-historical analysis', *Journal of Curriculum Studies*, 13(4).
(1983) Ball, S. J. 'Imperialism, social control and the colonial curriculum in Africa', *Journal of Curriculum Studies*, 15(3), 237–63.
(1987) Ball, S. J. 'Großbrittanien: Im Konflikt von Erzienhungs-knozepten', Der Deutschunterricht, 39(2), 45–52.
(1988) Ball, S. J. 'Staff relations during the teachers' industrial action: context, conflict and proletarianisation', *British Journal of Sociology of Education*, 9(3), 289–306.
(1990) Ball, S. J. 'Markets, inequality and urban schooling', *Urban Review*, 22(2), 85–100.
(1990) Ball, S. J. 'Putting politics back into micropolitics: a response to R.G. Townsend, *Curriculum Inquiry*, 20(2), 225–9.
(1990) Ball, S. J. 'Self doubt and soft data: social and technical trajectories in ethnographic fieldwork', in Allen, J. B. and Goetz, J. (eds), *Qualitative Research in Education: Teaching and Learning Qualitative Traditions*, College of Education, University of Georgia. Also in *International Journal of Qualitative Studies in Education*, 3(2), 157–72, and reprinted in Hammersley, M. (ed.) (1993) *Educational Research Vol. 1*, London, Paul Chapman.
(1990) Ball, S. J. 'The sociological implications of the education reform act; review essay', *British Journal of Sociology of Education*, 11(4), 485–91.
(1991) Ball, S. J. and Bowe, R. ' "When the garment gapes": policy and ethnography as process and practice', *Habitus*, 1(1), 55–64.
(1992) Ball, S. J. 'Lar Restauration Neo-Liberale et le systeme d'enseignement en Grand-Bretagne', *Sociales Critiques*, 3–4, 153–62.
(1992) Ball, S. J. and Bowe, R. 'Education, markets and professionalism: some reflections on recent policy developments in England and Wales', *Melbourne Studies in Education*, 1992, 56–62.
(1992) Ball, S. J. and Bowe, R. 'Subject departments and the "implementation" of National Curriculum Policy', *Journal of Curriculum Studies*, 24(2), 97–115.
(1993) Ball, S. J. 'Education, majorism and the curriculum of the dead', *Curriculum Studies*, 1(2), 195–214 (also published in *Socjologia wychowania* X11, Acta Universitatis Nicolai Copernici, Torun 1994).
(1993) Ball, S. J. 'Education markets, choice and social class: the market as a class strategy in the UK and US', *British Journal of Sociology of Education*, 14(1), 3–19.
(1993) Ball, S. J. 'Education policy, power relations and teachers' work', *British Journal of Educational Studies*, 41(2), 106–21.
(1993) Ball S. J. 'What is policy? Texts, trajectories and toolboxes', *Discourse*, 13(2), 10–17.

(1993) Gewirtz, S., Ball, S. J. and Bowe, R. 'Values and ethics in the education market place: the case of Northwark Park', *International Studies in Sociology of Education*, 3(2), 233–54.

(1994) Ball, S. J. 'Visions, costs and commonsense: whatever happened to the National Commission on Education?', *The Political Quarterly*, 65(3), 337–40.

(1994) Ball, S. J. 'What is criticism? A continuing conversation? A rejoinder to Miriam Henry', *Discourse*, 14(2) 108–10.

(1994) Ball, S. J., Bowe, R. and Gewirtz, S. 'Competitive schooling: values, ethics and cultural engineering', *Journal of Curriculum and Supervision*, 9(4), 350–67.

(1994) Bowe, R., Ball, S. J. and Gewirtz, S. 'Captured by the discourse? Issues and concerns in researching parental choice', *British Journal of Sociology of Education*, 14(1), 63–79.

(1994) Bowe, R., Ball, S. J. and Gewirtz, S. 'Parental choice, consumption and social theory: the operation of micro-markets in education', *British Journal of Educational Studies*, 42(1), 38–52.

(1994) Cribb, A., Bignold, S. and Ball, S. J. 'Linking the parts: an exemplar of philosophical and practical issues in holistic nursing', *Journal of Advanced Nursing*, 20, 233–38.

(1994) Gewirtz, S., Ball, S. J. and Bowe, R. 'Parents, privilege and the education market-place', *Research Papers in Education*, 9(1), 3–30.

(1994) Maguire, M. and Ball, S. J. 'Discourses of education reform in the UK and USA and the work of teachers', *British Journal of In-Service Education*, 20(1), 5–16.

(1994) Maguire, M. and Ball, S. J. 'Researching politics and the politics of research: recent qualitative studies in the UK', *International Journal of Qualitative Studies in Education*, 7(3), 269–86.

(1995) Ball, S. J. 'Intellectuals or technicians? The urgent role of theory in educational studies', *British Journal of Educational Studies*, 43(3), 225–71.

(1995) Ball, S. J. 'Parents, schools and markets: the repositioning of youth in UK education', *Youth: Nordic Journal of Youth Research*, 3(3), 68–79.

(1995) Ball, S. J., Bowe, S. J. and Gewirtz, S. 'Circuits of schooling: a sociological exploration of parental choice of school in social class contexts', *Sociological Review*, 43(1), 52–78.

(1995) Batteson, C. and Ball, S. J. 'Autobiographies and interviews as means of "access" to elite policy making in education', *British Journal of Educational Studies*, 43(2), 201–16.

(1995) Bignold, S., Cribb, A. and Ball, S. J. 'Befriending the family: an exploration of a nurse-client relationship', *Health and Social Care in the Community*, 13(3), 173–80.

(1995) Herring, R., Wilson-Barnett, J. and Ball, S. J. 'The role of Macmillan nurse tutors: an interview study with post-holders', *Journal of Palliative Nursing*, 1(4), 217–25.

(1996) Ball, S. J. and Gewirtz, S. 'Education markets, school competition and parental choice in the UK: a report of research findings', *International Journal of Educational Reform*, 5(2), 152–58.

(1996) Ball, S. J., Bowe, R. and Gewirtz, S. 'School choice, social class and distinction: the realisation of social advantage in education', *Journal of Education Policy*, 11(3), 89–113.

(1996) Bowe, R., Ball, S. J. and Gewirtz, S. 'La Eleccion de los padres, el consumo y teoria social: functionamiento do los micromercados en la educacion', *Proquesta Educativa*, 14 August. Flasco/Ediciones Novedades Educativas.

(1997) Ball, S. J. 'Good school/bad school: paradox and fabrication', *British Journal of Sociology of Education*, 18(3), 317–36.

(1997) Ball S. J. 'On the cusp: parents choosing between state and private schools', *International Journal of Inclusive Education*, 1(1), 1–17.

(1997) Ball, S. J. 'Policy sociology and critical social research: a personal review of recent education policy and policy research', *British Education Research Journal*, 23(3), 257–74.

(1997) Ball, S. J. and Gewirtz, S. 'Girls and the education market', *Gender and Education*, 9(2), 207–22.

(1997) Ball, S. J. and Gewirtz, S. 'Is research possible? Rejoinder to Tooley's "On school choice and social class"', *British Journal of Sociology of Education*, 18(4), 575–86.

(1997) Macrae, S., Maguire, M. and Ball, S. J. 'Whose learning society? A tentative deconstruction', *Journal of Education Policy*, 12(6), 499–510.

(1997) Reay, D. and Ball, S. J. 'Spoilt for choice: the working class and education markets', *Oxford Review of Education*, 23(1), 89–101.

(1997) Radnor, H., Ball, S. J. and Vincent, C. 'Whither democratic accountability? An investigation into teachers' perspectives on accountability in the 1990s with reference to their relationships with their LEAs and governors', *Research Papers in Education*, 12(2), 205–22.

(1998) Ball, S. J. 'Big policies/small world: an introduction to international perspectives on education policy', *Comparative Education*, 34(2), 119–30.

(1998) Ball, S. J. 'Introduction: international perspectives on education policy' – Guest editor – *Comparative Education*, 34(2), 117–18.

(1998) Ball, S. J. and Bowe, R. 'El curriculum nacional y su "puesta en practica": El papel de los departamentos de materias o signatures', *Revista de Estudios del Curriculum*, 1(2), 105–31.

(1998) Ball, S. J. and van Zanten, A. 'Logiques de marche et ethiques contexualisees dans les systemes scolaires francais et britannique', *Education et Societes*, 1(1), 47–72.

(1998) Ball, S. J. and Vincent, C. ' "I heard it on the grapevine": "hot" knowledge and school choice', *British Journal of Sociology of Education*, 19(3), 377–400.

(1998) Ball, S. J., Maguire, M. M. and Macrae, S. 'Race, space and the further education marketplace', *Race, Ethnicity and Education*, 1(2), 171–90.

(1998) Radnor, H., Ball, S. J. and Vincent, C. 'Local educational governance, accountability and democracy in the United Kingdom', *Education Policy*, 12(1–2), 124–37.

(1998) Reay, D. and Ball, S. J. ' "Making their minds up": family dynamics of school choice', *British Educational Research Journal*, 24(4), 431–48.

(1998) Reay, D., Bignold, S., Ball, S. J. and Cribb, A. ' "He just had a different way of showing it": gender dynamics in families coping with childhood cancer', *Journal of Gender Studies*, 7(1), 39–52.

(1999) Ball, S. J. 'Labour, learning and the economy: a "policy sociology" perspective', *Cambridge Journal of Education*, 29(2), 195–206.

(1999) Ball, S. J. 'The market form in United Kingdon education: information, values and political control', *La Revue Tocqueville*, 10(2), 89–100.

(1999) Ball, S. J., Macrae, S. and Maguire, M. 'Young lives, diverse choices and imagine futures in an education and training market', *International Journal of Inclusive Education*, 3(3), 195–224.

(1999) Maguire, M. M., Ball, S. J. and Macrae, S. 'Promotion, persuasion and class-taste: marketing (in) the UK post-compulsory sector', *British Journal of Sociology of Education*, 20(3), 291–308.

(2000) Ball, S. J. 'Performativities and fabrications in the education economy: towards the performative society', *Australian Educational Researcher*, 27(2), 1–24.

(2000) Ball, S. J., Maguire, M. and Macrae, S. 'Space, work and the "New Urban Economies" ', *Journal of Youth Studies*, 3(3), 279–300.

(2000) Reay, D. and Ball, S. J. 'Essentials of female management: women's ways of working in the education marketplace?', *Educational Management and Administration*, 28(2), 145–58.

(2001) Ball S. J. 'New youth, New economies, new inequalities', *Studies on Education and Society*, 11, 11–19.

(2001) Ball, S. J., Davies, J., David, M. and Reay, D. 'Decisions, differenciations et distinctions: vers une sociologie du choix des etudes superieures', *Revue francaise de pedagogie*, 136, Juillet–Septembre.

(2001) Maguire, M., Ball, S. J. and Macrae, S. ' "In all our interests": internal marketing at Northwark Park School', *British Journal of Sociology of Education*, 22(1), 35–50.

(2001) Reay, D., David, M. and Ball, S. J. 'Making a difference: institutional habituses and higher education choice', *Sociological Research Online*, 5(4), http//www.socresonline.org.uk/5/4.reay.html

(2001) Reay, D., Davies, J., David, M. and Ball, S. J. 'Choice of degree or degrees of choice?: class, race and the higher education choice process', *Sociology*, 35(4), 855–74.

(2001) Vincent, C. and Ball, S. J. 'A market in love? Choosing pre-school childcare', *British Educational Research Journal*, 27(5), 633–51.

(2002) Ball, S. J. 'School- based management: new culture and new subjectivity', *da invetigacao as practicas: estudos de natureza educacional*, 3(1), 59–76.

(2002) Ball, S. J. 'Textos, discursos y trayectorias de la politica', *Paginas*, 2(2–3), 19–33.

(2002) Ball, S. J., Davies, J., David, M. and Reay, D. ' "Classification" and "jugement": social class and the "cognitive structure" of choice of higher education', *British Journal of Sociology of Education*, 23(1), 51–72.

(2002) Ball, S. J., Reay, D. and David, M. ' "Ethnic Choosing": minority ethnic students and higher education choice', *Race Ethnicity and Education*, 5(4), 333–57.

(2002) Reay, D., Ball, S. J. and David, M. ' "Its taken me a long time but I'll get there in the end": mature students on access courses and higher education choice', *British Educational Research Journal*, 28(1), 5–20.

(2002) Tamboukou, M. and Ball, S. J. 'Nomadic subjects: young black women in Britain', *Discourse*, 23(3), 267–84.

(2003) Ball, S. J. 'The risks of social reproduction: the middle class and education markets', *London Review of Education*, 1(3), 163–75.

(2003) Ball, S. J. 'The teacher's soul and the terrors of performativity', *Journal of Education Policy*, 18(2), 215–28.

(2003) David, M., Ball, S. J., Davies, J. and Reay, D. 'Gender issues in parental involvement in student choices of higher education', *Gender and Education*, 15(1), 21–37.

(2004) Ball, S. J. 'Suorituskeskeisyys ja yksityistaminen jalkihiyvinvointivaltion koulutus-politiikassa', *The Finnish Journal of Education*, 35(1), 6–20.

(2004) Ball, S. J., Vincent, C., Kemp, S. and Peitakienen, S. 'Middle class fractions, childcare and the "relational" and "normative" aspects of class practices', *The Sociological Reveiw*, 54(4), 478–502.

(2004) Vincent, C., Ball, S. J. and Kemp, S. 'The social geography of childcare: making up a middle class child', *British Journal of Sociology of Education*, 25(2), 229–44.

Contributions to books

(1980) Ball, S. J. 'Initial encounters and the process of establishment', in Woods, P. E. (ed.), *Pupil Strategies*, London, Croom Helm.

(1980) Ball, S. J. and Lacey, C. 'Subject disciplines as the opportunity for group action: a measured critique of subject sub-cultures', in Woods, P. E. (ed.), *Teacher Strategies*, London, Croom Helm.

(1981) Ball, S. J. 'The teaching nexus: a case of mixed-ability', in Barton, L. and Walker, S. (eds), *School, Teachers and Teaching*, Lewes, Falmer Press.

(1982) Ball, S. J. 'The application and verification of participant observation case study', in Deakin University, *Case Study Methods 26–33, Perspectives on Case Study 4: Ethnography*, Deakin University Press.

(1982) Ball, S. J. 'Participant observation as a research method', in Deakin University, *Case Study Method: Readings 34–44, The Conduct of Fieldwork*, Deakin University Press.

(1983) Ball, S. J. 'Case study method: some notes and problems', in Hammersley, M. (ed.), *The Ethnography of Schooling*, Driffield, Nafferton Press.

(1983) Ball, S. J. 'A subject of privilege: English and the school curriculum 1906–35', in Hammersley, M. and Hargreaves, A. (eds), *Curriculum Practice: Sociological Perspectives*, Lewes, Falmer Press.

(1984) Ball, S. J. 'Beachside reconsidered: reflections on a methodological apprenticeship', in Burgess, R. (ed.), *The Research Process in Educational Settings: Ten Case Studies*, Lewes, Falmer Press.

(1984) Ball, S. J. 'Becoming a comprehensive: facing up to falling rolls', in Burgess, R. (ed.), *The Research Process in Educational Settings: Ten Case Studies*, Lewes, Falmer Press, pp. 227–46.

(1984) Ball, S. J. 'Comprehensives in crisis?', in Ball, S. J. (ed.), *Comprehensive Schooling*, Lewes, Falmer Press, pp. 1–26.

(1984) Ball, S. J. 'Conflict, panic and inertia: mother tongue teaching in England 1970–83', in Herrlitz, W. *et al.* (eds), *Mother Tongue Education in Europe, Studies in Mother Tongue Education1*, International Mother Tongue Education Network, National Institute for Curriculum Development, Enschede, Netherlands, pp. 160–93.

(1984) Ball, S. J. 'The making of a school subject: English for the English 1906–82,' in Goodson, I. F. (ed.), *Social Histories of the Secondary Curriculum: Subjects for Study*, Lewes, Falmer Press, pp. 53–88.

(1984) Ball, S. J., Hull, R., Skelton, M. and Tudor, R. 'The tyranny of the "devil's mill": time and task at school', in Delamont, S. (ed.), *Readings on Interaction in the Classroom*, London, Methuen.

(1985) Ball, S. J. 'Participant Observation with pupils', in Burgess, R. G. (ed.), *Strategies of Educational Research*, Lewes, Falmer Press, pp. 23–54.

(1985) Ball, S. J. 'School politics, teachers' careers and Educational change: a case of becoming a comprehensive school', in Barton, L. and Walker, S. (eds), *Education and Social Change*, Beckenham, Croom Helm, pp. 29–61.

(1985) Ball, S. J. and Goodson, I. F. 'Understanding teachers: concepts and contexts', in Ball, S. J. and Goodson, I. F. (eds), *Teachers' Lives and Careers*, Lewes, Falmer Press.

(1986) Ball, S. J. 'Relations, structures and conditions in curriculum change: a political history of English teaching', in Goodson, I. F. (ed.), *International Perspectives in Curriculum History*, Beckenham, Croom Helm.

(1986) Ball, S. J. 'The sociology of the school: streaming, mixed-ability and social class', in Rogers, R. (ed.), *Education and Social Class*, Lewes, Falmer Press.

(1987) Ball, S. J. 'English teaching, the state and forms of literacy', in Kroon, S. and Sturm, J. (eds), *Research on Mother-Tongue Education in an International Perspective*, Enschede, VALO-M.

(1988) Ball, S. J. 'A comprehensive school in a pluralist world – divisions and inequalities', in O'Keeffe, B. (ed.), *Building Walls or Building Bridges: Education for Tomorrow*, Lewes, Falmer Press.

(1988) Ball, S. J. 'Comprehensive schooling, effectiveness and control: an analysis of educational discourses', in Slee, R. (ed.), *Disruptive Behaviour and School Effectiveness*, Sydney, Macmillan.

(1988) Ball, S. J. 'Costing democracy: schooling, equality and democracy in Sweden', in Lauder, H. and Brown, P. (eds), *Education in Decline: Policies for Reconstruction*, Lewes, Falmer Press.

(1988) Stacey, M. and Ball, S. J. 'A portrait of twelve English lessons at Boundary School, England', prepared for the International Mother-Tongue Education Conference, University of Antwerp.

(1989) Ball, S. J., Kenny, A. and Gardiner, D. 'Literacy and democracy: policies and politics for the teaching of english', in Goodson, I. and Medway, P. (eds), *Bringing English to Order*, Lewes, Falmer Press.

(1989) Radnor, H., Ball, S. J. and Burrell, D. 'The certificate of pre-vocational education: an analysis of curriculum conflict in policy and practice', in Hargreaves, A. and Reynolds, D. (eds), *Policy and Practice in Contemporary State Education*, Lewes, Falmer Press.

(1990) Ball, S. J. 'Introducing Monsieur Foucault', in Ball, S. J. (ed.), *Foucault and Education*, London, Routledge.

(1990) Ball, S. J. 'Management as morale technology', in Ball, S. J. (ed.) *Foucault and Education*, London, Routledge.

(1990) Ball, S. J. 'Power, conflict, micropolitics and all that!', in Walford, G. (ed.), *Doing the Sociology of Education Vol. 2*, London, Routledge.

(1991) Ball, S. J. and Bowe, R. 'The micropolitics of radical change: budgets, management and control in british schools', in Blase, J. (ed.), *The Politics of Life in Schools*, Newbury Park, CA, Sage.

(1991) Bowe, R. and Ball, S. J. 'Doing what should come naturally: an exploration of LMS in one secondary school', in Wallace, G. (ed.), *Local Management of Schools: Policy and Practice*, Clevedon, Multi-Lingual Matters.

(1993) Ball, S. J. 'Culture, cost and control: self management and entreprenuerial schooling in England and Wales, in Smyth, J. (ed.), *A Socially Critical View of the Self-Managing School*, London, Falmer.

(1993) Ball, S. J. 'Leadership, governance and policy: England and Wales', in Crump, S. (ed.) *School-Centred Leadership*, Melbourne, Nelson, pp. 225–36.

(1993) Ball, S. J. 'The micropolitics of schools. in International Encyclopedia of Education (2nd edn) Husen, T. and Postlethwaite, N. (eds), Oxford, Pergamon.

(1993) Ball, S. J. 'Participant observation', in Husen, T. and Postlethwaite, N. (eds), *International Encyclopedia of Education* (2nd edn), Oxford, Pergamon.

(1993) Gold, A., Bowe, R. and Ball, S. J. 'Special educational needs in a new context', in Slee, R. (ed.), *The Politics of Integration*, London, Falmer Press.

(1994) Ball, S. J. 'Market forces and parental choice', in Tomlinson, S. (ed.), *Educational Reform and its Consequences*, London, IPPR/Rivers Oram Press.

(1994) Ball, S. J. 'Political interviews and the politics of interviewing', in Walford, G. (ed.), *Researching the Powerful in Education*, London, UCL Press.

(1994) Ball, S. J. 'Researching inside the state: issues in the interpretation of elite interviews', in Halpin, D. and Troyna, B. (eds), *Researching Educational Policy: Ethical and Methodological Issues*, London, Falmer.

(1995) Ball, S. J. 'Culture, crisis and morality: the struggle over the National Curriculum', in Atkinson, P., Davies, B. and Delamont, S. (eds), *Discourse and Reproduction: Essays in Honor of Basil Bernstein*, Cresskill, NJ, Hampton Press.

(1995) Ball, S. J. 'Mercados Educacionais, Escolha e Classe social:o mercado como uma estrategia de classe', in Gentili, P. (ed.), *Pedagogia da exclusao*, Petropolis, Voces, Brasil, (2nd edn 1998).

(1995) Ball, S. J. and Lacey, C. 'Revisiting subject disciplines as the opportunity for group action: a measured critique of subject sub-cultures', in Siskin, S. S. and Little, J. W. (eds), *The Subjects in Question*, New York, Teachers College Press.

(1995) Bignold, S., Cribb, A. and Ball, S. J. 'Creating a seamless web of care', in Richardson, A. and Wilson-Barnett, J. (eds), *Nursing Research in Cancer Care*, London, Scutari.

(1995) Bowe, R., Ball, S. J. and Gewirtz, S. 'Market forces, inequality and the city', in Jones, H. and Lansley, J. (eds), *Social Policy and the City*, Aldershot, Avebury Press.

(1995) Herring, R., Wilson-Barnett, J. and Ball, S. J. 'The two worlds of the Macmillan Nurse Tutor: contrasts and conflicts', in Richardson, A. and Wilson-Barnett, J. (eds), *Nursing Research in Cancer Care*, London, Scutari.

(1995) Jones, D. M. and Ball, S. J. 'Michel Foucault and the discourse of education', in McLaren, P. and Giarelli, J. (eds), *Critical Theory and Educational Research*, Albany, NY, SUNY.

(1995) Maguire, M. and Ball, S. J. 'Teacher education and education policy in England', in Shimahara, N. and Holowinsky, I. (eds), *Teacher Education in Industrialized Nations*, New York: Garland Publishing.

(1996) Ball, S. J. 'Analysing British reform policy in the 1990s', in Haug, P. (ed.), *Pedogogiki i ei Reformtid*, Volda, Norges forskningsrad.

(1996) Ball, S. J., Bignold, S. and Cribb, A. 'Death and the disease: inside the culture of childhood cancer', in Howarth, G. and Jupp, P. C. (eds), *Contemporary Issues in Death, Dying and Disposal*, London, Macmillan.

(1997) Ball, S. J. 'Markets, equity and values in education', in Pring, R. and Walford, G. (eds), *Reaffirming the Comprehensive Ideal*, Brighton, Falmer.

(1997) Macrae, S., Maguire, M. and Ball, S. J. 'Competition, choice and hierarchy in a post-16 market', in Tomlinson, S. (ed.), *Education 14–19: Critical Perspectives*, London, Athlone Press.

(1998) Ball, S. J. 'Cidadania global, consumo e politica educacional', in L. Heron da Silva (ed.), *A Escola cidada no contexto de globalizacao*, Petropolis, Editora Vozes.

(1998) Ball, S. J. 'Educational studies, policy entrepreneurship and social theory', in Slee, R. and Weiner, G. with Tomlinson, S. (eds), *School Effectiveness for Whom?*, London, Falmer.

(1998) Ball, S. J. 'Education policy', in Ellison, N. and Pierson, C. (eds), *British Social Policy*, London, Macmillan.

(1998) Ball, S. J. 'Performativity and fragmentation in "Postmodern schooling"', in Carter, J. (ed.), *Postmodernity and the Fragmentation of Welfare*, London, Routledge.

(1999) Ball, S. J. 'Industrial training or new vocationalism? Structures and discourses', in Flude, M. and Sieminski, S. (eds), *Education, Training and the Future of Work II*, London, Routledge (reprinted from *Education Politics and Policymaking*).

(1999) Ball, S. J. 'School management. Myth: good management makes good schools', in O'Hagan, B. (ed.), *Modern Educational Myths: The Future of Democratic Comprehensive Education*, London, Kogan Page.

(1999) Ball, S. J., Macrae, S. and Maguire, M. M. 'Young lives at risk in the "Futures market": some policy concerns from ongoing research', in Coffield, F. (ed.), *Speaking Truth to Power*, Bristol, Policy Press.

(1999) Marshall, B. and Ball, S. J. 'Tales of fear and loathing: teachers' work and recent educational reform', in Hammersley, M. (ed.), *Researching School Experience: Ethnographic Studies of Teaching and Learning*, London, Falmer.

(2000) Ball, S. J. 'The sociology of education: a disputational account – general introduction', in Ball, S. J. (ed.), *Sociology of Education: Major Themes* (in 4 volumes), London, RoutledgeFalmer.

(2000) Ball, S. J., Maguire, M. M. and Macrae, S. 'Worlds apart – education markets in the post-16 sector of one urban locale 1995–98', in Coffield, F. (ed.), *Differing Visions of a Learning Society*, Bristol, Policy Press.

(2001) Ball, S. J. 'Globaalit Toimintaperiaatteet ja kansalliset politiikat eureooppalaisessa koulutuksessa', in Jauhiainen, A., Rinne, R. and Tahtinen, J. (eds), *Koulutuspolitiikka Suomessa: ja ylikansalliset*, Turku, Suomen Kasvatustietcellinen.

(2001) Ball, S. J. 'Performativities and fabrications in the education economy: toward the performative society', in Gleeson, D. and Husbands, C. (eds), *The Peforming School: Managing, Teaching and Learning in a Performance Culture*, London, RoutledgeFalmer.

(2001) Ball, S. J. 'Schulwahl und Schulqual in der Grobstabdt: Zur Politik des "Elternrechts" auf Schulwalh', in Achs, O., Gruber, K.-H., Tesar, E. and Weidinger W. (eds), *Urban Education: Bildung und Schulentwicklung in Grobstadten*, Wein, Obv&hpt.

(2001) Ball, S. J. and Vincent, C. 'New class relations in education', in Demaine, J. (ed.), *Sociology of Education Today*, London, Palgrave.

(2002) Ball, S. J. 'Grandes Politicas, Un mundo pequeno: Introduccion a une perspectiva internacional en las politicas educativas', in Naradowski, M., Nores, M. and Andrada, M. (eds), *Nuevas Tendencias en Politicas Educativas: Estado, mercado and escuela*, Buenos Aires, Granica.

(2002) Ball, S. J. 'The teachers' soul and the terrors of performativity', in *Proceedings from the Twenty-sixth Annual Conference of the Association for Teacher Education In Europe*, Stockholm, Stockholm Institute of Education Press, pp. 43–63.

(2003) Ball, S. J. 'Education for profit and standards in education: the ethical role of markets and the private sector in state systems', in Oelkers. J. (ed.), *Futures of Education II: Essays from an Interdisciplinary Symposium*, Bern, Peter Lang.

(2003) Ball, S. J. 'Market mixes, ethical re-tooling and consumer heroes: education markets in England', in J. Oelkers (ed.), *Economy, Public Education and Democracy*, Zurich, Peter Lang.

(2003) Ball, S. J. 'Social justice in the head: are we all libertarians now?', in Vincent, C. (ed.), *Social Justice, Identity and Education*, London, RoutledgeFalmer.

(2003) Fischman, G. E., Ball, S. J. and Gvirtz, S. 'Toward a neoliberal education? Tension and change in Latin America', in Ball, S. J., Fischmann, G. E. and Gvirtz, S. (eds), *Crisis and Hope: The Educational Hopscotch in Latin America*, New York, RoutledgeFalmer.

(2004) Ball, S. J. 'The sociology of education: a disputational account', in Ball, S. J. (ed.), *The Routledge Falmer Reader in Sociology of Education*, London, RoutledgeFalmer.

Other publications

(1980) Ball, S. J. 'Using worksheets: problems and possibilities', in Beavis, R. and Weatherley, C. (eds), Worksheets and School Learning, Scottish Council for Educational Technology, *Occasional Working paper (8)*.

(1980) Ball, S. J. 'Work in a changing society: an approach through social studies', *The Social Science Teacher*, 9(3), 7–9.

(1987) Ball, S. J. 'Management vs. micro-politics: Griffiths and the mystification of control', *Radical Health Promotion*, 5, 14–19.

(1988) Ball, S. J. 'Schools of management (Thatcherism, management and the teacher)', *The English Magazine*, 20, 7–10.

(1990) Ball, S. J. 'Education, inequality and school reform: values in crisis!', *Inaugural Lecture*, London, Kings College London.

(1990) Ball, S. J. 'La Perspectiva micropolitca en el analisis de las organizaciones educativas', *I Congreso Interuniversitario de Organizacion Escolar Actas*, Areas y Departmentos de Didactica y Organizacion, Esolar de Cataluna, Barcelona.

(1990) Ball, S. J. 'A national Curriculum for the 1990s', *NUT Education Review*, Spring, 9–14.

(1991) Ball, S. J. 'Case study methodology, in research on mother tongue education: theorising the object', in Haueis, E. and Herrlitz, W. (eds), *Studies in European Standard Language Teaching*, Enschede, IMEN.

(1993) Ball, S. J. 'The education reform act: market forces and parental choice', *Education in the 1990s*, Sheffield, Pavic Publications.

(1993) Ball, S. J. 'Market forces in education', *Education Review*, 7(1), 8–11.

(1994) Ball, S. J. '…and this little piggy has none: education goes to market', *Education Today and Tomorrow*, 46(1), 2–4.

(1994) Ball, S. J. 'School competition, market choice and education markets in the UK', *UK–Japan Education Forum Newsletter*, 4(4/7/94), 1–10.

(1994) Bignold, S. Cribb, A. and Ball, S. J. 'Nursing families with children with cancer: the work of paediatric oncology outreach nurses', Report to Department of Health and Cancer Relief Macmillan Fund, London, CES/KCL.

(1994) Herring, R., Ball, S. J. and Wilson-Barnett, J. A *Review of the Changing Role of the Macmillan Nurse Tutor*, Report to the Cancer Relief Macmillan Fund, London, CES/KCL.

(1998) Ball, S. J. 'Ethics, self interest and the market form in education', in Cribb, A. (ed.), *Markets, Managers and Public Service? Professional Ethics in the New Welfare State*, Centre for Public Policy Research, Occasional Paper No. 1, London, King's College London.

(1998) Fitz, J. and Ball, S. J. 'Selection mechanisms in secondary education in Japan and England and Wales', *Working Paper No. 24*, School of Education, University of Cardiff.

(1999) Ball, S. J. 'Global trends in education reform and the struggle for the soul of the teacher!', *Education Policy Studies Series*, No. 17, Hong Kong Institute of Educational Research, Chinese University of Hong Kong.

(2000) Ball, S. J. 'Reading policy texts: an excavation of Michael Barber's "high expectations an standards for all – no matter what" ', *Education and Social Justice*, 3(1), 6–8.

INDEX